THE
MYTHIC
IMAGE

THE
MYTHIC
IMAGE

by JOSEPH CAMPBELL

assisted by M. J. ABADIE

PRINCETON UNIVERSITY PRESS

Copyright © 1974 by Princeton University Press, Princeton, New Jersey

All rights reserved

This work is number one hundred in Bollingen Series, sponsored by
Bollingen Foundation

Library of Congress Catalogue Card Number: 79-166363
ISBN: 0-691-09869-7

This book has been composed in Linotype Primer

Printed in the United States of America
by Princeton Polychrome Press, Princeton, New Jersey

TO
JOHN D. BARRETT
AND VAUN GILLMOR
CELEBRATING THREE DECADES
OF FRIENDSHIP
AND COLLABORATION

Contents

V. THE SACRIFICE

VI. THE WAKING   483

Preface

PICTURES invite the eye not to rush along, but to rest a while and dwell with them in enjoyment of their revelation. In the fashioning of this book, therefore, my thought has been to let the spirit of the pictures rule, and to arrange it so that the reader might enter into its pages at any turn he liked. The mythic themes illustrated are interpreted in the chapters, which are designed rather as settings for the works of art than as independent arguments; yet there is also an argument developed, which the reader need not—yet may—decide to add to his enjoyment of the visual forms.

This argument is, briefly, that through dreams a door is opened to mythology, since myths are of the nature of dream, and that, as dreams arise from an inward world unknown to waking consciousness, so do myths: so, indeed, does life. In Chapter I we open this door, through dream, to myth, and in Chapter II set apart two orders of myth: the first, comparatively simple, of the non-literate, oral, folk traditions, and the second, infinitely more complex, of the monumental, literate civilizations—chiefly of Europe and the Near East, India, the Far East, Middle and South America, culminating historically in the great triad of the "world religions," Buddhism, Christianity, and Islam. The founding structures of this immeasurably influential mythology are in Chapter II identified, and in Chapter III certain important differences between its Oriental and Occidental applications and interpretations are illustrated and discussed. Chapter IV then treats in detail of an Oriental approach through yoga to a psychological reading of the symbolisms of mythology; and to demonstrate the relevance of such a reading to Occidental as well as Oriental forms, I have illuminated the pages with illustrations of recent European as well as of Ancient and Oriental masterworks. This chapter is the climax of the book and is followed, Chapter IV, by a broadly ranging comparative survey of a series of both folk and literary treatments of an early, very widely known figure of the sacrificed god; and finally, in Chapter VI, we close with a consideration again of myth as dream, and as life, along with the paradoxical mystery of the waking.

My thanks for the extraordinary beauty of this volume, giving satisfaction to my wish that the reader should take delight in its art, are to Miss M. J. Abadie, whose own art, editorial skill, and loyal devotion through many trials and difficulties made possible a book in which the verbal and pictorial strains can be experienced simultaneously, in accord. The long task was hers, not only of procuring the pictures but also of designing the finished work; and what this book would have been without her hand I cannot now imagine. My sincere thanks go also to Mr. Mark Hasselriis for his elegant line drawings, the quality of whose art first caught my attention when it appeared in the great Egyptian volumes of the Bollingen Series (Bollingen Series XL). There is a radiance in his brush that is particularly appropriate to mythic subjects, and I was delighted when he let it be known that he would be happy to collaborate in the production of this volume too. My good friend Paul Jenkins, the artist, whose luminous works have opened for me a new window to the wonder of space, inward as well as outward, has enriched the volume with his drawing, "Mythic Image One," made especially for the introduction of Chapter IV. I wish to express my heart-felt appreciation also to Mr. P. J. Conkwright, of the Princeton University Press, whose unfailing interest and counsel through every stage of our labor made possible this elegant realization of the project, and to Mrs. Carol Orr, who super-vised the long and complicated task of seeing our work through the press.

Professor Yoshinori Takeuchi of Kyoto University and President Takaaki Sawa of the Kyoto University of the Arts are especially to be thanked for their kindness in approaching for me the Abbot of Daigoji and arranging with him and with a state photographer of the Nara National Museum to photograph the magnifi-cent Great Sun Buddha, here appearing as Figure 198. My thanks go, also, to the Reverend Abbot of Daigoji for his kindness in allowing this treasure of his temple to be photographed for reproduction in my pages. Professor Alex Way-man of Columbia University generously provided from his collection of photo-graphs the prints for Figures 266 and 300; Dr. Kenneth P. Emory, Director Emeritus of Polynesian Research at the Bernice Pauahi Bishop Museum in Hon-olulu, helped me to the photographs, appearing in Figures 392, 392a, and 392b, of three unique pieces in the Museum collection; T.G.H. Strehlow, Professor of Linguistics at the University of Adelaide (Australia), went to considerable trouble to recover from his files his negative of the ritual scene reproduced in Figure 168. Professor Martin Beek, of Amsterdam, kindly provided his own splendid photograph of the ziggurat of Dur Kurigalzu, Figure 73. For the lovely White Tara of Figure 297 my thanks are to Geshe Khyongla Losang; and for the four fine photographs very kindly made for us of the remarkable American Indian image illustrated in Figures 273 a,b,c,d, I am indebted to the very generous cooperation of Miss Karen Taylor, of the Office of Public Rela-tions, and Mr. Edmund R. Arnold, Director of Library Services, of Cornell Col-lege, Iowa. Miss Sophie Ebeid, whose splendid photograph made for us of Cheops' Pyramid and the Sphinx appears as Figure 13, likewise is one to whom especial thanks are due.

My longest standing debt—or investment, rather—of gratitude is to two dear friends and colleagues, the president and vice-president of the now inactive, once wonderful, Bollingen Foundation, John D. Barrett and Vaun Gillmor. For it was on the wings of their enthusiasm and imagination that my first idea of this work was brought to the condition of a project to be realized; and it has been only through their encouragement and support that I have been kept going these ten years. As the final number—C—of Bollingen Series, the book was to reflect and celebrate the whole delightful adventure in exploratory scholarship that had been opened, 1943, with the publication of *Where the Two Came to Their Father: A Navaho War Ceremonial*, Bollingen Series I, recorded by Maud Oakes, with my commentary, from the words and wisdom of an old medicine man, Jeff King, now gone to his Fathers. Indeed, the words and wisdom not only of Jeff King but of many others, dear and great friends who have passed away, have inspired and inhabit the pages of this book, and to them, in grateful memory, my deepest thanks are due. For the typing, retyping, and again typing of the manuscript in its various redactions, my thanks are to Miss Marcia Sherman; to Miss Donnie Brown for special help in locating a number of difficult subjects; and to my wife, Jean Erdman, not only for her judgment and advice in the shaping of the chapters, but also for many significant insights illuminating the imagery of the masterworks here gathered. Finally, in a book of this kind it may be allowed to thank also the Muses—of whatever time or land they may have been—who watched over and guided the work throughout, in that wonderful way the spirits have of letting one imagine that the ideas of their inspiration are one's own.

New York City   JOSEPH CAMPBELL
February 20, 1973

THE
MYTHIC
IMAGE

We are such stuff / As dreams are made on, and our little life / Is rounded with a sleep.

—SHAKESPEARE, "THE TEMPEST"

There is a dream dreaming us. —A KALAHARI BUSHMAN

The Chinese sage Chuang-tzu dreamt he was a butterfly and on waking wondered whether he then had been a man dreaming, or might not now be a butterfly dreaming it was a man.

That we come to this earth to live is untrue: We come but to sleep, to dream.

—AZTEC POEM, ANONYMOUS

La Vida es Sueño: "Life is a Dream" —TITLE OF A PLAY BY CALDERÓN

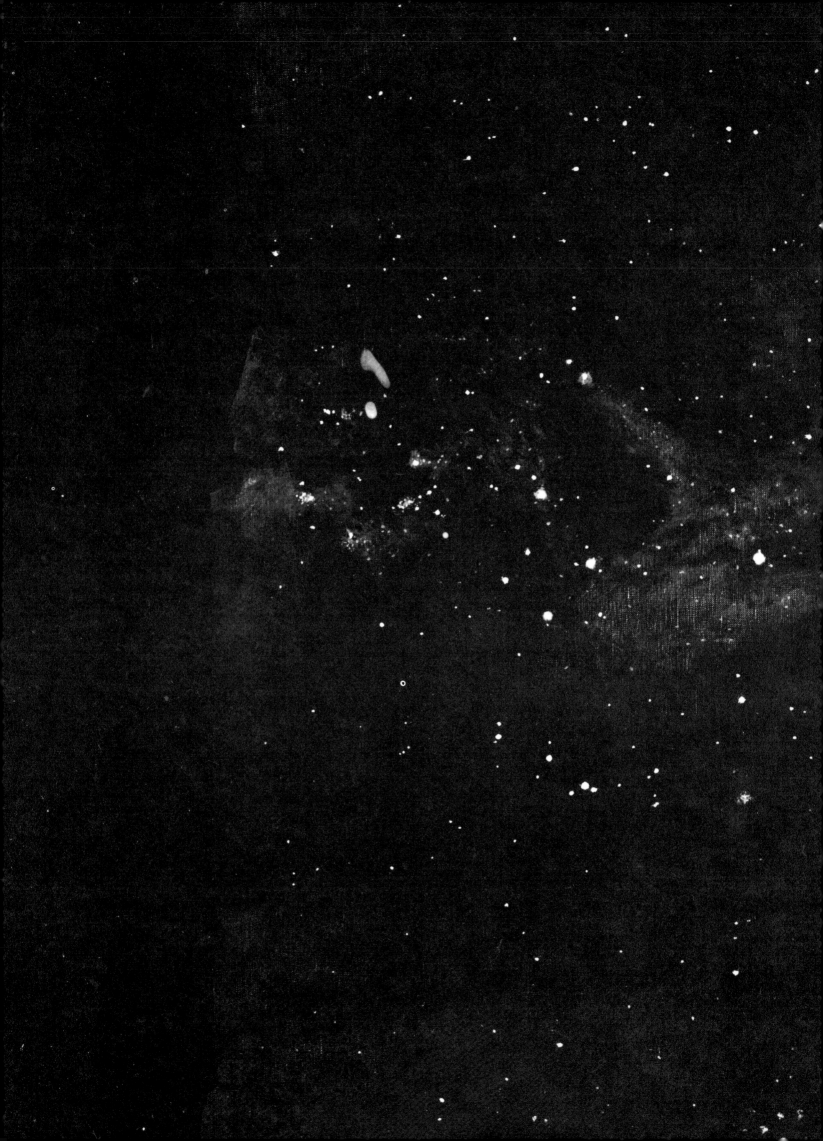

I. THE WORLD AS DREAM

The fateful slumber floats and flows
About the tangle of the rose;
But lo! the fated hand and heart
To rend the slumberous curse apart!

There lies the hoarded love, the key
To all the treasure that shall be;
Come fated hand the gift to take
And smite this sleeping world awake.

2. *Sleeping Beauty, from "The Briar Rose Series." Edward Burne-Jones.*
"The Briar Wood" (upper); "The Rose Bower" (lower)

3. *"The Moon King and His People." Rock Painting. Southern Rhodesia.*
   (See page 426 for discussion.)

4. *Vishnu Dreaming the Universe*

1. The Lord of Sleep

THE notion of this universe, its heavens, hells, and everything within it, as a great dream dreamed by a single being in which all the dream characters are dreaming too, has in India enchanted and shaped the entire civilization. The picture opposite Fig. 4 is a classic Hindu representation of the ultimate dreamer as Vishnu floating on the cosmic Milky Ocean, couched upon the coils of the abyssal serpent Ananta, the meaning of whose name is "Unending." In the foreground stand the five Pandava brothers, heroes of the epic *Mahabharata*, with Draupadi, their wife: allegorically, she is the mind and they are the five senses. They are those whom the dream is dreaming. Eyes open, ready and willing to fight, the youths address themselves to this world of light in which we stand regarding them, where objects appear to be distinct from each other, an Aristotelian logic prevails, and *A* is not *not-A*. Behind them a dream-door has opened, however, to an inward, backward dimension where a vision emerges against darkness. Are these youths, we might ask, a dream of that luminous god, or is the god a dream of these youths?

"The dream," wrote C. G. Jung, as though in elucidation of this Hindu work of art,

> is a little hidden door in the innermost and most secret recesses of the soul, opening into that cosmic night which was psyche long before there was any ego-consciousness, and which will remain psyche no matter how far our ego-consciousness may extend. For all ego-consciousness is isolated: it separates and discriminates, knows only particulars, and sees only what can be related to the ego. Its essence is limitation, though it reach to the farthest nebulae among the stars. All consciousness separates; but in dreams we put on the likeness of that more universal, truer, more eternal man dwelling in the darkness of primordial night. There he is still the whole, and the whole is in him, indistinguishable from nature and bare of all egohood.
>
> It is from these all-uniting depths that the dream arises, be it never so childish, grotesque, and immoral. So flowerlike is it in its candor and veracity that it makes us blush for the deceitfulness of our lives."[1]

A lotus hovers above the dreaming Indian god, as though growing from his body, and seated on its corolla is Brahma, the lord of light, apparent creator of this visible world, who with four radiant faces illuminates the quarters, giving visible shape to the figures of day as they rise from the night below. At his left (our right) is the frightening god Shiva, destroyer of illusions, riding with his goddess Parvati on their milk-white bull Nandi and followed by a member of his howling host, a young

Fig. 4 wind god or Marut; while at the Creator's right (our left) are the gods by whom the world-illusion is maintained: mighty Indra, the Indian counterpart of Zeus, on his four-tusked white elephant Airavata (the rain-bearing cloud from which the god lets fly his fiery bolts), and beside him, on a peacock, the young war god, Shiva's son, who is called Kumara, the "Chaste Youth," because wedded alone to his army. These are the leading Indian personifications of those universally revered powers that the poet Robinson Jeffers calls

> *the phantom rulers of humanity*
> *That without being are yet more real than what they are*
> *born of, and without shape, shape that which makes them:*
> *The nerves and the flesh go by shadowlike, the limbs and the*
> *lives shadowlike, these shadows remain, these shadows*
> *To whom temples, to whom churches, to whom labors and*
> *wars, visions and dreams are dedicate.*[2]

The figure at Vishnu's feet in the role of the virtuous Indian wife, massaging his right leg and so stimulating his cosmic dream, is the goddess Shri Lakshmi, "Beauty and Good Fortune," who is known also as Padma, "Lady Lotus." For it is actually she who has appeared symbolically in her husband's dream as the lotus wherein Brahma thrones. There is a hymn addressed to her as the matrix of phenomenality:

> *It is alone by Thy power*
> *That Brahma creates, Vishnu maintains,*
> *And at the end of all things,*
> *Shiva annihilates the universe.*
>
> *They, but for Thine aid, were powerless.*
>
> *Hence, Thou alone art the Creator,*
> *Maintainer,*
> *And Destroyer of this World.*[3]

For in dreams things are not as single, simple, and separate as they seem, the logic of Aristotle fails, and what is *not-A* may indeed be *A*. The goddess and the lotus are equivalent representations of this one life-enclosing sphere of space-time, wherein all things are brought to manifestation, multiplied, and in the end return to the universal womb that is night.

Behind the goddess at Vishnu's feet stands a female attendant holding the god's mace in readiness, at whose side, likewise in readiness, stands (in human form) the god's sky-carrier Garuda, the sun bird on whose back he will fly to those portions of Fig. 5 his dream from which cries come to him for aid—as opposite, where he appears soaring to the rescue of an elephant entrapped in a lotus pond by the coils of a serpent king and his spouse.

5. *Vishnu Rescuing the Elephant King*

The legend is told in *Bhagavata Purana* 8.2-4 of a mighty elephant ranging in a remote mountain forest with his herd, who, upon entering for a cooling bath a delicious lotus lake, became ensnared there in the coils of a serpent king. The trapped beast struggled long, unable to break free, and at last sent forth a prayer remembered from a former lifetime, to which the god whose dream is the universe immediately responded. In this scene the pious pachyderm is shown lifting a lotus spray in its trunk in praise of the appearance of its savior, while the serpent king and his queen, whose prodigious forms dwarf even that of the elephant, worshipfully surrender their victim to the god in whose dream they play but minor roles.

In the *Purana*, Vishnu is said to have flung his discus and cut off the serpent's head, who, released thus from his scaly form, was instantly reborn as a heavenly musician in a paradise of erotic bliss. However, in this elegant panel of classic grace there is no such scene of violence. Soaring on his sun bird, the dreamer of the world-illusion simply enters personally into this episode of his imagination (as might anyone, by illusion, the context of his own dream) and the work is done.

cf. Fig. 4
Fig. 6 Now, whereas the dreamer of Figure 4 is a god dreaming of his creatures, the one pictured below is a creature dreaming of his god; and again the question arises: Is Job a creature of Yahweh, or is Yahweh a creature of Job? Are the Pandavas figments of Vishnu's dream, or is Vishnu a figure of theirs? Are you and I, as we know ourselves, reflexes of some high mystery, and if so, is that mystery adequately represented in our imagination of "God"?

6. Job's Vision. William Blake

With Dreams upon my bed thou scarest me and affrightest me with Visions.[4]

Job's god in the poet Blake's engraving is pointing with one hand to the tablets of the law and with the other to the fires of hell; for in Blake's view a person's idea of God is necessarily a product of his own spiritual limitation, and Job, as we know his story, had been striving to interpret the calamity of his life in rational, legal terms, according to the laws of Moses—which, however, did not fit his case, since he had not violated those laws. As told:

> There was a man in the land of Uz, whose name was Job; and that man was blameless and upright, one who feared God, and turned away from evil. . . . And the Lord said to Satan, "Have you considered my servant Job, that there is none like him on earth, a blameless and upright man, who fears God and turns away from evil?"
>
> Then Satan answered the Lord, "Does Job fear God for nought? Hast thou not put a hedge about him and his house and all that he has, on every side? Thou hast blessed the work of his hands, and his possessions have increased in the land. But put forth thy hand now, and touch all that he has, and he will curse thee to thy face." And the Lord said to Satan, "Behold, all that he has is in your power; only upon himself do not put forth your hand." So Satan went forth from the presence of the Lord. (*Job 1:1, 2:3-7*)

This complacency of Job's god at the opening of the story was a reflex, according to Blake's view, of the very good man's own self-satisfaction in virtue; and the poet's name for such complacency is Selfhood. His name for Job's god as a reflex of that conceit is, therefore, The Great Selfhood, or Satan; hence, in this picture, the serpent and the cloven hoof. Blake's dreamer, that is to say, is an ego-bounded personality, interested in his own condition, comparable rather to the elephant affrighted by the serpent king of a lotus pond than to the "Self" beyond selfhood reposing on the cosmic sea, through whose recollection the elephant is to be saved.   Fig. 6   cf. Fig. 5   cf. Fig. 4

In sum: in the contrast of these pictured dreamers an opposition is suggested of two contrary points of view from which mythic forms can be interpreted. The figures in the Indian piece are conceived as symbols of cosmic import, whereas in Blake's engraving the god and his laws, along with the fires and demons of his hell, are but reflections of the dreamer's personal or ethnic limitations. Mythic forms, that is to say, may be regarded either as pointing past themselves to mysteries of universal import, or as functions merely of local ethnic or even personal idiosyncrasies. In India these two facets of all mythologies and their associated rites are known respectively as *marga* and *deshi*: marga meaning "path" or "way," the path or way to immortal knowledge; and deshi, "of the region; local or ethnic," the peculiar sectarian or historical aspect of any cult, through which it constellates a folk, a nation, or a civilization.   Fig. 4   Fig. 6

In the present work both aspects are regarded—as indeed they have to be, since universals are never experienced in a pure state, abstracted from their locally conditioned ethnic applications. It is, in fact, in their infinitely various metamorphoses that their fascination resides. And so, while it has been my leading thought in the present work to let sound the one accord through all its ranges of historic transformation, not allowing local features to obscure the everlasting themes, it has also been intended and arranged that the wonder of the revealed accord should not diminish our appreciation of the infinite variety of its transformations.

7. Shiva Maheshvara, The Great Lord

The living ground of all being is here personified in a sublime triadic image, 23 feet high, 19½ across, carved in high relief against the back wall of a great handhewn cave on an island in the harbor of Bombay. The profile at the beholder's left is male, that at the right, female; the visage at the center is of the eviternal source whence all pairs of opposites proceed: female and male, peace and strife, creation and annihilation.

"If it were possible," C. G. Jung has suggested, *"to personify the unconscious, we might think of it as a collective human being combining the characteristics of both sexes, transcending youth and age, birth and death, and, from having at its command a human experience of one or two million years, practically immortal. If such a being existed, it would be exalted above all temporal change; the present would mean neither more nor less to it than any year in the hundredth millennium before Christ; it would be a dreamer of age-old dreams and, owing to its immeasurable experience, an incomparable prognosticator. It would have lived countless times over again the life of the individual, the family, the tribe, and the nation, and it would possess a living sense of the rhythm of growth, flowering, and decay."*[5]

8. *Etruscan Pietà. 5th century* B.C.

2. The Lord of Death and Resurrection

9. *The Night. Jacob Epstein.* A.D. *1929*

cf. Fig. 4 AN Egyptian counterpart of the Indian figure of Vishnu dreaming on the cosmic Milky Ocean appears in the centuries-earlier mummy of Osiris in the scene of Figure 10. Here the newborn sun-god Horus-the-Child hovers in the risen solar disk above the mummy of his murdered father, which—like Vishnu on the cosmic snake—is couched on the crocodile-god Sebek of the abyss. At Osiris' feet, in the place of Padma-Lakshmi, is Isis, mother of the newborn child who, in Figure 11, is shown being born—like Brahma—from the corolla of a lotus. Twelve stars displayed between the crescent and full moon represent the nights of the moon's waxing, symbolic of rebirth, while lotus and papyrus sprouts springing from the crocodile stand likewise for resurgent life. Within the circle of the risen sun, seated behind the infant on a lion throne, is Min "of the uplifted arm," an ancient phallic deity, here symbolic of the procreative power of the dead and mummified Osiris: for it was only after he had been murdered by his brother Seth that Osiris, the Lord of both Death and Resurrection, begot his avenging son.

10. The Birth of Horus

11. Horus, Lotus-Born

12. Tut-Ankh-Amon Reborn as the Young Sun-God Nefertem

"I am Yesterday, Today, and Tomorrow, and I have the power to be born a second time. I am the divine hidden Soul who creates the gods, and who gives sepulchral meals to the denizens of the underworld, of the deep, and of heaven. I am the rudder of the east, the possessor of two divine faces wherein His beams are seen. I am the lord of the men who are raised up; the lord who comes forth out of darkness and whose forms of existence are of the house wherein are the dead. Hail, lord of the shrine that stands in the middle of the earth. He is I, and I am He" (*Book of the Dead, Chapter of the Coming Forth by Day*).[6]

13 (overleaf). The Sphinx and the Pyramids

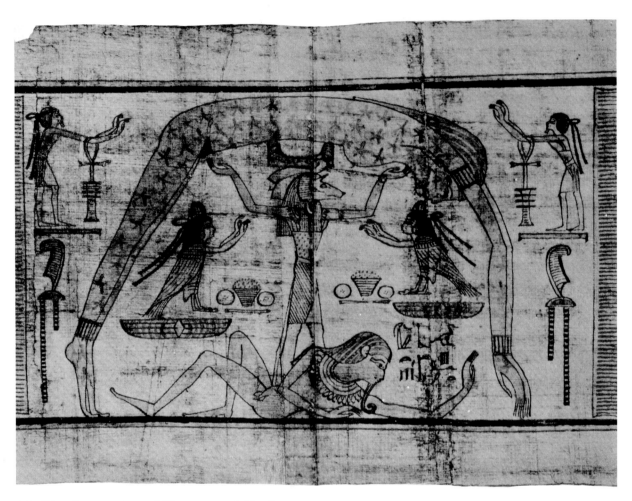

14. The Separation of Heaven and Earth

Above is the sky-goddess Nut, her body covered with stars; below, her spouse, the earth-god Geb, before whom there is an inscription reading "Geb, Prince of the Gods." Normally in Egyptian art the god elevating the sky goddess is the air-god Shu. Here, however, where his part is taken by an ape-headed figure with the "mountain sign" on his head, the reference would seem to be not only to the power of air, the life-breath (compare, in Figure 24, Hapy, the baboon, as guardian of the lungs), but also to the "Primordial Hillock" by which heaven and earth were first separated. To the right and left of this figure a soul-bird, Ba, lifts human arms in the attitude of prayer. Below each of these there is a feast sign, and before, two loaves of bread and a basket of fruit placed on a mat. Behind and before the goddess Nut are male figures in adoration, to whose outstretched arms the signs of life and stability are attached and below each of whom is the sign West.

The sign of life is, of course, the *ankh* ☥ and the sign of stability, the *Djed*-pillar ☩ ; while the West, direction of the sunset, is the quarter of the entrance to the Netherworld, where the dead enjoy a never-ending life.[7]

THE LEGEND OF ISIS AND OSIRIS

According to the best-known version of the ancient Egyptian legend, Osiris and his twin sister Isis, Seth and his twin sister Nephthys, were the progeny, all, of the sky-goddess Nut and her spouse, the earth-god Geb. They flourished in the first age of the world. And it was Osiris and his sister who bestowed on mankind the arts of civilization; he: agriculture, monumental architecture, writing, astronomy, and the calendar of rites; she: weaving, the preparation of foods, music, dancing, and painting. However, in the dark of one fateful night Osiris mistook his brother's wife for his own, and the child of that illicit union—the firstborn of Osiris—was the jackal-headed deity Anubis. Seth, enraged and with his mind fixed on revenge, prepared in secret a splendid sarcophagus exactly to his brother's measure, which he offered at the climax of a merry party as a gift to anyone it might fit. All tried; and the moment Osiris lay in it, seventy-two accomplices rushed in, clapped the lid on, sealed the coffer tight, and flung it into the Nile. Carried out to sea and drifting to the Syrian coast, it was cast ashore at Byblos, where immediately an erica-tree sprang Fig. 15 up, enclosing the precious casket in its trunk, which then became so beautiful, emitting such a fragrance, that the king of the city had it felled and made into a pillar for his palace.

15. *Osiris in the Erica Tree*

16. *Stupa. Kathmandu, Nepal*

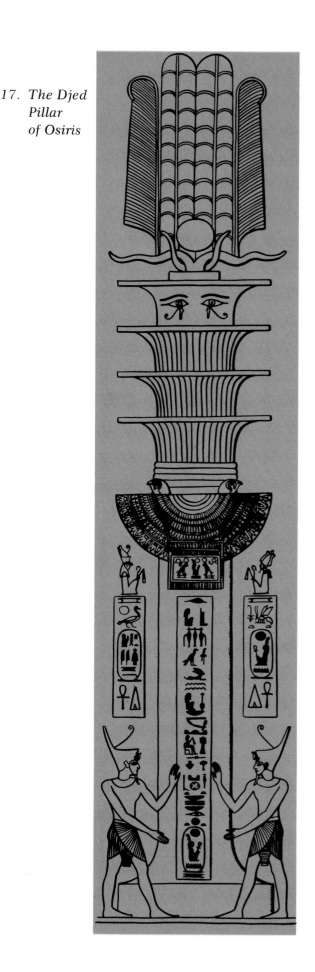

17. *The Djed
Pillar
of Osiris*

cf. Fig. 298 As the eyes of Osiris, looking from the Djed-pillar, tell of an eternal life not quenched by apparent death, so too the eyes of Buddha-consciousness, here gazing from this famous Buddhist stupa in Nepal. A stupa is basically a reliquary mound containing the relics of some Buddhist saint, and as the pharaoh entombed in a pyramid is believed to have passed to eternity, so also the saint enshrined in such a tomb. Both monuments symbolize the world mountain, that "mountain mother" from whom all living things appear and to whom they return in death. The great pagoda above stands for the stages of the heavens. And we note that the eyes of Buddha-consciousness peer out from a plane exactly between the earth-dome and the heavenly height, where the knowledge of time and the intuition of eternity come together. Analogously, in the Djed-pillar, it is by the interlocked horns of the cow (♀) and the ram (♂) that the solar disk is upheld.

The widowed Isis, meanwhile, searching everywhere in grief and desperation, arrived in the Syrian city and, on hearing there of the marvelous pillar, contrived to be appointed nurse to the newly born infant prince. She would give the child her finger to suck and at night gently place him in the fire to purge away his mortal parts and endow him with immortality; then, assuming the form of a swallow, she would go winging, mournfully chirping, around the pillar: until, one evening, the mother chanced upon this tender scene and, perceiving the case of her child in the fire, emitted such a startled shriek as broke the spell on the infant, who had to be rescued from incineration. The goddess made known who she was, begged to be permitted to extract her husband from the column, and had the coffer transferred to a royal barge. Then cruising with it homeward, she removed the lid, lay with her face to that   Fig. 18 of her dead spouse and, embracing him, weeping bitterly, conceived.

18. Isis with the Recovered Mummy of Osiris

19. Tut-Ankh-Amon

20. *Shrine in the Tomb of Tut-Ankh-Amon*

Fig. 13
Fig. 21

A second portion of this ancient tale to which the pyramids are monuments tells of the goddess hiding with the body of her lord in the papyrus swamps of the Delta and there giving birth to their son. She remained in mortal fear of Seth, who, having usurped his brother's throne, was now threatening to appropriate her as well, to com-

21. Isis in the Papyrus Swamps

Before the goddess stands Amon-Re, Creator and Lord of Eternal Light, presenting to her the ankh, the sign of life, while Thoth, behind her, grasping her right arm, offers the protection of magic. "From the fact that Amon-Re and Thoth are present," states E. A. Wallis Budge, "these gods representing the husband and witch doctor of modern days, we may assume that Isis suffered greatly, and that her labor was 'difficult.' This assumption is supported by the description of the birth of Horus given by Isis in her narrative on the Metternich Stele, in which her agony is insisted upon, as well as her loneliness."[8]

pel her to serve as his queen. And it came to pass that one night when the moon was full Seth pursued a wild boar into the Delta swamps, and there coming on the body of his brother, tore it in a rage into fourteen parts (one for each night of the waning moon), which he flung about far and wide. Whereupon the goddess, now twice bereaved, began a second wide-ranging search, this time accompanied, however, by her grieving sister Nephthys and the jackal-boy Anubis: and these three, scouting everywhere, recovered with the help of Anubis' nose all of Osiris but his phallus, which had been swallowed by a fish. According to one version of the tale, they buried each part where they found it—hence the numerous "tombs of Osiris." According to another, however, the parts were all brought together and reassembled as a mummy, through the magic of Anubis in the role of embalming priest.

Cf. Fig. 321

22. *The Embalming of Osiris*

The mummy lies on the lion couch with four jars of unguent beneath it. Anubis in the role of embalming wizard-priest bends over the deceased. Right and left are, respectively, Nephthys and Isis with their hands placed on *shen* signs symbolizing the solar circuit from day to night and renascent day.[9]

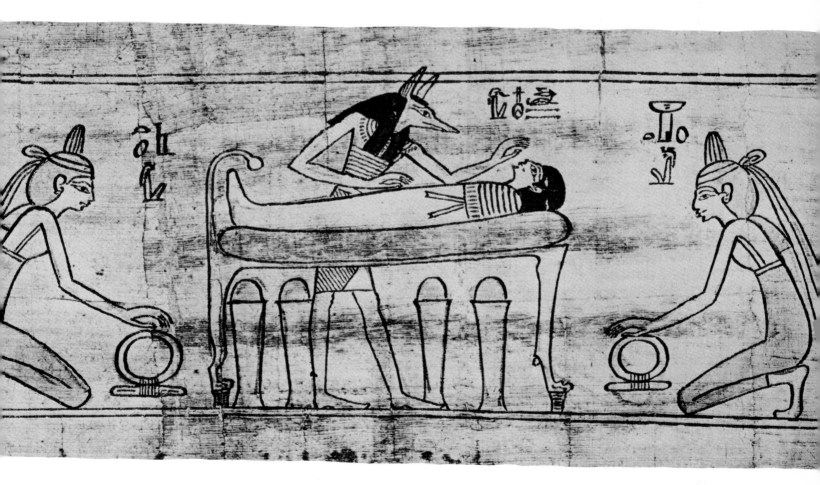

This two-layered scene summarizes the whole legend of the disappearances and restorations of Osiris. In the upper register the Djed-pillar stands between Isis and Nephthys, bearing the *Atef*-crown with horns and disk, and holding in human hands the crook and flagellum of pharaonic rule. Above the pillar is an inscription: "Osiris, Lord of Busiris, the Great God, Ruler of Eternity." This group is depicted between signs signifying West.

Below, projecting downward from the skyline, is the head of a hawk representing Horus and sending rays (shown as stars and red disks) pouring down upon the mummy. The latter is protected by the goddess Isis at its head and her sister Nephthys at its feet, while above are a vulture and a cobra, each with a basket of bread before it.

The vulture in Egyptian iconography is a form or aspect of the mother-goddess taking the dead back into her body for rebirth. Her name in this role is Nekhbet and, as such, she was patroness of the earliest capital of Upper Egypt. The patroness of the earliest capital of Lower Egypt, on the other hand, was the serpent-goddess Buto. As here represented, these two divinities stand as emblems of the union of The Two Lands.[10]

In the tomb rites the mummy of the deceased was identified with the mummy of Osiris, to be resurrected; and the union of The Two Lands under his single temporal lordship was taken to signify, by analogy, the union under his lordship in the afterworld of the two estates, life and death.

23. *Osiris in the Djed Pillar (upper); Revivification of the Mummy (lower)*

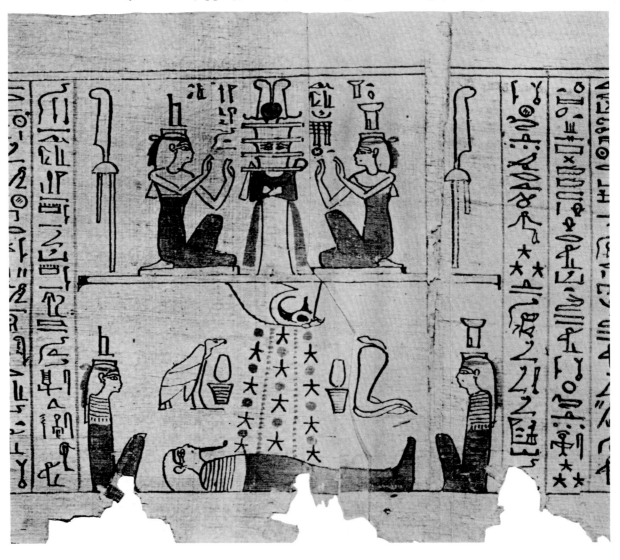

Horus, in the meantime, the second son, who was already a splendid youth (for these gods, you must know, mature rapidly), had overwhelmed his uncle Seth in a furious battle of revenge, during the course of which he had lost an eye—his left—but deprived his uncle of a testicle. And it was this sacrificed left EYE OF HORUS, when presented as an offering to the mummy of Osiris, that restored the deity to life—an eternal life, beyond the cycle of death and generation: so that now, enthroned forever in the Netherworld, he reigns there as lord and judge of the resurrected dead.

Fig. 390

Fig. 25

24. *Horus and His Sons before Osiris*

The figure with the head of an ass, stuck with knives and bound by his arms to a forked slave-stick, is Seth, conquered. The Minotaurlike figure behind Osiris is the god Serapis, a late, Ptolemaic (hence Hellenized) personification of the mystery of Osiris' identity with the sacred Apis Bull (the name Osiris plus Apis yields Serapis). He is in the role here essentially of the god Min "of the uplifted arm" in the scene of Figure 10, representing the continuing force of the pharaonic principle as it proceeds from father to son. Osiris wears the *Atef*-crown with horns and holds before him the *Uas*-scepter, flagellum, and shepherd's crook.

Horus, facing his father and Serapis, has behind him his four sons, Imesty, Hapy, Dua-motef, and Kebeh-senuf, each armed, like himself, with a knife. In Egyptian tombs the viscera of the deceased, removed during embalmment of the mummy, were stored in four so-called "Canopic jars" (named after an island town in Lower Egypt, on the western mouth of the Nile), the covers of which bore representations of the heads of these four sons. They contained, respectively, the liver (Imesty, with a man's head), lungs (Hapy, with a baboon's head: compare, in Figure 10, the ape in the role of the air god), stomach (Dua-motef, a dog's head), and intestines (Kebeh-senuf, head of a hawk). Osiris and the four sons of Horus are here standing imagelike on pedestals: they are potencies, respectively, of the past and future and, as such, associated not with the world of the now-living but the Netherworld of the dead and the yet-to-be.

Serapis and Horus, on the other hand, are standing squarely on this earth, Horus with the head of a hawk and wearing the tail of a bull. His hawk's head is a reference to his daily flight as the sun bird, east to west, at the close of which he passes into the earth, to become, next day, reborn. He is thus the one who "begets himself," the son who is one with his father, and is consequently known as the "bull of his own mother." That is the idea suggested by the bull's tail, which unites him by association with the procreative pharaonic force symbolized in Serapis.

In the upper register, Hunefer, the deceased, kneels in prayer before fourteen gods. These are: Re (the lord of eternal light); Tem (a sun god of night); Shu (the air god); Tefnut (Shu's sister and consort); Geb (the earth) and Nut (the sky); Horus, Isis, and Nephthys; Hu (a god of wisdom); Sa (a god of abundance); Uat-resu ("Road of the South"), Uat-meht ("Road of the North"), and Uat-Amenti ("Road of the West," i.e., to the Netherworld).

In the main scene the deceased is conducted by Anubis into the judgment hall of Osiris, where his heart is weighed against a feather of the goddess Truth, whose head appears atop the pole of the balance. Anubis tests the tongue of the balance, and before him stands a monster called Eater of the Dead, whose function it is to consume and thus annihilate all who fail the test. It is looking back for a sign to Thoth, who is recording the result; and finally, Hunefer, justified, is being introduced by Horus to Osiris.

The great god is seated in his shrine of fire, on a throne set beside the pure waters of the Netherworld, from which a lotus rises, bearing on its corolla the four young sons of Horus. Before the great god is the winged EYE OF HORUS, by virtue of which he was resurrected, and behind him stand the two goddesses of his legend, Nephthys at his left arm and Isis at his right. A cornice frieze of Uraeus serpents crowns the building.

The pictured texts are, first, a prayer recited by the deceased while his heart is being weighed; next, Thoth's announcement of the result; and finally, Horus' words to Osiris, introducing Hunefer with the assurance that the tongue of the balance never moved.[11]

25. *Osiris, Judge of the Dead. Hunefer Papyrus.* 1317-1301 B.C.

26. Introducing the Miracle. Paul Klee

3. The Wonder Child

THE recurrence of many of the best-loved themes of the older, pagan mythologies in legends of the Christian Savior was a recognized feature intentionally stressed in the earliest Christian centuries. The meaning, for example, of the ass and ox in the Nativity scene would in the fourth century A.D. have been perfectly obvious to all, since these were the beasts symbolic in that century of the contending brothers, Seth and Osiris. Their inclusion in the new setting would have signified, firstly, that in Christ opposites are reconciled: "I say to you, Love your enemies" (Matthew 5:44); and secondly, that in the birth, death, and resurrection of the new Savior

Fig. 27

Fig. 24

27. Nativity Scene. A.D. 4th century

the promises prefigured in the mere myths of the pagan gods had been historically, in actual fact, fulfilled: "For," as we read in a second-century text, the so-called Second Epistle of Peter, "we did not follow cleverly devised myths when we made known to you the power and coming of our Lord Jesus Christ, but we were eyewitnesses of his majesty" (II Peter 1:16).

Likewise, the Magi above, wearing the Phrygian cap then associated with the Persian savior Mithra, must have made the point that even the followers of that most threatening rival of the Christian mission had recognized and were now worshiping the newborn King. Thus the promises and aspirations of all the mysteries of antiquity were shown harvested in the gospel of this sole historic incarnation of the one and only true God. Fig. 27a
Fig. 28

27a. Detail of Figure 27

28. Head of Mithra

The night of December 25, to which date the Nativity of Christ was ultimately assigned, was exactly that of the birth of the Persian savior Mithra, who, as an incarnation of eternal light, was born the night of the winter solstice (then dated December 25) at midnight, the instant of the turn of the year from increasing darkness to light.

THE VIRGIN BIRTH

And not only the mythic motifs, but even the festival dates of the contemporary pagan mystery cults were openly adopted by the Christian Fathers. We learn from the fourth-century saint and churchman Epiphanius (ca. 315-402), for example, of an annual festival observed in Alexandria on January 6, the date assigned to the Epiphany and (originally) the Nativity of Christ, and to his Baptism as well. The pagan occasion was in celebration of the birth of the year-god Aion to the virgin goddess Kore, a Hellenized transformation of Isis. Her votaries would assemble, we are told, on the eve of January 6 in her temple, the Koreion, pass the night intoning hymns to the flute, and at cockcrow, bearing torches, descend joyously to the crypt to carry up on a bier her seated, naked idol with the signs of a cross and a star of gold marked on her hands, her knees, and her brow. This image would then be carried seven times around the temple, ever to the sound of hymns and the flute, until returned at last to the crypt. "And her votaries," states the Christian saint, "declare that the Virgin gives birth that day, that hour, to the Aion."[12]

cf. Fig. 6

29. *Phanes' Birth from the World Egg.*
A.D. *117-138*

Like Blake's image of Job's god, this divinity has cloven hoofs and is wrapped in the folds of a serpent, the head of which appears above his own. He holds in one hand a thunderbolt, in the other his messenger-staff; he is winged; the interior of the shell from which he is bursting is in flames; and on his breast is a lion mask. From his left side emerges the head of a ram and from his right that of a deer. Known as Aion, he is "the Lord of Ages"; and as Phanes, "the Shining One."* Iconographically interesting is the Phanes-Pan identification expressed in the goat-shaped feet.

Contemplating this image, one is to think of the veil of space-time (connoted by the girdle of the zodiac) as parting to reveal a personification of the ground of being; or (in the image of a human nativity) the vulva of Kore, the Virgin, giving birth to a god, fully grown. A meditation proper to such an epiphany would be: May I come, by this god, to the knowledge of my own radiant Truth enclosed in the coils of my temporal life.

* Cf. p. 221, Amitayus-Amitabha.

Meanwhile, from the Christian quarter of Jerusalem a like procession would have been trooping to celebrate in Bethlehem a night of worship in the cave alleged to have been the scene of Christ's Nativity; and in the morning at cockcrow, this procession, too, would have been chanting hymns, rejoicing in a virgin birth, on its way back to Jerusalem.[13]

30. Nativity with the Prophets Isaiah and Ezekiel. A.D. 1278-1318

A contemporary chronicler writes of the installation of this famous altarpiece:

"On the day that it was carried to the Duomo the shops were shut; and the Bishop bade that a goodly and devout company of priests and friars should go in solemn procession, accompanied by the *Signori Nove* and all the officers of the Commune and all the people; all the most worthy followed close upon the picture, according to their degree, with lights burning in their hands; and then behind them came the women and children, with great devotion. And they accompanied the said picture as far as the Duomo, making procession round the Campo as is the use, all the bells sounding joyously for the devotion of so noble a picture as this. And all that day they offered up prayers, with great alms to the poor, praying God and His Mother who is our advocate, that He may defend us in His infinite mercy from all adversity and all evil, and that He may keep us from the hands of traitors and enemies of Siena."[14]

THE MADONNA

The Madonna as mother of a child-savior is an iconographic figure of the greatest antiquity, which, however, is for some reason of much more frequent occurrence westward than eastward of Iran. The figure below, from Mesopotamia, is of the Late Fig. 31 Sumerian period, ca. 2000 B.C., and the beautifully animate, deeply felt Egyptian Fig. 32 rendition of the anguished solitude of Isis in her holy motherhood is of approximately the same date. Such pagan images of the great Near Eastern mother-goddesses played important roles in the shaping of the earliest Christian Madonna types; how- Figs. 33, 34 ever, as Professor André Grabar of the Sorbonne has recently shown, a more imme- diate influence on the artist-craftsmen responsible for the Christian formulation was exercised by the popular funerary art of third- and second-century Rome.

31. Mesopotamian Madonna. ca. 2000 B.C.

32. Isis with Horus. 2040-1700 B.C.

33. *Madonna and Prophet.* ca. A.D. 200

"A young woman, seated, head inclined with a motherly smile, holds on her lap a naked infant, who presses one hand to her breast and turns with a pretty movement of surprise to look behind. The woman is a Roman, beautiful and strong. Her sturdy arms are bare; her oval, regular features, rather large, are framed by a head of rich black hair, partly covered by a transparent veil. This already is the Madonna as she would be rendered by the artists of the Renaissance.

"Before her stands a man clothed in the robe of the philosophers, who carries in one hand a rolled manuscript and with the other points to a star. Have we here a Christian family scene, or a portrait of the Holy Family? No! It is of the prophet Isaiah prophesying before the Virgin and Child. For the star is the sun, to the rising of which Isaiah compared the coming of the Redeemer."[15]

> *The Lord himself will give you a sign. Behold, a virgin shall conceive and bear a son, and shall call his name Immanuel.*
>
> *The sun shall be no more thy light by day; neither for brightness shall the moon give light unto thee:*
> *But the Lord shall be unto thee an everlasting light, and thy God thy glory.*
> (Isaiah 7:14, 60:19; Douay version)

In the sense of the second of these verses, one could perhaps suggest that the star of the painting should be interpreted, not as the sun, but as the star of Bethlehem, the light of which was to surpass both sun and moon.

34. *Shepherdess and Child.*
   A.D. *3rd century. Rome*

"Before a small cottage," states Professor André Grabar of this piece, "one sees a family of shepherds; the shepherdess, seated, holds a young child in her arms. The sculpture is of the third century. For the historian of Christian iconography it is very precious, because it furnishes an example of the image of mother and child as it must have been commonly represented at this time; such a composition, among others, was used by the first image-makers for Mary holding the Child Jesus."[16]

Figure 33, for example, is a fresco from the ceiling of a Christian catacomb of about A.D. 200, and Figure 34, the fragment of a pastoral scene from a Roman pagan sarcophagus, is of approximately the same date. A second pagan formula appears below in a funerary stele which, as Professor Grabar points out, inspired a certain well-known Byzantine type of icon of the Virgin, the Nikopea, characterized by a frontal presentation with the child on the axis of the mother's body, cut just below shoulder height and enclosed in a medallion.[17]

Figs. 35, 36

35. Pagan Funerary Stele   *36. Byzantine Madonna (Nikopea)*

More largely viewed, not in local art-historical terms but as an archetype of world mythology, the earliest prototype of the Christian Madonna yet found can be seen in the interesting dual image opposite, which is from an extremely early neolithic town site of ca. 6000-5800 B.C., situated on the Anatolian plain of southern Turkey. As described and interpreted by Dr. James Mellaart, who unearthed it: "On the left a couple of deities are shown in embrace; on the right a mother holding a child, whose head is unfortunately lost. It is possible, if not probable, that the two scenes relate a succession of events; the union of the couple on the left and the intended result on the right. The goddess remains the same, the male appears either as husband or as son. This may be one of the earliest representations of the *hieros gamos*, the 'sacred marriage.' "[18]

Fig. 37

A great number of other figures of the mighty Asian Magna Mater appear in this extraordinarily early, richly documented neolithic site, of which Figure 38 may be taken as an example, particularly striking, with a perfect echo six millennia later in Rome and another in India, later still.

Figs. 39, 40

37. *Father-god, Mother-goddess, Divine Child. ca. 5750* B.C. *Çatal Hüyük*

38. *Enthroned Goddess, Giving Birth.*
ca. 5750 B.C. Çatal Hüyük

"Large clay figure of a goddess supported by two felines, giving birth to a child. An early example of the concept of the goddess as 'Mistress of Animals,' it was found in the grain bin of a shrine, where it may have been placed to promote the fertility of the crops by sympathetic magic."[19]

39. *Cybele, Mother of the Gods. Late Rome*

The great Phrygian goddess Cybele, mother of the slain and resurrected young Phrygian deity Attis. Her cult was early introduced to Greece (where she was identified with Rhea), and to Rome at the time of the Carthaginian Wars. Known generally as Mountain Mother as well as Mother of the Gods, her sanctuaries were on mountains, frequently in caves, her animals were lions, cf. Fig. 8 and her attendants Corybantes, half-human, demonic beings. Her priests, the Galli, were self-emasculated eunuchs, attired in female garb and wearing long hair, fragrant with ointment.

40 (opposite). *Indrani, Queen of the Gods.* A.D. 750-850

cf. Fig. 224

41. The Rest on the Flight into Egypt. Gerard David

INFANT EXILE

In the legend, recounted in the Matthew gospel, of King Herod's malice and the flight of the Holy Family to Egypt, an echo is to be recognized of the malice of Seth Fig. 21 and the refuge of Isis with her infant son in the Delta. These two legends are but two instances of an extremely popular theme known to students of world folklore as the infant exile motif, which has been documented from every quarter of the

42. Romulus and Remus, Discovered by Shepherds

earth. An early collaborator of Sigmund Freud, Otto Rank, published in his celebrated monograph *The Myth of the Birth of the Hero* (1922) a psychoanalytical interpretation of some seventy examples of this general theme (to which thousands could have been added), wherein five essential constituents were identified and discussed.

1. The infant is the offspring of noble or divine parents, or of a deity and earthly maiden.

2. Extraordinary difficulties attend the birth, occasioned commonly by the malice of either the father himself or some father surrogate such as a cruel uncle or king.

3. The infant is exposed (like Romulus and Remus, or like Oedipus), or otherwise sent or carried off, either alone or (as in the legends of Perseus and Danaë, the child Jesus and Mary) together with his mother.

Figs. 41, 42 4. The rejected ones are rescued, either by animals or by simple, usually rural, folk (in the Christian legend by both: the little donkey and the humble carpenter, Joseph).

5. In the end, the hero, now a youth returning to his proper home, either overthrows the father and sets himself in his place (Oedipus, Perseus, Christ's New Testament supplanting the Old), or becomes reconciled with the father and completes the father's work (the New Testament as fulfillment of the Old).

Rank compared this recurrent formula to a common fantasy of disturbed children, who, believing themselves to be infinitely finer and greater than their parents, imagine that they must actually be of noble, even divine, descent, but exiled or lost, and only adopted by this coarser pair that they have been taught to revere as parents.[20] And Freud then developing this thesis in his last masterwork, *Moses and Mono-*
Fig. 43 *theism*, noticed that whereas in all the other legends the adopting family is of lowly birth, in the Biblical tale of Moses the opposite is the case. Hence, by analogy, he argued, since in the case of the fantasizing child the *true* parents are those represented as adoptive, the true parents of Moses must have been Egyptians of the royal house, and the later fashioners of his legend only *wished* he had been a Jew.[21]

A prominent instance from the Greek tradition, preserved by Hesiod, is the
cf. Fig. 329 infancy of Zeus, where the cruel father Kronos (Saturn), having been warned that a son was to overthrow him, devoured his children, one by one, as soon as they were born. However, when the mother Rhea was to be delivered of Zeus, she fled to a cave in Crete where the goddess Earth received the child, and a stone wrapped in swaddling clothes was given to the father in its stead.[22] Or according to a version recorded
Fig. 44 by Strabo: a company of young warriors, the Kouretes, danced about the birth scene with a din of drums and clashing arms to screen the child's cries from his father's ears, and it was they who then carried the infant to Crete to be nursed and tended by nymphs.[23]

Fig. 45 The best-known Oriental example is the legend of the birth of the popular savior Krishna, as an incarnation of Vishnu, the world-dreamer.

43. *The Finding of Moses. Nicolas Poussin*

44. *Kouretes and the Infant Zeus*

THE LEGEND OF THE BIRTH OF KRISHNA

The wicked tyrant-king Kansa of Mathura, warned by a mysterious voice that the eighth child of his cousin Devaki would slay him, set a watch over her palace and as her children were born destroyed them, one by one, to the number of six.

Whereupon the goddess Earth, incensed by this outrage, assumed the form of a cow, and repairing to the summit of Mount Meru, the city of the gods, complained there to Brahma of the wickedness of the king. And the Lord of Light, rising from his lotus throne, immediately conducted his whole pantheon to the shore of the cosmic Milky Ocean, where he addressed in prayer the great reclining form of the Lord Vishnu, dreamer of the world-illusion, far out on the distant waves.

"O thou that art distinct from holy writ, twofold in nature, both possessed of form and without form; twofold, likewise, in wisdom: exoteric, esoteric, and the ultimate end of both; smallest of the least, largest of the large, omniscient, inspiring spirit of the arts and of speech: imperceptible, indescribable, inconceivable, pure, infinite and eternal, without name; who hearest without ears, seest without eyes, movest without feet, and seizest without hands, knowest all and art known by none; the common center of all things, in whom all exist! Just as fire, though one, is modified in many ways, so doest thou, O Lord, who art of one form, take upon thee all appearances. Thou art that supreme eternal state beheld by the wise with the eye of knowledge. There is nothing, O Lord, but thee. Unaffected by fear, anger, desire, weariness or sloth, thou art both universal and individual, independent and without beginning. Subject to no necessity, thou assumest forms, neither because nor not because of any cause. Pervader of the Universe, thousand-formed, thousand-armed, many-visaged, many-footed, who art nature, intellect, and consciousness, yet other, even, than the spiritual root of these, glory to thee! Do thou behold this Earth, oppressed, and show thy favor. Behold us all, these gods, prepared to do thy will. Only command, and lo! we are at hand."

The prodigious sleeper stirred, and his mighty right arm, lifting, plucked from his giant head two hairs, one white, one black, while a voice—infinitely inward—could be heard by all there assembled. "These two hairs," they heard, "shall descend upon the goddess Earth to relieve her of her burden: the white to become the seventh, and the black, the eighth child of Devaki, the chaste wife of the pious prince Vasudeva."

And indeed, that very night, the goddess Yoganidra, "Visionary Sleep of Spiritual Union," descended on the princess Devaki. And she conceived of the white hair her seventh child, Balarama, an incarnation in human form of the cosmic serpent Ananta. Shortly after which conception, to protect this seventh from the malice of the tyrant king, the same goddess Yoganidra transferred the precious foetus to the womb of Vasudeva's second wife, Rohini, who had been sent for protection across the broad river Jumna, to live there with a tribe of cowherds in the pleasant wood called Vrindavan.

And so the time came for the work of the black hair, which, rendering Devaki's eighth conception, produced an incarnation of the world-dreamer Vishnu himself. And on the moonlit holy midnight when that Being of Beings first appeared in this world in the radiant blue-black form of Krishna, clouds gathering emitted a low pleasing sound and let fall a rain of flowers; heavenly kettledrums resounded; celestial maidens danced to the pipes of airborne heavenly musicians; and all the earthly seas made a music of their own.

45. *The Infant Krishna and His Parents*

However, when Devaki's spouse beheld that child—four-armed and bearing in his hands a mace, a conch, a discus, and a lotus, blue-black as a dense raincloud and with invaluable stones embellishing his golden crown, wearing bracelets, armlets, and a radiant multitude of ornaments—Vasudeva's eyes bloomed wide in wonder. The parents addressed prayers of welcome to the child, but then prayed him, for the safety of all, to withdraw that holy godly form and put on a shape more human: who replied with gracious tenderness, and, growing silent, assumed before their marveling eyes the form of an ordinary babe.

Fig. 45

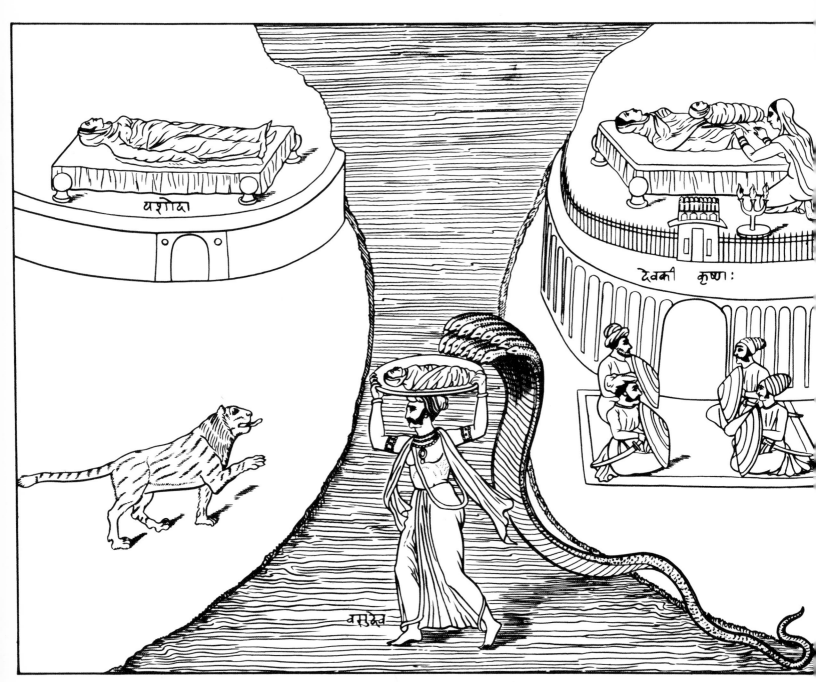

यशोदा

देवकी कृष्ण:

वसुदेव

46. *Krishna Carried over the Jumna by Vasudeva.*
Sanskrit: upper left, "Yashoda"; upper right,
"Devaki," "Krishna"; below, "Vasudeva"

Moreover, there had been born that night, across the holy river Jumna, a girl-child to Yashoda, chaste wife of the pious herdsman Nanda. And Devaki's spouse, Vasudeva, moved by supercelestial inspiration, gathered up his own newborn babe, Krishna, and made off with him into the night.

There was falling a heavy rain, and the many-headed cosmic serpent, following Fig. 46 solicitously father and child, spread above them his numerous hoods. The guards of the city gates had already been charmed by the goddess of visionary sleep, so that the company passed to the riverbank unhindered, where the Jumna, deep and wide as it was, with numerous dangerous whirlpools, grew still. The waters rose no higher than Vasudeva's knees. And when he had reached the opposite shore, where the entire camp of the tribe of cowherds slept deeply under Yoganidra's spell, he silently and swiftly placed his infant beside Yashoda and, taking up her girl-child, returned as he had come. So that when the lovely young woman woke, she found that she had been delivered in sleep of a son as black as the dark leaves of a lotus, and together with her husband she rejoiced.

But now the guards of the city, hearing the cries of a newborn infant in the princess Devaki's palace, quickly informed their tyrant-master Kansa, who, repairing thither immediately, ripped the girl-child from the protesting mother and flung it against a rock—where, instead of bursting, it rose, expanding, and, assuming the form of a goddess with eight arms, each flourishing a weapon—a bow, a trident, arrows, a shield, a sword, a conch, a discus, and a mace—began to laugh ever expanding; laughed terribly and laughed again. "What good to you now," the vision cried triumphantly, "to have hurled me, O Kansa, to the ground? He who is to kill you is already born!"

For it was herself, the goddess Yoganidra, now decorated with garlands, jewels, and emitting rare perfumes, who had assumed this birth for this purpose; and laughing, laughing on—hymned by the choirs of both sky and earth—she dissolved in air and disappeared.

Alarmed, trembling, altogether unstrung, the king returned in desperation to his palace to issue a terrible command: namely, that a search throughout the whole world should be made for whatever newborn infants might be found upon this earth.

"And let every boy-child," he commanded, *"in whom signs of unusual vigor appear* Fig. 47 *be slain."*[24]

47. *Massacre of the Innocents (detail). Peter Paul Rubens*

4. The Mighty Goddess

Fig. 48 This figure from Tibet is a type of Buddhist savior known as a Tara, said to be the personification of a tear of divine compassion. The title itself has two distinct meanings, "savior" and "star." In the first sense it derives from a Sanskrit verbal root *trī*, which means "to cross or traverse (as, a river), to transport, surpass or overcome"; also, "to liberate," and "to escape." Compare the Latin *ter-minus*, "boundary, limit, terminal, term," as personified in the Roman deity Terminus, presiding over boundaries. And in the second sense, "star," the title is drawn from a second Sanskrit verbal root, *stṛī*, which means "to scatter, expand, or spread out (as light)," and is related to our English "star, aster, and strew."[25] One is to think of this gentle figure as an apparition from the ultimate bound of the world-dream, come to liberate our hearts and minds from its binding spell of illusory joys and fears.

Now the Indian term for "illusion," *māyā*—from the verbal root *mā*, "to measure, to measure out, to form, to create, construct, exhibit or display"—refers to both the power that creates an illusion and the false display itself. The art of a magician, for example, is maya; so too the illusion he creates. The arts of the military strategist, the merchant, actor, and thief: these also are maya. Maya is experienced as fascination, charm; specifically, feminine charm. And to this point there is a Buddhist saying: "Of all the forms of maya that of woman is supreme."[26]

As a cosmogonic principle—and as a feminine, personal principle, also—maya is said to possess three powers:

1. A Veiling Power that hides or conceals the "real," the inward, essential character of things; so that, as we read in a sacred Sanskrit text: "Though it is hidden in all things, the Self shines not forth."[27]

2. A Projecting Power, which then sends forth illusory impressions and ideas, together with associated desires and aversions—as might happen, for example, if at night one should mistake a rope for a snake and experience fright. Ignorance (the Veiling Power), having concealed the real, imagination (the Projecting Power) evolves phenomena. And so we read: "This power of projection creates all appearances, whether of gods or of the cosmos."[28]

These first two powers, concealing and projecting, can be compared to those properties of a prism by which sunlight is transformed into the colors of a rainbow. Arrange these seven colors on a disk, spin it, and they will be seen as white. So too, when viewed a certain way, the phenomena themselves may reveal what normally they veil; which demonstrates:

3. The Revealing Power of maya, which it is the function of art and scripture, ritual and meditation, to make known.

48. Tara

"*For I have learned,*" wrote the poet Wordsworth in his "Lines Composed a Few Miles above Tintern Abbey . . . (July 13, 1798),"

> *To look on nature, not as in the hour*
> *Of thoughtless youth; but hearing oftentimes*
> *The still, sad music of humanity,*
> *Nor harsh nor grating, though of ample power*
> *To chasten and subdue. And I have felt*
> *A presence that disturbs me with the joy*
> *Of elevated thoughts; a sense sublime*
> *Of something far more deeply interfused,*
> *Whose dwelling is the light of setting suns,*
> *And the round ocean and the living air,*
> *And the blue sky, and in the mind of man:*
> *A motion and a spirit that impels*
> *All thinking things, all objects of all thought,*
> *And rolls through all things. Therefore am I still*
> *A lover of the meadows and the woods,*
> *And mountains; and of all that we behold*
> *From this green earth; of all the mighty world*
> *Of eye, and ear,—both what they half create,*
> *And what perceive; well pleased to recognize*
> *In nature and the language of the sense*
> *The anchor of my purest thoughts, the nurse,*
> *The guide, the guardian of my heart, and soul*
> *Of all my moral being.*[29]

Or as in the Indian *Chhandogya Upanishad*:

> It is below, it is above; it is to the west, it is to the east, it is to the south, it is to the north: it is, in fact, this entire world. . . .
>
> And truly, the one who sees this, thinks this and understands this, takes pleasure in the Self, is joined to the Self, knows bliss in the Self: such a one is autonomous. He has unlimited freedom in all worlds.
>
> But those who think otherwise than this are ruled by others, inhabit perishable worlds, and in all worlds are unfree.[30]

49. Landscape with a Bridge. Thomas Gainsborough

50. *Playing the Lute in Moonlight. Ma Yüan*

"Why does a virtuous man take delight in landscapes?

"It is for these reasons:

> that in a rustic retreat he may nourish his nature;
>
> that amid the carefree play of rocks and streams, he may take delight;
>
> that he may constantly meet in the country fishermen, woodcutters, and hermits, and see the soaring of the cranes, hear the crying of monkeys.

"The din of the dusty world and the locked-in-ness of human habitations are what human nature habitually abhors; while, on the contrary, haze, mist, and the haunting spirits of the mountains are what human nature seeks, and yet can rarely find. . . .

"Having no access to landscapes, the lover of forest and stream, the friend of mist and haze, enjoys them only in his dreams. How delightful then to have a landscape painted by a skilled hand! Without leaving the room, at once, one finds oneself among the streams and ravines."[31]

Under the Yangtzu Bridge, where the river overflows,
The willow-tendrils show forth their hue, insensitive to man's gray hair.
Throughout Spring, rain and snow have kept away the scenery lovers;
Yet throughout Ch'ing-Ming season, the plum-blossoms will preserve and flourish.

Aging and being useless, I have grown attached to my friends;
But year after year, my friends have diminished like stars and seagulls.
Suddenly Master Wang turns to me with an astonishing statement of his mind,
I will therefore give him my observation of the Min River . . .[31a]

51. Spring on the Min River. Tao-chi

Figures 53 and 54 show the Madonna, the Virgin Mother of God, in an unforgettable way, as a vehicle of the Revealing Power of maya. In the picture-language of the Christian church, the Veiling and Projecting Powers are typified in Eve and the serpent, by whom Adam was seduced and turned from his immortal life in God; while the Revealing Power is represented in the Virgin, the Madonna, "changing Eva's name," i.e., reversing her effects, as declared in a popular Catholic hymn:

Ave maris stella,	Hail, bright Star of ocean,
Dei mater alma,	God's own Mother blest,
Atque semper Virgo,	Ever-sinless Virgin,
Felix caeli porta!	Gate of heavenly rest!
Sumens illud Ave	Taking that sweet AVE
Gabrielis ore,	Which from Gabriel came,
Funda nos in pace,	Peace confirm within us,
Mutans Heva nomen.[32]	Changing EVA's name.[32]

Through Eve the gates of that garden were closed where God "walked in the cool of the day," and the very beauty of the female thereupon became "the Devil's Door." To which catastrophe, the answer was given in Mary, whose virginity became God's door, and whose motherhood "Heaven's Gate." "Spiritual Vessel," she is named in the Litany of Loreto: "Vessel of Honor, Singular Vessel of Devotion, Mystical Rose, Tower of David, Tower of Ivory, House of Gold, Ark of the Covenant, Gate of Heaven," and, like the Buddhist Tara, "Morning Star."[33]

Fig. 57

Fig. 52

cf. Fig. 218

Throughout centuries of Christian thought two contrary traditions of interpretation have contended in the reading of such symbols. The first we may term the historical, or prosaic, where the images are understood to refer to historical events; the second, the experiential, psychological, or poetic, referring not to what once *was*, but to what *is*, now and forever; not to any segment of phenomenality, present or past (where *A* is not *not-A*), but inward, to experienced and possible states and crises of consciousness, illumination and delusion (where *A* is indeed *not-A*, since what is mirrored in the imagery is one's own inward reality and truth).

Fig. 55

In terms of the first tradition of interpretation, there actually *was* a prehistoric garden of Eden, where the fall of mankind occurred; an actual earthly paradise. There was actually, also, a deluge, survived by Noah in his ark; after which God selected a certain historic people to become the sole vehicle of his will on earth. And in the fullness of time, a daughter of that priestly race, remaining physically virgin, bore a son who was literally God. And it was actually and only through the incarnation, crucifixion, death, and (literal) resurrection of that divine being that mankind was restored to the grace of God, which had been forfeited in the garden.

Today many are finding it difficult to accept such mythic themes, so read, when all the known facts of history, biology, astronomy, and physics appear to stand against them. Hence, even among the orthodox there is becoming evident an increasing tendency to invoke, when faced with irrefutable facts, the alternate, poetic tradi-

52. *Christ in the Virgin's Womb*

53. *Vierge Ouvrante (closed)*

54. *Vierge Ouvrante (open)*

Fig. 59 tion of hermeneutics. For instance, the assumption of Mary physically to heaven is, in the light of what we know today, impossible as fact. However, as a mythological image transcending the popular notion of an absolute dichotomy of nature and spirit (*A* is not *not-A*: man is not God), it makes once again the point that had already been made (though canonically disregarded) in the doctrine of the Incarnation, where in the person of Jesus not only was the idea of the absolute distinction of the opposed terms God and man refuted, but the point was also made that one should realize, like Jesus, this coincidence of opposites as the ultimate truth and substance of oneself, as in the words, for instance, attributed to Jesus in the early Gnostic *Gospel According to Thomas*:

> If those who lead you say to you: "See, the Kingdom is in heaven," then the birds of heaven will precede you. If they say to you: "It is in the sea," then the fish will precede you. But the Kingdom is within you and it is without you. If you will know yourselves, then you will be known and you will know that you are the sons of the Living Father. But if you do not know yourselves, then you are in poverty and you are poverty. (80:19-81:5)
>
> Whoever drinks from my mouth shall become as I am and I myself will become he, and the hidden things shall be revealed to him. (98:28-30)
>
> His disciples said to Him: When will the repose of the dead come about and when will the new world come? He said to them: What you expect has come, but you know it not. (90:7-12)
>
> Cleave a piece of wood, I am there; lift up the stone and you will find me there. (95:26-28)
>
> The Kingdom of the Father is spread upon the earth and men do not see it. (99: 16-18)[34]

Meister Eckhart (1260?-1327?) made the same fundamental point a millennium later, speaking from his pulpit on the virgin birth: "It is of more worth to God, his being brought forth spiritually in the individual virgin or good soul, than that he was born of Mary bodily. But this involves the notion of *our* being the only Son whom the Father has eternally begotten. When the Father begat all creatures he was begetting me; I flowed out with all creatures while remaining within in the Father."[35]

Compare the idea of Figure 4. Compare, also, the following couplet of the cherubic seventeenth-century mystic Angelus Silesius (1624-1677):

> *Of what use, Gabriel, your message to Marie,*
> *Unless you now can bring the same message to me!*[36]

Fig. 52 Viewed in this light, the little Virgin Mother (of a date only shortly following Meister Eckhart and also of the Rhineland) must be read as pointing *through* the image of the legendary Mother of God finally to the inward truth-to-be-known of each Fig. 54 of us. And in the *Vierge ouvrante* the same possibility is suggested, of an inward realization through which the deluding (Concealing and Projecting) force of maya, which binds us to the outward, temporal, merely historical aspects of experience,

55. *Adam and Eve, Expelled from the Garden of Eden. Masaccio*

might be dissipated and a prospect opened to an inward dimension of ineffable mystery and wonder. Beheld first in the way of waking consciousness, holding in her left hand the apple of Eve's sin, the "world apple," she is the earthly mother of her mystery child; but then, *ouverte*, she reveals herself—and by reflection, each of us, insofar as we have followed Eckhart's sermon—as the bounding horizon of all forms and names, even those that are known as God.*

"In my birth," as Meister Eckhart has said, "all things were born, and I was the cause of my own self and all things . . . and if I had not been, then God had not been either."[37]

And in the words again of Silesius:

> *God is my center when I close him in;*
> *My circumference when I melt in him.*[38]

It is in this poetic, mystic, spiritual sense that the symbols of the Christian message can be read in concord with those of the other mythological traditions of mankind, and it will therefore be in this sense that we shall treat of them in the present work. Thomas Mann, in the first volume of his mythological tetralogy *Joseph and His Brothers*, coined the term "Moon Grammar" to capture the sense of this order of thought and communication. "Daylight," he wrote, "is one thing, moonlight another. Things take on a different look beneath the moon and beneath the sun. And it well might be that to the Spirit the light of the moon would appear to yield the truer illumination."[39]

---

* Compare the text to Figure 12.

56. *Mulier Janua Diaboli*

"For the monk," writes Emile Mâle to this piece, "woman is almost as powerful as the devil. She is his instrument, and he makes use of her to ruin saints. Such were the sentiments of the great abbots and reformers of the monastic orders. All were in fear of woman; they did not want the monk to be exposed to her temptation, all too sure that he would succumb. 'To live with a woman without incurring danger,' said Saint Bernard, 'is more difficult than to resuscitate the dead.'

"And to what lengths did they not go in their precautions! The rules of Cluny did not permit a woman, for any reason whatsoever, to cross the bounds of a monastery. The rules of Cîteaux are still more severe; for a woman might not even appear there at the gate of the monastery: the brother serving as porter was instructed to refuse such a woman alms. So that in self-defense the Cistercian even goes so far as to fail in charity. If a woman comes into the church, the service is to be suspended, the abbot deposed, and the brothers sentenced to fast on bread and water. . . .

"There is a capital in the cathedral of Autun," Mâle continues, "showing a young man staring at a woman unveiled. The artist did not know how to endow his heroine with beauty, yet has given her a sort of sinuous grace. She turns to cast an eye in the direction of her victim, letting a ribbon float behind her. But at that very moment the devil appears and grips the young man by the hair; he is now and henceforth his master. And it can be seen that the woman is his accomplice; for her hair, bristling like Satan's, makes known the daughter of hell."[40]

57. *The Triumph of Venus*

The psychologist Erich Neumann, in his volume *The Great Mother*, has commented on this painting. "The nude Venus within the *mandorla* symbolizing the female genitals appears to a group of men of different periods who were known as great lovers. The ambivalence of the whole . . . is made evident by the strange genii that accompany the Goddess. These winged creatures, late forms of the bird-shaped souls over which the Goddess rules, are Cupids, but they have ugly birds' claws. These feet, which were formerly a natural part of the bird's body, now produce the effect of an archaic vestige whose significance is evil. Birds' menacing claws are among the rending attributes of the Archetypal Feminine as siren and harpy; here, as is frequently the case, they have been transferred to the male companion figures. In the Renaissance picture the genii bearing weapons and birds' claws are symbols of the voracious impulses revolving around the Golden Aphrodite, who enchants and ruins the men ensnared in her earthly paradise."[41]

58. Sin.
Franz Stuck

59. *Mary, Queen of Heaven*

IA ORANA MARIA

60. *Ia Orana Maria (We Greet You, Mary). Paul Gauguin*

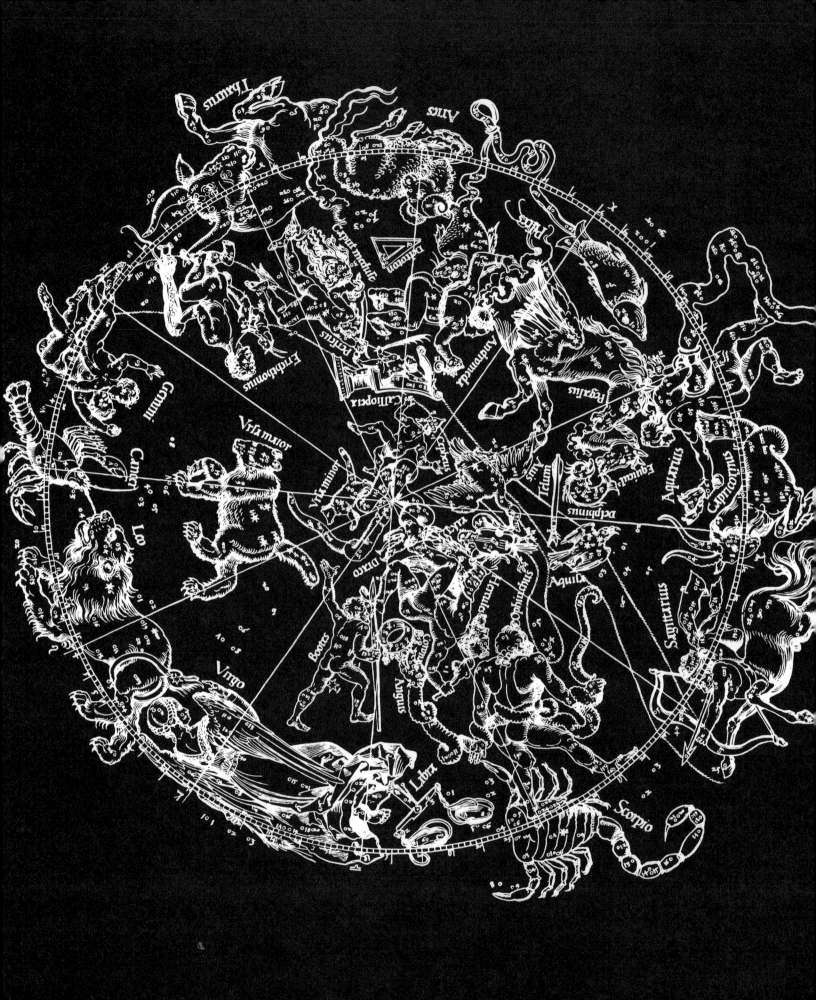

II. THE IDEA OF A COSMIC ORDER

1. Literate and Nonliterate Traditions

ONE explanation that has been proposed to account for the appearance of homologous structures and often even identical motifs in the myths and rites of widely separate cultures is psychological: namely, to cite a formula of James G. Frazer in *The Golden Bough*, that such occurrences are most likely "the effect of similar causes acting alike on the similar constitution of the human mind in different countries and under different skies."[1]

There are, however, instances that cannot be accounted for in this way, and they suggest the need for another interpretation: for example, in India the number of years assigned to an eon* is 4,320,000; whereas in the Icelandic *Poetic Edda* it is declared that in Othin's warrior hall, Valhall, there are 540 doors, through each of which, on the "day of the war of the wolf,"** 800 battle-ready warriors will pass to engage the antigods in combat.[2] But 540 times 800 equals 432,000!

Moreover, a Chaldean priest, Berossos, writing in Greek ca. 289 B.C., reported that according to Mesopotamian belief 432,000 years elapsed between the crowning of the first earthly king and the coming of the deluge.[3]

No one, I should think, would wish to argue that these figures could have arisen independently in India, Iceland, and Babylon.

A second approach to interpretation has therefore been proposed, based on the observation that at certain identifiable times, in identifiable places, epochal transformations of culture have occurred, the effects of which have been diffused to the quarters of the earth; and that along with these there have traveled constellations of associated mythological systems and motifs.

The most important and far-reaching cultural mutation of this kind in the history of the human race was that which occurred in Mesopotamia about the middle of the fourth millennium B.C., with the rise in the lower reaches of the twin rivers Tigris and Euphrates, of a constellation of city-states governed by kings according to a notion of cosmic order and law derived from a long-continued, systematic observation of the heavens. Towering temples symbolic of a new image of the universe made their appearance at that time—the first examples of monumental architecture in the history of civilization; and it was within the precincts of those sanctuaries that the members of a new type of highly specialized, heavenward-gazing priesthood invented, ca. 3200 B.C., writing, mathematical notation (both sexagesimal and decimal), and the beginnings of a true science of exact astronomical observation.

---

* A "Great Cycle" (*Mahayuga*) of cosmic time.
** I.e., at the ending of the cosmic eon, Wagner's *Götterdämmerung*.

61. *Tomb of Pharaoh Zoser. ca.* 2630 B.C.

Attributed to the genius of the pharaoh's vizier, Imhotep, this brilliant white limestone pyramid, gleaming like the moon, is the oldest stone structure in existence. It is about 411 feet long at the base, 358 feet wide, and some 204 feet high. The burial chamber (the substructure) is cut 90 feet down into the limestone beneath and lined with prodigious granite blocks. A fortified wall (lower right) once surrounded the precincts, some 30 feet high and a mile or so in circumference, faced with a fine white limestone masonry of small bricklike blocks, to imitate the mud brick walls of an archaic fortified town. Within were various temples, chapels, secondary tombs, galleries, and colonnades (lower left), all in perfectly worked, perfectly finished white stone.

Having remarked a mathematically calculable regularity in the passages of the planets through the constellations of the fixed stars, these first systematic observers of the heavens conceived—in that specific period, in that specific place, for the first time in human history—the grandiose idea of a mathematically determined cosmic order of greater and lesser, ever-revolving cycles of celestial manifestation, disappearance, and renewal, with which it would be prudent for man to put himself in accord. Hence the relationship even now of religious festivals to astronomically Fig. 62 based calendars; also, the notion of laws and mandates handed down from on high. Hence, too, the imitation of heavenly circumstance in the costumes and procedures of royal courts: solar crowns, star-bedecked robes; monarchs and their queens revered as gods and, vice versa, deities revered as kings and queens.

cf. pp. 141ff.   This life-transfiguring concept of a celestially based political and social order reached Egypt ca. 2850 B.C. with the founding of the First Dynasty; Crete on one hand, India on the other, ca. 2500 B.C.; China, ca. 1500 B.C., with the Shang Dynasty; and America, apparently ca. 1200 B.C., with the abrupt appearances in Middle and South America of the Olmec and Chavín culture complexes.

It is noteworthy, furthermore, that whereas today the sun at the vernal equinox stands in the constellation of the Fish (Pisces), in the century of Christ it was in the Ram (Aries), and two millennia earlier had been in the Bull (Taurus). This almost imperceptible slippage at the slow but steady rate of one degree in 72 years* is what is known as the "precession of the equinoxes." To complete one cycle of the zodiac—or, as it is called, one "Great" or "Platonic Year"—requires 25,920 years; which sum, divided by 60,** yields, once again, the number 432. So that the mythological count of 432,000 years not only cannot have been the product of any psychological archetype or elementary idea, but must have been discovered only through centuries of controlled astronomical observation.

Therefore, it is necessary in every study of mythology to distinguish clearly, as a first principle of method, between literate and nonliterate orders; and further—in relation to the latter—to recognize a distinction between truly primitive traditions, such as those of the bushmen of the Kalahari desert, and those, like the Polynesian, that are, at least in part, regressed, i.e., provincial forms, survivals and local transformations of traditions originally stemming wholly or in part from one or another of the major matrices of literate civilization.

The present work is devoted chiefly to the literate traditions: firstly, because for these we possess dependable written interpretations from the hands of those who developed and employed them; secondly, because it is necessary to become acquainted with the main figures, themes, and motifs of the literate traditions before attempting to distinguish between primitive and regressed features in the nonliterate. But finally and principally, because it has actually been from the one great, variously inflected and developed literate world-heritage that *all* of the philosophies,

* Compare, in the Osiris legend, the number of Seth's accomplices (above, p. 21).
** One *soss*, the founding unit of the old Mesopotamian sexagenary scale, still used for the measurement of circles, whether of space or of time.

theologies, mysticisms, and sciences now in conflict in our lives derive. These are in origin one; one also in their heritage of symbols; different, however, in their histories, interpretations, applications, emphases, and local aims.

62. *The Law Code of Hammurabi.*
1728-1686 B.C. *Babylon*

As interpreted by André Parrot, Curator-in-Chief of Oriental Antiquities at the Louvre:

"The law-giver king had himself represented at the top of the black basalt stele on which the two hundred and eighty-two clauses of his Code are engraved with exquisite precision. Standing in the attitude of respect, with his right arm raised, he appears before the god of justice, Shamash, whose shoulders are aflame and who holds in his right hand the attributes of power, the rod and circle, while he dictates the Law to the king. Impassive and majestic, Shamash gazes intently at the man who acts as his representative on earth, and who, though exacting obedience from his fellow men, must, himself, obey his god. The setting of the scene is not in the plain but on a mountain, indicated by the triple line of imbrications on which the god's feet rest. Here the sculptor has brilliantly succeeded in rendering the atmosphere of the colloquy, serene and dignified but governed also by a 'categorical imperative' with which the king had no choice but to comply. And looking at this scene, we are inevitably reminded of Moses, on Mount Sinai, receiving the tables of the law."[4]

2. The World Mountain

Figs. 61, 73 UNDOUBTEDLY the most striking symbolic features of the earliest high culture centers of both the Old World and the New were the great temple towers and pyramids rising high above the humble rooftops clustered about their bases. These were in every case prodigious edifices, which in their building must have required the labor Fig. 63 of thousands. The little scene below (left) shows work proceeding on one of the earliest ziggurats, that of the old Sumerian city of Kish, early third millennium B.C.; and we note that a god, floating in his celestial craft, is waiting above for the tower Fig. 64 to be finished so that he may disembark and descend. At right, in a work of a slightly later date, a deity in a strange puntlike barge cruises the waters beneath the earth. Fig. 65 And at far right a sun god is represented in two aspects: first, as he rises from the

63. *The Ziggurat of Kish.*
   Early 3rd millennium B.C. *Sumer*

In the lower register, where the building of the temple tower is in progress, six figures suffice to represent the whole company involved. "The one seated at the left," states André Parrot in his discussion of this scene, "is nude to the waist and wears a little skirt of the archaic Sumerian kind. He is presenting to a laborer similarly garbed a brick and and a jar containing either water or the mortar. Two more workers bearing jars on their heads are on their way to the work area, transporting the water or mortar; and two masons are at work there, constructing the ziggurat, four of the stages of which have already been completed. These are delineated in their diminishing importance by the number of vertical architectural lines, respectively 6, 5, 4, and 3, the fifth stage, still in progress, being nearly done. . . ."[6]

64. *Night-sea Journey of the Solar Barge.*
   2350-2150 B.C. *Akkad*

Whereas the god of Figure 63 is sailing a celestial sea, the deity of the present scene is traversing the waters beneath the earth, as suggested by the fish. The stern of his craft terminates in a serpent's head, the bow in the body of his boatman. Aboard are various pots, agricultural implements, and a standing, sphinxlike, human-headed lion, who like the Egyptian sphinx of slightly earlier date (Fourth Dynasty, 2600-2480 B.C.) may rep- cf. Fig. resent the solar power inherent in divine kingship. In any case, the seated deity steering the boat has solar rays pouring from his shoulders, while a goddess with grain growing from her body, standing on a plane slightly above that of the waters, holds in one hand a threefold spray of the tree of life.

deep, and next, ascending the cosmic mountain to its peak. For in the view of the old Sumerian astronomical observers, the universe was neither flat nor a sphere, but in the form of a great mountain rising in stages from an infinite sea; and it was this glorious world mountain, marked in its stages by the orbits of the circling spheres—the moon, Mercury, Venus and the sun, Mars, Jupiter, and Saturn—that the imposing temple towers were designed to reproduce in local, visible form. Nor were the abyssal sea and cosmic mountain composed of inanimate matter; they were living creatures. In a Late Sumerian cuneiform text of ca. 2000 B.C. inscribed on a tablet now in the Louvre the name of the goddess-mother of the universe, Nammu, is denoted by an ideogram signifying "sea," and she is given praise as "the mother who gave birth to Heaven-and-Earth [*ama tu an-ki*]."[5] Moreover, a second tablet of about the same date preserved in the University Museum, Philadelphia, tells that when this "Heaven-and-Earth" emerged from the primal sea, its form was of a mountain whose summit, Heaven (An), was male, and lower portion, Earth (Ki), female; further, that from this dual being the air-god Enlil was born, by whom the two were separated.

Fig. 66

> *The lord whose decisions are unalterable,*
> *Enlil, who brings up the seed of the land from the earth,*
> *Took care to move away Heaven from Earth,*
> *Took care to move away Earth from Heaven.*[7]

But this, almost to the letter, is the myth preserved in the classical legend of Earth and Heaven, Gaia and Ouranos, separated by their son Kronos. We recognize it, also, in the ancient Egyptian representation of the separation of Heaven and Earth by the air-god Shu, or, as in Figure 14, by a god bearing on his head a mountain sign—except that in Egypt the sexes of the world-parents are reversed, Heaven (Nut) being female, and Earth (Geb) male.

Fig. 14

65. Sun-god Ascending the World Mountain.
2350-2150 B.C. Akkad

At the left is the water-god Enki, enthroned in his "sea house." At the extreme left his porter attends the gate. Between these two the sun god appears in two aspects: first emerging from the sea house, then ascending the world mountain. The swastika-like crooked knee and sawtoothed weapon are his well-known signs. One foot planted on the back of a winged lion, he steps with the other on the shoulder of a crouching human form. Rays of light pour from his shoulders, streams of water from those of Enki. Ascending the heavenly mount, the god carries in one hand his mace, while with his other he exchanges a greeting with Enki, to whose realm below he is now to return.

66. *Ziggurat of Nippur.* 2050-1950 B.C. *Restoration Drawing*

This celebrated ziggurat, dating in its final form from Late Sumerian times, was dedicated to the patron of Nippur, Enlil, the Lord of Air, who reigned from the summit of the world mountain and was in that period the leading power of the pantheon. Situated with its angles oriented to the quarters of the earth, the majestic sanctuary in this final phase of its long career was composed of three main elements: a forecourt, the main court, and, within the latter, the ziggurat.

The quadrangular forecourt had two gates, an outer, facing the holy river Euphrates, and an inner, leading to a main court slightly trapezoidal in form. In the middle of the forecourt stood a welcoming temple, and in the eastern corner of the main court another smallish building that the excavators named (after the elements of offering and libation) the "House of Honey, Milk, and Wine." A large ground-level temple occupied the northern corner of this splendid interior esplanade.

The ziggurat, built largely of unfired brick —but with a massive facing of fired brick some 4½ feet thick—rose from a large rectangular base, approximately 62 yards broad and 43 deep. Towering in five stages, in imitation of the cosmic mountain, it bore on its summit a heavenly chamber furnished to welcome and accommodate the god. A stairway for his divine descent to the ground-level temple served equally for his priests' ascent to his dwelling above.

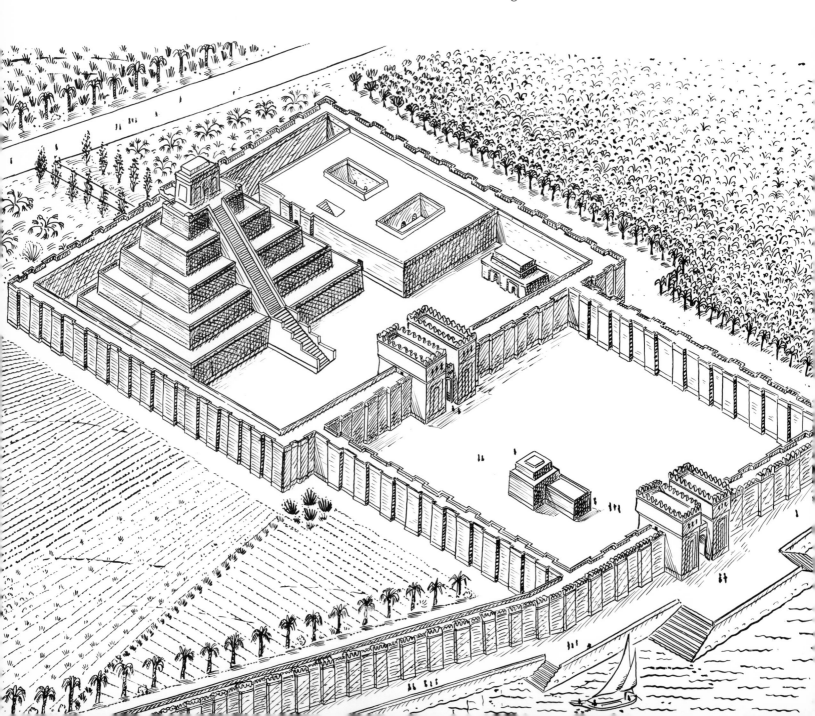

As rendered in the classical account of the separation of Heaven and Earth, Father Heaven (Ouranos), having begotten on the earth-goddess Gaia a generation of Titans, refused to let them be born, shoving each child back as it appeared, until the tortured mother, groaning with pain, eventually thought of a plan. Fashioning a sawtoothed sickle of flint, she proposed this weapon to her sons—of whom the only one courageous enough to attempt the awesome deed was the eldest, Kronos. Accordingly, when the father, bringing night with him, next descended, stretching out, and lay hugely over his goddess, this bold son reached with his left hand from his hiding place and, seizing his father, holding in his right the sickle,

> *with its long blade edged like teeth,*
>   *he swung it sharply,*
> *and lopped the members of his own father,*
>   *and threw them behind him*
> *to fall where they would. . . .*[8]

In Polynesia, remarkably, the same primordial separation of Sky and Earth is reported in equally dramatic terms, of which accounts those of the Maori of New Zealand are the best known. There it is told that Rangi Nui, the Sky, lay upon Papa-tu-a-nuku, the Earth, so closely that their offspring, becoming impatient of darkness, met together to consider what should be done. As retold by Antony Alpers in his *Maori Myths and Tribal Legends*, the first proposal, offered by the war-god Tu-matauenga, was to kill the parents; but Tane-mahuta, the god and father of forests and of all things that inhabit forests, argued rather for separating the primal pair. "Let the Sky," he said, "become a stranger to us, but let Earth remain close, as our nursing mother." And this was the plan accepted.

First Rongo-ma-tane, god and father of the cultivated food of men, rose up and strove to force the heavens from the earth. When Rongo had failed, next Tangaroa, god and father of all things that live in the sea, rose up. He struggled mightily, but had no luck. And next Haumia-tiketike, god and father of uncultivated food, rose up and tried, without success. So then Tu-matauenga, god of war, leapt up. Tu hacked at the sinews that bound the Earth and Sky and made them bleed, and this gave rise to ochre, or red clay, the sacred color. Yet even Tu, the fiercest of the sons, could not with all his strength sever Rangi from Papa. So then it became the turn of Tane-mahuta.

Slowly, slowly as the kauri tree did Tane rise between the Earth and Sky. At first he strove with his arms to move them, but with no success. And so he paused, and the pause was an immense period of time. Then he placed his shoulders against the Earth his mother, and his feet against the Sky. Soon, and yet not soon, for the time was vast, the Sky and Earth began to yield. The sinews that bound them stretched and ripped. With heavy groans and shrieks of pain, the parents of the sons cried out and asked them why they did this crime, why did they wish to slay their parents' love? Great Tane thrust with all his strength, which was the strength of growth. Far beneath him he pressed the Earth. Far above he thrust the Sky, and held him there. As soon as Tane's work was finished the multitude of creatures were uncovered whom Rangi and Papa had begotten and who had never known the light.[9]

Figs. 66, 67 It was the function of the Mesopotamian temple towers to heal this break and on festival occasions to link the separated pair for the restoration of fruitfulness. According to Herodotus' description, fifth century B.C., of the great temple tower of the Babylon of his day, the building stood behind a wall of great strength in a compound a quarter of a mile square and with gates of solid brass.

> In the middle of the precinct there was a tower of solid masonry, a furlong in length and breadth, upon which was raised a second tower, and on that a third, and so on up to eight. The ascent to the top is on the outside, by a path that winds round all the towers. When one is about half way up, one finds a resting-place and seats, where persons are wont to sit some time on their way to the summit. On the topmost tower there is a spacious temple, and inside the temple stands a couch of unusual size, richly adorned, with a golden table by its side. There is no statue of any kind set up in the place, nor is the chamber occupied of nights by any one but a single native woman, who, as the Chaldaeans, the priests of this god, affirm, is chosen for himself by the deity out of all the women of the land.

> They also declare (but I do not believe it) that the god comes down in person into this chamber, and sleeps upon the couch. This is like the story told by the Egyptians of what takes place in their city of Thebes, where a woman always passes the night in the temple of the Theban Zeus [Amon-Re]. In each case the woman is said to be debarred all intercourse with men. It is also like the custom at Patara, in Lycia, where the priestess who delivers the oracles, during the time that she is so employed (for at Patara there is not always an oracle),[10] is shut up in the temple every night.

> Below, in the same precinct, there is a sitting figure of Zeus [Babylonian Bel Marduk], all of gold. Before the figure stands a large golden table, and the throne whereon it sits as well as the base whereon the throne is placed are likewise of gold. The Chaldaeans told me that all the gold together was 800 talents' weight. Outside this temple are two altars, one of solid gold, on which it is lawful to offer only sucklings; the other, a common altar, but of great size, on which the full grown animals are sacrificed. It is also on the great altar that the Chaldaeans burn the frankincense, which is offered to the amount of 1,000 talents' weight every year, at the festival of the god. In the time of Cyrus there was likewise in this temple the figure of a man, eighteen feet high, entirely of solid gold.[11]

67. *Babylon of Nebuchadnezzar II. 604-562* B.C. *Restoration Painting by Maurice Bardin.*

Fig. 68

Fig. 69

Figs. 70-72

The early Sumerian seal below shows the holy moment of the mystic bed where the god and goddess of sky and earth—possibly incarnate in the persons of a priest and priestess, king and queen, or king and priestess (the dedicated woman named by Herodotus)—are joined in divine connubium as they had been at the beginning of time. The slightly later Akkadian scene depicts the ritual of the sacred drink, preparatory to the culminating sacrament of the bed. In Figures 70-72 we have a superb contemporary representation of the whole ascent and meeting at the summit of a temple tower, with indications of the animal and harvest offerings, the gate and priestess of the summit-chamber, the cortege of approaching priests (always naked in Sumerian rites), and the welcome of the arriving high priest or king.

68. *Marriage of Heaven and Earth. Early 3rd millennium* B.C. *Sumer*

69. *The Ritual Drink. 2350-2150* B.C. *Akkad*

70. *The Warka Vase. 4th-3rd millennium* B.C. *Sumer. Extended Drawing. (See Figure 71)*

"This, the oldest ritual vase in carved stone that has so far been discovered in Mesopotamia," writes André Parrot, "can be dated to round about 3000 B.C. It initiates us into the atmosphere of the age and with it we get for the first time a notion of the way in which man entered the presence of his gods. . . .

"The theme is the cult of the goddess Innin, here represented by her emblems: two bundles of reeds, which, placed side by side, symbolize no doubt the entrance of a temple. A long line of offering-bearers is approaching it: naked men carrying baskets of fruit and vegetables, and vases. One of them leads the way and immediately behind him is a dignitary whose face has unfortunately been brok-

en off. Presumably he was the king of the city or its high priest. His long-tasseled belt is held up like a train by an attendant, and he is greeted by a woman just come out of the temple, perhaps the goddess herself, but more probably, in our opinion, the High Priestess. Behind her, within the sacred precinct, is a great pile of offerings: baskets and dishes of fruit, animal shaped vases, and other objects. More problematical are the two rams bearing small figures. Finally, in the lowest band, we see a procession of animals moving along a strip of fertile land which, given the luxuriance of the barley and other vegetation, is evidently on the riverside."[12]

Fig. 72

71. *The Warka Vase.*
(See Figure 70)

72 *(opposite). Detail (top register) of Figure 71*

The word "ziggurat," by which such towering Mesopotamian structures are des- Fig. 73
ignated, is from the Babylonian verb *zagaru*, meaning "to be tall, to be lofty," and—
contrary to the view of the authors of the Biblical tale of Babel (Genesis 11:1-9)—
such towers were not meant to storm the heavens but to elevate the mind and heart
to supernal contemplation and to provide, as well, a scale of descent for the gods
to come down to earth. As expounded by one of the master scholars and interpreters
of this archaic view of the universe and its mystery, the late Alfred Jeremias of the
University of Leipzig:

> The whole cosmos is regarded as pervaded by a single life, in such a way that Figs. 74, 75
> there is a harmony recognized between the upper and lower modes of Being and
> Becoming. The informing thought of the Sumerian world feeling is: "What is above
> is below"; and from this two directions of spiritual movement are projected: the
> Above comes downward, the Below mounts aloft. The spatial symbol of this world
> feeling is the stepped Sumerian temple-tower with its various cosmological names,
> such as, "Temple of the Seven Conveyers of the Commands of Heaven and Earth,"
> "Temple of the Foundation of Heaven and Earth," etc., the stages of the tower cor-
> responding to the different levels of doctrine of the ranges of the upper world.
>
> Moreover, the entirety of the Above and Below is thought of as filled with spiritual
> godly presences, which pass as "heavenly energies" upward and downward. The
> visible yet unattainable celestial bodies are regarded as the material nuclei of
> heavenly forces. And man, too, is a spiritual being: an "image of divinity" veiled in
> earthly clothing, consigned however to death, since the gods "kept life to themselves"
> and "denied eternal life" to mankind. All human Being and Becoming is guided
> from on high. . . .
>
> Accordingly, the earthly order corresponds to the heavenly. Every priest-king in
> his own domain (which is a miniature of the cosmos) is by the grace of his god a
> consummate image of the godhead. And this idea lives on even after the high
> symbolic period passes. Every throne is the image of a heavenly throne. The king's
> court reflects that of his god. As steps are mounted to a throne, so one mounts the
> stages to heaven. Moreover, the same thought can be recognized in the structure
> of any temple. The forecourt leads to the sanctuary, and the sanctuary to the inner
> shrine, where the image represents the seat of the supreme god. The spatial symbol-
> ism of such a temple-form corresponds to that of the ziggurat projected on a flat sur-
> face: the penetration ever deeper inward being equivalent to the ascent ever higher
> aloft.[13]

This old Sumerian idea of the graded stages of a universal manifestation of divinity, symbolized in the towering ziggurats and understood to correspond to grades in
the powers of human consciousness, survived through many transformations of
myths and monuments, not only throughout antiquity, but also (in the Orient) even
to modern times. And not only were the gods of unequal majesty, but the substance
of the mountain itself became denser and less luminous in the long descent from
the summit to the plane of earth.

73. *Ziggurat of Dur Kurigalzu. 14th century* B.C. *Near Baghdad, Iraq*

74. *Kudurru. 12th century* B.C.   75. *Figure 74. Extended Drawing*

In the Babylonian boundary stone shown here, for example, the manifestations of deity on the six stages of the world mountain are displayed in descending series, from the governing spheres above—symbolized (left to right) by the planet Venus of the goddess Ishtar, the lunar crescent of the moon-god Sin, and the solar disk of Shamash—downward, stage by stage, to the elements of the watery abyss. The huge serpent winding up the left side of the sculptured stone cannot be seen in a frontal view, but bends across the top to present its head above the cup of the crescent moon. And as in the Indian image of the reclining world-dreamer Vishnu, above whose head the five cobra hoods of the cosmic serpent Ananta bend, so the reptile here is symbolic of the primal generative waters that surround the universe, support it from beneath, and rain down upon it from on high. Turn the present picture on its side and the parallel becomes perfectly evident.

Fig. 4
cf. Fig. 29

Now the fluency of the serpent suggests water, and its continually flashing forked red tongue suggests flame, the life-giving fire inherent in fertilizing waters. Moreover, the moon is compared to a cup, continually filled with and emptied of ambrosial fiery fluids of which sacramental intoxicants are the extract—which is perhaps why Noah, the moon man who had sailed his moon boat on the cosmic sea, planted a vineyard immediately when the waters had abated, became drunk, and lay uncovered in his tent (Genesis 9:20-21). The moon is lord of the tides of life, both the oceanic ebb and flow and the rhythms of the womb. Shedding its shadow, furthermore, as the serpent its skin, it is the high celestial sign of the same triumphant power of life as that represented in the serpent sloughing death.

As represented in this *kudurru*, the star, the moon, and the solar disk above the Figs. 74, 75 summit of the world mountain stand for the ultimate governing powers of the cosmos. Impersonal, mathematically moved, their destiny-shaping orbits are beyond the reach of prayer. Hence the main divinities addressed in temple and court rituals are of the next two stages down.

On the first of these lower stages are three chapels, or as interpreted by some, three thrones supporting turbans of the deities designated, who are Anu, Lord of the Great Above; Enlil, of the Air and Earth; and Ea (Enki, Oannes), of the "House of Water."

Next below are the seats and symbols of the special patron gods of Babylon: first Marduk, son of Ea, patron god of the city, whose animal is a dragon; next Marduk's son and messenger, the god of writing and wisdom, Nabu, whose animal here is a goat; and finally Ninhurshag-Ninlil, the goddess-queen herself, the Mountain Mother.

The following two ranges are of this earthly plane, first of the atmosphere all about us and then of the earthly powers below ground. On the first we see the standards of the guardians of the four world quarters. The bizarre hawk's head at the left and double-lion column beside it are the emblems of two heroic monster-slayers, Zamama of Kish and Ninib of Nippur; the enshrined image of a horse's head is of some foreign, perhaps Aryan, warrior god; and the miserable eagle to the right is surely also of some war god, as yet, however, unidentified. Below ground sits the goddess Gula, from behind whom the cosmic serpent rises. She is the patroness of herbs, healing, and burgeoning life, as her flowered garment shows. Hands lifted in a gesture of prayer, she sits with her dog, defender of homes, while before her a Scorpion Archer mounts guard at the uttermost bound of the earth, i.e., the shore of the cosmic sea, fending off daemonic powers and so protecting both the rising and the setting sun.

Beneath all, in the abyssal sea itself at the base, are the symbols of the four elements of which all things above are composed: at the right, the lamp of Nusku, a god of fire; at the left, the bull and thunder-sign of Ramman-Adad, an air and storm god; below, the scorpion, earth-dwelling dealer of death; and above, the swimming tortoise, here supporting with his little feet the entire cosmic mountain.[14] These are clearly mythological prototypes of the later classical four elements. The tortoise, of the watery element, is an animal associated with Ea, the water god. The scorpion corresponds to the guardian Scorpion Archer of the earth-goddess Gula. Ramman-Adad is an air god akin to the lord of the atmosphere, Enlil. And the lamp of the fire-god Nusku, intentionally shaped to suggest a crescent moon, refers by this sign to the heavenly fires of the night sky, the lamps of the high heavenly father Anu.

Thus the entire universe, finally, whether viewed in its highest or in its lowest aspect, is a reflex, according to this ancient view, of four elementary powers; the same that we have already found personified of old in the four great gods of the earliest literate civilization known to us: Anu (light or fire), Enlil (air), Ea (water), and the Goddess (earth).

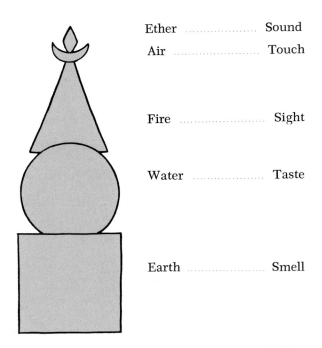

Ether .... Sound
Air .... Touch

Fire .... Sight

Water .... Taste

Earth .... Smell

76. *Components of the Buddhist Stupa*
The number of the elements in the Indian system is five: first, space or ether, experienced as sound, from which the other four proceed by devolution in the following sequence: air, experienced through touch; fire, through sight; water, through taste; and earth, through smell. These primary five, however, are of a subtle quality imperceptible to the gross senses. To compose their perceptible gross counterparts, they combine in

the following way: "By dividing each subtle element into two equal parts and subdividing the first half of each into four equal parts, then adding to the unsubdivided half of each element one subdivision of each of the remaining four, each element becomes five in one" (*Panchadashi* 1.27).

These gross elements are named according to their principal components, but since each contains portions of each of the rest, they all affect all the senses.[15]

air		ether		ether		ether		ether	
fire	ether	fire	air	air	fire	air	water	air	earth
water		water		water		fire		fire	
earth		earth		earth		earth		water	

The poet stands before the walls and cathedral of his city, gesturing toward the gate of Hell, from which the church and his book are to save us. A company of the lost, herded by devils horned like heathen gods, is descending to the pit. Behind stands the mountain of purgatory in the perfect form of a ziggurat; on its summit is the earthly paradise in the figure of a sacred marriage, while above the moon and other celestial lights are ranged in the order of Dante's own progress to the heaven of the beatific vision.

78. *Temple (view from the west).* A.D. *12th century. Arunachaleshvara, South India.*

79. *Detail (of interior) of Figure 78*

In the shrine at the right reposes an image of Nandi, Shiva's bull, facing the entrance to a temple of his lord (outside the picture, to the left). In the background towers a temple gate symbolic of the world mountain, supporting on its summit the high chamber of Shiva and his consort Parvati, "Daughter of the Mountain." Beneath this multistoried structure we are to imagine equivalent ranges descending deep into the earth. And as in Dante's vision, so here: the abyss, the world mountain, and the heavenly stages are understood to represent, respectively, states of spiritual pain, exaltation, and beatitude.

81. Detail of Figure 80 (center of the west façade)

80. Borobudur, Java. A.D. 8th-9th century

This richly ornamented Buddhist temple is conceived in the image of the world mountain. Ascending its stages, the mind of the pilgrim visitor is elevated from earthly to transcendental concerns. Around its sculptured base are representations of the pleasures and sorrows of earthly life, the sufferings in the ranges of hell, and the joys of the storied heavens. The first gallery then exhibits scenes from the life of the Buddha Shakyamuni, who achieved and taught release from the unending round of rebirths. Mounting further, we are inspired by the pictured legend of a princely youth in quest of illumination, consulting various great teachers; higher still is the biography of the Buddhist sage Asanga (fifth century A.D.), who gained release through a vision of the Future Buddha Maitreya.

On the summit-platforms, high above the earthly plane, are three circles of bellshaped tabernacles enclosing "Meditation Buddhas," which are reminders of the Buddha-wisdom that is resident in each of us, only waiting for our minds to waken inward and be drawn spontaneously to that center of interior peace which is actually already ours.

82-83. *Ankor Wat.* A.D. *early 12th century. Cambodia.*
At left, air view from the west;
above, air view from the northwest

84 (opposite). *The Temple of Heaven. (Hall of Prayers for an Abundant Harvest, top center.)* A.D. *17th century. Peking, China*

85. *Hall of Prayers for an Abundant Harvest. Detail of Figure 84*

86. *Mayan Temple.* A.D. 292-869. *Tikal, Guatemala. Restoration Drawing by Tatania Proskouriakoff*

The long, very steep flights of steps of the Mayan temple towers, mounting heavenward to symbolically ornamented chambers, suggest comparison with the Mesopotamian ziggurats and have consequently occasioned professional as well as popular speculation. Not only the architecture but also the mythology of the Middle American representations of the world mountain can be compared with the symbolic forms both of the ancient Near East and of India. "The Maya," states one of the leading students of this culture, the late Sylvanus G. Morley, "conceived the world as having thirteen heavens, arranged in layers, the lowest being the earth itself. Over each presided one of the Thirteen Gods of the Upper World or Oxlahuntiku—meaning in Maya, *oxlahun*, 'thirteen,' *ti*, 'of,' and *ku*, 'god' (here 'gods') and by association 'heaven.' In addition to the thirteen upper worlds there were nine underworlds, also arranged in layers, over each of which presided its own special god, one of the *Bolontiku* or Nine Gods of the Lower World, meaning in Maya, *bolon*, 'nine,' *ti*, 'of,' and *ku*, 'god.' The ninth and lowest underworld was Mitnal, ruled by Ah Puch, the Lord of Death. . . ."[16]

cf. Fig. 66

Above and beyond the highest heaven, furthermore, was the ultimate source and essence of all, known as *Hunab ku*, whose name itself, combining *hun*, "one," *ab*, "state of being," and *ku*, "god," proclaims the mystery of a transcendence of all temporal changes and oppositions.

"The Maya Paradise," Morley continues, "is described as a place of delights, where there was no pain or suffering, but on the contrary an abundance of good foods and sweet drinks, where grew the *yaxche*, or sacred tree of the Maya (the *ceiba*), under the branches and grateful shade of which they could rest and forever cease from labor. The penalty exacted from those whose lives had been evil was that they had to descend into a lower region called Mitnal—the Maya Hell. There devils tormented them with hunger, cold, weariness, and grief."[17]

When such analogies—and they are innumerable—are contemplated, associating the mythologically inspired civilizations of Middle and South America with those of trans-Pacific Asia, the inevitable question arises: Can so many exact correspondences, touching every aspect of life, science, the arts, and ceremonial custom, even manners of dress, details of ornament, and symbols of authority, have come into being simply as a consequence of (to repeat the earlier quote from Frazer) "similar causes acting alike on the similar constitution of the human mind in different countries and under different skies"? Can it be assumed that the human nervous system is "programmed" to such a degree? Many think not, rejecting the possibility of an absolutely separate development of two flowerings in so many ways alike. In the biological sciences no such possibility would be allowed. How, then, diffusionists argue, in the cultural-historical?

87. *Acropolis.* A.D. *300-900. Copan, Honduras.*
Restoration Drawing by Tatania Proskouriakoff

88. *Temple Area (view from the north).* A.D. 950-1460. *Chichen Itza, Yucatan. Restoration Drawing by Tatania Proskouriakoff*

89. *"El Castillo" (Temple of Kulkulcan). Detail of Figure 88.*

90. *Toltec Temple of Quetzalcoatl (detail). ca.* A.D. *800. Teotihuacan, Mexico*

3. The World Mountain in Middle America

THE earliest known artificial mountain in the American hemisphere was constructed about 800 B.C. as the dominant shrine of an altogether mysterious, geometrically ordered ceremonial complex situated on a tiny, sandy, swamp-surrounded islet, hardly thirteen hundred yards across and two and three-quarter miles long, in a region of tropical forest, high annual rainfall, sluggish rivers and extensive swamps, some nine miles up the Tonala River, which separates Tabasco from Veracruz. The questions of why such a site should have been chosen for a sanctuary, who the people can have been who chose it, where their already highly developed sculptural art, building techniques, and religious notions can have originated, and what possible relationship they can have had to the comparatively primitive peoples of the undeveloped neighborhood, remain, one and all, unanswered. As first reported, in 1959, the base of the impressive adobe pyramid, which at that time was heavily overgrown, was thought to be rectangular.[18] A second study, however, in 1967, after a clearing away of the forest cover, revealed the curiously fluted, nearly circular, conical form shown here.[19] It has now been suggested that the monument may have been designed to imitate some specific feature of the natural landscape, and a possible model has been found in the fluted volcanic cinder cones of the nearby Tuxtla Mountains,

Fig. 91

91. Olmec Pyramid (air view from the southeast). ca. 800 B.C. La Venta, Tabasco, Mexico.

some forty miles to the west of this forest site. In relation to our present theme, however, it little matters whether a natural mountain somewhere else or a builder's imagination at work in the precincts of La Venta itself supplied the architectural model for this unprecedented pyramid. The *idea* involved in either case would have been of an artificial hill dominating a geometrically organized ceremonial center; and our question consequently must be of the source as well as the sense of this *idea*. Can it have originated in the New World independently of the Old? What mythology can it have served? And of what sort, to what purpose, were the rituals that were enacted in these plazas?

92. *Olmec Ceremonial Center. 1200-800 B.C. (Olmec period). La Venta, Tabasco, Mexico.*

This group of monuments consists of an alignment of mounds and plazas some 700 yards long, its centerline leaning about 8 degrees westward of true north, and its dominant feature a huge adobe mound in the form of a roughly circular fluted pyramid approximately 420 feet in diameter and 103 feet high. Mounds A-4 and A-5 are each about 95 yards long, 3 feet high, and 53 feet across the top. They appear to have been terraced, the lower terraces paved with immense limestone slabs, some as much as 10 inches thick and weighing 300 to 400 pounds. Originally A-3 and A-2 were rectangular platforms, the former some 60 to 75 feet long, 40 feet wide, and 2½ feet high; the latter has not been described. Between these was a broad rectangular court surrounded by a kind of fence of columnar basalt pillars set upright along the top of a low wall of adobe bricks.[20] A leading authority suggests between 800 and 700 B.C. as the date of the building of the pyramid, "which would have been," he writes, "about the mid-point of the site's use. . . . It is possible, even probable, that the La Venta pyramid is the largest construction in all of Mesoamerica dating from early in the first millennium B.C."[21]

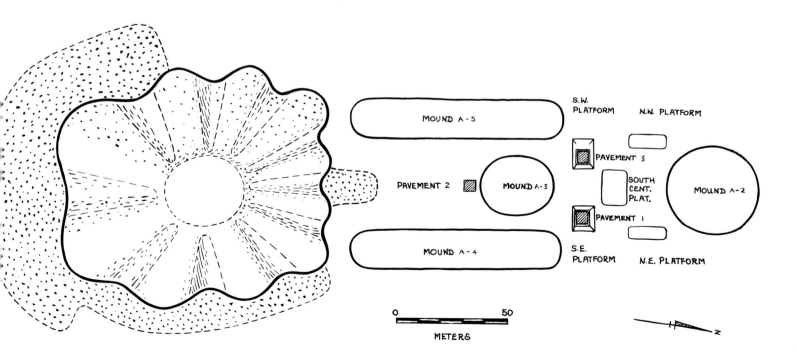

MOUND A-5

S.W. PLATFORM   N.W. PLATFORM

PAVEMENT 3

PAVEMENT 2   MOUND A-3   SOUTH CENT. PLAT.   MOUND A-2

PAVEMENT 1

MOUND A-4

S.E. PLATFORM   N.E. PLATFORM

0   50
METERS

Fig. 93   Four prodigious basalt heads add to the enigma of this site and its civilization; not only because of their size, but also because of their features, which are of a Negroid or Polynesian cast, whereas most of the figures of this so-called Olmec culture complex show a race of Mongoloid affinity. Eight more monuments of this kind have been found on related sites: two at Tres Zapotes, five at San Lorenzo, and one (unfinished) at San Miguel, the smallest being about five feet high (Monument Q, Tres Zapotes) and the largest (Monument 1, San Lorenzo) nine and a half. Dr. Matthew Stirling of the Smithsonian Institution, one of the leading investigators of this culture, has pointed out that the realistic treatment of the heads precludes the probability of their representing gods:

> Each has an individual quality and was probably the portrait of a prominent leader. The expressions differ; some are stern, some are placid, one is smiling. In two instances at least, the teeth are shown; usually the iris is indicated by a circle in low relief on the eyeball. All wear a close-fitting, helmet-like headdress, some rather elaborately decorated, some plain. . . . The majority have ear ornaments: a circular earspool or a rectangular bar through the lobe. All heads share one feature: a perfectly flat, plain surface a foot or more in width extending vertically up the middle of the back. This might indicate that the heads were meant to be set up against a wall, a possibility borne out by the fact that in most cases they were designed to be viewed from in front or at a three-quarter angle. The features appear rather flat when seen in full profile.[22]

93. Olmec Colossal Head. La Venta, Tabasco, Mexico

The great blocks of stone from which these huge heads were carved had to be transported to their present sites from quarries many miles away: so, too, the materials for the numerous basalt columns variously placed about, and for the ponderous limestone slabs incorporated in the platforms. It has been recognized that the little swamp-surrounded, sandy isle of the ceremonial center itself can hardly have supported more than a small resident group of priests or priestly rulers, master craftsmen, sculptors, and builders, together with their personal servants. Hence, the larger labor force must have been recruited from villages round about—whether by force or by religious persuasion alone, there is no one to tell.[23]

94. *Olmec Sarcophagus (now destroyed). La Venta, Tabasco, Mexico*

Nor can the really great tradition of sculptural masterworks have sprung spontaneously to view, full blown, from the conditions of this forest site; or even from those of the whole complex of Olmec sites so far discovered and investigated. No signs have been found anywhere of a period of development; yet no one who has ever set foot inside a gallery, studio, or museum would fail to recognize and regard with awe the art of such a piece as, for example, Figure 95. Whether in basalt colossi or in miniatures of jade, the unfailing mastery displayed in Olmec art is consummate —and the artists worked, furthermore, as the laborers quarried, without metal tools.

Figs. 97, 98

95. *Olmec "Wrestler." Veracruz, Mexico*

The nature and function of the rites enacted in the precincts are all but impossible to surmise. They involved, among other enigmatic enterprises, the burial at great depths, in various quarters of the sanctuary, of both massive and smaller offerings, meticulously covered with layers of differing kinds of soil: the great jaguar-sarcophagus seen here, for example; layers of studiously arranged, carefully shaped and polished stone blocks; layers of celts and other valuable objects carved of jade and serpentine; ceramic vessels and, in separate locations, half a dozen or so remarkable concave stone mirrors, highly polished and hollowed in such a way that it would have been possible to use them to reflect and focus solar rays to ignite a fire.[24] The most amazing of all these buried offerings, however, is the miniature ritual scene of sixteen figurines and six long polished jade celts that was unearthed from beneath the court pavement (Pavement 1) just west of the middle of the northeast platform, and is shown in Figure 96. As described by the excavators:

Fig. 94

Fig. 96

> The long slender celts, all of jade, stood upright edge to edge along the east and southeast edge of an ellipse 20 inches along its north-south diameter and 14 inches east-west. The figurines also were standing upright. One of them, typically Olmec stylistically, but of very unusual material, was placed so that it stood with its back against the row of celts. The other 15 figurines, two of jade and the rest of serpentine, were placed in front of this figure. A file of four was set up as though passing in review from north to south. The 11 other figurines are arranged in a semicircle along the western side of the ellipse, watching.
>
> The feet of the figurines and polls of the celts were embedded in a small, slightly mounded hump of reddish-brown sand which, as an extensive layer, constituted part of the fill underlying the rose-colored floors [of the sanctuary]. After the celts and figurines had been placed in position the feet and lower legs of the figures and the polls of the celts were buried about 1½ inches in the reddish-brown sand to hold them upright. The whole offering was covered with white sand. At this point the white sand was mounded up so that it covered the figurines and extended outward, in the form of an elliptical lens, some distance north and south. A thin brown sand layer was then used to fill out the surrounding area level with the top of the white sand mound in which the figurines were buried. The area was then leveled off and covered over.[25]

Mounted exactly as it had stood for more than two thousand years beneath Pavement 1 of the La Venta sanctuary, the mysterious little scene is now on exhibit in the National Museum of Mexico; and although thus brought to the light of our own day, it is still enclosed in its own great darkness. To what end was it made? Who or what are its eunuchoid participants? What are they doing? And why were they thus interred?

If we may judge from this little scene and from the features generally characteristic of Olmec jade figurines, the solemn rituals of this earliest New World high culture complex were conducted by an order of priests of eunuchoid physique, associated in some way with a jaguar cult that involved the sacrifice of young boys whose

96 (overleaf). Olmec Buried Offering of Figurines in Ritual Scene. La Venta, Tabasco, Mexico

97. *Olmec Priest with Jaguar Boy. Mexico*

98. *Olmec Were-Jaguar Figurine. Necaxa, Puebla, Mexico*

100 (opposite). Olmec "Quintuplet Altar." La Venta, Tabasco, Mexico

99. *Olmec Jaguar God.*
Veracruz, Mexico

Figs. 97-101ciated in some way with a jaguar cult that involved the sacrifice of young boys whose heads were deformed (artificially?) in such a way as to suggest the features of a jaguar—possibly a mythic jaguar-child. A number of theories have been proposed to account for the prominence of this jaguar theme in Olmec art; and of these, two deserve special mention.

The first refers to the prevalence even today of a were-jaguar concept among North and South American Indian tribes. Briefly stated: both shamans and jaguars are believed to have supernatural powers, and to such a degree that, as Professor Peter Furst of the University of California has put the case: "shamans and jaguars are not merely equivalent, but each is at the same time the other."[26] It is possible, therefore, according to this view, that the curiously eunuchoid body forms and feline features of the Olmec figurines refer not to actual human models but to a mythological concept, "the supernatural jaguar qualities inherent in the priest or shaman, his spiritual bond and identity with the jaguar, and his capacity, unique among men, of crossing the boundary between animals and humankind by achieving total spiritual transformation."[27] To be noted in addition, however, is the fact that among many of both the North and the South American Indian tribes the leading shamans are not infrequently transvestites—not only wearing women's clothes and living as women, but even, in some cases, having been physically transformed into *mujerados*, "womanized ones," by means of an intensive daily regimen practiced upon them in adolescence of unremitting, debilitating masturbation;[28] so that indeed the were-jaguars of Professor Furst's observation may also have been artificially "womanized" androgynes, and the body forms of the Olmec figurines based on natural models after all.

The second relevant theory is based on the evidence of two mutilated works of sculpture in the round discovered at separate sites in southern Veracruz, representing a jaguar, ceremonially attired, in sexual intercourse with a human female.* One thinks immediately of the escapades of Zeus as a bull, a serpent, or a swan, and the obvious implication of the Olmec works then would appear to be that they illustrate some legend of a mythic sacred marriage wherein the godly role was played by a were-jaguar, jaguar-god, or shaman, the offspring of which *hieros gamos* would then have been either a single incarnate jaguar-boy or a host of such jaguar sons.

Fig. 101In Figure 101 a bearded personage, ponderously crowned and bearing a ceremonial mace, stands surrounded by such a company, of which he is obviously the lord—as is Shiva, in India, of the young wind gods, the Maruts; and in Europe, Othin, of his night-flying Howling Host.

Fig. 102A further and particularly striking illustration of the possibility of Old World mythological motifs recurring in the New appears in Figure 102, where a Middle

---

* The published photographs of the two mutilated images are unfortunately all but impossible to make out, so badly battered are the fragments. However, the monuments have been excellently described by their discoverer, Dr. Matthew W. Stirling. See opposite page.

Monument 1 at Río Chiquito

"Monument 1 was lying in the village of Tenochtitlán (Veracruz) when we first saw it. According to the natives it was found in the vicinity of the nearby group of large mounds. The sculpture apparently represents an anthropomorphic jaguar seated on a human figure lying on the back cross-legged. Presumably the lower figure is that of a woman, and the act of copulation is depicted. This identification would be much less certain were it not for the fact that we later found a much more realistically carved monument (Monument 3, Potrero Nuevo) representing the same subject. The upper figure of Monument 1 is carved in the full round and considerably more care is used in forming it than is the case with the lower figure, which is flattened and somewhat angular. The jaguar is shown with a long trailing ornament hanging down the lower part of the back and what appears to be a headdress hanging over the back of the neck. The heads of both figures are missing, as are the forearms of the upper figure. The sculpture proper is mounted on a low flat base."

Monument 3 at Potrero Nuevo

"Monument 3 was found . . . on the high elevation west of Potrero Nuevo. The subject, which is similar to Monument 1, Río Chiquito, apparently represented copulation between a jaguar and a woman. The figure of the woman is represented lying on the back with knees drawn upward along the abdomen and with bent elbows, the hands extending upward. The head, hands, and feet are missing. The body of the jaguar is missing except for the hind feet, the lower part of a double back ornament, and a tail. Ornaments in the form of bands with a decorative attachment in the rear are worn about both ankles. The portions of the jaguar which remain are much more animalistic than in Monument 1, Río Chiquito; the feet, claws, and tail definitely identifying the subject. As in the similar monument, this one is mounted on a low flat base. Although badly broken, enough remains to indicate that in its complete form Monument 3 must have been a strongly carved and striking piece of sculpture. The episode represented must have been an important feature of Olmec mythology. It is particularly interesting in view of the frequent representation of part human and part jaguar figures in Olmec art, these often having infantile characteristics. . . ."[29]

101. Olmec Stele. La Venta, Tabasco, Mexico

cf. Fig. 4
cf. Fig. 10

cf. Fig. 5

cf. Fig. 13, 103

cf. Fig. 253

cf. Figs. 123ff.

American counterpart of both the Hindu vision of Vishnu on the serpent and the earlier Egyptian scene of Osiris on the cosmic crocodile is to be seen.

The feathered serpent portrayed here combines the natures of the two traditional animal vehicles of Vishnu, the sun-bird Garuda of the upper worlds and the serpent Ananta of the lower, while the jaguar mask of the seated human figure suggests both Vishnu in his incarnation as the "Man-Lion" and the leonine Egyptian sphinx, symbolic of pharaonic rule.

Moreover, the little bag or bucket extended in the right hand of this seated jaguar-man has been identified as probably a container of powdered copal*—used to this day in Mexico as incense, the usual ritual symbol (known to Egypt and India as well as to both pagan and Catholic Rome) of the odor of sacrifice as a fragrance pleasing to gods.

Further: the left hand of this seated figure is held somewhat awkwardly (as remarked by the archaeologist-discoverers, "turned at the wrist with the palm out"),[30] in a gesture that in the Orient would be everywhere interpreted as the "boon-bestowing hand-posture" (*varada-mudra*) of a divinity; and the fact that the Olmec artist even over-strained his art to render it in the profile of his relief suggests that the gesture must have had some such ritual meaning in Middle America as well.

* A resinous substance prepared from the sap of certain trees.

102. *Olmec Stone Tablet. La Venta, Tabasco, Mexico*

103 (right). *Vishnu, the Man-Lion.*
   A.D. *8th century*

104 (below). *Vishnu, the Man-Lion.*
   A.D. *19th century*

The legend is of an atheistic king named "Golden Garment," who through the power of yoga had become sole sovereign of the universe, overthrowing even the gods. But he had an intensely pious son named "Joyful Excitement," who was an absolutely faithful devotee of the cosmic dreamer Vishnu; and the wicked father's repeated attempts to put this irritating youth out of the way were miraculously, one and all, frustrated.

One fateful day, when his son declared that Vishnu was everywhere, the king challenged him to explain why, if that were so, the god was not visible in a pillar of the palace, which he thereupon struck with his fist. The column split and out sprang Vishnu in a terrible form, part lion, part man. A brief but furious battle ensued, which ended with the belly of the king ripped open and the lion-god consuming his guts with relish. The episode is portrayed comically in the popular Kathakali plays and described at length in the *Bhagavata Purana*.

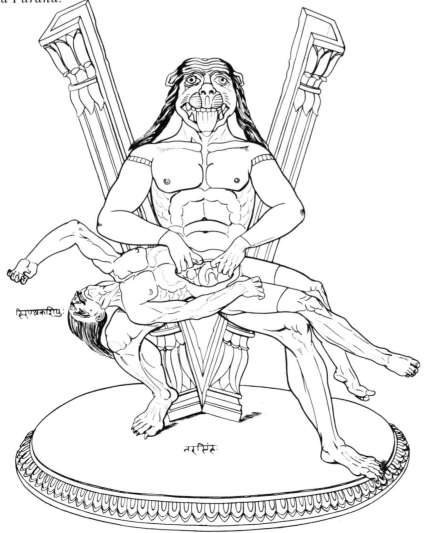

THE LEGEND OF THE ''FACE OF GLORY''

The Indian legend of the "Face of Glory" begins, like that of the Man-Lion, with the case of an infinitely ambitious king who through extraordinary austerities had gained the power to unseat the gods and was now sole sovereign of the universe. His name was Jalandhara, "Water Carrier," and he conceived the impudent notion of challenging even Shiva, the supreme sustainer of the world. (In the Man-Lion legend this was the role of Vishnu. The present legend belongs to the mythology of Shiva.) The king's idea was to demand that Shiva should surrender to him the goddess Parvati, his wife, and to this end he sent as messenger a terrible monster called Rahu, "the Seizer," whose usual role is to seize and eclipse the moon.

Rahu approached the Lord of Life and Death, and when he had stated Jalandhara's demand, the god simply widened that third eye between his brows, whereupon a flash of lightning shot forth, striking the earth and taking the form of a lion-headed demon whose alarming body, lean, huge, and emaciated, gave notice of insatiable hunger. Its throat roared like thunder; its two eyes burned like fire; the mane, disheveled, floated far and wide into space. Clearly its strength was irresistible. Rahu was aghast and did the only thing left for him to do. He threw himself on Shiva's mercy, and the god—for such is the way of gods—granted protection.

This, however, only created a new predicament, since the ravenous half-lion, who was nothing if not hunger incarnate, now had nothing to eat. And he, too, turned to the god, imploring him to furnish a victim. Whereupon Shiva, with one of those inspirations such as occur only to the greatest, suggested that the monster should eat himself—to which work the prodigy immediately turned and the gorgeous banquet began.

Commencing with his feet and hands, continuing through his legs and arms, the monster, ravenous and unable to stop, let his teeth go right on chopping through his belly, chest, and even his neck, until there was nothing left but a face. And the god, who had been watching with delight this epitomization of the self-consuming mystery that is life, smiled, when the feat had been accomplished, upon what remained of that creature of his wrath, and said to it: "You shall be known henceforth as Kirttimukha, 'Face of Glory,' and shall abide forever at my door. No one who fails to worship you will ever obtain my grace."[31]

"Kirttimukha," Heinrich Zimmer states in commenting on this legend, "was first a special emblem of Shiva himself and a characteristic element on the lintels of Shiva temples. Presently, then, the 'Face' began to be used indiscriminately on various parts of Hindu shrines as an auspicious device to ward off evil. . . .

"This monster is a match for any evil. The principle symbolized in its eloquent deed, once grasped by the mind and assimilated by the faculties, will protect against both spiritual and physical disaster in the deepest darknesses of the jungle of the world."[32]

And we have the comment, also, of Ananda K. Coomaraswamy: "The Kirttimukha as the Terrible Face of God, who as the Sun and Death both generates and devours his children, is analogous to the Greek Gorgoneion and the Chinese T'ao t'ieh, the 'Glutton.' "[33]

106 (opposite). "Face of Glory" (Kirttimukha). A.D.13th century. Over Temple Doorway. Panataran, Java

107 (far right). "Face of Glory" (Kirttimukha). A.D. 8th century. At Top of Stairway (detail of Figure 81). Borobudur, Java

105. *"Face of Glory" (Kirttimukha).*
A.D. *13th century. Reverse of a*
Shivaite Image

108. T'ao-t'ieh Mask Worn as Headgear.
13th-12th century B.C.

109. T'ao-t'ieh Mask Analyzed (see Figure 110)

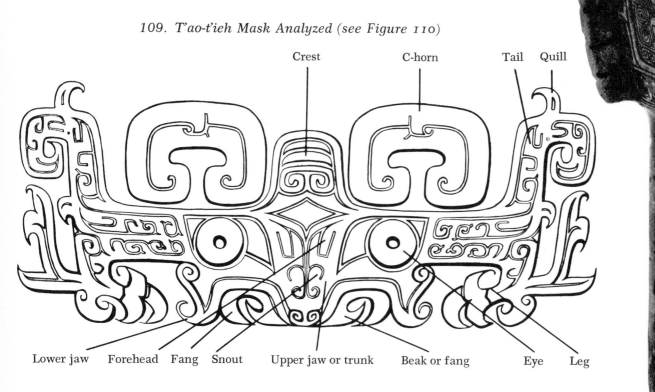

Crest   C-horn   Tail   Quill

Lower jaw   Forehead   Fang   Snout   Upper jaw or trunk   Beak or fang   Eye   Leg

Chinese accounts of the meaning of the *t'ao-t'ieh* mask are unclear and conflicting. There is a work, supposedly of the fourth century B.C., by a certain historian, Tso chuan, which tells of dangerous spirits at large in the hills and wastes, and of how these were depicted on the sacrificial cauldrons of the legendary emperor Yü the Great, to let people know what they looked like. Another ancient work, the *Lü shih ch'un ch'iu*, thought to date from a century later, states that "On Chou vessels there was put a *t'ao-t'ieh* with a head but no body. He is eating a man and thinks he is going to swallow him; but already his own body has been destroyed.

The object of the design was to warn people that the hour of disaster was at hand."

William Willetts, from whose *Foundations of Chinese Art* I have taken these two statements, warns against the temptation to relate this ancient Chinese motif to similar forms known elsewhere. "The idea," he writes, "of a connexion between the *t'ao-t'ieh* and similar forms in the art of Mycenae, Persia, India, and Amerindia has often been mooted and is of course extremely attractive, but it should be resisted as far as possible. On Chinese bronzes the mask may in one sense represent the sacrificial animal; in another . . . it may symbolize 'an appalling tigerlike monster intended to avert evil.' "[36]

In the light, however, not only of the visual likeness but also of the ancient Chinese commentator's statement about the *"t'ao-t'ieh* with a head but no body. . . . his own body already destroyed," it is not easy to follow Professor Willetts' unexplained advice to reject out of hand all thought of any possible connection between the Chinese and other variants of this mythic figure. The makeshift anthropological term "convergence," which has been used by many to "explain" (without explaining) such appearances all over the world of identical mythic motifs—and not only individual motifs, but even great constellations of motifs, in association, furthermore, with identical religious practices—just won't do any more! Science is concerned to search out and identify causes; and the term "convergence" points to no cause, but only to the *effect* of a cause. What then are the *causes* of convergence? In some cases, psychological laws common to mankind; in others, historical connection by diffusion. In the case of the Chinese t'ao-t'ieh, Indian "Face of Glory," classical Medusa, and Middle American jaguar mask, the evidence, it seems to me, points to diffusion.

110. *T'ao-t'ieh Mask on Sacrificial Vessel.*
Shang Dynasty, 1523-1027 B.C.

cf. Figs. 105-115

The South American counterpart of the Mexican Olmec culture is the no less mysterious Chavín culture of Peru, equally abrupt in its fully formed appearance and of roughly the same very early period, ca. 800-400 B.C. The type site is Chavín de Huantar in the North Highlands, and the range includes the Peruvian coast, from the Chicama Valley in the north to Curayacu, some thirty miles south of Lima. As in the Olmec sphere, the dominant mythic figure is the jaguar-man, again with the characteristic cleft head. Moreover, there is even at one site (Punkurí in the Nepeña Valley) a monument strongly suggesting the Olmec theme of the jaguar god and his bride;* namely, "a terraced platform with a wide stairway, on which stands a feline head and paws, modeled in the round from stone and mud, and painted. At its feet is the skelton of a woman who is believed to have been sacrificed. Higher up are clay-plastered walls made of conical adobes, bearing incised designs of Chavín character."[34]

In the neighborhood of San Agustín, Colombia, the same theme has recently been found represented in both prehistoric sculpture and present-day folk legend. See Gerardo Reichel-Dolmatoff, "The Feline Motif in Prehistoric San Agustín Sculpture," in *The Cult of the Feline*, edited by Elizabeth P. Benson (Washington, D.C.: Dumbarton Oaks Research Library and Collection, 1972), pages 54-55.

The prevailing view of modern scholarship is that the earliest Chavín sites reveal influences from the Olmec. It is also possible, however, that the two represent related but independent "seedings" from a common source—possibly, as Professor Robert Heine-Geldern of the University of Vienna has pointed out in numerous publications, from contemporaneous Early Chou China, with later influences then arriving, century after century, from Southeast Asia as well.[35] In contrast, however, to the Olmec finds, among which no works in metal have appeared, those of the Chavín complex include many elegant examples of a highly competent, graceful craftsmanship in silver and gold.

* Cf. pp. 114-115, above.

Chavin Metalwork. ca. 800 B.C.
111 (upper left). Gold Breast Ornament
112 (upper center). Gold Breastplate
113 (upper right). Gold Embossed Crown
114 (lower left). Gold Ear Ornaments
115 (lower right). Silver Jaguar Face

Striking evidence of a direct influence from China to Mexico—difficult to reject, but also difficult to evaluate because of the disparity of dates—is provided by what would appear to be an identity of decorative motif in certain Chinese sacrificial vessels of the Late Chou period and a number of works in the so-called Tajín style of Classic Mayan art. The fact, furthermore, that the sacrificial scene of Figure 117 is engraved on the back of a mirror would seem to reinforce the evidence of a continuity. Professor Heine-Geldern has discussed such apparent connections in many learned publications, as have a number of other authorities, Dr. G. F. Eckholm of the American Museum of Natural History, for example, and the late artist-anthropologist Miguel Covarrubias.[37] Certain other authoritative scholars are still reluctant, however, to concede the probability of any significant trans-Pacific influence.[38] The problem is a fascinating one; and when considered in relation to the whole vast catalogue of cosmological, architectural, mythological, ceremonial, sociological, folkloristic, and philosophical parallels that unite (or at least appear to unite) the two worlds of Eurasia and Middle America, the accord is surely marvelous, however regarded: whether as evidence of cultural seeds carried in early times from one shore of the Pacific to the other, or as the result simply of a prodigious concatenation of what American anthropologists are loosely calling "convergences," resemblances arrived at accidentally by peoples altogether out of touch with each other. A sensible suggestion for the judgment of such evidence was proposed many years ago by the old master A. L. Kroeber. "The first observation to be made," he wrote in his volume *Anthropology* in 1923, "is that resemblance must not be too close if independent development is to be the explanation. . . . If the resemblance includes any inessential or arbitrary parts, such as an ornament, a proportion that so far as utility is concerned might be considerably varied but is not, a randomly chosen number, or a name, the possibility of independent development is wholly ruled out. Such intrinsic features would not recur together once in a million times."[39]

118 (left). *Yu Vessel.*
  Shang Dynasty, 1523-1027 B.C.

119 (right). *Rear view of Figure 118*

The remark cited previously concerning the t'ao-t'ieh "with a head but no body. . . . Figs. I eating a man" cannot have referred to this creature precisely, since there is here a body as well as a head, but it does suggest an association. Moreover, on the back of this piece there is an exceptionally fine t'ao-t'ieh design, and as A. K. Coomaraswamy noted in his comment, quoted earlier, on the Indian tale of Kirttimukha, the Chinese term *t'ao-t'ieh* is translated "Glutton."

Interpreters have differed as to whether the animal represented here is meant to be eating or protecting the human being, who appears, indeed, to be rather more pleased than discomposed by what is occurring. However, the tiger in China, like the jaguar in Mesoamerica, is a beast symbolic of earth, and as such representative (whether male or female) of the female, receptive, *yin* principle in nature; the *yang*, the male, being represented by the dragon—as by the Feathered Serpent in America. And we perceive that in this wonderful piece, symbolic of the sacrifice it was designed to serve, there are serpents of many kinds curling everywhere over the two bodies, together with auspicious spiral, thunder, and labyrinth motifs.

Let us turn back to the Olmec jaguar- Fig. 9. sarcophagus and, looking for a while at that, then for a while at this, and then back to that again, let us call to mind the meaning of our own word "sarcophagus," which is from the Greek *sarx, sarkos*, "flesh," plus *phagein*, "to eat." The old Greek reference was to a certain kind of stone believed to have the property of consuming the flesh of dead bodies and therefore used for coffins, wherein the bodies of the dead were to be returned to earth, Mother Earth. Analogously, in the symbolism of the jaguar-coffin the body was to be returned to the Mother by way of her consuming animal aspect or agent. Likewise in this Chinese piece, it is the feline symbol of the consuming power of Mother Earth that is seen taking her willing child back to her bosom.

The initiatory lesson of the sacrifice, we have seen, is acquiescence, and not merely acquiescence but a willing participation in the holy mystery and precondition of existence; which is, namely, the process of life consuming life—as in the image of the "Face of Glory" and also, apparently, in the Chinese t'ao-t'ieh. That is the meaning, too, of the burning of incense: release of the fragrance of surrender, which lifts to greet the nostrils of that "One" beyond and above, whose will is accomplished in this manner on earth. There are the lines of an unknown Aztec poet:

> Let us consider things as lent to us,
> oh friends: only in passing are
> we here on earth.
> Tomorrow or the day following (as
> Your heart desires, O Giver of
> Life!) we shall go, my friends,
> to His home.[40]

The Indian *Taittiriya Upanishad* presents the idea with a little more enthusiasm:

> Oh, wonderful! Oh, wonderful! Oh,
> wonderful!
> I am food! I am food! I am food!
> I am a food-eater! I am a food-eater!
> I am a food-eater!
> I am a fame-maker! I am a fame-
> maker! I am a fame-maker!
> I am the first-born of the world order,
> Earlier than the gods, in the navel of
> immortality!
> Who gives me away, he indeed has
> aided me!
> I, who am food, eat the eater of food!
> I have overcome the whole world!
>
> He who knows this, has a brilliantly
> shining light.
> Such is the mystic doctrine![41]

120. *Yu Vessel (profile view of Figure 118). Shang Dynasty,* 1523-1027 B.C.

121. *Mochica Jar. ca.* A.D. *500. North Coastal Peru*

Maps 1-4

The argument for Asian influences in the cultures of Middle America received dramatic support in December 1960, when pottery sherds and stone figurines in a style identified as Japanese, ca. 3000 B.C. ("cord-marked," Middle Jomon ware), were unearthed on the coast of Ecuador at a site known as Valdivia,[42] these being the earliest signs either of pottery or of works of art yet discovered in the New World. A likely pattern of diffusion has been charted from this coastal site, both southward to Peru and northward to the Caribbean, whence the culture seems to have been carried (perhaps following the Gulf Stream) to the mouth of the Savannah River in Georgia ("Stallings Island" ware, ca. 2400 B.C.).[43]

About 2000 B.C. a second landing along the same Ecuadorean coast, a few miles north of the first, at Machalilla, brought a second ceramic style, together with a curious Asian custom of intentional skull deformation that became in time the hall-mark of the most highly developed Amerindian civilizations, the Inca, Maya, and Aztec; and the typical traits of this culture, too, passed northward on the Gulf Stream, landing in Florida, on the shores of the St. John's River.[44]

A third trans-Pacific company seems to have arrived about 1500 B.C. on the west coast of Guatemala, there to leave sherds of a later Japanese Jomon style known as Horinouchi ware[45]—soon after which (in the words of one leading authority) "the American cultures received a shock that was to change their character profoundly . . . the sudden introduction of a religio-political system demanding great public works."[46]

This was the Olmec complex of La Venta and the other early sites of Tabasco and Veracruz, where (to continue in the words of Professor James A. Ford), "a remark-able ceremonial complex, infinitely advanced over anything else in the Americas at that date, had developed by 1200 B.C." Professor Ford has classified this suddenly present, monumental culture stage as "Theocratic Formative," distinguishing it sharply from that of the earlier East Asian (neolithic) imports, which he terms "Colonial Formative." "We are in ignorance as to what sparked the Olmec civiliza-tion," he states.[47] However, he mentions with approval Professor Heine-Geldern's recognition of Chinese stylistic forms and iconographical motifs in later Meso-american works,[48] and allows, with respect to the Olmec tradition as well, that "an Asiatic origin for this entire new religious complex is not to be ruled out."[49] Heine-Geldern identified not only Chinese but also Hindu-Buddhist influences in the arts of Middle America, dating from periods as early as ca. 800 B.C. to as late as A.D. 1219.

In sum, the whole broad course of the large historical reconstruction suggested by these two authorities may be outlined roughly as follows:

I. COLONIAL FORMATIVE PHASE

Ca. 3000 B.C.: Valdivia Culture, Coastal Ecuador

Middle Jomon ware from Kyushu, Japan; ceramic and stone figurines. There is reason to suspect that this arrival was in the nature of an exploring and colonizing expedition involving a number of individuals of both sexes and varied skills. "The ceramic arts do not degenerate," Ford notes, ". . . but after about 2300 B.C. pottery is actually better made than the contemporary wares on the Japanese islands."[50] Diffusion followed almost immediately, southward to the Peruvian coast (Guañape, ca. 2340 B.C.) and northward to the Caribbean (Puerto Hormiga, ca. 2915 B.C.), whence the passage, possibly by stages, to the mouth of the Savannah River (ca. 2400 B.C.).

Ca. 2000 B.C.: Machalilla Culture, Coastal Ecuador

Possibly "a second colonizing venture from some unknown point on the coast of Asia."[51] Another pottery style; also the practice of deforming the skulls of babies by applying pressure to back of the head and to the frontal region. "The custom spread into North America to the Pueblo peoples of the Southwest and the Mississippian peoples of the East. In the Amazon Basin, some remote tribes still continue the practice."[52] The Valdivia and Machalilla traditions coexisted in apparent peace for some five hundred years (2000-1500 B.C.). Machalilla diffusion to the shores of the St. John's River in Florida was already taking place ca. 2000 B.C.

Ca. 1500 B.C.: Horinouchi Type Ceramic, West Coast Guatemala

Very brief appearance in Guatemala of a style remarkably similar to one flourishing at this time in central Japan.[53]

II. THEOCRATIC FORMATIVE PHASE

Ca. 1200-500 B.C.: Olmec Culture, Tabasco and Veracruz

"It is not known with certainty where this first appeared, but the Olmec region on the Gulf coast of Mexico seems to be the best

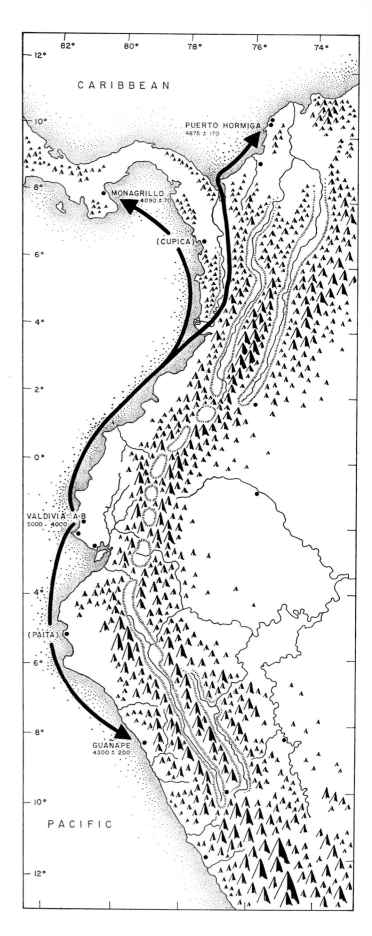

Map 1. Earliest New World Pottery Sites.
3000-2000 B.C. (Arrows indicate likely routes
of diffusion.) (1) Valdivia (Coastal Ecuador),
ca. 3000 B.C.: pottery and figurines resembling Japanese "Jomon" products of same
date (see *Map* 2). (2) Puerto Hormiga (North
Coast, Colombia), ca. 2900 B.C.: wares
showing many Valdivia traits. (3) Guañape
(North Coast, Peru), ca. 2350 B.C.: crude
wares showing a few Valdivia traits. (4)
Mongarillo (Pacific Coast, Panama), ca.
2100 B.C.: strong Valdivia-Puerto Hormiga
affinities. (5) and (6) Paita (North Coast,
Peru) and Cupica (West Coast, Colombia):
wares of later periods incorporating early
Valdivia traits.[61]

guess." "There is no hint of earlier developmental stages that would lead to the unique features of Olmec." "It was the Olmec who provided the Maya with the long count cyclical calendar."[54] (For the last, see below, pp. 148-149.)

Ca. 800-200 B.C.: Chavín Culture, Coastal and Highland Peru

Evidence suggests, states Ford, that there was direct communication from the Olmec to the Chavín areas, having little or no immediate effect, however, on the lives of the peoples between. The emphasis in Chavín is on the pyramid, rather than the arrangement of mound structures about courts: large stepped pyramids decorated with niches containing sculptured figures or with large stone slabs carved in bas relief. Three symbolic animals dominate: a jaguar with prominent canine teeth, a bird (possibly the condor), and the serpent.[55]

Ca. 800-333 B.C.: Chinese Influences Evident

Middle and Late Chou Dynasty contributions, stemming probably from the coastal states of ancient China, Wu and Yüeh, evident particularly in the Tajín style of Mexico and Chavín of Peru. It is in this period that metal work (in gold) and weaving first appear in South America.[56]

Ca. 333 B.C.-A.D. 50: Dong-son Influences

When Yüeh lost its independence in 333 B.C. the trans-Pacific voyages were taken up by Yüeh's immediate neighbors in northeastern Indochina, the Dong-son, ancestors of the present day Vietnamese. Throughout the Andean region of South America, from Panama to northern Chile and northwestern Argentina, Dong-son influences are more conspicuous than Chinese.[57]

Ca. A.D. 50-220: Han Chinese Influences

The Dong-son voyages may have come to an end with the final conquest of Tonkin and North Annam by China. Pottery types of Guatemala, in particular, closely resemble those of Han. The dissolution of the Han empire seems to have terminated China's trans-Pacific role.[58]

III. CLASSIC AND POSTCLASSIC MESO-AMERICA (Maya, Toltec, Aztec, etc.)
Ca. A.D. 220-1219: Southeast Asian, Hindu-Buddhist Influences

When the Chinese voyages to Mexico and Central America were discontinued, the adventure was immediately assumed by the Hinduized peoples of Southeast Asia. The relations seem to have been particularly close between Cambodia and the Maya and Olmec areas between the seventh and tenth centuries; though they may have continued to the twelfth. "Could their rupture have been caused," Heine-Geldern asks, "by the political catastrophe of the Khmer empire after the death of Jayavarman VII around 1219 A.D.?"[59]

It would seem, then, that we can reasonably suggest that the mythologies underlying and represented in the art forms of the high cultures of Middle America were finally not merely similar to those of ancient Greece and the Orient, but actually of one piece with them—a remote provincial extension of the one historic heritage and universal history of mankind. And for the possibility that there may also have been significant early trans-Atlantic contributions from Europe and the Near East, there is the evidence (discussed by Dr. Cyrus H. Gordon, among others) of a Minoan inscription found in Georgia (ca. 1500 B.C.), a Canaanite notation in Brazil (ca. 531 B.C.), a Hebrew inscription of Roman date at Bat Creek, Tennessee, and a Roman sculptured head of about A.D. 200, professionally excavated from the stratified remains of a pyramid at Calixtlahuaca, Mexico.[60]

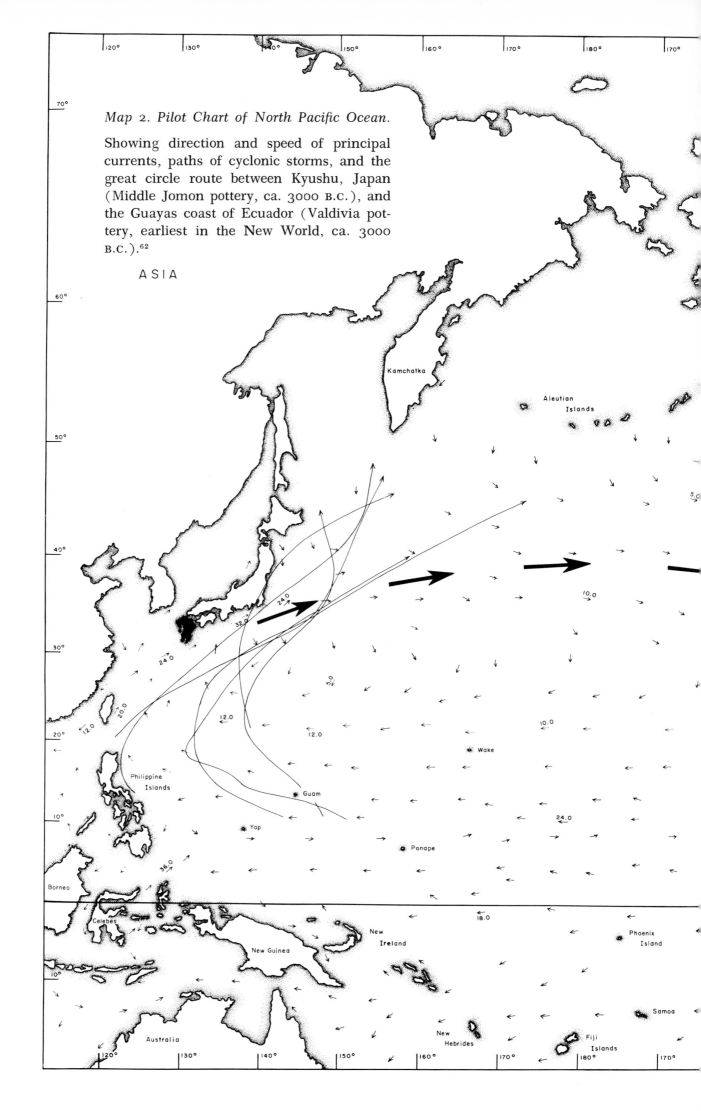

Map 2. Pilot Chart of North Pacific Ocean.

Showing direction and speed of principal currents, paths of cyclonic storms, and the great circle route between Kyushu, Japan (Middle Jomon pottery, ca. 3000 B.C.), and the Guayas coast of Ecuador (Valdivia pottery, earliest in the New World, ca. 3000 B.C.).[62]

ASIA

Kamchatka

Aleutian
Islands

Philippine
Islands

Wake

Guam

Yap

Ponape

Borneo

24.0

18.0

Celebes

New
Ireland

Phoenix
Island

New Guinea

Samoa

Australia

New
Hebrides

Fiji
Islands

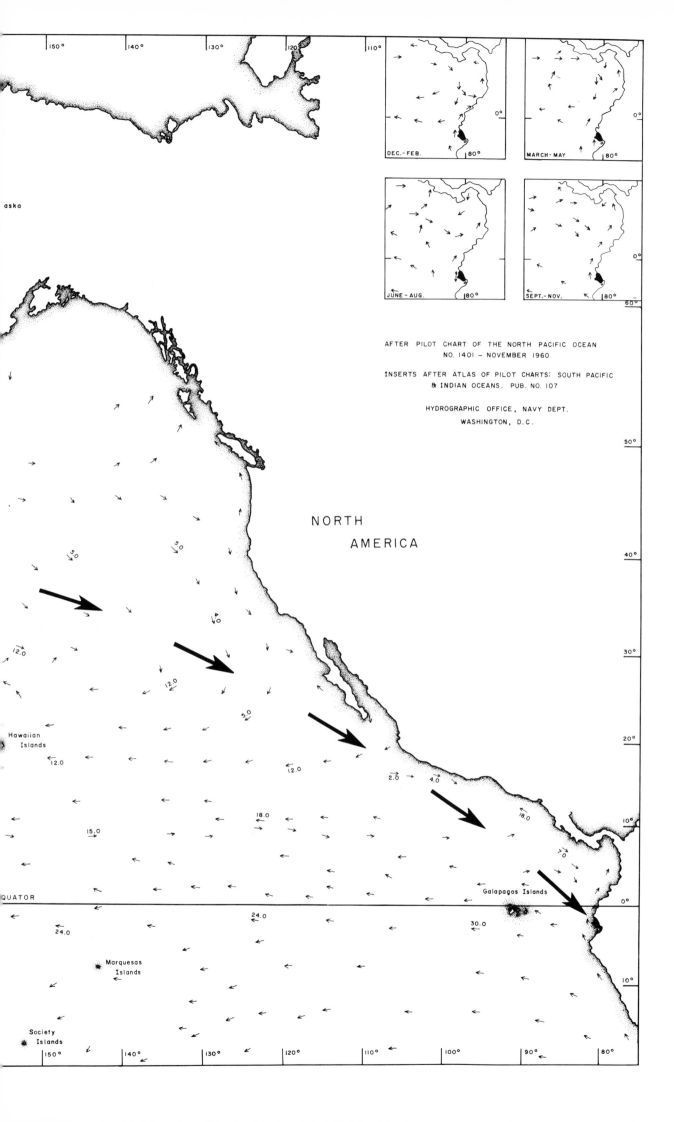

AFTER PILOT CHART OF THE NORTH PACIFIC OCEAN
NO. 1401 – NOVEMBER 1960

INSERTS AFTER ATLAS OF PILOT CHARTS: SOUTH PACIFIC
& INDIAN OCEANS. PUB. NO. 107

HYDROGRAPHIC OFFICE, NAVY DEPT.
WASHINGTON, D.C.

NORTH
AMERICA

DEC.- FEB.
MARCH- MAY
JUNE - AUG.
SEPT.- NOV.

Hawaiian
Islands

Galapagos Islands

EQUATOR

Marquesas
Islands

Society
Islands

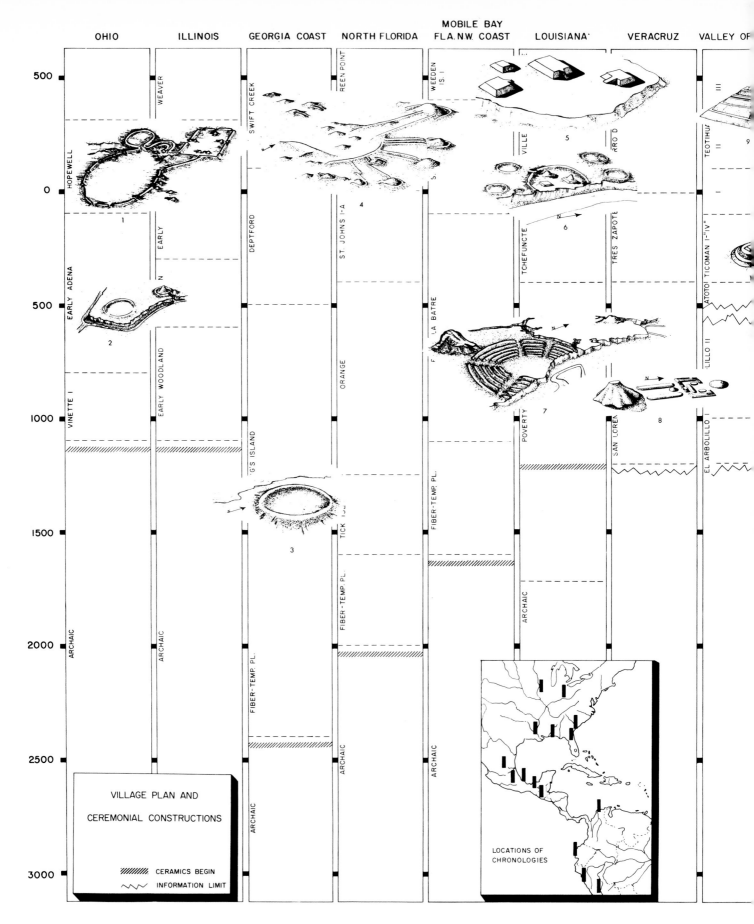

VILLAGE PLAN AND
CEREMONIAL CONSTRUCTIONS

▨▨▨▨ CERAMICS BEGIN
∿∿∿ INFORMATION LIMIT

LOCATIONS OF
CHRONOLOGIES

Map 3. Early New World Village Sites and Ceremonial Centers. ca. 3000 B.C.-A.D. 500. The very early Puerto Hormiga village site (item 17) is described as a ring measuring 84 yards in diameter north to south and 93 east to west, formed from "the careless, unplanned discarding of shells and other refuse" around an orderly circle of dwellings. Earlier American settlements show little or no evidence of any such village plan, where-

as a number of circular middens of this kind, of both earlier and later dates, have been found in Japan.[63] The earliest monumental ceremonial centers in America date from the Olmec period, ca. 1200-400 B.C., and arose not only on the Gulf coast of Veracruz (item 8), but also simultaneously at "Poverty Point" on the Lower Mississippi (item 7), where a large circular town three-fourths of a mile in diameter has left six concentric

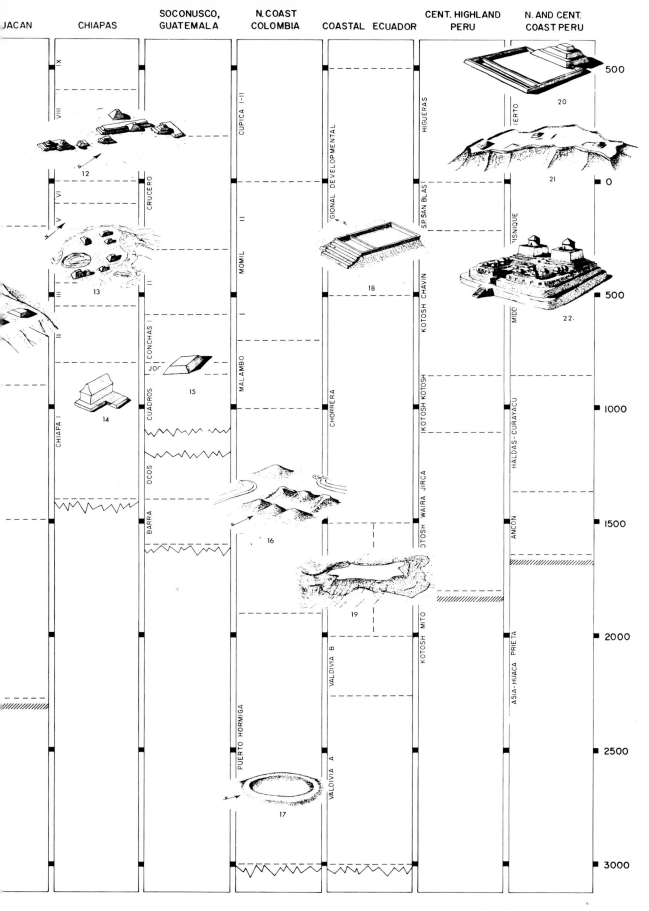

ridges in alternating layers of normally deposited refuse and intentionally added soil. To the west of this great center is an immense mound, apparently a bird effigy, about 75 feet high; and about a mile to the north there is another birdlike mound, about 59 feet high. Air photographs show that the plan of this early site was perfectly symmetrical and its axial orientation, furthermore, exactly that of the contemporary Olmec ceremonial centers of Mexico, namely 8 degrees west of true North. Huge earthworks of various, often unknown, uses subsequently arose in many other parts of North America (items 1-6), while in Mexico, Middle America, and South America (items 9-15, 18, and 20-22) highly styled monumental ceremonial centers of adobe, concrete, and stone were being erected.[64]

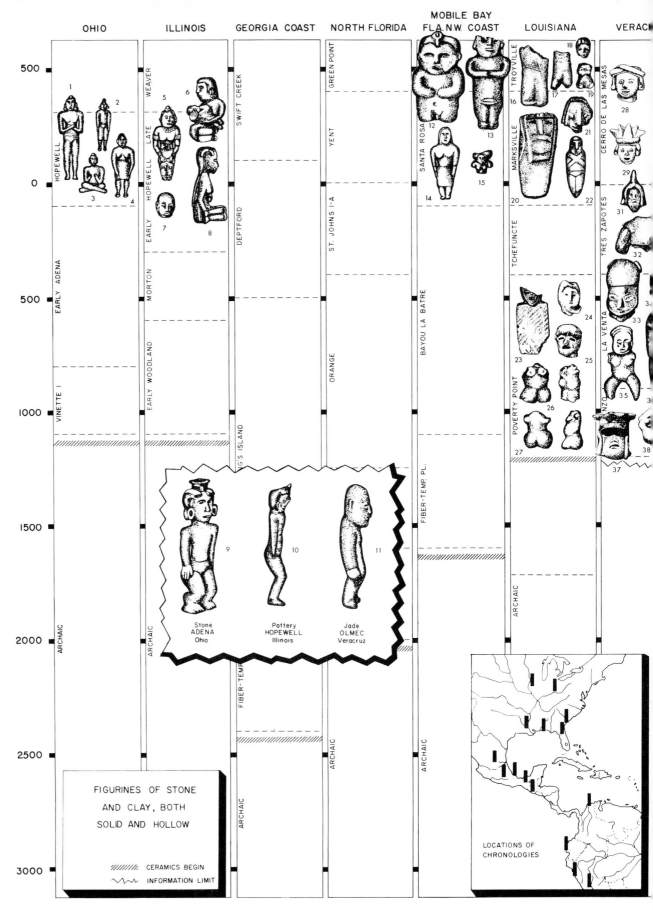

FIGURINES OF STONE
AND CLAY, BOTH
SOLID AND HOLLOW

///////// CERAMICS BEGIN
∿∿∿ INFORMATION LIMIT

Stone
ADENA
Ohio

Pottery
HOPEWELL
Illinois

Jade
OLMEC
Veracruz

LOCATIONS OF
CHRONOLOGIES

Map 4. Early New World Figurines. ca. 3000 B.C.-A.D. 500. The earliest known New World figurines (items 85 and 86) are of stone and resemble those of the Japanese Middle Jomon period. Pottery figurines appear later (items 83, 84, etc.) and are generally of nude females, sometimes obviously pregnant. Fig-

urines are rare in early Peru, as also in Colombia. Throughout Mexico, on the other hand, they abound from ca. 1500 B.C. onward (items 28-61), those bearing Olmec features commonly being of carved jade. In the United States the earliest known figurines are from the so-called "Poverty Point" period

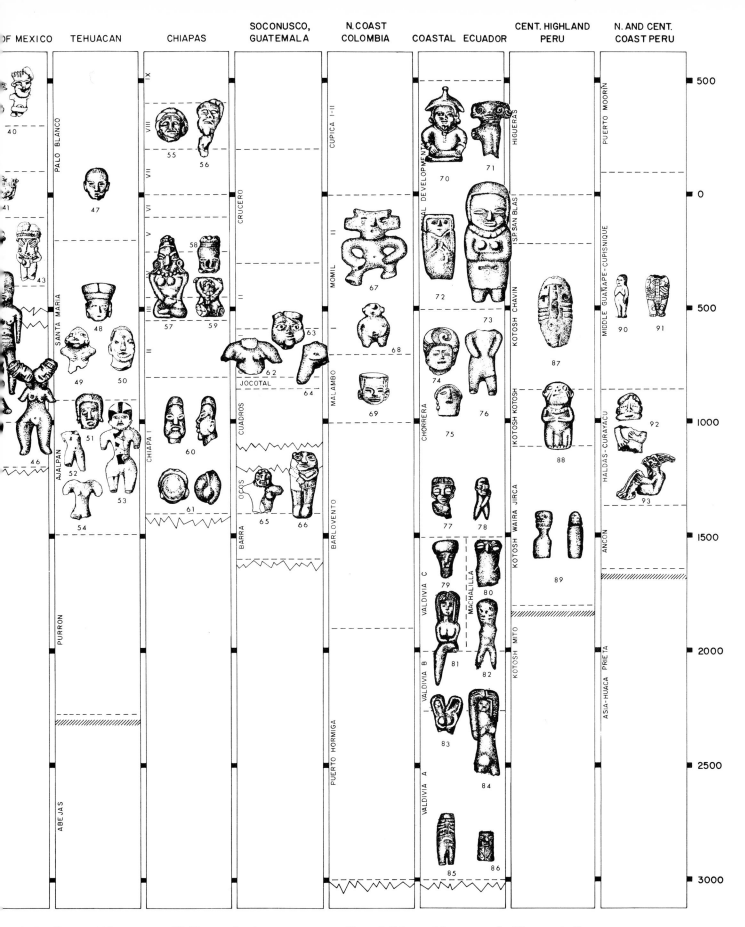

of the Lower Mississippi Valley culture complex, ca. 1200-400 B.C. (items 23-27), and are contemporary with the Olmec works of the southern shores of the Gulf. Farther north and very much later, in Ohio and Illinois, ca. 100 B.C.-A.D. 500, not a few of the Adena and Hopewell figurines (items 1-10) still exhibit evidences of Olmec influence (items 9-11)[65]—the short legs and bent-knee stance, by the way, being characteristic features of the primitive arts of Oceania and Africa as well.

122. *Vishnu and Lakshmi on the Cosmic Sea*

The style is of the popular 19th century mass-produced Anglo-Indian colored prints. Below are the names, Vishnu, Brahma, Lak-

shmi. Four-headed Brahma holds in one hand a lustral spoon; books of the Veda in his others. Above is again his name.

123. *Brahma the Creator*

Adored by celestial rishis, the god in this work of a classic period exhibits in three hands a rosary, lustral spoon, and jar of am-

brosia; the fourth is in the boon-bestowing posture. At his knee is the wild gander, his special vehicle of flight.

4. The Calendric Round

CORRESPONDING to the spatial order of the world mountain, the four quarters, and the ever-cycling spheres, there is everywhere an associated temporal order of precisely measured days, months, years, and eons.

In India, for example, where the first form to appear in the lotus of Vishnu's dream is seen as Brahma, it is held that when the cosmic dream dissolves, after 100 Brahma years, its Brahma too will disappear—to reappear, however, when the lotus again unfolds. Now one Brahma year is reckoned as 360 Brahma days and nights, each night and each day consisting of 12,000,000 divine years. But each divine year, in turn, consists of 360 human years; so that one full day and night of Brahma, or 24,000,000 divine years, contains 24,000,000 times 360 or 8,640,000,000 human years, just as in our own system of reckoning the 24 hours of a day contain 86,400 seconds—each second corresponding to the length of time, furthermore, of one heartbeat of a human body in perfect physical condition.[66] Thus it appears not only that the temporal order written on the faces of our clocks is the same as that of the Indian god Vishnu's dream, but also that there is built into this system the mythological concept of a correspondence between the organic rhythms of the human body as a microcosm and the cycling eons of the universe, the macrocosm.

Fig. 123

Every day of a Brahma lifetime of 100 Brahma years, the god's eyes slowly open and close 1,000 times. When they open a universe appears, and the moment they close it fades, appearing, enduring, fading, and disappearing thus in a cycle of four stages called *yugas*, named in descending series after the four throws of a die:

Krita, 4, "the lucky throw"
Treta, 3
Dvapara, 2
Kali, 1, "the worst"

These correspond to the four ages in our own classical tradition, of gold, silver, bronze, and iron; also to the meaning of the prophetic dream attributed in the Book of Daniel to King Nebuchadnezzar of Babylon; which was of an idol "mighty and of exceeding brightness," the head of which was "of fine gold, its breast and arms of silver, its belly and thighs of bronze, its legs of iron, its feet partly of iron and partly of clay" (Daniel 2:31-33).[67]

The four ages of the Indian cycle are described in the sacred books as follows:

Krita Yuga, a golden age of 4,000 divine years, preceded by a dawn of 400 years and followed by a twilight of equal length; in sum, 4,800 divine years, during the whole of which the Cow of Virtue stands on all four legs, men are perfectly virtuous, and the laws of caste strictly honored.

Treta Yuga, one quarter less virtuous, blissful, and long; in sum, including its dawn and twilight, an age of 3,600 divine years, when the Cow stands on three legs.

Dvapara Yuga, a second quarter gone, and the Cow is balanced on two legs; a period lasting, with its dawn and twilight, but 2,400 divine years.

Finally *Kali Yuga*, our own world age: wicked and consequently miserable, with the Cow of Virtue on one leg. And just as in the prophecy of Daniel it is declared that the races of this age "will mix with one another in marriage," so in the sacred texts of India the fourth period is characterized by "the mixture of castes." This lawless terminal age, declining toward catastrophe, is believed to have commenced on February 17, 3102 B.C., and it will endure, including its dawn and twilight, only 1,200 divine years.

Translating, now, divine into human years, we arrive at the following sums:

$$4,800 \times 360 = 1,728,000 \text{ human years}$$
$$3,600 \times 360 = 1,296,000 \quad " \qquad "$$
$$2,400 \times 360 = 864,000 \quad " \qquad "$$
$$1,200 \times 360 = 432,000 \quad " \qquad "$$

12,000 divine = 4,320,000 human years = 1 Great Cycle or Mahayuga

Furthermore:

1,000 Mahayugas = 1 daytime (or 1 night) of Brahma (1 *kalpa*):
i.e., 12,000,000 divine years or 4,320,000,000 human years.

360 days and nights of Brahma (720 kalpas) = 1 Brahma year:
i.e., 8,640,000,000 divine or 3,110,400,000,000 human years.

100 Brahma years = 1 Brahma lifetime:
i.e., 864,000,000,000 divine or 311,040,000,000,000 human years.

At the close of each Brahma lifetime, Brahma and all dissolve into the body of the cosmic dreamer, who remains then absorbed in dreamless sleep for a period equal in length to another Brahma lifetime—until presently something within him stirs, the lotus dream again unfurls, and all begins anew. Moreover, in the distances of infinite space innumerable lotus universes are everywhere unfurling, flowering, and fading, each with its Brahma, as on a boundless lotus lake. Nor in the infinitudes of time will there ever be an end—as in the past there was no beginning—of this flowering and fading of Brahma worlds.

When the time arrives for the reabsorption of such a lotus dream into the timeless state of deep dreamless sleep within the body of the world-dreamer, the work of destruction is absolute. As told in the *Matsya Purana*, reviewed and retold by Heinrich Zimmer in a chapter on "The Waters of Non-Existence":

In this Indian conception of the process of destruction, the regular course of the Indian year—fierce heat and drought alternating with torrential rains—is magnified to such a degree that instead of sustaining, it demolishes existence. The warmth that normally ripens and the moisture that nourishes, when alternating in beneficent co-operation, now annihilate. Vishnu begins the terrible last work by pouring his infinite energy into the sun. He himself becomes the sun. With its fierce, devouring rays he draws into himself the eyesight of every animate being. The whole world dries up and withers, the earth splits, and through deep fissures a deadly blaze of heat licks at the divine waters of the subterranean abyss; these are caught up and swallowed. And when the life-sap has entirely vanished from both the egg-shaped cosmic body and all the bodies of its creatures, Vishnu becomes the wind, the cosmic life-breath, and pulls out of all creatures the enlivening air. Like desiccated leaves the sear substance of the universe leaps to the cyclone. Friction ignites the whirling tumult of highly inflammable matter; the god has turned into fire. All goes up in a gigantic conflagration, then sinks into smoldering ash. Finally, in the form of a great cloud, Vishnu sheds a torrential rain, sweet and pure as milk, to quench the conflagration of the world. The scorched and suffering body of the earth knows at last its ultimate relief, final extinction, Nirvana. Under the flood of the God-become-Rain it is taken back into the primal ocean from which it arose at the universal dawn. The fecund water-womb receives again into itself the ashes of all creation. The ultimate elements melt into the undifferentiated fluid out of which they once arose. The moon, the stars, dissolve. The mounting tide becomes a limitless sheet of water. This is the interval of a night of Brahma.

Fig. 124   Vishnu sleeps. Like a spider that has climbed up the thread that once issued from its own organism, drawing it back into itself, the god has consumed again the web of the universe. Alone upon the immortal substance of the ocean, a giant figure, submerged partly, partly afloat, he takes delight in slumber. There is no one to behold him, no one to comprehend him; there is no knowledge of him, except within himself.[68]

124. Vishnu Sleeps

125. End of the Aeon

Above is a Middle American representation of the same cosmic event from Fig. 125 the so-called Dresden Codex of the Mayas. "Here," states Sylvanus G. Morley, "we see the rain serpent, stretching across the sky, belching forth torrents of water. Great streams of water gush from the sun and the moon. The old goddess, she of the tiger claws and forbidding aspect, the malevolent patroness of floods and cloudbursts, overturns the bowl of the heavenly waters. The crossbones, dread symbol of death, decorate her skirt, and a writhing snake crowns her head. Below with downpointed spears, symbolic of the universal destruction, the black god stalks abroad, a screeching owl raging on his fearsome head. Here, indeed, is portrayed with graphic touch the final all-engulfing cataclysm."[69]

Along the top of the page are two rows of signs of a type known to scholars as "serpent numbers," because of their common occurrence in association with a serpent symbol; and like the lengths of years of the Indian yugas, mahayugas, and kalpas, these are prodigious sums referring to astronomical cycles. Moreover, like the Indian cycles within cycles, the serpent numbers of the Mayan codices are features of a calendric order based on a complex system of intermeshing rounds,* the historic origins of which are not known. Based on a duodecimal, rather than sexagesimal, mathematical system, and featuring the number thirteen instead of twelve, the Mesoamerican reckonings yield different sums from the Babylonian; yet in every other way the two systems are remarkably alike.

"The Maya codices were made of the bark of a tree called in Maya *copo* (*Ficus cotonifolia*), pounded into a pulp and held together with some sort of natural gum as a bonding substance. They were made in long strips. . . . A coating or wash of fine white lime was applied to both sides of this mangled-bark paper strip, which was folded like a screen, and on the smooth glossy finish thus obtained columns of glyphs and pictures of gods and ceremonies were painted in many colors: dark red, light red, blue, yellow, brown, green, and an intense, almost lustrous black.

"The pages are divided into two, three, and sometimes four horizontal sections by red lines, and the order of reading was across the pages from left to right, always in the same horizontal section until the particular matter being treated, perhaps to be likened to a chapter, was finished. These so-called 'chapters' sometimes extend across as many as eight or more consecutive pages or folds. The codices were bound between decorated boards to protect the rather fragile bark-paper, and when they were completely opened out they were quite long. . . . The Codex Dresdensis is 11¾ feet long and has 39 leaves, or 78 pages, 4 of the pages being blank."[70]

Now it is of interest to note that on pages 51 through 58 of this codex there is apparently an "eclipse table," representing correlations of lunar and solar cycles, which matches in a manner that has not yet been explained certain inaccurate calculations of the Han Chinese.[71] For eclipse cycles were of the gravest concern to the Chinese calendrical astronomers as well as to the Mayan, since, as Professor Nathan Sivin of the Mas-sachusetts Institute of Technology remarks in a thoroughgoing study, *Cosmos and Computation in Early Chinese Mathematical Astronomy*:

"The form in which the [Chinese] calendrical art was transmitted was decisively conditioned, as in Mesopotamia, by the importance of astrology to the security of the state. Celestial phenomena which could not be predicted were ominous in the fullest sense of the word: they were omens. Every solution to a problem of astronomical prediction meant removal of one more source of political anxiety. . . . The ability to predict moved celestial events from the realm of the ominous to that of the rhythmic and intelligible. The Emperor was thus enabled to know Nature's Tao so that his social order might be kept concordant with it. Failure of the official system to predict was necessarily a sign of moral imperfection, a warning that the monarch's virtue was not adequate to keep him in touch with the celestial rhythms. The Chinese theory of the natural order and the political order as resonating systems, with the ruler as a sort of vibrating dipole between them, imposed on the history of astronomy an insatiable demand for increased precision—far exceeding, in the area of the calendar, any conceivable agricultural, bureaucratic, or economic necessity."[72]

In Middle America, also, it was apparently some such mythological notion of celestial and human accord that inspired the unremitting application of the leading minds of the civilization to astronomy; and remarkably enough, it now appears that the Mayan table registered in the Dresden Codex matches to a fault the Han Chinese. According to the so-called "phase coincidence cycle"

cf. Figs 146

* See text to Figure 128.

of the Han astronomers, 135 lunations equal 23 lunar eclipses. That is to say, 23 such eclipses will occur every 135 lunar months;[73] whereas according to the Middle American figure, 69 (3 times 23) lunar eclipses occur every 405 (3 times 135) lunations: the Mayan figures simply triple the Chinese; the proportions are exactly the same.

But the interesting fact is that this coincidence cannot possibly have been founded on independent histories of exact astronomical observation, since, as Professor Sivin has remarked with reference to the Chinese equation, the figures do not correspond to the facts that would have been observed.[74] "Twenty-three eclipses," he points out, "is almost one and a third times as many as actually take place, and close to two and a half times as many as could have been noted by the Chinese observers unless they had a branch observatory in Boston or thereabouts."[75]

Would it be too much, then, to suggest that the undiscovered origins of the Middle American calendric system should be looked for not in Mexico but in Cathay? In any case, the underlying mythologies of a mathematical order governing earth as well as heaven are the same. Figure 126 is a chart used by Joseph Needham and Wong Ling in their study *Science and Civilisation in China* to illustrate the world diffusion of astronomical learning from Babylon.[76] We do not know when the earliest Middle American calendar was composed. Alfonso Caso appears to suggest a date in the first half of the first millennium B.C., in early Zapotec-Olmec times.[77] Such a dating would require only an extension of Needham's chart to the east, out of China, during the Middle or Late Chou centuries (772 to 221 B.C.), which is exactly the period suggested for such influences by the findings of Professor Heine-Geldern.[78]

126. *The Development of Astronomy*

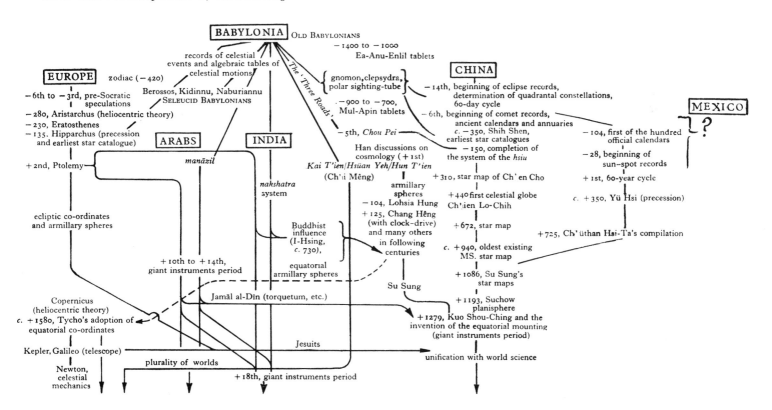

We do not know the name of this god, nor that of the prostrate dwarf at his feet. On the reverse is a date reading from the top downward, commencing with the second glyph: 8 baktuns, 14 katuns, 3 tuns, 1 uinal, 12 kins. The sign at the top refers to a month. The last five glyphs are noncalendrical. The Mayan terms kin, uinal, tun, etc. are to be understood as follows:

20 kins (days)   1 uinal
(1 Mayan month)
18 uinals   1 tun
(360 days = 1 conventional "year")*
20 tuns   1 katun
(7,200 days = 20 conventional "years")
20 katuns   1 baktun
(144,000 days = 400 conventional "years")
20 baktuns   1 pictun
(2,880,000 days = 8,000
conventional "years")

These are the measures of time that appear on dated Mayan monuments. Beyond are the higher, so-called serpent numbers, used in such advanced cosmological calculations as those of the Dresden Codex:

20 pictuns   1 calabtun
(57,600,000 days = 160,000
conventional "years")
20 calabtuns   1 kinchiltun
(1,152,000,000 days = 3,200,000
conventional "years")
20 kinchiltuns   1 alautun
(23,040,000,000 days =
64,000,000 conventional "years")

The sum on the Leyden Plate represents, therefore, 8 times 400 plus 14 times 20 plus 3 times 1, which equals 3,483 conventional "years"; plus 20 plus 12 days; which number of "years," corrected, comes to 3,433 true years. But the basal, starting, or zero date of the Mayan chronology was 3113 B.C.; so that the inscription on the Leyden Plate corresponds to our date of A.D. 320. All of which means, as Professor Morley has remarked, that the Mayas started their chronology from a date nearly three thousand years earlier than the probable date of the invention of

* Compare Indian conventional "year," p. 143.

127. *The Leyden Plate*

their calendric system. "Therefore," he suggests, "it seems much more likely that Maya chronology began with some hypothetical event, rather than with an actual historical occurrence. Possibly it may have commenced with a supposititious event like the creation of the world. . . . Perhaps it may even have been counted from the supposed date of the birth of their gods, in which indefinite and remote past we must leave this question as yet undetermined."[79]

128. Reverse of Figure 127

What strikes me, however, is the fact that in India our present world age, the Kali Yuga,* is supposed to have commenced on February 17, 3102 B.C., which is but eleven years before the Mayan basal date.

"The astronomical aspect of the yuga," states Professor Hermann Jacobi in an article on the Indian system, "is that, in its commencement, sun, moon, and planets stood in conjunction in the initial point of the ecliptic, and returned to the same point at the end of the age. The popular belief on which this notion is based is older than Hindu astronomy."[80] Is it not possible that a similar consideration may have determined the Mayas' selection of their basal date?

It is perhaps worth remarking, also, that the dates 3102 and 3113 B.C., when transferred to Mesopotamia, align almost exactly with the dates for the invention of the arts of writing, mathematics, and astronomical reckoning there: the time and place of the initiation of this whole remarkable effort to translate celestial mathematics into the ordering principle of life on earth.

The Roman philosopher Seneca, discussing the Babylonian cosmology of Berossos,* informs us that "Berossos states that everything takes place according to the course of the planets, and he maintains this so confidently that he determined the times for the conflagration of the world and for the flood. He asserts that the world will burn when all the planets that now move in different courses come together in the Crab, so that they all stand in a straight line in the same sign, and that the future flood will take place when the same conjunction occurs in Capricorn. For the former is the constellation of the summer solstice, the latter of the winter solstice; they are the decisive signs of the zodiac, because the turning points of the year lie in them."[81]

"This Babylonian doctrine," notes Alfred Jeremias in commenting on this text, ". . . has spread over the whole world. We find it again in Egypt, in the religion of the Avesta, and in India; traces of it are discovered in China, as well as in Mexico and among the savage nations of South America. To refer these phenomena back to 'elementary ideas' such as may arise independently among different peoples, will not hold good in view of the circumstance that we have to do with ideas connected with definite facts which rest on continued astronomical observations. Babylonia was, moreover, according to a constant tradition, the home of astronomy ('Chaldean wisdom'), and there the science of the stars formed the basis of all intellectual culture."[82]

* Above, p. 72.

All of the Mesoamerican calendric systems—the Mayan, the Aztec, and others—were based on the intermeshing of four revolving cycles: the first, a week of 13 days; the second, a month of 20, which, intermeshing with the first, forms a third, a cycle of 13 times 20 or 260 days; and this, in turn, intermeshes with the cycle of the natural year.

The weekday numbers and monthday names of the Aztec series are as follows:

13 Weekday Numbers   20 Monthday Names

1 week	1	Crocodile	
	2	Wind	
	3	House	
	4	Lizard	
	5	Serpent	
	6	Death	
	7	Deer	
	8	Rabbit	
	9	Water	
	10	Dog	1 month
	11	Monkey	
	12	Grass	
	13	Reed	
	1	Jaguar	
	2	Eagle	
	3	Vulture	
	4	Movement	
	5	Flint knife	
	6	Rain	
	7	Flower	
	8	Crocodile, etc.	

Going on in this way, no combination of number and name will be repeated until 13 times 20 or 260 days have passed, which period is known to scholarship by the Aztec term *Tonalpohualli*. Next, this completely artificial cycle is geared to the natural year of 360 days plus 5, which yields in Aztec reckoning a year of 18 months of 20 days each, plus 5 so-called Empty Days. Not until 4 times 13 or 52 of these Aztec years have passed do the same number and day name recur on the first day of a year; and this unit of 52 is known as a "Knot of Years." At its termination, all fires are extinguished and a new flame is kindled on the breast of a sacrificial victim.

But this is not all; for in addition, there is a fifth cycle to be observed: that of the appearances and disappearances of the planet Venus as the morning and evening star, the celestial sign of Quetzalcoatl, the Feathered Serpent. Venus rises as the morning star for a period of roughly 240 days, then disappears for roughly 90, reappears as evening star for another period of about 240 days, disappears again for 14, and finally reappears as the morning star to begin the cycle anew. All of which adds up to a sum of 584 days (one synodal revolution), and not until 65 of these have elapsed will the same Aztec day number and name recur on the first day of a cycle. But 65 times 584 days is exactly 104 years, that is to say, two knots of 52 years—obviously a very great and dangerous occasion! For it will be at one of these cosmic junctures that the intermeshing will break and the world dissolve.

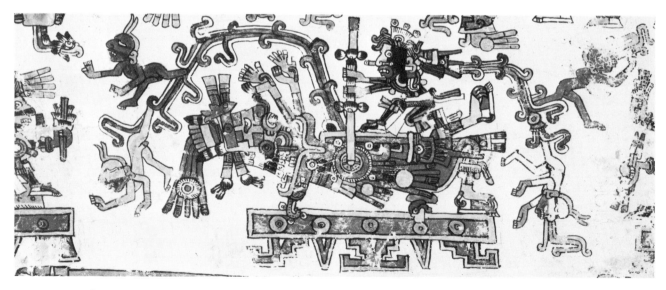

129. *Quetzalcoatl Drilling Fire on the Body of the Fire-goddess*

Beside the Aztec Calendar Stone following I have placed for comparison an Etruscan ceiling lamp of a date two thousand years earlier. The central gorgon mask is in both symbolic of the mystic sun: not the sun of day but the power behind it, source and end of all life. And the emanating circles then represent the ranges of existence. First—in the lamp—is the range of the earth and its life: four groups of beasts, each of a griffin and lion tearing a third beast to pieces. A ring of waves and eight dolphins tells of the world-surrounding sea, beyond which the element air is represented by the guardians of the quarters and points between: eight winged sirens, each on a triple-stepped base with lines signifying rain, alternating with eight pipe-playing sileni. And finally, above the head of each siren and silenus ten stars and a sun suggest the heavenly element, fire, while on the upper side of the lamp there would be burning sixteen flames of real fire.

The great Aztec calendar, in contrast, is carved from a block of porphyry more than twelve feet in diameter and weighing over twenty tons. Its pivotal solar mask is set in a hieroglyph, "4 Olim," which denotes both the predetermined day on which the present world age is to end and the manner of its termination; for the word *olim*, "movement, motion," means also "earthquake." The two earlike projections at either side of this mask show hands tipped with eagle claws, clutching human hearts. The sun was pictured as an eagle, and the offerings sustaining his flight were hearts. Four quadrangular glyphs flaring from the rim of this symbol of the will-in-nature refer to four mythological eons supposed to have preceded our own; and as Dr. Eduard Seler, one of the great founding scholars of Middle American research, has observed with undisguised amazement, the powers represented in these four correspond to the very elements hypothesized by the Greek philosopher Empedocles as the "roots," *ritsomata*, of all things. "The four distinct prehistoric and precosmic ages of the Mexicans, each oriented," Seler notes, "toward a different direction of the heavens, are astonishingly related to the four elements, earth, wind, fire, and water, known to classical antiquity and which even now determine the way in which the civilized people of East Asia look upon nature."[83]

In the ring of twenty signs immediately encircling this demiurgical center appear the day names of the Aztec twenty-day month, commencing at the upper left and rotating counterclockwise:

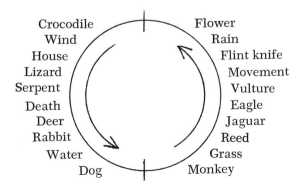

130. The Calendar Stone of the Aztecs. A.D. *1479*

Spearlike indicators of the quarters and the four points between spring from the next two circles—which have not, to my knowledge, been explained: the first a circle of pentagrams grouped in arcs of ten, the second a ring of what in the Orient would be lotus petals, grouped also in arcs of ten. Beyond is an open area where signs of celestial lights and clouds appear; and finally, the whole is enclosed by two great feathered serpents, with their rattlesnake tails at the top and open jaws, showing human heads within, confronting each other below.

On the outside of the carved serpent rim, and so not visible in the photograph, are representations of a goddess known as Itzpapalotl, "Obsidian Butterfly." She is a goddess of the stars—those points of light that mark the ultimate reach of human

131. Etruscan Ceiling Lamp. 5th century B.C.

sight and thought, beyond which is the "Place of Light Where He-who-gives-light Hides Himself";[84] whereas within the bounding double serpent rim, "The gods battle," as one authority says of the mystery, "and their struggle for supremacy is the history of the universe."[85]

Now it is in the sequence of the four prehistoric world ages represented on the Calendar Stone by the four quadrangular glyphs flaring from the central gorgon mask that the wars of the world-governing gods are synopsized. Commencing with the upper righthand sign and progressing counterclockwise, they are described in the relevant texts as follows:

Fig. 132   1. The first age, known as "4 Jaguar," the day name of its predestined end, was a brutish period of giants living on acorns, during which the sun-carrier was the god Tezcatlipoca of the night sky, whose name means "Smoking Mirror," and whose animal, the jaguar, is symbolic of the element earth. The period lasted 13 times 52 or 676 years and ended when Tezcatlipoca, its sun-carrier, was struck down by Quetzalcoatl and turned into a jaguar that devoured all the giants. The world quarter associated with this first world age is the North, and its colors are black and red.

Fig. 133   2. The second period, "4 Wind," began when Quetzalcoatl became sun-carrier and it lasted, like the first, 13 times 52 or 676 years, closing when Quetzalcoatl, defeated by Tezcatlipoca, became a hurricane and carried away many people. All those remaining became monkeys. The world quarter associated with this second world age is the East, its element is air, and its color the yellow of dawn. In the glyph on the Aztec Calendar Stone the head of its deity is shown with an open mouth, signifying wind.

Fig. 134   3. In "4 Rain," the next age, the sun-carrier was Tlaloc the rain god, "He-who-makes-things-sprout," appointed by Tezcatlipoca. His world period lasted only 7 times 52 or 364 years, concluding when he was overcome by Quetzalcoatl; whereupon he sent down a rain of fire that transformed his people into turkeys. Thus the element here is fire (as in lightning), the designated world quarter the South, and the color the white of day. The glyph on the Calendar Stone shows Tlaloc's head composed of serpent forms and rain.

Fig. 135   4. "4 Water," last of the prehistoric ages, had as sun-carrier Tlaloc's wife, the goddess of flowing waters, known as Chalchiuhtlicue, "She-of-the-robe-of-green-jewels," whom Quetzalcoatl appointed to the post. Her season, which endured but

Fig. 136   6 times 52 or 312 years, concluded with a deluge lasting 52 years more, when it rained so hard and so long that the heavens fell and the people became fish. Water was the element of this terminal age, its world quarter the West, and its color blue or blue-green.

Thus the guardian power of each of the four world quarters gained in turn possession of the sun, only to succumb to the power opposite; whereupon each was overtaken by the negative, uncontrolled, destructive aspect of its own element. Earth, the world support and base, became the swallower of all things. Air, the breath of life, became a devastating wind. Fire that descends from heaven tempered as the fire-of-life in lifegiving rain came down as a rain of flames. And finally, Water, gentle mothering vehicle of the energies of birth, nourishment, and growth, became a deluge.

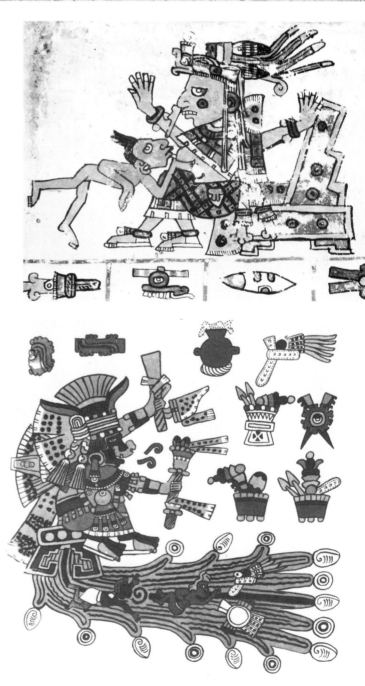

132 (upper left). Tezcatlipoca, the Jaguar

133 (upper right). Quetzalcoatl, the Great Wind

134 (center left). Tlaloc, the Rain-god

135 (center right). Chalchihuitlicue,
the Water Goddess

136 (lower right). Chalchihuitlicue
Sending the Deluge

After which the time fell due for the dawn of our own world age, the age of historic man, whose day name, "4 Movement," announces both the character of the period and the day and manner of its destined end. Its glyph is at the center of the Calendar Stone, enclosing the gorgon mask, and as connoted by this pivotal place, where it is not opposed to any one of the others but axial to all, its years were to be full of strife. Open to influences from all quarters at once, it was to be a more complex, alive, and dynamic age than any of the earlier four; and in the very circumstances of its inauguration, furthermore, warning was given of the importance of unremitting sacrifice for its continuation.

For following the mighty rains, which had lasted so long that the heavens had fallen, there was need for a completely new creation. The Lord Quetzalcoatl, there-fore, descended to the Netherworld, Mictlan, to confront the Lord of Death, Mictlan-tecuhtli; and returning with a parcel of human bones, he presented these to the all-encompassing goddess-mother of the universe, the Lady of the Serpent Skirt. She ground them up, poured them into a precious vessel of clay into which Quetzalcoatl bled his member, and then, with all the gods practicing penances, a new people came into being. "For our sake," declares a native text, "the gods did penance."

Fig. 137

Fig. 138

137. *Mictlantecuhtli, Lord of the Dead*

This monstrous form has been explained as "the embodiment of the cosmic-dynamic power that, in the struggle of opposites, bestows life and thrives on death: a struggle so compulsive and essential that its fundamental and final meaning is war."[86]

As in the ancient Mesopotamian idea of the world mountain as the body of the goddess-mother of the universe,* so here: this is an image of the universe as the goddess-mother of all being. The skull between navel and genitals represents the power that generates, supports, and consumes all things on this earth-plane, death (the sacrifice) thus corresponding to the sense of the sun mask at the center of the Calendar Stone. The hands opened in the four directions represent the boons of life going forth to all quarters, while the two hearts between are the same as those clutched in the talons of the

* Above, p. 77.

solar eagle of the Calendar Stone.** Below, in the massive legs, are the underworlds, the nine Aztec hells; while above, in the region of the dual yet single head, are the thirteen heavens culminating in that "Place of Duality," Omeyocan, where the ultimately transcendent "One" becomes the "Lord-Lady of Duality," Ometecuhtli Omecihuatl, who is in essence identical with the power of the pivotal skull.

> *You are in heaven: you uphold the mountain.*
> *The plane of Earth is in your hands.*
> *Awaited, you are always everywhere.*
> *You are prayed to: you are invoked.*[87]

So addressed, this deity, at once female and male, transcendent yet the center of all, the "mirror that illumines all things," is given praise with "flower and song."

** See text to Figure 130.

138. Coatlicue, "Goddess of the Serpent Skirt"

Fig. 140   However, the new sun refused to move until a sacrifice had been offered, and for the sake of the whole new universe a little deity named Nanahuatzin, "the Pimply One," the god of syphilis, hurled himself into a huge fire and became by that act the sun-bearer of this last and present age. But that single sacrifice—even though

Fig. 139   of a god—was not enough. To keep the sun moving, continuing sacrifices are required, and to this end the holy institution of war has been established for the gathering of victims, whose hearts torn living from their opened breasts are daily tossed as flowers of gratitude to the "Giver of Life."

139. Heart Offering to the Sun-god

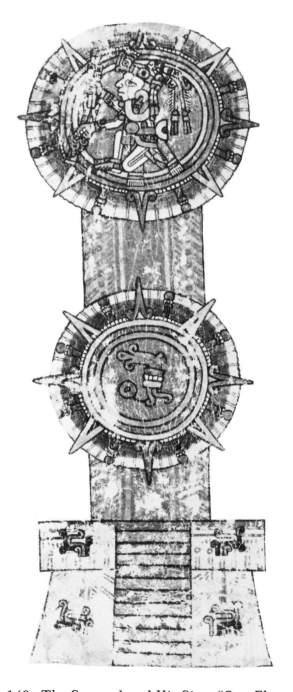

140. The Sun-god and His Sign, "One Flower"

Now do I hear the words of the coyolli bird
  as he makes answer to the Giver of Life.
He goes his way singing, offering flowers,
  and his words rain down
  like jade and quetzal plumes.
Is it this that pleases the Giver of Life?
Is this the only truth here on earth?

These lines of the Aztec poet Ayocuan Quetzpaltzin convey a sense of the existential terror of this awesome civilization. *In xochitl in cuicatl,* "flower and song," Figs. 141, 142 was the Aztec metaphor for poetry, "the only truth here on earth"; and both the sacrifice and the "flowery war" were of the essence of that mythopoesy. Aztec warriors were priests; so too were the players of the sacred ball game. In every Middle American civilization from the Olmec period onward an unremitting meditation on the mystery of death in life appears to have been the primary inspiration.

142. Xochipilli, "Flower Prince"

141. Xochipilli, God of the Flower Feast

According to Eduard Seler, Xochipilli, the god of flowers and food supplies, was the patron particularly of players, singers, dancers, painters, and artisans of all classes. Moreover, his stone effigies were set up in the ball courts. He is represented here as he appeared in the annual flower festival, wearing his characteristic helmet mask of the blue-plumaged, high-crested bird known as the *quetzalcoxcoxtli*, carried in state on a royal palanquin of abundant maize and preceded by his herald, a musician sounding the conch. He is said to have been born in the West, the land of the great goddess, of water and mist, and of maize.[88]

Life is but a mask worn on the face of death. And is death, then, but another mask? "How many can say," asks the Aztec poet, "that there is, or is not, a truth beyond?"

cf. Figs. 1, 4

We merely dream, we only rise from a dream:
It is all as a dream. . . .[89]

143. Drum and Flute Song to the Sacrifice

The head on the pyramid is that of the maize god. It rests upon the sign *caban*, meaning earth. The smoke of incense rises from the jar resting on its nose.

144. Carved Jadeite Head, in the Olmec style

145. Bronze Mirror-back. Han Dynasty, 202 B.C.-A.D. 220

The classical Chinese renditions of the common heritage of cosmological themes have generally a beautifully geometrical quality of their own, abstract and impersonal, with little of the Indian tendency to erotic personification—until later, after the Indian Buddhist missions arrive in the early centuries A.D. Here the mound in the center is symbolic of the axial mother mountain, the world navel, the Greek *omphalos*; and the four petals in the four directions again suggest, as they would in India, the world lotus. The earth in the old Chinese view is quadrangular; heaven is circular. Here, within the quadrangular field of earth, twelve studs, suggesting secondary centers, alternate with ideograms of the Twelve Earthly Regions or Branches (the north being at the top), while in the circular field of heaven we find again twelve studs, besides a dozen gracefully stylized animal forms in linear relief, and the so-called TLV devices, from which this type of Han Dynasty bronze mirrorback takes its name. The T's represent the gates of the four quarters. The swastikalike L signs, suggesting a rotation of the heavens, mark the quarters of the heavenly horizon, and the v signs mark the points between. Professor Schuyler Cammann has shown that the symbolism of these mirrors relates to the ritual duties of the emperor serving as the harmonizing pivotal figure of the realms of heaven, earth, and man;[90] so that, once again, we have in this harmonious abstract composition a reflex of the ancient Mesopotamian theme of a universal concord uniting heaven and earth, recognized in the social order and honored as the guide for all human life.

The animals represented are as follows, commencing at the upper left (northern quarter) and circling counterclockwise: (1) and (2) the so-called "Somber Warrior" (*hsüan-wu*), image of a snake mating with a tortoise; (3) a tiger; (4) a gazelle (sitting on the western L); (5) a kind of griffin; (6) a fairylike human form; (7) a phoenix, perched on the southern L; (8) another phoenix; (9) a bird; (10) a sort of harpy; (11) a dragon; and (12) a unicorn.

5. The Revolving Sphere of Space-Time

In Hindu and Buddhist thought the elements recognized are five: space or ether, cf. Fig. 76 and in descending order, air, fire, water, and earth, to each of which there has been assigned one of the five senses: hearing, touch, sight, taste, and smell; so that the macrocosmic and the microcosmic orders are coordinate—which is an idea basic to yoga, as to all traditional Indian thought and culture.

And in China, too, the elements are five, though not the same. They are wood, fire, earth, metal, and water, usually understood as giving rise to each other in that order: wood producing fire by being consumed as fuel; fire producing earth by yielding ashes; earth producing metal by fostering the growth of metallic ores within its rocks; metal producing water by secreting or attracting dew when metal mirrors are exposed at night; and water then producing wood again by entering into the substances of plants.[91]

146. *Hsi Brothers and Ho Brothers Commissioned by the Emperor Yao to Organize the Calendar and Pay Respect to the Celestial Bodies. Late Manchu Illustration of the Legendary "Book of Documents" (Shu Ching)*

Moreover, in the Chinese cosmological view as in the Aztec each element is related to a world quarter, a division of time, and a color: wood to the East, spring, and green; fire to the South, summer, and red; metal to the West, autumn, and white; water to the North, winter, and black; while earth, at the center, is yellow. China itself is the "Kingdom of the Center" and hence coordinator of the universe, at that pivotal point in the revolving sphere of space-time where all pairs of opposites come together: fire and water, metal and wood, motion and rest, heaven and earth. And as in the Aztec mythic order, so too in the Chinese: to each quarter and its element there has been assigned a mythic personage who stands for its special quality; and as the cosmic wheel revolves these powers have followed one another in succession to the pivotal Chinese throne—as we know, for example, from a work of the fifth century B.C., *The Book of the Master Tsou on Coming into Being and Passing Away*:

> When some new dynasty is going to arise Heaven exhibits auspicious signs to the people. During the rise of Huang Ti, the Yellow Emperor, large earthworms and large ants appeared. He said, "This indicates that the element Earth is in the ascendant, so our color must be yellow, and our affairs must be placed under the sign of Earth." During the rise of Yü the Great, Heaven produced plants and trees that did not wither in autumn and winter. He said, "This indicates that the element Wood is in the ascendant, so our color must be green, and our affairs must be placed under the sign of Wood." During the rise of T'ang the Victorious a metal sword appeared out of the water [Excalibur!]. He said, "This indicates that the element Metal is in the ascendant, and our affairs must be placed under the sign of Metal." During the rise of King Wen of the Chou, Heaven exhibited fire, and many red birds holding documents written in red flocked to the altar of the dynasty. He said, "This indicates that the element Fire is in the ascendant, so our color must be red, and our affairs must be placed under the sign of Fire." Following Fire, there will come Water. Heaven will show when the time comes for the *ch'i* [breath, vital force] of Water to dominate. Then the color will have to be black, and affairs will have to be placed under the sign of Water. And that dispensation will in turn come to an end, and at the appointed time, all will return once again to Earth. But when that time will be we do not know.[92]

According to the Greek system of four elements, two activating principles, love and strife, communicate motion to the quaternity, love uniting and strife sundering. And here again we find that in the course of time the elements succeed one another in dominance. "For," as Empedocles states, "they prevail in turn as the circle comes round, pass into one another, and grow great in their appointed turn."[93]

Heraclitus, on the other hand, saw fire as the elemental activator of all, and strife, not love, as the principle that brings opposites together and so sustains the universe. "We must know that War is common to all, and Strife is Justice, and that all things come into being by Strife."[94] And again (suggesting the words of the famous "Fire Sermon" of his contemporary, the Buddha): "This world, the same for all, was not made by any god or man, but was always, and is, and shall be an everliving Fire, with measures of it kindling and measures of it being extinguished."[95]

In the Aztec, Mayan, and general Middle American view, love, in the sense of Empedocles, plays no cosmic role whatsoever. On the contrary, as in Heraclitus, it is rather strife that holds opposites together: strife and strife alone supports and constitutes the world process. And this mystery of strife was supremely symbolized both in war and in the sacred ball game—each with its symbolic consummation in its concluding dyad, DEFEAT/VICTORY. Hence the hieratic priestly costume and decorum

Fig. 147

of the Mesoamerican ball player. Hence, too, the culminating sacrament of the ball

147. Sacrifice in the Ball Court.   Mayan Classic period, A.D. 292-869

At the right sits the umpire, at the left, the presiding deity, Death. In the center, above, descending to receive the proffered heart, is the figure of the sun god as an eagle. Compare the style of the decorative border with that of Figures 111-112.

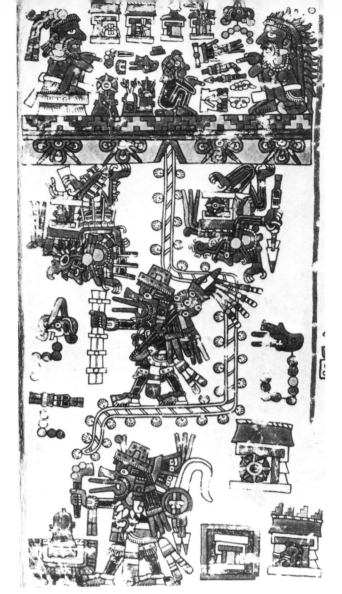

148. *Quetzalcoatl Descending the Ladder from Omeyocan. Mixtec. Pre-Columbian*

court, where the defeated captain is the sacrificial victim and the victor the sacrificing priest. The ceremonial stone phalli of the heavily vestured players of this panel —which is rendered, by the way, in a style revealing Chinese (Early Chou) affinities—signify battle-fervor, not sexual zeal. The strongly phallic male-female (*lingam-yoni*) accent so prominent in Hindu religious art and worship is missing from the Middle American scene, and from Shang and Chou China as well. cf. Figs. 116, 117

And yet, in a different way, the male-female polarity is indeed in both traditions recognized as attesting to an even more essential duality than the battle principle of contending masculine opposites—as, for instance, in the Aztec symbol of the Goddess of the Serpent Skirt and the Chinese of the interacting yang and yin. The Fig. 138 ultimate source and ground of all being was personified by the Aztecs in a transcendent-immanent dual divinity known as Ometeotl, "God of Duality," dwelling in Omeyocan, the "Place of Duality," at the summit of the world mountain, "where Fig. 148 duality begins," and around which the whole sphere of this mighty universe unceasingly revolves. Quetzalcoatl is seen first (above) as a child receiving instruction from the Lady and Lord of that highest place, and then descending to earth as an incarnation of their message. In prayer those two aloft were addressed as two aspects of the one substance of all life: Tonacatecuhtli Tonacacihuatl, "Lady-of-our-flesh Lord-of-our-flesh"; and recognized also as "She-who-is-clothed-in-black He-who-is-clothed-in-the-color-of-blood," which is to say, the night sky and the sun.[96]

cf. Figs. 61, 66, 67, 76-90, 149

The image of an axial ladder let down through an opening in midsky, as though from the golden sun-door of noon to the navel of the earth, is a universal mythological motif, the mythic prototype, in fact, of the stairway of the temple tower. At the summit, the place of the union (or identity) of heaven and earth, eternity and time, where the two are one and the One becomes two, Quetzalcoatl sits in the naked state symbolic of unconditioned being. His posture is that of a child listening, but also talking, to its parents. Between them, receiving their words, he is at the coming together of their powers—each of the two, meanwhile, representing but one half of the dual appearance, in the place "where duality begins," of that ultimate "One" which is finally neither one nor many but unmeasured. Reuniting their powers in himself (as their son), he thus actually transcends them as an image of that which, anteceding them, is beyond both twoness and oneness, beyond imaging, beyond thought, beyond the categories even of "being," "nonbeing," and "beyond." And he is in this sense verily a paradox, an incarnation of the Inconceivable, as he descends the ladder of manifestation to this earth, voluntarily assuming, in descending, the limitations inevitably imposed upon life by the conditions of time and space. These are represented in the tokens of his powers, which in the regions above are all about him as potential, and which in the course of his descent are taken on as the masks represented in the ritual gear of his cult and expounded in his myth.

In this relief from the ruined stupa at Bharhut the gods, soaring in the sky, are attending the Buddha's descent to earth. For three months he has been teaching them in their heaven, to which he had mounted to pay a visit to his mother, who, like the mother of Quetzalcoatl, died shortly after her son's birth. Three ladders are represented, because he is accompanied in his descent by Brahma on his right and Indra on his left, each with an attending host. The person of the Buddha himself, however, was never represented in this early period of Buddhist art, and so we do not see him here. As explained by Heinrich Zimmer, "The pertinent text for this tradition is that of the Ceylonese *Sutta Nipata*: 'For him who [like the sun] has set, there is nothing any more with which he can be compared.' There is nothing any more by means of which he can be represented: his footprint, like the twilight, only gives evidence of a vanished sun."[97]

The Buddha is to be imagined as descending the middle ladder, where the impress of the soles of his feet marked by the Buddhist symbol of the wheel appear on the topmost and lowest rungs. We are actually watching him, that is to say, as he comes invisibly down, and the pious community at the bottom is watching too. "Thus," to quote Zimmer again, "no single particular moment, but time itself, flowing on, is an intrinsic factor in this dynamic composition."

149. Return of the Buddha from Trayastrimshat Heaven. Early 1st century B.C.

150. *The Crucifixion. Francesco del Cossa.* A.D. 1470-1475

One is reminded by the legend of this alien god-made-flesh of the words of Paul to the Philippians, telling of that other, "who, though he was in the form of God, did not count equality with God a thing to be grasped, but emptied himself, taking the form of a servant, being born in the likeness of men. And being found in human form he humbled himself and became obedient unto death, even death on a cross" (2:6-8).

151 (opposite). Shrine Panel, Temple of the Cross

THE LEGEND OF THE FEATHERED SERPENT

Quetzalcoatl, according to the ancient legend, was born of the virgin Chimalman, one of three noble sisters in the Toltec city of Tollan to whom the God-above-gods once appeared under his form known as "The Morning." The other two were terrified; but on Chimalman the Presence breathed and she conceived. Giving birth, however, she died, and is now, therefore, in that heaven of heroes to which warriors who die in battle, women who die in childbirth, and victims sacrificed on the temple altars are translated. She is there worshiped under the honorable title "Chalchihuitzli," "Precious Stone of the Sacrifice."

Fig. 153 Her son was endowed at birth with speech, as with all knowledge and wisdom; and in later life, reigning as the priest-king of Tollan, he was of such purity of heart that his nation flourished wonderfully through the whole length of his reign. Fair of feature and white of beard, he was the teacher of all the arts of life as well as inventor of the calendar. His marvelous temple-palace comprised four radiant apartments: that of the East was yellow with gold; the South, white with shell and pearls; the West, blue with turquoise and jade; and the North, red with bloodstone. Moreover, the building was set above a majestic river that passed directly through Tollan, so that the godly king might descend at midnight to bathe in its pure waters; and the place of his bathing was known as "In the Painted Vase."

But now, the legend goes on to relate, when his long life-season was accomplished and the time for his predestined fall drew nigh, he made no move to delay or evade it; and though he must have known his destiny, as written in the stars, he was strangely taken by surprise.

There came to his palace a young god, Tezcatlipoca, bearing a mirror wrapped in the skin of a rabbit (the animal whose form is seen in the shadows on the face of the moon), who said to the palace servants: "Go tell your master, I have come to show him his own flesh."

Informed of this, Quetzalcoatl answered: "What does he call my own flesh? Go and ask." But when the vigorous young god came in: "Welcome youth. Whence do you come?" the elder said in greeting. "You have put yourself to much trouble. What is this, my flesh, that you would show me?"

"My Lord and my Priest," the youth replied, uncovering his mirror, "look now Fig. 154 upon your flesh! See yourself as you are seen!"

And when Quetzalcoatl beheld his face, wrinkled, aged, and full of sores, he was appalled. "How is it possible," he asked, "that my people should see me without fright?"

154. *Quetzalcoatl, Lord of Death (rear view of Figure 153)*

Tezcatlipoca had brought a potion, brewed by the magic of the goddess Mayahuel of the agave plant from which pulque is extracted. Pleading illness when the vessel was offered, the old god-king declined; but then pressed merely to taste with the tip of his finger, he did so and was overcome. He took and lifted the whole bowl, drank and became drunk, and then sent for his sister Quetzalpetlatl, who, when she arrived, was given the bowl as well; and she also drank. Reason thus erased, those two sank together to the floor, and at dawn Quetzalcoatl said in shame: "I have sinned. I am not fit to rule."

Having burned his palace of the four fair world colors, buried his treasures in the neighboring mountains, turned his chocolate trees to mesquite, and told his multi-colored birds to fly on ahead, in deepest sorrow Quetzalcoatl, the Feathered Serpent, departed. At a certain place along the way he rested, and looking back at his City of the Sun, Tollan, he wept. His tears went through the rock, and he left in that place the mark of his sitting and the impress of his palms. Farther on, he was chal-lenged by necromancers, who would not allow him to pass until he had left with them the arts of working silver, wood, and feathers, and of painting. When he crossed the mountains, many of his attendant dwarfs and humpbacks died of cold. At another place he met Tezcatlipoca and was challenged to a ball game—which he lost. And at still another he aimed an arrow at a large *pochotl* tree; the arrow, too, was a pochotl tree, and when it penetrated the first, the two together formed Quet-zalcoatl's sign, a cross.

Fig. 155

Fig. 152

*155. Quetzalcoatl Dancing Before Tezcatlipoca.
Aztec. Pre-Columbian*

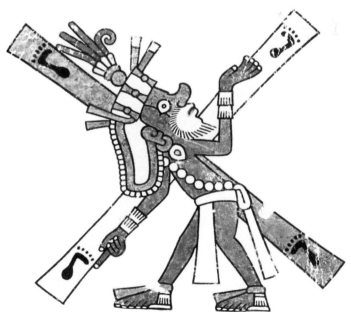

*156. Yiacatecuhtli, "Lord of the Vanguard."
Aztec. Pre-Columbian*

Fig. 158

Fig. 157

cf. Fig. 102

cf. Fig. 132

cf. Fig. 155

cf. Figs. 158-160

cf. Fig. 4

cf. Fig. 130

Thus he passed along, leaving many signs and place-names behind him, until, arriving at last where the sky, land, and water come together, he sailed away on a raft of serpents; or, according to another version of the end, his remaining attendants built a funeral pyre into which he cast himself, and as the body burned, his heart departed, after four days reappearing as the morning star.[98]

The miracle of this transformation of Quetzalcoatl's heart is here illustrated. In the center, a pair of intertwined feathered serpents support two tiny reclining figures of the dead Quetzalcoatl, each holding a copal bag. Reminded of the masked Olmec god seated on a feathered serpent and holding out a copal bag, we have to recognize here a continuity of some twenty-five hundred years, from ca. 1000 B.C. to A.D. 1500. The only change is the substitution of a wind-god mask for the earlier jaguar mask; and when it is considered that the old Olmec symbol of the jaguar has in Aztec mythology simply gone over to Tezcatlipoca, the Feathered Serpent's counterplayer, this change is small enough—especially since such counterplayers are generally, and in this mythology explicitly, the polarized aspects of a single force.

Quetzalcoatl in the abyss of death, reposing on his own serpent-form—like Vishnu on the serpent Unending—is enclosed in a design representing his feathered neck-ornament; and this entire composition is then set inside a great quadrangle representing the body of the death-goddess Mictlancihuatl. At the top, center, her head appears facing upward in profile, black, with open mouth and blazing eye. Beneath its chin is the "face" of a swallowed heart, emitting smoke. At the four corners are the rain gods (Tlalocs) of the four directions: North, upper right, with an agave plant behind him, the plant from which the potion was drawn that upset the fallen god's reason; West, upper left, before a blossoming tree of some kind; South, lower left, before a tree that is bearing fruit; and East, lower right, before another blossoming tree. We are to think of the god as having disappeared from earthly view as the evening star, swallowed by the great mouth of the northwest horizon. However, at the base of the composition, where the body of the goddess opens, the double serpent reappears, disgorging the two masked human forms, thus sending Quetzalcoatl forth again to rise in the southeast as the morning star.

The whole rectangular body of the goddess Death is pictured as the night, embellished gorgeously with stars; and encircling its interior are the day signs of the Aztec twenty-day month. Commencing at the upper right (within the circle at the end of the northern Tlaloc's bone dagger) and proceeding counterclockwise, the signs are: death (encircled), deer, rabbit, water, dog, monkey (encircled), grass, reed, jaguar, eagle, vulture (encircled), movement, flint knife, rain, flower, crocodile (encircled), wind, house, lizard, serpent.[99]

157. Quetzalcoatl's Heart in the Underworld, Transformed into the Morning Star. Aztec. Pre-Columbian

159. *Vishnu Seated on the Cosmic Serpent.*
A.D. *578. India*

160. *Muchalinda Buddha.* A.D. *12th century. Cambodia*

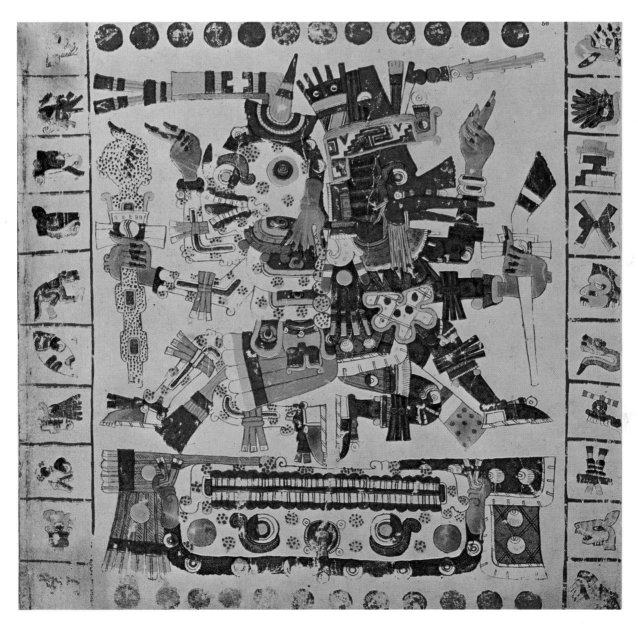

161. The Dual Lords of Life and Death, Quetzalcoatl-Mictlantecuhtli. Aztec. Pre-Columbian

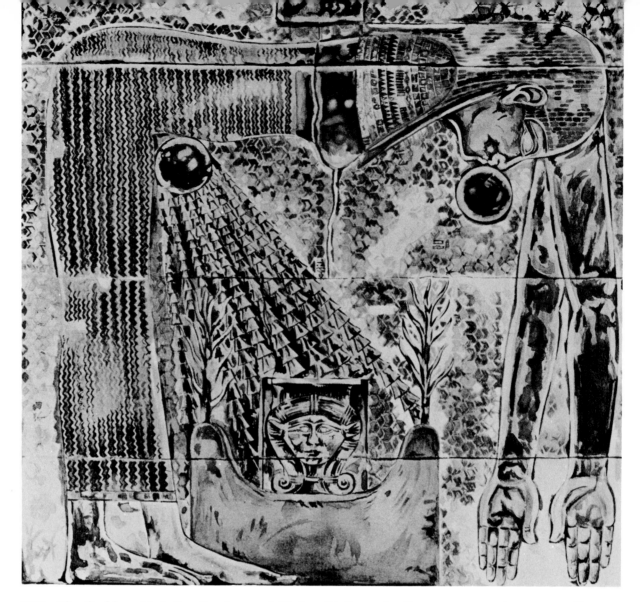

162. *The Goddess Nut, Swallowing and Giving Birth to the Sun.* A.D. *1st-4th century. Egypt*

163. *Pietà.* A.D. *14th century. Italy*

164. Christ of the Apocalypse. A.D. *12th century. Chartres Cathedral*

Thus the point is again made that we have already found illustrated in the Aztec Calendar Stone, of time and space together as composing the body of the universal goddess. They are of one spherical form and measurement in this Mexican cosmology, as they were in the Mesopotamian system from which our own sexagesimal manner of measuring circular space and time is derived. Furthermore, the idea of a great star-spangled goddess swallowing and giving birth to a god symbolic of the resurrection is exactly what is represented in the ancient Egyptian image of Nut Fig. 162 swallowing and giving birth to the sun. The idea is implicit also in the Christian medieval sequence of the Pietà and the Apocalypse. And if one considers that the Figs. 163, 164 four "living beasts" of the Apocalyptic vision, as represented above on the west portal of Chartres Cathedral (the bull of Luke, lion of Mark, eagle of John, and manlike angel of Matthew) are adaptations to Christian iconography of the four Chaldean zodiacal signs of the world quarters (the Bull, Taurus, of the vernal equinox and eastern quarter; Lion, Leo, of the summer solstice and southern quarter; Eagle or Scorpion, Scorpio, of the fall equinox and western quarter; Water Carrier, Aquarius, of the winter solstice and the north), corresponding thus to the four Tlalocs at the corners of Figure 157—the equivalence of the Aztec, Chaldean, and medieval- cf. Fig. 157 Christian symbols is complete, and the Christ of the Second Coming is shown born of a matrix that is cosmic. Interpreted in these terms, the Jesus of the Gospels, born of a human virgin mother—like Quetzalcoatl of Chimalman—was a foreground manifestation, a compassionate "stepping down" to human-historical proportions, of the same mystery which in the Second Coming, born of the body of Space-Time— like Quetzalcoatl of Mictlancihuatl—is revealed in its macrocosmic magnitude.

And finally, to pursue this theme one step farther: as all the temples of antiquity make visible to mortal eyes the grand lines of the order of nature, so, too, the architecture of Chartres. The cathedral, in the form of a great cross, is oriented to the four quarters, with its altar facing east and with every detail, whether of proportion or of ornamentation, controlled and inspired by a Platonic-Pythagorean concept of the laws of number governing the universe. By these laws, made audible in music and visible in architecture, the soul is brought to accord with both its own spiritual nature and the universal ground; for, in the words of John of Salisbury, Bishop of Chartres from 1176 to 1178, "The soul is said to be composed of musical consonances." And further: it is by laws of musical proportion that (again to cite the learned bishop), "the heavenly spheres are harmonized and the cosmos governed, as well as man."[100] We are to recognize, therefore, translated into stone and stained glass in the noble Gothic visions of those richly inspired years, both "a 'model' of the cosmos as the Middle Ages perceived it,"[101] and a model of the Christian soul in accord.

And in the same way, to the same religious end, the ziggurats of Babylon and the temple towers of both India and Mexico were models of a spatial-temporal universe, ordered mathematically to coincide with the laws of a cosmic harmony that are equally of man's moral nature. And yet, too, there is to be sensed about all such buildings the knowledge of a ground or meaning transcending such laws, made present architecturally not in the forms of majestic stone, but in the great silence surrounding and inhabiting those forms. Just as in the legend of Christ and the Virgin to whose mystery the cathedrals arose, so also in the legends to which the temple gongs are resounding, there is signified the knowledge of a seed or part within ourselves and all things that is antecedent to time and space, part and parcel of eternity, and which, like the everlasting light that in the sun, the moon, and the morning star seems to rise and set according to laws, never dies but is ever renewed. Begotten as it were of fire and wind, born as it were of water and earth, it is what lives in all lives, but also antecedes and survives them.

All accounts agree, therefore, that the vanished Quetzalcoatl is to return. From the shining East he will one day arise with a feathered, fair-faced retinue, to resume his reign and the guardianship of his people. For those same irreversible laws of time that brought to pass the dissolution of his glorious palace-city Tollan must also inevitably bring about its restoration.

165. *Chartres Cathedral*

6. The Center of Transformation

THE idea of a sacred place where the walls and laws of the temporal world may dissolve to reveal a wonder is apparently as old as the human race. And as an instance of the way in which such a mystic point becomes known we may take the Old Testament story of Jacob's dream.

Fig. 166
Cf. Figs. 148, 149

Having just gained, by device, the birthright of his elder brother, the young favorite of his father left Beer-sheba in haste for Haran, and at the close of the first day "lighted," we are told, "upon a certain place, and tarried there all night, because the sun was set; and he took of the stones of that place, and put them for his pillow, and lay down in that place to sleep. And he dreamed, and behold a ladder set up on the earth, and the top of it reached to heaven: and behold the angels of God ascending and descending on it. And, behold, the Lord stood above it, and said, 'I am the Lord God of Abraham thy father, and the God of Isaac: the land whereon thou liest, to thee will I give it, and to thy seed; and thy seed shall be as the dust of the earth, and thou shalt spread abroad to the west, and to the east, and to the north, and to the south: and in thee and in thy seed shall all the families of the earth be blessed. . . .' And Jacob awaked out of his sleep, and he said, 'Surely the Lord is in this place!' And he was afraid, and said, 'How dreadful is this place! This is none other but the house of God, and this is the gate of heaven.' And Jacob . . . took the stone that he had put for his pillow, and set it up for a pillar, and poured oil upon the top of it. And he called the name of that place Beth-el [The House of God] . . ." (Genesis 28:10-14, 18-19, KJV).

Fig. 167
In Egyptian thought every tomb was the site of a heaven ladder of this kind, up

166. *Jacob's Ladder. Early Christian*

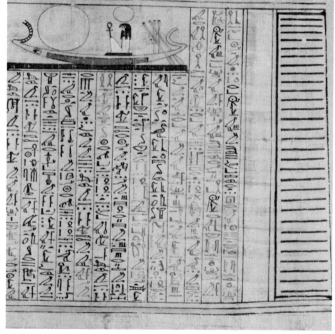

167. *The Ladder from Earth to Heaven. 16th century* B.C.

which the soul of the awakened dead would mount to its eternal place in the ever-circling barge of Re. So we read in the Pyramid Texts of 2350-2175 B.C. (the earliest mythological texts known): "The deceased ascends on the ladder that Re, his father, made for him" (Utterance 271:390a). "They bring the ladder for the deceased; they set up the ladder for the deceased; they raise up the ladder for the deceased. . . . He ascends on the hips of Isis; he climbs up on the hips of Nephthys. His father, Atum, lays hold of the arm of the deceased" (480:995a-c, 996c-997a). And again: "The deceased goes to his mother Nut [the Sky]; he climbs upon her in this her name of 'Ladder'" (474:941a-b). "Every spirit, every god who shall open his arms to the deceased will be on the ladder of the god. United for him are his bones, assembled for him are his limbs; the deceased has sprung up to heaven on the fingers of the god, lord of the ladder" (478:980).[102]

But not all such visionary gateways open upward. Below is shown a sacred place of Fig. 168 the Northern Aranda of Australia, marking the site where, at the dawn of the world, the totem ancestor of the Bandicoot people sprang from the earth, leaving behind a great gaping hole filled with the sweet dark juice of honeysuckle buds.[103] And

168. *Sacred Ground Painting. Australia*

Three Northern Aranda tribesmen, cere-monially attired, sit before a sacred ground-painting representing the Ilbalintja Soak on the Burt Plain, some thirty miles northwest of Alice Springs. There, according to legend, in the very beginning, when all was dark-ness, Karora, the Bandicoot totem ancestor, lay at rest in everlasting sleep. Over him the soil was red with flowers, overgrown with many grasses; and from the midst of a patch of purple flowers just above his head there rose a decorated sacred pole that swayed to and fro. This was a living creature covered with smooth skin, like the skin of a man. And at its root lay Karora's head.

Though asleep, the ancestor was thinking: desires flashed through his mind, and Bandi-coots began coming then from his navel and armpits. Bursting through the sod above, these sprang there into life, and at that mo-ment the first dawn also appeared. The sun rose, flooding all with light. And with that, Karora thought also to rise. He burst through the crust that had been covering him and the gaping hole that he left behind became Ilbalintja Soak.

The ground of this painting has been hard-ened with men's blood, drawn from their sexual organs and arms. The white circles are of down. The kneeling men have just per-formed in three different ceremonies: the central figure is a Bandicoot ancestor with the decorated pole overhead; the other two have been acting in different sun totemic ceremonies and wear the headgear of those rites. For Ilbalintja is regarded as the site where both the Bandicoot totem and the sun originated.[104]

Fig. 169   a rock face along the shore of a Canadian lake registers the vision there of a god who is apparently Manabozho, the Great Hare, the earthly Trickster Hero of the Algonquins, whose adventures supplied Longfellow with many episodes of his "Song of Hiawatha."

Clearly, the occurrence of such visions over the whole inhabited earth requires no explanation in terms either of racial or of cultural diffusion. The problem is, rather, psychological: of that depth of the unconscious where, to quote the words of C. G. Jung, "man is no longer a distinct individual, but his mind widens out and merges into the mind of mankind—not the conscious mind, but the unconscious mind of mankind, where we are all the same."[105]

169. The Great Hare. Rock Painting. Ontario, Canada

However, when the concept of such a holy site or center is found joined to that of a mathematically structured universe, symbolized (as discussed earlier) in the imagery of a cosmic mountain oriented to the quarters of a zodiac, a derivation either proximate or remote from ancient Mesopotamia must be suspected—as, for Fig. 170   instance, in the painting, opposite, made in 1931 by Standing Bear of his friend Black Elk at the mythical center of the earth.

170. Black Elk's Vision of Himself. Painting by Standing Bear

"Then I was standing on the highest mountain of them all, and round about beneath me was the whole hoop of the world. And while I stood there I saw more than I can tell and I understood more than I saw; for I was seeing in a sacred manner the shapes of all things in the spirit, and the shape of all shapes as they must live together like one being. And I saw that the sacred hoop of my people was one of many hoops that made one circle, wide as daylight and as starlight, and in the center grew one mighty flowering tree to shelter all the children of one mother and one father. And I saw that it was holy." Black Elk said that the mountain he stood upon in that vision was Harney Peak in the Black Hills. "But anywhere," he then added, "is the center of the world."[106]

The picture by Standing Bear was painted half a century after the Oglala Sioux had been settled on their reservation; hence it is possible that it was influenced by Christian sources. However, Black Elk's vision itself occurred in 1872, when the Oglala were still a tribe of buffalo-hunting nomads (in 1876 he participated in the defeat of General Custer at Little Big Horn), and there is no end of evidence for the antiquity in America of the idea of the world center and four directions. According to Black Elk, who was the last Keeper of the Sacred Pipe of the Oglala Sioux, the colors of the four directions are as follows: the West, blue or black; the North, white; the East, red; and the South, yellow.[107]

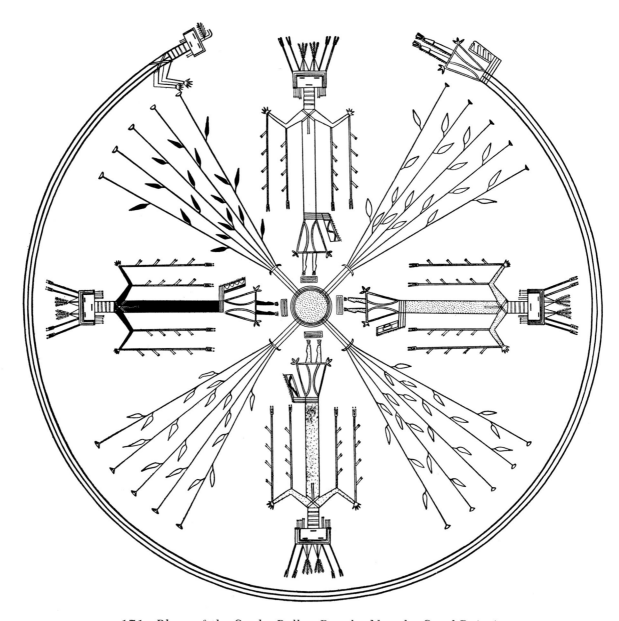

171. Place of the Snake Pollen People. Navaho Sand Painting

The center is blue water with bands of white foam, and the colors of the four Snake Pollen People are those of the four directions: white, the East (above); blue, the South (to our right); yellow, the West (below); and black, the North. The white figure is male and is named Snake Tracks; the blue, female, is Blue Sky; the yellow, male, is called Where They Built the Fire; and the black, female, is Rain Came Over Where Fire Is. Their caps represent the Two Pointed Rocks on the summit of Mount Taylor, and from their arms hang strands of horsehair, attached to which are deer tracks. The plants are medicine herbs. The encircling guardian form is that of Rainbow Man.

The use of such a sand painting in connection with a curing ceremonial (a two-day, five-day, or occasionally nine-day chant) has the effect of harmonizing a disordered spirit, returning the patient to the "Pollen Path of Beauty" by setting him in accord again with the powers of the universe, which are the same, finally, as his own. The chief use of the Beautyway chants and rites, to which this painting belongs, is against what are known as snake infections: aching feet, legs, arms, back, and waist, swollen ankles and knees, itching skin, painful urination, dry throat, mental confusion, fear, and the loss of consciousness.[108]

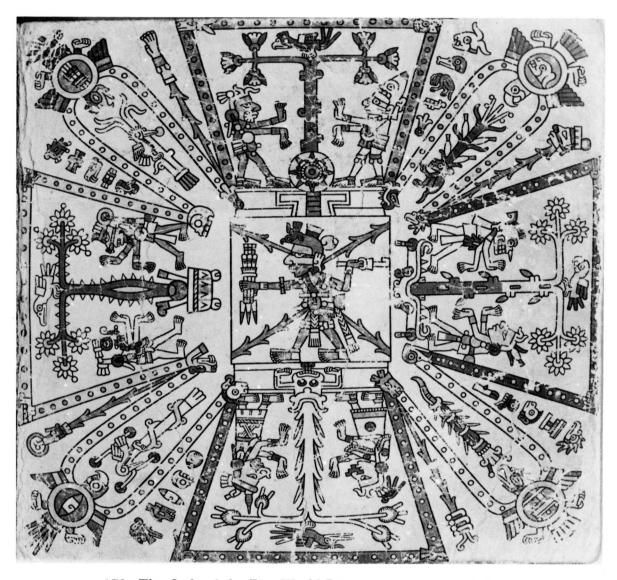

172. *The Gods of the Five World Directions. Aztec. Pre-Columbian*

The directions are East (above), North (left), West (below), and South (right). The birds atop the trees are, respectively, a quetzal, an eagle, a colbiri bird, and a parrot; the colors of the trees are turquoise blue, blue, white, and half-blue, half-white. The objects under the trees are a sun disk, a bowl containing sacrifices, a mythic creature symbolic of the pulque god, and a symbol of the open jaws of the earth. The god in the center is Xiuhtecuhtli, the Old Lord, God of Fire, the same who appears at the belt of the world goddess Coatlicue. In his right hand are his spears, in his left his throwing stick, and from his body flames go forth.

From the corners, food and medicine plants proceed, topped by birds bearing day signs on their bodies: * upper left, reed; lower

left, flint; lower right, house; and upper right, lizard. To the left of each of these corner devices are the five day signs associated with the quarter in question. Commencing at the upper left and reading each stack from bottom to top: East: crocodile, reed, serpent, movement, water; North: jaguar, death, flint, dog, wind; West: deer, rain, monkey, house, eagle; and South: flower, grass, lizard, vulture, rabbit.

It is of interest to note that the number of dots appearing in each length of frame is twelve, and that the hand postures of the eight deities attending the four trees are those known in India as "fear-dispelling" (*abhaya-mudra*) and "boon-bestowing" (*varada-mudra*).

* See text to Figure 157.

173. *Griffin at the Tree of Life*

174. *The Dragon of the Hesperides*

175. *Two Genii Fertilizing the Tree of Life*

In many cases the center is conceived as an axis (*axis mundi*) extending vertically to the pole star and downward to some pivotal point in the abyss. Iconographically, it may be represented as a mountain, a stairway or ladder, a pole, or very commonly a tree. It is symbolized in our Christmas tree, with the pivotal star at its summit, bounteous gifts appearing beneath, and the Christ child, greatest gift of all, in the crèche at its base; while below, as we may imagine, are its roots in the fiery abyss.

cf. Fig. 224   But equally, it is symbolized in the Cross.

176. *Crucifixion. Albrecht Dürer*

In the Old Norse *Poetic Edda* this axial tree is named Yggdrasil, Steed (*drasil*) of Othin (*Ygg*), because the god Othin (Woden, Wotan) hung on it nine days to gain the wisdom of the runes. In his own words:

> *I ween that I hung on the windy tree,*
> *Hung there for nights full nine;*
> *With the speer I was wounded, and offered I was*
> *To Othin, myself to myself,*
> *On the tree that none may ever know*
> *What root beneath it runs.*[109]

At the root of Yggdrasil a "worm" or serpent gnaws and on the summit perches an eagle, while running up and down its trunk is an everlasting squirrel:

> *Ratatosk is the squirrel who there shall run*
> *On the ash-tree Yggdrasil;*
> *From above the words of the eagle he bears,*
> *And tells them to Nithhogg beneath.*
> *Four harts there are, that the highest twigs*
> *Nibble with necks bent back;*
> *Dain and Dvalin, Duneyr and Dyrathror. . . .*[110]

Santa's reindeer, no less!

There is the idea also of an inverted tree with its root above, in eternity, as described in the Indian *Katha Upanishad*:

> *Root above, branches below: this primal fig-tree!*
> *Pure indeed is its root: it is* brahman, *known*
> *as the Immortal.*
> *In it rest all the worlds:*
> *No one soever goes beyond it.*
> *All this, verily, is that tree.*[111]

John of Ruysbroeck (1293-1381) employs such an image in writing of the spiritual efforts of the mystic: "and he must climb into the tree of belief, which grows downward, since it has its roots in the godhead."[112] Also, in the chief medieval text of the Kabbalah, the *Zohar* (ca. A.D. 1280), we are told of an inverted tree. "Happy," it is there declared, "is the portion of Israel, in whom the Holy One, blessed be He, delights and to whom he gave the Torah of truth, the Tree of Life. Whoever takes hold of this achieves life in this world and in the world to come. Now the Tree of Life extends from above downward, and it is the Sun which illumines all."[113]

Fig. 178   Dante on the sixth ledge of his world mountain of purgatory passed an inverted tree, which he describes as "a tree that we found in the mid road, with apples sweet and good to smell. And as a fir-tree tapers upward from branch to branch,

177. *Dante at Hill of the True Cross*

178. *Dante at Inverted Tree*

so downward did that: I think, in order that no one might go up."[114] And there was a voice calling from that tree, forbidding anyone to eat of its fruit.

Again, in the Earthly Paradise on the summit of the mountain, where heaven and earth come together as at the summit of a Mayan pyramid or a Mesopotamian ziggurat, there was found the tree from which Adam and Eve plucked the fateful Fig. 179 fruit: "a plant," as the poet tells, "despoiled of flowers and of other leafage on every bough. Its tresses, which the wider spread the higher up they are, would be wondered at for height by the Indians in their woods."[115] And to this arid tree there came, as he declares, a chariot symbolic of the church, drawn by a griffin whose dual nature, at once bird and beast, was a likeness of the dual nature of Christ, at once God and man. And when that griffin had drawn its chariot to that tree the cf. Fig. 173 plant was renewed, "as is the world in spring."

179. *Griffin and Chariot at Mystic Tree of Paradise*

Now it is of the essence of the image of the axial point or pole that it should symbolize the way or place of passage from motion to rest, time to eternity, separation to union; but then also, conversely, rest to motion, eternity to time, unity to multiplicity. Hence in the Biblical Eden the imagery is of *two* trees: "the tree of life also in the midst of the garden, and the tree of knowledge of good and evil" (Genesis 2:9). In Titian's painting of the fall this tree is shown as a dividing medium through which what is one becomes seen as two. The one tempter appears in two aspects. So also, of course, does man, who has already become male and female. And by what the latter differently perceive they are moved to opposite reactions: the woman to desire, the man to apprehension and fear. She reaches beautifully for the gift of a child; he, startled by what looks like a pair of serpent tails, extends to her a hand of caution. Adam and Eve were expelled from the garden lest they should "take also of the tree of life, and eat, and live for ever" (Genesis 3:22); and Yahweh, moreover, after their expulsion, "placed at the east of the garden of Eden the cherubim and a flaming sword which turned every way, to guard the way to the tree of life."

Fig. 180

In Buddhist legend, on the other hand, the whole sense of the teaching is that one should penetrate that guarded gate and discover that tree—the *Bodhi*-tree, the tree of the "Waking to Omniscience," which is the very tree beneath which the Buddha sat when he opened to mankind the way of release from those same two conditions (desire and fear) that in Titian's work are represented as pertaining to the fall. And is it not interesting to remark that in the Buddha legend, too, a

180. The Fall of Man. Titian

tempter appeared in the precincts of that tree?—a tempter, moreover, of two aspects, who appeared before the Blessed One first as Kama, the Lord of "Lust," exciter of desire, and then as Mara, "Death," provoker of fear.

A famous representation of this crucial episode of the Buddha legend is found Fig. 181 in a mutilated but still legible work of very early Buddhist art, rescued from the ruins of a once magnificent stupa at Amaravati, above the delta of the River Kistna. The person of the Buddha is not depicted in this rendering of the scene, he being that one, absolutely egoless, "who like the sun has set," so that "there is nothing any more with which he can be compared." He is to be imagined as enthroned beneath the axial tree on the "Immovable Spot," where opposites converge as at the hub of a great turning wheel; and the lord whose names are Desire and Death, the ruler of all in this moving world, has arrived to attempt to unseat him.

In the panel the two temptations are represented as though occurring simultaneously. At the lower right, where in Titian's painting Eve stands, we can still make out the mutilated form of one of Kama's three voluptuous daughters, displayed before the Blessed One to move him to desire. Behind her there were once to be seen her two sisters and on the elephant in the background the beautiful god Kama himself, with his elephant-boy behind him. And if the Blessed One had thought "I," he would also have thought "They." He, however, was no longer an ego. He remained unmoved, and the first temptation failed.

181. The Assault of Mara

The antagonist, therefore, transforming himself into King Death, let loose against the Blessed One his army of fiends and ogres—seen here threatening at the left, in the place of Titian's Adam, with their lord Mara behind them on his elephant. But again, there was no ego present to be moved. In consciousness the Blessed One had—so to speak—moved back and away, through the very stem of the tree, leaving the two great panels of the lures and threats of life to persevere, as harmless and inconsequent as the reflex of a mirage.

Fig. 182   In Christian thinking the counterpart of the second tree of the garden is the Cross, and the abandoned body of Christ in Mary's arms at its foot is the perfect correlate of the empty seat beneath the Buddhist tree of awakening to omniscience: the mother's sorrow in this Pietà being the end term of the yearning for a child in Titian's Eve. Again, as in the old Buddhist book of sayings:

> *From attachment springs grief,*
> *From attachment springs fear,*
> *For the one free from attachment*
> *There is no grief; and whence fear?*[116]

However, if any one could follow all the way, to the ultimate term of all these

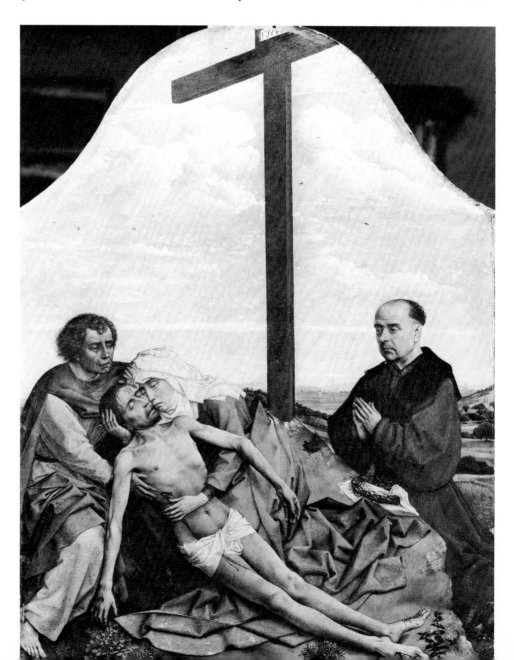

182. Pietà

183. *Coronation of the Virgin*

teachings of transcendence—with the Buddha passing beyond desire and fear and with the crucified Christ to at-one-ment with the Father—surely it would be found that when *all* pairs of opposites have been left behind, then duality and nonduality, egolessness and egohood, heavenly truth and earthly truth have been left behind as well. This, finally, is the meaning of the gentle scene of the coronation Fig. 183 of Christ's earthly virgin-mother Mary in heaven. She has risen carnally to that spiritual height where he, in union with the Father, turns again with a gesture of total affirmation to the mother of his earthly body and crowns her heaven's queen.

Below is a classical rendition of the same transcendent theme, in which appear Fig. 184 the two divine forms of Dionysos and his mother Semele, the goddess Earth. The god, we observe, is in "the full bloom of his youth, not elderly though bearded, coeval with fair Semele"[117]—as might be said of the young god of the Christian coronation scene as well. For in these eviternal figures temporal categories are transcended, youth and age, cause and effect—as in Dante's prayer to the Virgin at the opening of his last canto: "Virgin Mother, daughter of thine own Son, humble and exalted. . . ."[118]

184. *Dionysos and Semele*

And when such a realization of the nonduality of heaven and earth—even of non-being and being—will have been attained and assimilated, life-joy will pour from all things, as from an inexhaustible cup. Ego sacrificed, it is given back, and the waters of deathlessness are released to be carried in all directions. That is the wisdom for which Othin hung nine days on the World Ash and gave his left eye;* and that in general is the mystical-psychological sense of the sacrifice in all high religions, the Mayan-Aztec as well as Hindu, Buddhist, and Christian, and in Judaism in the *Akedah*, the holy symbol of Abraham's interrupted sacrifice of his son.

Figs. 185-187

* Compare the Eye of.Horus, above, pp. 29-31.

185. *Dionysos Riding a Bull*

186. *Dionysian Episode*

But the wines of immortality are, for mortals, heady fare. "No one but a Greek," wrote Jane Harrison to this amusing scene, "could have conceived this lovely little vase painting from an oinochoë in the Boston Museum of Fine Arts. . . . A beautiful maiden is the center of the scene. She is a worshipper of Dionysos. In her left hand is a tall thyrsos and she holds a cup of Dionysos, the kantharos, in her right. It is empty, and she seems to ask the Satyr who stands before her to refill it from his oinochoë. But he will not, she has had too much already. Over her beautiful head, slightly inclined as if in weariness, is inscribed—and who but a Greek would have dared to write it?—her name 'Kraipale' [Drunken Headache]. Behind her comes a kindly sober friend bearing in her hand a hot drink, smoking still, to cure her sickness."[119]

187. The Good Shepherd Bearing the Milk Pail

As the cherubim of the Assyrian seal (Figure 175) carry in hand little pails or baskets of the pollen, fruit, or ambrosia of the tree of life, and the satyr of Figure 186 an equivalent *oinochoë* of Dionysos' heady wine; so in this fresco of the catacombs the Christian Savior, whose "flesh is meat indeed" and whose "blood is drink indeed" (John 6:55), bears a little pail of the milk of paradise. He is among his lambs. To left and right are the trees of paradise. "As the child is vivified by honey and milk," we read in the Epistle of Barnabas, "so the faithful by the Word" (Barnabas 6:12).

And we have also the words of Hermes, from the pagan *Corpus Hermeticum*:

> God filled a mighty Cup with Mind and sent it down, joining a Herald to it, to whom He gave command to make this proclamation to the hearts of men: "Baptize thyself with this Cup's baptism, whatsoever heart can do so: thou that hast faith thou canst ascend to Him that hath sent down the Cup; thou that dost know for what thou didst come into being!"
>
> As many then as understood the Herald's tidings and doused themselves in Mind, became partakers in the Gnosis; and when they had "received the Mind" they were made "perfect men." But they who do not understand the tidings, these, since they possess the aid of Reason only and not Mind, are ignorant wherefor and whereby they came into being.[120]

Compare with these ambrosial pails and cups the little copal pouch held out by the Olmec jaguar-man.

Fig. 188 The sixth-century floor mosaic of the now-famous ruins of the Beth Alpha Synagogue near Galilee, discovered and excavated in 1929, renders in three extraordinary panels a pictorial exposition of the Akedah, the most holy moment of Abraham's binding of his son, as the fundamental Old Testament lesson of the meaning of sacrifice. This quaint work has been discussed by a numerous company of scholars; most notably by the late Professor Erwin R. Goodenough in his monumental *Jewish Symbols in the Greco-Roman Period*,[121] where it serves as a kind of Rosetta Stone to a formerly unsuspected pictorial tradition. Not a little surprising is the fact that such a violation of the commandment against graven images (Exodus 20:4) should have been thought proper for the inner chamber of a synagogue, directly before the very apse or shrine of the Torah. The damaged inscription at the entrance reads, in Greek: "May the craftsmen who carried out this work, Marianos and his son Hanina, be held in remembrance"; and in Aramaic: "This mosaic was laid down in the [. . . .] year of the reign of the Emperor Justin." Justin I reigned from 518 to 527, Justin II from 565 to 578. In either case, the mosaic is thus definitely placed as of the sixth century A.D.

It is bordered, like an oriental rug, with a decorative design of lozenges and of stems and leaves enclosing a number of symbolic figures:

pomegranates and bunches of grapes (1)
baskets (2)
a fish (3)
three drinking horns (4)
a hen with her chicks (5)
long-legged birds (6)
beasts nibbling grapes (8)

Flanking the Greek and Aramaic inscriptions at the bottom stand a lion and a bull, facing inward as part of the marginal decoration rather than outward as portal guardians; but one searches in vain for the other two of the usual four "living creatures." Professor Goodenough has remarked the appearance of a number of these figures in other iconographic traditions of the period: in the Christian context, for example, the basket of bread with grapes (9) would have been read as a eucharistic reference; so too, another bunch of grapes (10) and a fish with open mouth (11), directly in front of the sanctuary. The hen with her chicks (5) is familiar from the Gospels: "O Jerusalem, Jerusalem. . . . How often would I have gathered your children together as a hen gathers her brood under her wings . . . !" (Matthew 23:37; Luke 13:34). Three cups or drinking horns (4) suggest not only a sacramental meal, but even a trinitarian theme.

Fig. 189 Most amazing of all, however, is the appearance of the Roman sun-god Helios, driving his heavenly *quadriga*, as the central figure of the entire composition. He is

188. Mosaic. Inner Room, Beth Alpha Synagogue. Near Galilee

surrounded, furthermore, by all the pagan signs of the zodiac and figures of the seasons, each with its name in Hebrew. Aries, Taurus, and Gemini are at the god's left shoulder. Cancer is directly over his head, Leo and Virgo are to his right. Libra, Scorpio, and Saggitarius come next. Capricorn (damaged) is directly below. Aquarius and Pisces complete the round. The personages at the corners are the seasons. They appear over the wrong signs, however, and that (I would say) says a lot! Spring, at the upper left, with a bird before her, pecking at a plant, presides over the signs not of springtime but of summer. Summer, with a basket of field produce and fruit, is watching over autumn. Autumn, meanwhile, with a bird perched on her right shoulder and two wine jars on her left, a tree nearby, and again certain fruits before her, appears above the signs of winter; while Winter is found, with a little branch bearing two leaves, in the place of spring.

The problem of the religious significance of Helios, the zodiac, and the seasons to a Jewish community of that time is not easy to resolve. The fact that the astronomical references were so little understood that the seasons are out of place suggests that neither an interest in Greek science nor a knowledge of Chaldean astrology can have contributed much to the inspiration of this icon. Professor Goodenough suggests an approach through the mystical tradition. "In general," he points out, "the astronomical religion of that period saw three chief values in the heavenly bodies and their changes as reflected upon earth in the seasons. The first was one of circular or cyclic determinism, the heavenly causation of all things earthly. As still in astrology, one's character and fate were considered set by the signs under which one was born and did various crucial acts. Secondly, the seasons and the cycle of the heavenly bodies suggested death from life, and life from death, that is the hope of immortality, as sunrise, the east, the seasons, and the germination of seeds still make a comforting allusion when we bury our dead. And thirdly, the mystic saw in the planets, as well as in the heavenly bodies in general, a great ladder to the world beyond. The hope, in material terms, was to be able to rise and share in the great cycle with Helios and the stars; or, in immaterial terms, to climb beyond the material universe altogether to the immaterial."[122]

Some thought of that kind may have supplied the inspiration for this panel. However, it is perfectly clear that in this particular application of the symbols the sun-door guarded by the pagan god was to be understood, not as an end, but as a gate of passage leading through and beyond the natural world of space, time, and Figs. 190, 191 causation; while in the upper and lower panels, where the presence of the Living God beyond the natural world, on the one hand, and the holiness of Jewish life within it, on the other, are represented, the figures employed are not of the general Hellenistic heritage but specifically and authentically Jewish. Thus the reference of the gentile symbol has been reduced to an essentially secular, allegorical level, and in the place of its native mystic connotation, as symbolic of that Light of Lights

189. *Zodiac Panel. Beth Alpha Synagogue*

which is of the mind and of all things—"For in the All," as we read in the roughly contemporary pagan *Corpus Hermeticum*, "there is naught that is not God: wherefore, neither size, nor space, nor quality, neither form, nor time, surroundeth God, since He is All, and All surroundeth all, and permeateth all"[123]—there have been substituted strictly Jewish emblems of the law made known through Moses.

Fig. 190 Opposite, the curtains of a sanctuary separate to reveal the portal of a Torah shrine, duplicating thus through a Jewish symbol the meaning that would already have been represented to pagans in the sun-door; and below, where the lesson is one of the absolute submission of Israel to Yahweh, the figure is of the Akedah, Abraham's interrupted sacrifice of his son. As Professor Goodenough points out, it was altogether fitting that the men entering this inner chamber of their synagogue should traverse these three instructive panels, representing in contemporary terms their own way of approach to God.

"Mystics," he reminds us, "who follow the Perennial Philosophy have always tended to see three stages in mystic ascent, stages which have most generally been called purgation, illumination, and unification. The three stages here might well be given the names purgation, ascent, and arrival." "No mystic," he adds, "would have objected to the change."[124]

The change, however, *does* make a difference. What it refers to is a sequence sufficiently different to announce a theme unknown to gentile mystical thought; namely, that God is not immanent in nature and of one substance with the mind, but a power transcendent and absolutely "other," not to be sought and found within Fig. 191 through illumination, but revered and served as "up there." And the nature of the required service is taught in the first, the lowest, of these three panels, which is not simply of purgation—spiritual *katharsis*, as a Greek or Roman might have thought of it—but specifically of the Akedah, which is here the focal symbol of the whole mosaic.

For the Akedah, Abraham's sacrifice, is the archetype, the legendary prototype, of Israel's submission to God's will, and the altar—the altar specifically of the Akedah —is a Hebrew transformation of the idea of that cosmic center which in classical terms would have been known as the world navel, as Dr. Bernard Goldman of Wayne State University reminds us in an illuminating study of this unique mosaic entitled *The Sacred Portal*:

> In Jewish lore the site of Abraham's sacrifice was given profound significance. The Palestinian Aramaic version of the Hebrew Bible text (Targum Yerushalim) on Genesis 8:20* identified the same site as holding the altars built by Adam and Noah. The sages continued the identification: Abraham went to the altar upon which Adam had sacrificed, upon which Cain and Abel had sacrificed, upon which Noah and his sons had sacrificed. The sanctity of the location was even further multiplied, for it was the ground upon which the Temple of Solomon was to rest! . . .
>
> Hence, the congregation of Beth Alpha on entering the synagogue, may have been reminded not only of the Sacrifice of Abraham, but also of the consistent tradition of sacrifice in Judaism as well as the alignment of the Akedah with the promised site for the most holy of all buildings, the Temple of Jerusalem. In this manner, the flaming altar of the scene could well be taken as a sign of the Temple which was unique in that it contained the high altar of sacrifice. Written in the Midrashim,

* "Then Noah built an altar to the Lord, and took of every clean animal and of every clean bird, and offered burnt offerings on the altar."

190. *Sacred Portal Panel. Beth Alpha Synagogue*

We here recognize from the common treasury of mythological images the two guardian lions; also the two little trees of paradise, to each of which a tiny bird has flown, here representing allegorically "the hope of all of us."[125] We note the two curtains drawn back at either hand (that to our left destroyed) to reveal the ultimate symbol of the godhead: a portal of two panels behind which the Word of the Living God (Torah) is to be assumed. Two unidentifiable birds, possibly phoenixes, appear to be climbing up the roof, but the other elements scattered about are strictly of the temple and synagogue: two seven-branched candelabras (*menorah*), two ram's horns, two incense shovels, and, in the foreground, two bundles of branches (*lulab*) with attached citrus fruits (*ethrog*). From the peak of the gable hangs an eternally burning lamp. Below this there is a decorative shell. Three wine cups stand above the portal and projecting to either side are hornlike forms, recalling the horns of ancient altars.[126]

191. The Sacrifice of Isaac. Beth Alpha Synagogue

At the left stand two young servants: "Then Abraham said to his young men, 'Stay here with the ass; I and the lad will go yonder and worship, and come again to you'" (Genesis 22:5). Abraham, Isaac, and the ram are labeled in Hebrew, and beside the hand of God are the first words of the prohibition: "Do not stretch forth. . . ." The hand reaches out from a dark cloud that is sending four rays of light to the world below and three into heaven above, the orderly nature of heaven being signified by the regular spacing of its trees, while on earth there is an irregular scattering of vegetation. "The cloud is the source, and the hand, along with or without the rays, is the symbol of the procession of divinity from the source to mankind and the world in general. So while the hand is entirely below the line of heaven in the Beth Alpha scene, the round dark source, which we may by a compromise call the 'cloud of unknowing,' is properly only in part below that line, and casts its purest rays above it."[129] The altar, already blazing, is at the right.

the rabbinical exegetical literature on Scriptures, is the spiritual significance of the Akedah: the fate of Israel is symbolized by the story of Abraham's sacrifice. . . .[127]

Thus in relation to the ageless concept of the axis mundi a new dimension, that of linear, historic time, has been substituted in this precious mosaic for the cyclical, space-time figure of the earlier and more generally followed Mesopotamian cosmology. Moreover, this linear theme was carried into the Christian tradition as well. The Cross of Christ on the "Hill of the Skull," Calvary or Golgotha (Latin *calvaria*, "skull"; Aramaic *gūlgūlthā*, also "skull"), was planted, according to Christian legend, on the site of the burial of Adam's skull; so that the blood of the Savior, baptizing as it were the patriarch of the whole human race, thereby redeemed mankind, and drove an axis backward to the dawn of time as well as forward to the promise of an end.

cf. Fig. 151

As Professor Goldman reminds us, the Christian Fathers saw in the sacrifice of Isaac a prefiguring of that of Jesus: "as the ram was sent by divine will to be a substitute offering for Isaac, so was Christ sacrificed in place of all mankind."[128] And so in the Akedah panel of the Beth Alpha mosaic we find the ram, significantly enough, directly beneath the sun-door, on the very vertical of the axis, fixed to its tree as was Jesus to his Cross—both the tree and the cross (as mentioned earlier) being figures of the axis mundi, and the ram, furthermore, one of the traditional Near Eastern animal avatars of the world-sustaining sun.

cf. Fig. 188

Figs. 192-195

192. *The Lamb Triumphant.*
A.D. *12th century. Germany*

In the center is the Lamb, symbolic of the Resurrected Christ. The four rivers of Paradise flow from the quarters: Pishon (above), Gihon (left), Hiddekel (right), Euphrates (below). The corner medallions are of the cardinal virtues: Prudence (upper left), Fortitude (lower), Temperance (lower right), Justice (upper). The four panels show the evangelists and their emblems: Matthew (upper left), Mark (lower left), Luke (lower right), and John (upper right).

193. *"The Ram in the Thicket."*
2050-1950 B.C. *Sumer*

Not a ram, actually, but a goat: one of a pair found together in the largest of the royal "death pits." They probably faced each other as parts of a single composition, each secured to its flowering shrub by a silver chain (now completely decayed) made fast around its fetlocks. From behind the shoulder of each a solid gold stump rises that was evidently the base of something that has now disappeared. Thus they would have been the "vehicles" or "supporters" of some divinity or divine scene.

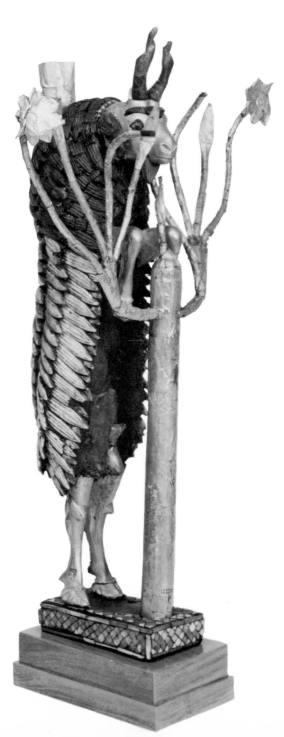

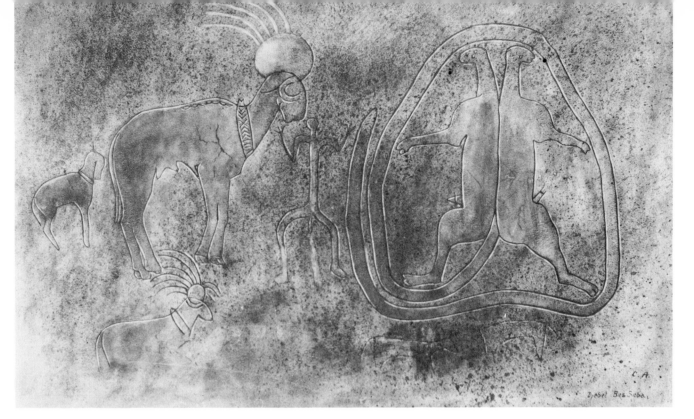

194. *Worship of the Sun-ram. Late Paleolithic Petroglyph. Saharan Atlas Mountains, Algeria.*
(The sun-symbol appears to have been added at a later, possibly early neolithic, date.)

195. *Amun, Creator and Sun-god, as a Ram, Protecting the Pharaoh Amenhotep III.*
1413-1337 B.C. Egypt

III. THE LOTUS AND THE ROSE

196. *Dante Led Before God in the Heavenly Rose*

In form then of a pure white rose
the holy host was shown to me
which in His own blood Christ made His
bride. (Paradiso 31.1-3)[1]

1. The Flower Scepter

Fig. 196   DANTE beheld the host of paradise as a rose, pure white, with angels "like a swarm of bees" descending into it and rising up again, "to where," as the poet writes, "their love forever abides." And when his eyes, following their upward flight, dared to gaze long into the Supreme Light, marveling, he beheld there the beatific vision Cf. Figs. 4,   of the Trinity.[2] For as Brahma, the Creator with four heads, is throned in India 123   on the lotus of Vishnu's dream, so above the rose of Dante's soars the vision of a God in three persons—to the knowledge of whom the poet has been brought through his rapture in the beauty of an earthly woman.

197. The Madonna in Majesty. Laon Cathedral, France

"The Virgin of the twelfth and early thirteenth century is a queen," observes Emile Mâle. "On the west portal of Chartres and the Saint Anne portal of Notre Dame de Paris, she appears enthroned in royal solemnity. She wears the crown upon her head, holds the flowering scepter in hand, and supports the infant sitting on her knee. Thus she is shown also in the window of Chartres known as 'la belle verrière' and in a beautiful window of Laon. Our early artists evidently were striving to embody the saying of the doctors: 'Mary is Solomon's throne. . . .' The artists of no period knew better how to communicate grandeur to the imagery of the mother of God."[3]

Above is an early thirteenth-century stained glass window. The flower scepter in the right hand of the Madonna enthroned—who herself is the living throne of her son—corresponds symbolically to the lotus in the left hand of the Buddhist god-

Fig. 197

198. Tara. Bihar, India

dess opposite. This Tara has appeared in compassion from the rim of the world-
illusion as a guide to release from its sorrows. Seated on a lotus throne supported
by a pair of lion caryatids symbolic of the "lion roar" of the wisdom of the Buddha,
she holds her right hand open in the "boon-bestowing" posture, while above the lotus
in her left there floats the figure of a saving Buddha. Analogously, the crown on
the Virgin Mother's head makes known her celestial character, the infant on her
knee corresponding to the Buddha in the Oriental icon. But she is clothed, also, in
the earthly garb of the young woman of Palestine to whom the angel came. For as
in her child, true God and true man, so in her, contradictions are transcended:
motherhood and virginity, humanity and divinity, earth and heaven. More noble
than the angels, of whose choirs she is the heavenly queen, she is praised by them—
pure spirits, knowing nothing of temporality—as she appears in this radiant glass,
which, though of earthly stuff, is yet transparent of solar light and thus itself an
agent of the "revealing power" of maya.*

Fig. 198
cf. Fig. 48
cf. Fig. 39

Fig. 197

Following is a Javanese Buddhist image of the same date as the Virgin of Laon. Fig. 199
It is a portrait statue of Queen Dedes of the Singasari Dynasty, in the character of
Prajnaparamita, a mythic being symbolic of the sweetness of the "Wisdom (*prajna*)
of the Yonder Shore (*paramita*)." The lotus at her left shoulder supports the book
of the teaching of this revelation from beyond illusory opposites. Her hands meet
in a gesture known as "link of increase" (*kataka-vardhana*), the meaning of which
is "juncture," "marriage," and "coronation."⁴ With the fingers of each hand held in
the posture called "opening in a link" (*kataka-mukha*), suggesting the holding of
a pearl or flower, the tips of the two middle fingers are brought gently together—left
below, right above—in a symbolized coincidence of opposites.

As interpreted by Heinrich Zimmer in one of his memorable lectures on the symbolism of Indian art:

> Whereas Shri-Lakshmi [at Vishnu's feet] represents earthly fulfillment and bliss, cf. Fig. 4
> Prajnaparamita, her Buddhist counterpart, represents the fulfillment and bliss of
> the transcendental sphere, which is attained by shattering the passion-ridden igno-
> rance of our limited, individualized modes of existence, and going, in realization,
> beyond the phenomenal illusion of the personality in its surrounding world. Just
> as Lakshmi is a manifestation of the universal mother of life in her benevolent, life-
> bestowing, life-increasing aspect, so is Prajnaparamita the source and embodiment
> of the deeper life and reality, which is transcendental. She sends out rays of enlight-
> ening wisdom that bring release from the agonies of our limited consciousness, bound
> to the round of rebirth. . . . This Buddhist, Indo-Javanese counterpart of the Western
> symbol of Sophia, Divine Wisdom, is the most spiritual manifestation of the maternal
> principle.

* See above, p. 52.

199 (overleaf). Queen Dedes as Prajnaparamita. A.D. *late 13th century. Java*

199a. Detail of Figure 199

The poise of the sculptured figure, its spirituality, the balance and harmony of its contours, including those of the halo and throne, and the convincing musicality of its proportions, which voice an indescribable serenity and bliss, are derived directly from a classical formula of the Indian Gupta period. . . . The lovely, perfectly symmetrical countenance is a model of beauty in complete harmony with the idea that it conveys, yet full of the vitality of a serenely living being. It is no sheer symbol or hieroglyph, but the portrait of an actual woman. . . .

In 1220 A.D. the ruling king of Singasari was overthrown by an adventurer, Ken Arok, who married Queen Dedes and ascended the throne under the name of Rajasa Sang Anurvadhumi. In 1227 he was killed, after many conquests but a very brief reign. And the chief treasure that remains to us from his time is this image of his consort as the Shakti of the Adi Buddha.[5]

The important Sanskrit term *shakti*, meaning "power, capacity, energy, faculty, or capability," has here been used in a technical sense basic to all Oriental religious thinking; namely, to denote the energy or active power of a male divinity as embodied in his spouse. Carried further (by analogy), every wife is her husband's shakti and every beloved woman her lover's. Beatrice was Dante's. Carried further still: the word connotes female spiritual power in general, as manifest, for instance, in the radiance of beauty, or on the elemental level in the sheer power of the female sex   cf. Fig. 59
to work effects on the male. It is operative in the power of the womb to transform seed into fruit, to enclose, protect, and give birth. Analogously, on the psychological plane, it is the power of a woman to bring a man to his senses, to let him see himself as in a mirror, to lure him to his realization—or destruction: for it is the power, also,   cf. Fig. 419
to bewilder and destroy. Goethe epitomized the idea in his frequently quoted concluding lines of *Faust*:

> *Das Ewig-Weibliche*
> *Zieht uns hinan.**

* *The Eternal Feminine*
  Draws us onward.

Fig. 200   This figure is a Japanese vision of the Buddha whose shakti is Prajnaparamita: the Adi Buddha, here in the aspect known as Mahavairochana, "Great Illuminator" (Japanese Dainichi Nyorai, "Great Day Thus Come"). James Joyce in *Finnegans Wake* refers humorously to this supreme Buddha and his shakti as "adi and aid."[6] *Adi* meaning simply "first," whether in the sense of "beginning" or of "preeminent," this Buddha Supreme is a personification of the *Dharmakaya*, "Law Body" of the universe, which though screened from us by the obscuring and projecting powers of maya is nevertheless the ground, substance, support, and reality of all being and of all things. The proper way to think of it is—paradoxically—*not* to think of it; for all thought is conditioned by maya, that is to say by concepts, categories, and the laws of grammar, whereas the reference of the term Dharmakaya is beyond categories, even beyond those of "being" and "nonbeing"; indeed, beyond the category "beyond." Hence the terms I have just used, namely "ground," "substance," "support," and "reality," do not describe it. One might think or speak of it (which, however, is no "it") as a "void" in the sense of "without characteristics," or as *nirvana*, "blown out," in the sense approximately of *deus absconditus*. Positively conceived, however, it is termed the Dharmakaya, and this, personified, is what is pictured as the Adi Buddha.

Note that beneath the lotus on which this highest Buddha sits there is another lotus, inverted. This is to be understood as the summit of a dome viewed from on high, the dome of the heavens *under* which we dwell. It is here revealed to be a reflection of the lotus—the shakti—of the Adi Buddha, mirrored inverted in the waters of our lives. Ideally we are to think of our own clarified consciousness as that Buddha; and of our supporting world, our shakti, as the lotus on which he is enthroned. Whereas actually, realistically regarded, our consciousness is clouded, and the lotus on which we sit—or rather, within which we are enclosed—not only is inverted but also is unopened, even miserably damaged, as an effect of the limits of our minds and of the consequent hopes and fears, desires and aversions, that have shaped our imperfect lives.

"If the doors of perception were cleansed," wrote William Blake in *The Marriage of Heaven and Hell*, "every thing would appear to man as it is, infinite. For man has closed himself up, till he sees all things thro' narrow chinks in his cavern."[7] The same thought appears in words attributed to the Chinese Zen Buddhist patriarch Hui-neng (A.D. 638-713): "Our pure mind is within the depraved one";[8] and again, a millennium later, among the sayings of the Japanese Zen master Hakuin (1685-1768): "This very earth is the Lotus Land of Purity, and this body is the body of the Buddha."[9] Compare the words attributed in the Thomas Gospel to Jesus: "The Kingdom of the Father is spread upon the earth and men do not see it."[10]* James Joyce in *Ulysses* suggests the same idea when, viewing the word "dog" transformed through the mirror of his art, he shows it reversed as GOD.[11] The image is a very old one, of this phenomenal world as a reflex in the medium of our reflecting minds of supernal forms in reverse. "As in a mirror, so it is seen here in the Self." (*Katha Upanishad*, 6.5)

* See above, p. 62.

200. *Dainichi Nyorai.* A.D. *1175. Japan*

Fig. 199

Fig. 199a

Fig. 200

And the same, exactly, is the message of this image of an earthly Javanese queen as shakti of the Adi Buddha (as also of the mother of Jesus crowned in heaven by her Maker, who on earth was the fruit of her womb). The hand posture of the Buddhist queen draws heaven and earth together at the point where the middle fingers of her two hands lightly touch. This "juncture," as it is called, corresponds to that in the Buddha image where the two supporting lotuses, upright and inverted, come together. Also in the hand posture of the Adi Buddha himself a simpler, stronger statement is made of the same mystery—in the way, however, not of reflection but of absorption. Before his heart, the lifted left forefinger is clasped in the right fist, representing the manner in which—on the plane *above* that of the overturned reflection—the projected image is taken back into its source. In Japanese this posture is known as the "knowledge sign." Esoterically interpreted, the five fingers of the right hand symbolize the elements of which all things of the material world are composed. The little finger is earth; the ring finger, water; middle finger, fire; index finger, air; and thumb, the void. The lifted index of the left hand, imitating the flame-symbol of the Adi Buddha himself, stands for the sixth element, mind (Japanese *chi*, Sanskrit *manas*). Brought together in this way the two hands represent the nonduality of the spiritual world (*kongōkai*) and the matrix or material world (*taizōkai*), which can be also read in the act of sexual union, wherein "each is both."[12]

Fig. 201

On Queen Dedes' throne we note, finally, on the lower base, in alternating series, the signs of a lotus and a reliquary shrine, the former symbolic of this world of burgeoning life in the vortex of rebirths (*samsara*), and the latter, release from the round (*nirvana*). So do they appear to us as opposites in this world of waking consciousness. Looking, however, upward to the saving figure above, we are told by the hand posture, "link of increase," that in the Wisdom of the Yonder Shore these two are linked in a "marriage" fruitful of life. In the words of Hui-neng: "If you are desirous of the truly immovable, the immovable is in the moving."[13] The rich throne, accordingly, is embellished with floral forms, and the earthly queen is bejeweled as a goddess.

201. Base of Queen Dedes' Throne (detail)

2. The Flower Support

THUS one may think of these symbolic flowers and their blossoming as referring either to the macrocosmic order, the flowering of the universe within whose bounds we dwell, or to the microcosmic opening of an individual's consciousness to its own potential amplitude. And in this second sense the lotus affords an especially fortunate symbol. Lotuses of many colors and forms, blue, pink, yellow, and white, originating from the muddy floor of a lake, grow slowly to the surface. Those at the bottom are not yet in bud; others, rising, are beginning to show signs of opening. More, below the surface, are at the very point of unfolding; while above, riding on the breeze-rippled waves, are those that have at last come to the light. Many are still closed, others open to the sun.

The next figure shows the Buddha of "Immeasurable Age and Light" (Amitayus-Amitabha, known in Japanese as Amida)* presiding over the lotus lake of his Western Paradise, "the Land of Joy," where according to his legend all who had ever in their lives called upon or meditated on his name are in rapture seated upon lotuses, floating before him on the surface of a boundless lake, irradiated by his sunlike presence shining from the western shore. And he is there attended by a multitude of perfected Bodhisattvas—whose "essence" (*sattva*) is "illumination" (*bodhi*). These are dispatched as rescuing scouts to lead souls from the toils of illusion to that lake of joy.

The legend of this joy-giving savior—the most popular Buddha figure today in the whole of Eastern Asia—assigns his earthly career to an eon infinitely earlier than that of our present universe, when a very great Buddha named Lokeshvararaja, "King and Lord of the World," had appeared and was somewhere teaching. Among those seated in a circle listening to his discourse was a monk named Dharmakara, "Mine of Virtue," who one day rose from his seat, having drawn his robe over one shoulder, and, approaching the Buddha, knelt with his right knee to the earth, stretched forth his reverently joined hands and, giving praise to the One Thus Come, prayed to be immediately endowed with the highest perfection of knowledge.

Fig. 202

* Cf. p. 34 (Fig. 29), Aion-Phanes, "Lord of Ages," "The Shining One."

Whereupon that blessed Buddha, knowing the good dispositions of the monk named Mine of Virtue, taught him for a full ten million years the doctrines and excellencies of the Buddha-lands of eighty-one-hundred-thousand-million times ten million Buddhas, concentrating the virtues of all those lands and Buddhas in the qualities of one Buddha-land, his own; after which the monk Dharmakara bowed his head to the feet of that Buddha, circled respectfully around to the right, and walked away from the Blessed One.

For a period of five world eons he meditated, maturing in his instructed mind the perfections of a Buddha-land eighty-one times more immeasurable, more noble, more excellent than the perfection of eighty-one-hundred-thousand-millions of ten million Buddha-lands: and when he had done all this, he returned to where the King and Lord of the World was still teaching and, again bowing before him, made known what he had accomplished.

The Buddha therefore said to him: "Preach, O Monk; the One Thus Come allows it! Now is the fitting time."

But that monk, then and there, refused to embrace Buddhahood unless, when he had done so, the Buddha-land of his accomplishment should fulfill certain unprecedented conditions which he described to the Blessed One as the excellencies of the Buddha-land that he would expect to be his own when he would have gained both for himself and for all beings the full perfection of knowledge.

Fig. 203   Every being in that Buddha-land should be of one color, gold, and there should be no death, no hell, no brute creation, demons, ghosts, or titans. Every being should have memory of all former births and be endowed with the highest spiritual powers: divine sight, divine hearing, knowledge of the deeds and thoughts of all beings, having no idea of property, but established in perfect truth. Moreover, the beings in that paradise should be innumerable. And further: this marvelous monk, Mine of Virtue, would refuse for himself illumination unless the measure of his light should be immeasurable, the measure of the lives of all in his Buddha-land immeasurable, and the measure of his own life immeasurable as well; unless innumerable Buddhas in Buddha-lands innumerable should glorify his name, and unless those hearing his name, and with serene thought meditating on it, should be able, at the instant of death, to behold him standing before them: unless, furthermore, all those directing their thought to rebirth in his radiant Buddha-land—even those entertaining that thought no more than ten brief times in their lives—should at the moment of death be reborn there, to bring their stock of merit to maturity; and unless, when so reborn, they should be released from all further births—except as desired by those, devoted to all beings, who might wish to return to perform in all worlds the duties of a Bodhisattva, bringing beings innumerable to enlightenment.

Fig. 203 Those perfected in that Buddha-land should have everything they wanted; be omniscient in reciting the wisdom of the Law, acceptable to all Buddhas as worshipers and celebrants; have bodies strong as adamantine thunderbolts; and find the beauty of that Buddha-land immeasurable. Even the least should be able to contemplate the bodhi-tree (a hundred leagues or more in height), and be possessed of perfect knowledge. One hundred thousand vases made of every kind of jewel should be there, filled with various sweet perfumes and emitting incense pluming skyward. Showers of fragrant jewel-flowers should pour down from music-clouds sweetly sounding, and the pleasures there should be far beyond anything known to either gods or men. Finally, that perfect monk, Mine of Virtue, would refuse release for himself unless all those in all other worlds or Buddha-lands who had even once heard his name might obtain, until achieving Buddhahood, whatever rapture in thought they desired, joy and gladness in their lives, whatever teaching of the Law they wished to hear, noble births, and endurance in spiritual effort.

And when Dharmakara had so vowed before the Buddha Lokeshvararaja, the earth trembled and hundreds of celestial instruments sounded, sweet sandalwood powder scattered from on high, flowers showered down, and a voice was heard that called from on high: "You shall be a Buddha in the world."

And indeed: from every pore of the monk's body poured a perfume of lotuses, and the auspicious signs of buddhahood appeared upon him. Moreover, most wonderful of all, from the palms of his hands and hairs of his head all manner of precious things poured forth: scents and incense, flowers, garlands, flags, banners and umbrellas, cloaks and vestments; viands furthermore, and drink, food and sweetmeats, pleasures and enjoyments of all kinds. Nor has that One Thus Come, that Buddha Being, passed away to this day, but in the western quarter, distant from our present world by a hundred-thousand-million times ten million Buddha-lands, he shines over the lotus lake Sukhavati, "the Land of Joy," as the Buddha Amitayus-Amitabha, surrounded by Bodhisattvas innumerable and adored by unnumbered saints.[15]

A bit baroque for our taste, perhaps, and I have cut it down considerably! To be remarked, however, is the idea of all these (to us) supernatural marvels proceeding, not from divinities, but from a fully realized human being. For in Buddhism as in Hinduism there is no ontological distinction between gods and men; nor even between gods, men, and beasts, plants, minerals, and planets. As declared in Ovid's *Metamorphoses*, in words attributed to the Greek sage Pythagoras: "The spirit wanders, comes now here, now there, and occupies whatever frame it pleases. From beasts it passes into human bodies, and from our bodies into beasts, but never perishes."[16] The godlike powers of the Buddhas and Bodhisattvas (and in Hinduism of the gods) are to be thought of as potential within us all; not *gained*, but *recovered*, or in the Platonic sense "recollected," when the impediments of ignorance (the obscuring power of maya) will have been either slowly purged away or suddenly transcended: our birth, as Wordsworth has said, having been "but a sleep and a forgetting."

204. Amida Raigo Tapestry

"A favored subject in the art of the Japanese 'Pure Land' (Jodo) sect was the Raigo, or Descent of the Savior Amida directly to the devotee at the moment of death.

"The orientation of the earlier *Raigos* is toward the spectator, as if he were the dying person, as in the great *Raigo* triptich at Kōyasan. Here the large figure of Amida accompanied by twenty-five Bodhisattvas floating on clouds faces the spectator and moves toward him, a movement indicated by the perspective of the clouds as they rise and recede to the left and top of the central panel. The vision hovers above a landscape clear at the lower left but barely visible at the right. But the landscape is a small part of the picture, confined to an unobtrusive place, so that the whole effect is a rather more iconic than realistic presentation of an imagined scene. Details of the figures reveal . . . a marked development of decorative detail, color, and realism. The music-playing angels are particularly interesting. They are shown in poses observed from nature, dancing or playing their instruments, and puffing out their cheeks as they blow into the more difficult wind instruments. . . .

"The *Raigo* is a subject that perhaps first appeared in Japanese art about 1053 on the doors of the Phoenix Hall [the original main hall of the Byōdō-in Temple, Kyoto]. The likelihood is very strong that the *Raigo* is a Japanese contribution, even invention, and it represents one of the most lyrical visions of deity achieved by any faith. The essential part of the *Raigo*, in contrast to the secret and forbidding nature of the esoteric icon, is that the Buddha comes to the spectator, reversing the attitude of the esoteric sects. The Amida is not merely approachable; he approaches the spectator, and the picture represents the vision of the dying believer whose soul is received and welcomed into his Western Paradise by the Buddha."[11]

In a Buddhist meditation text called the *Amitayur Dhyana Sutra, Guide to the Contemplation of Amitayus*, it is told that all who ever in their lives utter the name of this radiant Buddha will be reborn on one of his lotus lakes. If in their lives they have been virtuous, their lotuses will be open; if not the buds will be closed, and they within. However, the radiance of the sunlike Buddha shining like a setting sun that never sets, filling all of that paradise with his golden illumination, penetrates the meditation cells of the unopened buds, as do also the musical sounds of the rustling jewel trees on the jeweled shores of those Buddha-lakes, and the music of the innumerable banners rippling in the pellucid skies, flying from jeweled galleries to the number of five hundred million, from each of which gods and goddesses are sending forth celestial songs. Musical instruments playing by themselves are hung in the open sky, while the multicolored jewel birds of many orders in that Buddha-land chirrup sweetly, and the multicolored waters of the jewel lakes ripple gently among rising and falling lotus buds, lotus stalks, and lotus leaves: all variously resounding, yet in one harmonious symphony modulating this one song of immortal Buddha wisdom: "All is impermanence; all is without an individual self"— until, penetrated by that Buddha light, that jewel song and its melody, those meditating in locked lotus buds abandon the notion of anything to be saved, anything to be held to, anything to be done, and their lotus stems, released from the octopus tentacles of their selves-of-sleep, lift flowers to the surface, opening to the sun, with themselves sitting as Buddhas on the corollas, rapt in selfless realization of the Self that is no self and the Void that is no void.[17]

Thus the lotuses of those floating on the waters of Amida's Western Paradise are the signs of their own flowerings to perfection. So too, the lotus of Amida himself is symbolic of his own Buddhahood. However, in the beautiful little Japanese shrine opposite we note behind Amida's head a second lotus—the sun; as Dr. Sherman E. Lee, Director and Curator of Oriental Art at The Cleveland Museum of Art, has remarked in elucidating this image: "the equation—lotus equals sun—is one which the beginning student of Far Eastern iconography learns first."[18] It refers to the macrocosmic sun—up there—but also to the microcosmic sun—in the chamber of the heart. For as stated in the Indian *Maitri Upanishad*:

Figs. 205-207

> The course of the inner Self is measured by the course of the outer Self . . . and the course of the outer Self is measured by the course of the inner Self. For, as has been said: "Now, that golden Person within the sun who looks down upon the earth from his golden place is He who dwells within the lotus of the heart and eats food." He who dwells within the lotus of the heart and eats food is the same as that solar fire dwelling in the sky, called Time, the invisible, which eats all things as its food.
> What is that lotus, and of what does it consist?
> That lotus is the same as space: the four quarters and four intermediate quarters are its petals. The Breathing Spirit and the Sun, these two, strive to approach each other.[19]

205. Tachibana Shrine

The Buddha Amitayus-Amitabha (Japanese, Amida), flanked left and right by the Bodhisattvas Avalokiteshvara (Kwannon) and Maitreya (Seishi), overlooking the lotus lakes of the Western Paradise. The lady-in-waiting at the Imperial Court for whom this lovely shrine was created, Tachibana-no-Michiyo, died in the year 733.

206, 207. Tachibana Shrine (detail). Screen (upper); Base (lower)

Seated in relaxed postures midway toward the top are figures contemplating various aspects of this Buddhaland. All at the top, on the other hand, are seated in the one posture of immobile indrawn rapture, while at the bottom are to be seen the tentacles of octopuses reaching from beneath the waters.

The octopus was a favorite, gracefully rendered form in the ceramic arts of ancient Crete (opposite). With its eight arms, like rays radiating to the quarters and the four intermediate points, it is a kind of deep-sea solar symbol, negative to its high celestial counterpart: not pouring light forth, illuminating, but holding, grasping, taking to itself, and swallowing. At the base of the Tachibana screen the tentacles—their power broken—are releasing the lotus stems.

The lotus, then, symbolizes both the sun as the heart of space and the heart as the sun of the body, both moved by the same indwelling self (*atman*). And accordingly, the lotus open to the sun symbolizes the fully flowered knowledge of this mirrored truth, while the lotuses in bud mark stages of approach to its realization.

208. Cretan Amphora. ca. 1500 B.C.

The poet Robinson Jeffers has written of this mystery in his poem "Roan Stallion," using, however, a more modern metaphor:

> The atoms bounds-breaking,
> Nucleus to sun, electrons to planets, with recognition
> Not praying, self-equaling, the whole to the whole, the microcosm
> Not entering nor accepting entrance, more equally, more utterly, more
> incredibly conjugate
> With the other extreme and greatness; passionately perceptive of
> identity. . . .[20]

Fig. 205 The lifted right hand of the Buddha of the Tachibana shrine is in the "fear-dispelling" posture, the open left in the "boon-bestowing." Seated as he is between the two lotuses of sky and earth, the universe and the individual, bearing witness thus in his one person to their consubstantiality, he may be compared to his Christian counterpart Christ, as at once true God and true man, born of that "Mystical Rose," the Virgin. For indeed, the rose of the Occident corresponds symbolically to the lotus of the East.

Fig. 209
cf. Fig. 201 Opposite is another Japanese image of the "Great Sun Buddha," Mahavairochana, called in Japan "Great Day Thus Come," Dainichi Nyorai, as a personification of the manifestation of the heart and light of the universe. The pattern of the background here is of crossed thunderbolts (which shatter phenomenal forms), having lotus blooms at their crossings (giving rise to phenomenal forms). Over this symbolic ground of the coincidence of opposites three luminous circles ride: the largest, white, representing the void of nonbeing; the second, the rainbow horizon of being; and the last, the cycling eon of becoming. Before the latter, then, perfectly seated on the pure white thousand-petaled lotus of the ultimate degree of bliss, is the first and highest personification of the heart and light of the universe, the Great Sun Buddha, Dainichi Nyorai. At his navel hangs the Wheel of the Law, the *Dharma Chakra*, by which all things are maintained in motion; and luminous in his jeweled crown are the five world-guardian Buddhas of the world center and four quarters.

cf. Fig. 196 Compare with this vision that of Dante,* when, standing in the white celestial rose, he gazed upward into the light.

> Within the profound and clear substance of the lofty Light there appeared to me three circles of three colors and one dimension; and each seemed reflected in the other, as one rainbow in another, and the third seemed of fire that was equally breathed out from here and there.
> O how inadequate is speech, and how feeble toward my conception! and to call it feeble is not even enough in relation to what I saw.
> O Eternal Light, which sole in Thyself abidest, sole Thyself understandest, and by Thyself understood and understanding, lovest and smilest on Thyself!
> That circling, so generated, appearing threefold, like reflected light, when my

* Above, p. 212.

209. *"Great Sun Buddha."* A.D. *13th century.*
Daigo-ji. Kyoto, Japan

eyes had gazed on it a while, seemed to me painted within—in its own very color—with our [human] image, for which reason my gaze was given to it altogether. Like the geometer who applies himself wholly to squaring the circle and cannot find, for all his thought, the formula required, so was I in relation to that new wonder: I wished to see how the image corresponded to the circle and how it set itself there: but my own wings were not for that flight—had it not been that my mind was smitten by a flash, in which its wish was realized.

High fantasy here failed of power; but now my desire and will were revolving, like a wheel that is moving smoothly, by the Love that moves the sun and the other stars.[21]

The date of this vision of Dante, A.D. 1300, is less than a century later than that of Dainichi Nyorai of Daigoji, Kyoto, which in turn is of the same date as the glorious blaze of the great "Rose of France" of the northern transept of Chartres Cathedral, opposite. There, in the center, sits the Virgin, crowned, the scepter of world rule in her right hand and her left supporting the infant Christ. She is in this vision the "Mystical Rose" of the litany, vehicle and support of the revelation of God, the very "Gate of Heaven"; and she is looking down into her church, where—as Henry Adams observed, gazing up from the choir into the clear blues and reds of this great wheel of light—"she sees us on our knees and knows each one of us by name."[22]

Fig. 209
Fig. 210

210. Rose of France. A.D. 1200. Chartres Cathedral. France

"The Rose of France shows in its center the Virgin in her majesty. . . . Round her in a circle, are twelve medallions; four containing doves; four six-winged angels or Thrones; four angels of a lower order, but all symbolizing the gifts and endowments of the Queen of Heaven. Outside these are twelve more medallions with the Kings of Judah, and a third circle contains the twelve lesser prophets. . . .

"Beneath the rose are five long windows. . . . The great central figure, the tallest and most commanding in the whole church, is not the Virgin, but her mother Saint Anne, standing erect . . . and holding the infant Mary on her left arm. . . .

". . . Saint Anne has at either hand a royal court of her own, marked as her own by containing only figures from the Old Testament. Standing next on her right is Solomon, her Prime Minister, bringing wisdom in worldly counsel, and trampling on human folly. Beyond Wisdom stands Law, figured by Aaron with the Book, trampling on the lawless Pharaoh. Opposite them, on Saint Anne's left, is David, the energy of State, trampling on a Saul . . . ; while last, Melchisedec, who is Faith, tramples on a disobedient Nebuchadnezzar. . . ."[23]

211. *Shri Lakshmi*

3. The Waters Beneath and Above

HERE is a fine South Indian bronze representing the native Indian prototype of those Fig. 211 female saviors who have gone forth both by sea to Indonesia and by land into China and Tibet, Korea and Japan, with the gospel of the Buddhist faith. She is the same, a thousand years later, whom we have already seen both in her flower form, as the lotus of her husband Vishnu's dream, and in her human, as the Indian wife massag- cf. Fig. 4 ing Vishnu's leg. Here, however, she stands before us in her own right, alone, in the guise of an Indian queen, holding the fingers of her right hand in exactly the kataka-mukha posture that we have learned from the fingers of the Javanese Queen cf. Fig. 199a Dedes, where it rendered a message of the Wisdom of the Yonder Shore.

The signal in the present instance, however, is of only one hand, the right, where it represents the holding of a flower, while the left hand is simply out there at the end of that elegant left arm, held wide to accommodate the glorious sway of the great physi- cal left haunch—which, finally, when all has been said and seen, is the focal beauty and theme of the composition. The lady is standing in a gracefully affected *tri- bhanga*, "three bend," posture, which from the Gupta period became standard in India for both male and female presentations. The obvious accent on the full breasts and magnificent hips—in contrast to the emphasis on hands and head in the image of Queen Dedes—points to the role and meaning of this dark angel from the watery depths, who is the active power, the shakti, not of any world-transcending illumina- tion but of the world-generating will.

In the words of Heinrich Zimmer:

> Rising from the depths of water and expanding its petals on the surface, the lotus (*kamala, padma*) is the most beautiful evidence offered to the eye of the self-en- gendering fertility of the bottom. Through its appearance, it gives proof of the life- supporting power of the all-nourishing abyss. This is why the goddess Lotus (*kamalā, padmā*) is an appropriate consort or shakti of Vishnu—Vishnu being the cosmic water itself, the infinite ocean of that liquid life-substance out of which all the differenti- ated phenomena and elements of the universe arise, and back into which they must again dissolve.[23]

Fig. 212

Cf. Figs.
213, 214

Below is an earlier view—some fifteen hundred years earlier—of the same dream-goddess Universe as she rose at the beginning of the present cycle of world ages, like Aphrodite from the waters; or like William Blake's dolorous Utha. And we note that here it is not Brahma but the goddess who is seated on the lotus of which she is the personification. Thus enthroned, elevating a lotus in her right hand, she rests her left foot on a lotus footstool in such a way as to expose the lotus of her sex, while two flanking lotuses support elephants, earthly cousins of the rain-bearing clouds, which are pouring heaven's waters upon her from jars lifted in their trunks.

212. Padma-Lakshmi. Detail of Figure 213

Lady Lotus, rising from the watery depths, is here becoming endowed with the radiance of a Tara: a Tara, however, of special sort. For she is not, like the messenger of Figures 48 and 198, an apparition from beyond the sphere of illusion, but herself a personification of the whole context of this sphere. Her womb is the field of space, her heart the pulse of time, her life the cosmic dream of which each of our own lives is a reflex; and her charm is the attractive power, not of a *yonder* shore, but of *this*. In short: in Biblical terms, she is Eve; or rather, Eve extended to be the mother, not only of mankind, but of all things, the rocks and trees, beasts, birds and fish, the sun and moon and stars. And the ritual bath here being bestowed on her is a baptism "changing Eva's name."*

* See above, p. 58.

Just as in the Christian rite of baptism, Fig. 216, the "natural man" is "born again" from waters—heavenly blessed—in the virgin womb of the font, so in this Indian vision of the Goddess of Nature rising from the primal sea there is bestowed on her a second water-birth from the spiritual sphere above. For this work of the first century A.D. ornaments a Buddhist shrine, not a Hindu. Hindu divinities are personifications chiefly of the powers of nature and the structuring laws of the Indian social order—the caste system, and so forth—which are regarded as of a piece with the order of nature, not to be altered by human arrangement but as natural and holy as the laws that govern the orders of life of the various animal species. In Buddhism, on the other hand, the personified powers are primarily those of *con-sciousness*—neither of the will implicated in the universal dream nor of the obscuring and projecting powers that bring the dream into existence,* but consciousness, both apart from the dream and operating within it as the *releasing* power of maya.

Fig. 212

* See above, p. 52.

213. *The Great Stupa. Sanchi, India*

214. The Birth of Aphrodite

215. *Utha Emerging from the Sea. William Blake*

216. *Baptism*

Fig. 212   Miss Universe, that is to say, is now to be the shakti, not of an abyssal unregen-
erate will to life, but of a luminous, clarified consciousness. The center out of
which the forms and acts of creative willing are to stem is to be shifted from
cf. Fig. 211 the pelvic region (the beautiful loins of Shri-Lakshmi) to the head (the luminous
cf. Fig. 199 hands and face of Queen Dedes Prajnaparamita), as it has been transferred ritually
in Christianity as well, from the physical initiation of the circumcision rite to the
spiritual of baptism. Hinduism, like Judaism, is basically a racial religion: one is

born a Jew, born a Hindu. Buddhism, on the other hand, is, like Christianity, a religion founded on belief: a credal religion, hence a world religion, open to all equally, no matter of what mother born. And that, finally, is the meaning of the symbol of the virgin birth. It is neither of race nor of caste, but absolutely of the spirit, from aloft—as in the strange scene below.

217. *The Dream of Queen Maya*

The subject here—in one of the earliest monuments of Buddhist art, ca. 100 B.C.— is the dream of the Buddha's mother, Queen Maya, the night she conceived the Savior. She thought she saw descending through her sleep from the heaven of the highest gods (where the reincarnating monad of the one now to become the Buddha had been dwelling between incarnations) the form of a glorious white elephant, radiant, with four brilliant tusks, which on reaching the earth walked thrice around her bed in the auspicious sunwise direction, struck her right side with its trunk, and entered the womb.

Fig. 217

There is an old myth about elephants, telling how once upon a time they could fly and change shape like clouds. One day, however, a great flock alighted on the branch of a prodigious tree, beneath which an ascetic named Long Austerity was teaching. The branch broke and fell, killing a number of his pupils; whereupon the elephants simply winged to another bough and the yogi, righteously indignant, roundly cursed the entire race, dooming them to the loss of their powers both of flight and of changing shape. So that today, elephants are actually clouds condemned to walk the earth.[24] And they are revered in India as blessings, bringers of fertility and life, since when their relatives the clouds arrive to visit them, the boon of rain descends.

Now, of course, the boon of life represented in the Buddha is of a higher, more spiritual order than that of the popular elephant cult, and yet it too is a boon of *life*. Accordingly, just as in the Christian sacrament of bread and wine the earlier vehicles of "earthly" life have been changed into "spiritual" sustenance, so in the Buddhist image of the "coming down" of the Savior, his vehicle is the elephant of the earlier "earthly" order—now, so to speak, transubstantiated, rendered radiant, and descending from on high.

The Buddhist scene on the page preceding, of the first century B.C., can be com-
Fig. 218 pared to that of the Annunciation painted by a sixteenth-century German artist, Bartel Bruyn. Conducted by the Holy Spirit in the shape of a radiant white dove, the little Savior, already bearing his Cross, here comes flying to his intended mother on a beam of light that illuminates her face, while the angel, equipped with heaven-
cf. Fig. 52 ly wings, speaks to her those famous winged words:

Ave, gratia plena, Dominus tecum: Hail, full of grace, the Lord is with thee.

218. *The Annunciation. Bartel Bruyn*

Fig. 219   In the Roman Catholic service annually celebrating, on March 25, "this greatest event in history," the following Alleluia, in response to the pronouncement of the angelic salutation, signifies the import of the miracle in the image of a blossoming plant.

"The rod of Jesse has blossomed!" So the paean begins. "A virgin has brought forth God and man. God has given peace, reconciling in Himself the lowest with the highest. Alleluia."[25]

The Tree of Jesse window of Chartres Cathedral, opposite, represents the testament of art to this miracle, "changing Eva's name." At the base reclines Jesse, sleeping like the Vishnu of Figure 4, the tree of his descendants rising from his body like the lotus from the Indian god. Above, however, not one but six symbolic stages blossom forth; the first four, of King David and the Old Testament phase of the epic of redemption: God's preparation of a priestly race, a people dedicated not to the sins of this world but to Himself, to become the worthy natural vessel of His supernatural seed. The flowers of this phase are red; and the symbolic personages, standing for justice and the law, appropriately masculine. Whereas above, opening the second phase, the Virgin Mother Mary of the New Testament and Roman Church appears, pure vessel of God's mercy and of the restoration of mankind to grace, blossoming white. Above all of which, then, in the place of Brahma on the lotus throne of Figure 4, is the Savior himself, her Son, who is here comparable, however, rather to the Adi Buddha of Figure 200, enthroned above *two* lotuses, than to the Hindu Brahma, above *one*.

Fig. 218   Accordingly, in the painting by Bartel Bruyn, lilies of two colors, red and white, appear in the vase at the Virgin's knee, inscribed with the monogram of the crucified Incarnation, IHS,[27] while the third spray, also in the vase, signifies the Paraclete, God's spirit in His church, the vessel itself being an equivalent of the womb of clay—this blessed Mother Earth, wherein the whole drama of redemption is being unfolded.

Moreover, this artist of Meister Eckhart's Rhineland has celebrated in his symbols the elevation, or sublimation, not only of the racially oriented Old Testament heritage, but also of the classical pagan, of which Christianity is equally the heir. The Angel Gabriel's wand—which is raised at the midpoint of the composition in such a way that its relevance to the role of the dove is unmistakable—is ornamented with

Fig. 220   the emblem of the messenger of Olympus and guide of souls to eternal life: the wand of interlacing serpents (the caduceus) of the Greek god Hermes of the winged heels.

219. *The Tree of Jesse. Chartres Cathedral*

"There shall come forth a shoot from the stump of Jesse, and a branch shall grow out of his roots. And the Spirit of the Lord shall rest upon him, the spirit of wisdom and understanding, the spirit of counsel and might, the spirit of knowledge and the fear of the Lord. . . . In that day the root of Jesse shall stand as an ensign to the peoples" (Isaiah 11:1-2,10).

Of this prophecy Emile Mâle states:

"The artists of the Middle Ages. . . . Combining the verses of Isaiah with the genealogy of Jesus Christ, as given in the Gospel according to Saint Matthew . . . depicted a great tree rising from the belly of Jesse asleep; along the stem of which they showed the kings of Judah in stages; above the kings, the Virgin, and above her, Jesus Christ, to whom they gave an aureole of seven doves, to remind us that in him repose the seven gifts of the Holy Ghost. . . . Moreover, to complete their composition the artists placed beside Christ's ancestors according to the flesh those according to the spirit, and so in the stained glass of Saint-Denis, Chartres, and Sainte-Chapelle, one sees beside the line of the kings of Judah that of the prophets, fingers lifted, who announced the Savior to come."

"In an article in the *Revue de l'art ancient et moderne*, 1914, Vol. I, pp. 91ff.," Professor Mâle adds in a footnote, "I have discussed the origins of the Tree of Jesse. There I have shown that the motif seems to have been conceived by the Abbé Suger himself, since the earliest Tree of Jesse known is in a window of Saint-Denis (anterior to 1144), this window of Chartres being a little later, and but a copy."[27]

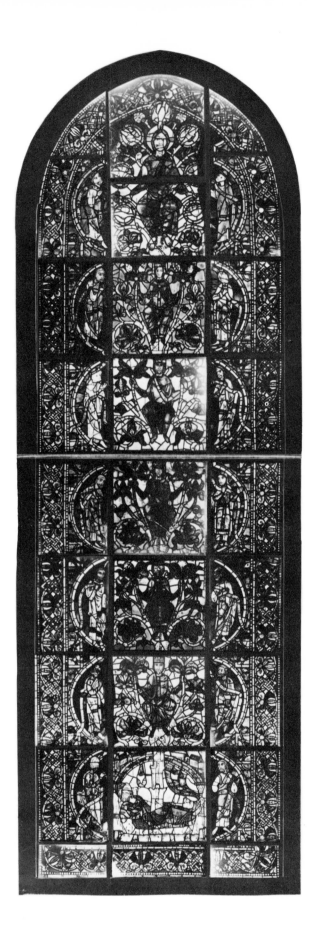

Fig. 220   This archetype of the mystagogue of rebirth, holding in his right hand his wand
of the mysteries, bears on his left arm the twice-born infant of those rites, the god
of bread and wine, Dionysos, many of the elements of whose iconography were
carried forward in the Christian Mass.

220. *Hermes Bearing the Infant Dionysos on His Arm*

Here Dionysos appears in the character of the deified grape—not, however, as in the Christian doctrine of transubstantiation, brought down from above, from "out there," changing the "natural substance" of the grape into the altogether different "divine substance" of a god; but showing forth, in the way rather of a transfiguration, the immanent divinity that had been there in the grape all along.

Fig. 221

cf. Fig. 224

221. *Dionysos, The Deified Grape*

Fig. 222   In this illustration of the famous Homeric legend of Dionysos in the ship one
cf. Fig. 219   sees a prototype of the Tree of Jesse motif; while in the Antioch chalice of the earliest

222. *Dionysos at Sea*

As the story is told in *Homeric Hymn* 7: The god was standing on a promontory in the form of a youth in his first bloom when Etruscan pirates put to shore and, pouncing on the lad, bound him and bore him off. But at sea the bonds fell from his limbs, wine began pouring through the ship, a grapevine burgeoned up the mast, and ivy curled about the oarlocks. The youth, becoming a lion, roaring, tore the captain apart, while the rest, leaping overboard, became dolphins.

Christian centuries the idea of Christ himself as the mystical fruit of the vine is celebrated. We note the garland of flowers, in full bloom, around the upper margin of the composition.

Fig. 223

223. "Chalice of Antioch"

"I am the true vine, and my Father is the vinedresser. Every branch of mine that bears no fruit, he takes away, and every branch that does bear fruit he prunes that it may bear more fruit. . . . Abide in me, and I in you. As the branch cannot bear fruit by itself, unless it abides in the vine, neither can you, unless you abide in me. I am the vine, you are the branches. He who abides in me, and I in him, he it is that bears much fruit, for apart from me you can do nothing" (John 15:1-2, 4-5).

Fig. 224   Finally, a thirteenth-century Swiss church door again represents this transformed Dionysian theme, the immediate inspiration for which is from the words of Christ to his apostles at the Last Supper:

This is my body. . . . This is my blood of the covenant . . . poured out. . . .

"And as they were eating, he took bread, and blessed, and broke it, and gave it to them, and said, 'Take; this is my body.' And he took a cup, and when he had given thanks he gave it to them, and they all drank of it. And he said to them, 'This is my blood of the covenant, which is poured out for many. Truly, I say to you, I shall not drink again of the fruit of the vine until that day when I drink it new in the kingdom of God'" (Mark 14:22-25).

224 (opposite). Christ as a Cluster of Grape

225. *The Alchemical Red-and-White Rose, Birthplace of the "Filius philosophorum"*

4. The Golden Seed

> *Take the flower Roses, white and red.*
> *And joyne them well in won bed.*
> *So betwixt these Roses mylde.*
> *Thou shalt bring forth a Glorious chylde.*

So we read in the alchemical scroll reproduced here, where the white of the "spiritual" flower is represented as contained *within* the red. The idea expressed appears to be a counterpart of the Buddhist meditation inscribed on the prayer wheels of Tibet: OM MANI PADME HUM: "OM: The Jewel [of Buddha consciousness] in the Lotus [of the world]: HUM."* For like the sages of the Orient for whom this visible-audible world is not the creation of a god apart, but the sensually apprehended form of divinity itself—as told, for example, in these words:

> *This living presence is to be known as*
> *a part of any hundredth part of*
> *the point of a hair subdivided hundredfold:*
> *Yet it partakes of infinity.*
>
> *Neither female, male, nor yet neuter,*
> *whatever body it assumes,*
> *in that it becomes contained . . .*[28]

*For the syllables OM and HUM, see below, pp. 356-360, and 379.

and again:

> *Though hidden in all things,*
> *That Self [atman] shines not forth,*
> *Yet is seen by subtle seers*
> *Of superior, subtle intellect . . .*[29]

—so the European medieval alchemists thought of the "gold," the "uncommon gold" (*aurum non vulgi*), of their psycho-metaphysical transmuting process as actually immanent in all things, simply released, i.e., revealed, through the various distillations and fermentations of their alchemical "work." In the *vas hermeticum*, the retort "hermetically" sealed, processes were initiated that were intended only to accelerate and fulfill, not to oppose, the travail of nature—which was namely to render from the elements of its soil a "golden flowering" of the spirit. Hence the *vas* in which the work was accomplished can be likened to a second womb, and the inauguration of the process to a spiritual begetting, the product of which was to be a "child" conceived of art and brought by art to birth, a "virgin birth."[30] All of which is to say that the gold of alchemy, as the old masters ever insisted, was not the same as that of the merchants, not the common gold, *aurum vulgi*, of the markets of the world, but the "gold of philosophy," *aurum philosophicum, aurum mercurialis, aurum nostrum, aurum volatile*; gold, in other words, such as only art bestows through its transfiguration of the world as commonly known.

Fig. 226

226. *The Transformations of Mercurius*

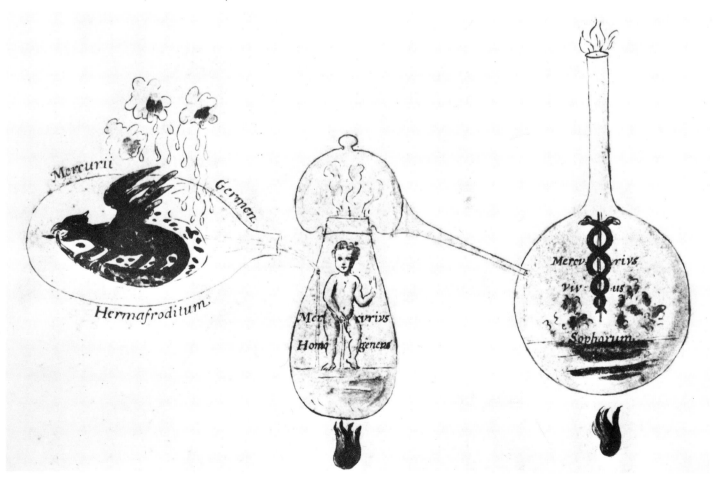

corrũpitur, neɋ ex imperfecto penitus fecundũ
artem aliquid fieri poteft. Ratio eft quia ars prĩ
mas difpofitiones inducere non poteft, fed lapis
nofter eft res media inter perfecta & imperfecta
corpora, & quod natura ipfa incepit hoc per ar
tem ad perfectionẽ deducitur. Si in ipfo Mercu
rio operari inceperis vbi natura reliquit imperᵉ
fectum, inuenies in eo perfectionẽ et gaudebis.

Perfectum non alteratur, fed corrumpitur.
Sed imperfectum bene alteratur, ergo corrupᵉ
tio vnius eft generatio alterius.

Speculum

227. *Lunar Queen and Solar King*

Fig. 227   In the figure above, which is an alchemical counterpart of the baptismal image of Figure 216, the waters from beneath are contributing to the symbolized spiritual *opus* no less than is the flower descending from above. "Art," as we are told in the text, "is unable to establish the primary arrangements." Art, that is to say, though inspired from above, cannot begin its work *ab initio*, independently of nature. "Our philosopher's stone is something," the text goes on to explain, "midway between perfected and unperfected bodies; and what Nature herself initiates is by art carried to perfection. If you set to work on that state of Mercurius where Nature has left imperfection, you will arrive at its perfection and rejoice. What is perfect does not alter, but is destroyed. However, what is imperfect does indeed alter. Hence the destruction of the one is the generation of the other."

The aim of the alchemists, then, was to achieve not a terminal perfection but a process ever continuing, of which their "stone," the *lapis philosophorum*, should become at once the model and the catalyst: a process whereby and wherein all pairs of opposites—eternity and time, heaven and hell, male and female, youth and age—should be brought together by something "midway between perfected and unperfected bodies." As C. G. Jung has commented in elucidation of these curiously symbolic texts to which he devoted a very great part of the studies of his later years: "The alchemist thought in strictly medieval trichotomous terms: anything alive—and his *lapis* is undoubtedly alive—consists of corpus, anima, and spiritus. The *Rosarium* remarks that 'the body is Venus and feminine, the spirit is Mercurius and masculine'; hence the anima, as the 'vinculum,' the link between body and spirit, would be hermaphroditic, i.e., a *coniunctio Solis et Lunae. . . .*"

The sun, as symbol of the light of consciousness, is identified with the masculine power here symbolized in the king, while the moon, the power of the tides of life both in the sea and in the womb, is the principle personified in the queen. Continuing with Jung, in discussion of this figure: "From all this it may be gathered that the queen stands for the body and the king for the spirit, but that both are unrelated without the soul, since this is the *vinculum* which holds them together."[31]

Interestingly, the Latin *vinculum*, "link," would be in Sanskrit *kataka*, the name of the hand posture of Queen Dedes as Prajnaparamita, "the Wisdom of the Yonder Shore," marking the mystery-point of the juncture of the lotus and its reflection.

Jung states of the king and queen opposite:

> If no bond of love exists, they have no soul. In our pictures the bond is effected by the dove from above and the water from below. These constitute the link—in other words, they are the soul. Thus the underlying idea of the psyche proves to be a half bodily, half spiritual substance, an *anima media natura*, as the alchemists call it, an hermaphroditic being capable of uniting the opposites, but who is never complete in the individual unless related to another individual. The unrelated human being lacks wholeness, for he can achieve wholeness only through the soul, and the soul cannot exist without its other side, which is always found in a "You."[32]

It is to be noted that the female receives her initiation from the right hand of

228. *Paradise*

Figs. 229, 230   the male and the male his from the left of the female, while the signs here given are of their contrasting modes of experiencing the new flowering: his generative powers wakened by the arrow of Mercurius in his side, and her reflective by the apprehension of death.

229 (*opposite*). *The State of Adam, as the Male Aspect of the Primal Androgyne, Pierced by the Arrow of Mercurius*

230 (*below*). *The State of Eve, as the Female Aspect of the Primal Androgyne, Under the Influence of the Apprehension of Death*

231. The Dream of the Virgin

Fig. 231   Above is a fifteenth-century "Dream of the Virgin," showing Christ crucified on a dreamlike tree of life growing from his mother's side, with birdlike angels among its boughs and on its summit the nest of the pelican, feeding its young with blood drawn from its own breast (an allegorical reference to Christ's sacrifice and his

Fig. 232   saving grace in the sacrament of the altar). Opposite, in the Northwest Indian Greco-Buddhist sculptural style of ca. A.D. 200, is a representation of the Buddha born from his mother's side while she stood clinging to the bough of a tree—and a

Fig. 233   Chinese version, five centuries later, of the same mythological event.

232. *Birth of the Buddha. ca.* A.D. *200. Gandhara, India*

233. *Birth of the Buddha.* A.D. *618-907. Northwest China*

According to the earliest known version of the Buddhist nativity legend,* the young Queen Maya, having carried the world savior in her womb for exactly ten lunar months and desiring to give birth to her child in her mother's home, was being transported in a golden palanquin by her company of attendants along a road beautified for the journey with banners, streamers, and flowering trees set out in pots, when they came to a glorious pleasure garden of sal-trees that was at that moment in full bloom. There were among its fragrant boughs humming swarms of bees of the five colors, flocks of birds of various feather, flying, fluttering, and warbling: and the young queen, wishing to pause in that delightful spot, descended from her palanquin and entered the pleasure grove, surrounded by her company.

Whereupon, at the foot of a giant sal-tree the pains of her time overtook her, and when she reached upward with her right hand, a flowery bough of that tree bent down, like the tip of a well-steamed reed, and, grasping it, the young queen, standing, gave birth to her child, who came forth from her right side.

Four pure-minded Mahabrahma gods, who had instantly descended, received the infant on a golden net and placed him before his mother, giving praise. "Rejoice, O Queen!" they said. "There has been born to you a mighty son." From the sky two pure streams of water fell, refreshing the child and its mother, after which the infant, standing upright, facing east, strode forward seven steps, pointed upward with his right hand, downward with his left, and shouted with a noble voice the victory shout of all the Buddhas:

Fig. 234

Worlds above, worlds below! The chief in all the worlds am I![33]

234. *The Child Buddha.* A.D. *13th century. Japan*

* Recorded in a Ceylonese text of ca. 80 B.C.

Figs. 235-237 Shown here are earth and tree divinities from the ruins of the early stupa at Bharhut, India, their date, early first century B.C., being approximately that of the nativity legend just related. We note that the goddesses are all in the pose of Queen Maya

Fig. 238 in the birth scene. The famous bracket figure of the later "Great Stupa" at Sanchi is also in this pose. Her date is ca. A.D. 100; that of the birth scene of Figure 232, a century later. What is the meaning of this pose?

It is derived from an ageless magical rite whereby, to stimulate the vital sap of a tree and cause it to blossom and bear fruit, a young girl in her own blossom time

235. Earth Divinity, Kubera Yaksha. *236. Tree Goddess, Chandra Yakshi.* *237. Tree Goddess, Chulakoka Devata.*

would entwine its trunk, draw down a bough, and deliver with her heel a sharp little kick at the root. These dryads are depicted, then, in the act of rousing in this magical way the trees to which they are attached. And the fact that the Buddha's mother giving birth is also represented in this pose signifies that in her the mothering power of nature (which has been represented from time out of mind in the tree and earth divinities of the popular imagination) became fruitful of its highest good; i.e., the golden fruit of the seed of Buddha-consciousness which is at the heart of the lotus of this world: OM MANI PADME HUM.

238. *Bracket Figure, The Great Stupa.* A.D. *100. Sanchi, India*

239. *The Sacrifice. ca.* 2000 B.C. *Indus Valley*

Sir John Marshall, excavator of the early Indus Valley site from which this seal derives, points out that what we see here are, on one side, "the figures of a man and woman, the former standing with a sickle-shaped knife in his right hand, the latter seated on the ground with hands raised in an attitude of supplication"; and he comments: "Evidently the man is preparing to kill the woman, and it is reasonable to suppose that the scene is intended to portray a human sacrifice connected with the Earth Goddess depicted on the other side, with whom we must also associate the two genii, whom I take to be ministrants of the Deity."[34]

The Indus script has not been deciphered. However, the signs on the two sides of this seal are identical, suggesting that the scenes are indeed related. We know, furthermore, of a mythic theme of practically worldwide distribution telling of a divine being slain or sacrificed, whose body, cut up and buried, becomes the source of certain basic food plants; and the usual ceremonies in commemoration of this mythological event have everywhere involved the ritual killing, dismemberment, and even eating of a human victim identified with the voluntarily sacrificed god.[35] Almost certainly, what is depicted on this seal is an ancient Indian version of such a rite; and the likelihood is the greater inasmuch as human sacrifice continued to be practiced openly in India until 1835, when forbidden by law. Moreover, animal sacrifices continue there to the present, particularly in worship of the Goddess Kali.

Buddhists, on the other hand, will have nothing to do with the sacrificial killing either of human beings or of beasts; for in the Buddhist view, what must be sacrificed are the fears, desires, and self-interest of the sacrificer himself. And yet, the line of descent from this early ritual scene to the much later figure of Queen Maya giving birth to the Buddha is clear and direct. Also, in its westward branch, the line leads to the Dream of the Virgin.

240. *Veneration of the Tree Goddess. ca.* 2000 B.C. *Indus Valley*

The meaning of this scene is unknown. However, a number of its elements bear comparison with well-known features of the contemporary Mesopotamian-Egyptian culture complex: the horned headgear, the sphinx motif, the number (seven) of attendant deities (or perhaps priestesses), and the association of a goddess with a vegetation theme; also, the very idea of a stamp seal. As described by one authority:

"Here a horned goddess is shown in the midst of a *pipal,* or sacred fig-tree, before which another horned deity is kneeling and doing obeisance. Both the goddess and her worshiper wear long plaits of hair, have their arms adorned with many bangles, and in the case of the latter, and possibly of the former as well, there is a floral or leafy spray springing from the head between the horns. Behind the worshiper a goat with a human cf. Fig. face looks on with evident interest. A row of seven spirits, or deities, facing the opposite way to the scene above, occupies the whole of the lower register of the seal-amulet, each figure wearing a sprig on the head, a long pigtail behind, but no horns."[36]

242. *The Birth of Adonis. Bernardino Luini.*
A.D. *15th century. Italy*

Ovid recounts in his *Metamorphoses* (10. 298-518) the legend of how the princess Myrrha, daughter of King Kinyras of Cyprus, conceived for her father an incestuous love, which with the aid of her nurse she contrived to satisfy, first on a festival night when her father was drunk with wine, and then eleven nights following, repeatedly, until the king, desiring at last to know what his mistress looked like, brought in a light and (as Ovid tells) "beheld his crime and his daughter."

Appalled and speechless, Kinyras reached for his sword; but his daughter had already fled. She had conceived, and full of shame prayed the gods to let her be nowhere, among neither living men nor the dead. And some divinity—Zeus possibly, more probably Aphrodite—in pity turned her into the tree that weeps the fragrant gum known as myrrh.

In due time the growing child inside caused the tree to swell in mid-trunk, where it cracked and gave forth its burden—whom naiads gently received, laid on a bed of leaves, and annointed with his mother's tears.

243. The Goddess "Abundance."
A.D. *2nd century. Mathura, India*

"In its general attitude and style," notes Heinrich Zimmer, "this work is related closely to the standing images of yakshas, nagas, and other divinities of the popular religion that we have seen on the railing posts of the early Buddhist sanctuaries, from the first century B.C. to the second A.D. [Figures 235-238]. The attitude is full of a significant sweetness and charm, personifying nature in her fostering, lovable aspect. With her hands the goddess indicates the two chief functions of the maternal principle: the left supports a nourishing breast while the right indicates her sex—a gesture resembling that of the Balinese goddess of maternity and fertility [Figure 244], and reminding one, also, of a kindred posture of the realm of Western art, namely that of the Venus de' Medici [Figure 247]. The goddess in the Classical rendition exhibits her body in splendid nakedness, but at the same time, with a spontaneous or coquettish bashfulness, screens her bosom and loins with her two arms and hands.

"I cannot but feel," Zimmer goes on to remark of the Western piece, "that this completely secularized posture—obviously devoid of any such symbolism as prevails in the Hindu and Balinese images—derives somehow from the background of the more archaic attitude, and may in fact be a semiconscious reminiscence of an older, widely spread classic conception of the goddess of life, fertility, and love; the same posture having been preserved in Oriental art, on the other hand, with full consciousness and understanding."[37]

It is interesting to compare with this thought the interpretation of the classical piece suggested by the art historian Sir Kenneth Clark.*

* See below, pp. 272-274.

243a. *Rear view of Figure 243*

Two birds of fair plumage, friends close
    bound,
Grasp close the selfsame tree.
One of them eats its luscious fruit,
The other, not eating, watches.

There where those two fair-plumaged
    ones
Flutter in ambrosial pasture,
The Lord Protector of this whole world
    came
To me: to this fool, the All Wise.

Of that tree where those fair-plumaged
    ones,
Enjoying its fruit, come to nest,
The topmost tip bears the sweetest fruit,
To which no one, not knowing the Lord,
    can attain.
        (Rig Veda I.164.20-22)

244. Rati, "Erotic Delight."
A.D. *19th century. Bali*

In this Balinese image, states Heinrich Zimmer, "the goddess of maternity and fertility . . . is indicating, with a traditional twofold symbolic gesture, the two main functions of the female principle. One forearm lifts the breasts that nourish the creatures she brings forth, while the other hand, placed at the lower abdomen, immediately above the organ of generation, presses the ever-pregnant womb. The sensual mouth, with its half-open lips and broadening gap at the left corner, has a voluptuous, dolorous trait, suggesting simultaneously the delights of love and conception and the pangs and throes of birth. The figure exhibits, frankly, all the innocent shamelessness of archaic mother figures, but in addition—or so it seems—the challenging, calm, watchful, and consciously exhibitionistic attitude of a curiously demonic, suprahuman harlot. The hideous and grotesque features are suffused with a sinister, devilish allure of sex. Full possession by the animalic force in man and life has been expressed without a single redeeming trait.

"The figure is executed," Zimmer continues, "in a sophisticated manner, which evolves its effects through a minuteness of lavish detail in dress; there is a blend of wild and frantic naturalism with an acute sense for ornamental outlines and design. The style is overripe and highly conventionalized. Nevertheless, it is full-blooded and still possessed of vigor. The smooth, costly incrustation of the richly decorative surface veils a volcano of indomitable force surging from the infrahuman sphere in man. Sheer nature, blending beauty with hideousness, charm with the grotesque, ambivalent and ambiguous, beyond or beneath human moral and social values and commands, is made manifest in this figure as the perennial antagonist to the purely human value of society, ethics, family, and the spiritual pursuits of mankind.

"The image, though by no means isolated in the art of Bali, is one of its most challenging and meaningful specimens. The archaic concept of the motherly principle of the universe, which found an abstract, solemn, and highly dignified expression in the neolithic images and their descendants, has here assumed a very challenging attitude: rawly protesting, as it were, against the lofty doctrines of release and transcendent redeeming wisdom, which, in the forms of Buddhist and yogic asceticism, were the most conspicuous and forceful products, in that period, of the masculine spirit. After millenniums of the struggle of the gurus to disengage man from the brutish thrall of the demonic powers of sheer nature, these—unabated, unconquered, and unreconciled—still were there. And they are both shocking and attractive. Not even attempting to conceal what is grotesque and hideous, they show forth triumphantly the basic monstrousness and ambivalence of life."[38]

244a. Rear view of Figure 244

Sir Kenneth Clark's discussion of the sense and origin of the classic pose of these three figures differs *toto caelo* from Zimmer's.* His argument opens with a comparison of the Knidian Aphrodite with the Capitoline and proceeds then to the Venus de' Medici.

"The classic nude, which Praxiteles invented," he writes, "became, in less sensitive hands, the conventional nude, and as we try to look at his *Knidian Aphrodite* we seem to see a forest of marble females, filling a vast conservatory with their chaste, monotonous forms. . . . In fact, these figures do not usually derive from the *Knidian*, but from two Hellenistic statues of great celebrity, the *Capitoline Aphrodite* and the *Medici Venus*. Fundamentally, these are versions of the Praxitelean idea, but they involve an important difference. The *Knidian* is thinking only of the ritual bath she is about to enter. The *Capitoline* is posing. Herself self-conscious, she is the product of self-conscious art. Her pose, whenever it was evolved, is the most complete solution in antique art of certain formal problems presented by the naked female body; and it is worth trying to see how this has been achieved.

"The variations on the *Knidian* are subtle, but decisive. The weight has been transferred from one leg to the other, but is more evenly distributed, so that the axes of the body are nearly parallel. The action of the *Knidian*'s right arm has been given to the *Capitoline*'s left, but both heads look in the same direction. Finally, the most obvious change, the arm of her 'free' side, instead of holding her drapery, is bent over her body, just below her breasts. All these changes are designed to produce compactness and stability. At no point is there a plane or outline where the eye may wander undirected. The arms surround the body like a sheath, and by their movement help to emphasize its basic rhythm. The head, left arm, and weight-bearing leg form a line as firm as the shaft of a temple. Approach the *Knidian* from the direction to which her gaze is directed, and her body is open and defenceless; approach the *Capitoline*, and it is formidably enclosed. This is the pose known to history as the

* See p. 268.

III · 272

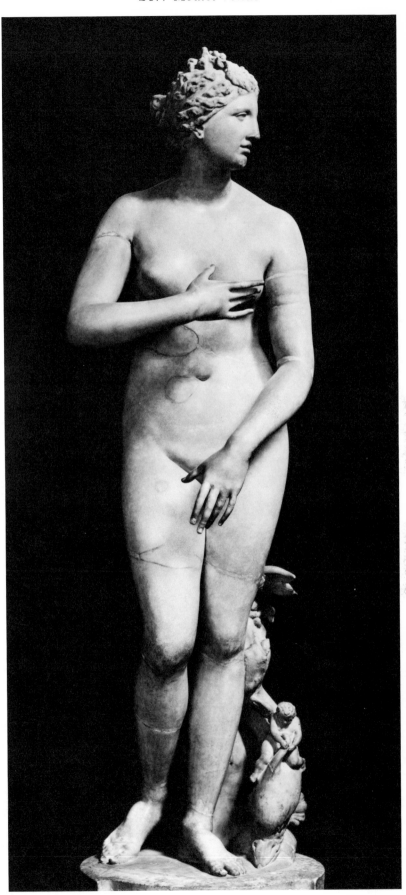

Venus Pudica, the Venus of Modesty, and although the *Capitoline* is more carnally realistic than the *Knidian*, and the action of her right hand does nothing to conceal her magnificent breasts, a formal analysis shows that the title has some justification. We can see why in later replicas this attitude was adopted when the more candid nudity of Praxiteles would have given offense. We can also understand why, through all the misfortunes and mutations Venus was to suffer during two thousands years, this impregnable design was the chief survivor.

"Curiously enough, it owes a great part of its authority in post-Renaissance art to a version in which the rhythmic completeness of the whole is almost lost: the famous *Venus dei Medici*, which so long reigned unchallenged in the tribuna of the Uffizi. The breakdown of rhythm is partly owing to a faulty restoration of the right arm, which, in an effort genuinely to cover the breasts and deserve her reputation for modesty, is bent at too sharp an angle and does not sustain the flow of movement round the body. But at every point the *Medici Venus* is stilted and artificial. The physical opulence of the *Capitoline* has been reduced to refined complacency. The line of the body tapers up to the tiny, Praxitelean head, with the vapid elegance of a Victorian fashion plate. It was perhaps inevitable that for two centuries this modish elegance should have been confused with ideal beauty. In the literature of praise the *Medici Venus* fills almost as many pages as the *Apollo Belvedere*, and with less reason. Byron, who considered the ideal 'all nonsense,' devoted to the *Venus* a stanza of *Childe Harold*:

> We gaze and turn away, and know not
>   where,
> Dazzled and drunk with Beauty, till the
>   heart
> Reels with its fulness; there—for ever
>   there—
> Chained to the chariot of triumphal Art,
> We stand as captives, and would not
>   depart.

> Away!—there need no words, nor terms
>   precise,
> The paltry jargon of the marble mart,
> Where Pedantry gulls Folly—we have
>   eyes.

"In fact," the art historian flings back, "Byron was not using his eyes at all and, like most people of his class and temperament, had himself been gulled by fashion."[39]

248. *Ancestral Figure. Easter Island*

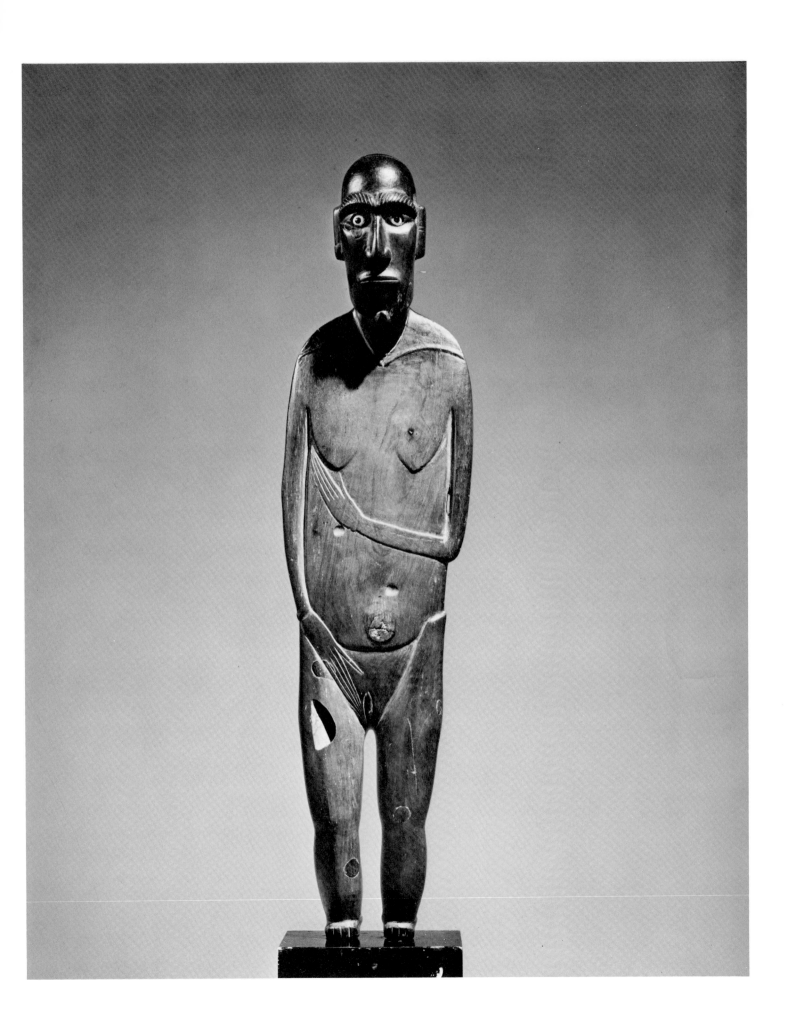

IV. TRANSFORMATIONS OF THE INNER LIGHT

1. Psychology and Yoga

THERE are three points of accord that make it possible to speak of modern depth psychologies in the same context with yoga. First, there is the idea that the fate of the individual is a function of his psychological disposition: he brings about those calamities that appear to befall him. Next, there is the idea that the figures of mythology and religion are not revelations from aloft, but of the psyche, projections of its fantasies: the gods and demons are within us. And finally, there is the knowledge that an individual's psychological disposition can be transformed through controlled attention to his dreams and to what appear to be the accidents of his fate.

Fig. 244 The mastery of the dark, demonic powers of sheer nature, mentioned by Zimmer in his discussion of the Balinese goddess, was in India attempted and in large measure accomplished, on one hand through enforcement of the ruthless social disciplines of caste, and on the other by an equally ruthless application of the disciplines of yoga to the spiritual unfoldment of those found gifted for the adventure. And although in our Western centuries of outward progress in physical sciences and in the forging of humanistic social institutions, we have long left the Orient behind, on the inward psychological side it is we who today have most to learn. As C. G. Jung states in his Foreword to D. T. Suzuki's *Introduction to Zen Buddhism*: "It is a well-known fact that the problem of spiritual 'healing' has been seriously occupying the most venturesome minds of the East for more than two thousand years, and that in this respect methods and philosophical doctrines have been developed which simply put all Western attempts in the same line into the shade."[1]

Furthermore, it is becoming increasingly apparent as we advance in our knowledge of Asia that in the yogic lore of India and Tibet, China and Japan, we may have a master key to the inward dimensions of *all* symbolic forms. As Chapters II and III have shown, the mythological systems of the great civilizations share a significant body of motifs, many of which may have been derived from a single historic source: the mathematically structured astronomical systems of the Early Bronze Age Near East. What esoteric interpretations the priestly fashioners and guardians of those systems may have attributed to their creations we do not know. However, we do know that in India, as early as the ninth century B.C., an essentially psychological interpretation was being given to the imagery of all myths and rites. In the words of the *Brihadaranyaka Upanishad*: "Whoever worships another divinity than his self, thinking, 'He is one, I am another,' knows not."

> This that people say, "Worship this god! Worship that god!"—one god after another!
> All this is his creation indeed and he himself, all gods. . . . He is entered in the

249. The Buddha in Meditation. A.D. *3rd-4th century. Ceylon*

universe even to our fingernail-tips, like a razor in a razor-case, or fire in firewood. Him those see not, for as seen he is incomplete. When breathing, he becomes "breath" by name; when speaking, "voice"; when seeing, "the eye"; when hearing, "the ear"; when thinking, "mind": these are but names of his acts. Whosoever worships one or another of these knows not; for as one or another of these he is incomplete.

One should worship with the thought that he is one's self, for therein all these become one. This self is the footprint of that All, for by it one knows the All—just as, verily, by following a footprint one may find cattle that have been lost. . . . One should reverence the self alone as dear. And he who reverences the self alone as dear—what he holds dear, verily, will not perish.[2]

cf. Fig. 12   Something similar would seem to be implied in the Egyptian song of the self cited above; so also, in Christ's words in the Gnostic *Thomas Gospel*: "I am the All, the All came forth from me and the All attained to me. Cleave a piece of wood, I am there; lift up the stone and you will find me there. . . . Whoever drinks from my mouth shall become as I am and I myself will become he" (95:24-28, 99:28-29).[3] We know that in the curing rites of the Navaho, where the patient walks or sits on mytho-

cf. Fig. 171   logical sand paintings, he identifies himself with the mythic beings depicted; and when the old Sioux medicine man Black Elk told how he had once in vision beheld

cf. Fig. 170   himself standing on "the highest mountain," at "the center of the world," he added: "But anywhere is the center of the world." Indeed, wherever one turns in the world, unmistakable signs appear of the realization by "subtle seers with superior, subtle intellect" of that "indwelling Self," as the Hindus say, "which shines not forth, though It is hidden in all things."[4] However, the only systematically developed *psychological* formulation of the grades of this realization is that of the Indian yoga of the "Serpent Power"—the Kundalini—which is basic to all the religious arts of both the Hindu and the Buddhist East.

Following Jung's observation, therefore, that methods and philosophical doctrines have been developed by the most adventurous minds of the East "which simply put all Western attempts in the same line into the shade," I am going in the present chapter to let the Kundalini system serve as guide to an appreciation of the psychological insights of certain well-known Occidental, as well as Oriental, works of art treating mythological themes. Thus, whereas in Chapter I the imagery discussed was of generally known "elementary" or "universal" ideas (the world-dream, world-dreamer, great mother, miraculous child, and resurrected hero), and in Chapters II and III of specifically high culture themes (the mathematical round of space-time and waking of the spirit to a life transcending that round), here the concern will be with the psychological dimension of mythological thought and themes. Chapter V, then, will treat of the use of such psychologically based symbols in magical rites; and finally, in Chapter VI, we shall return to the topic of man's achievement of release from the bondages of life's dream.

2. The Serpent Guide

THE basic treatise on yoga is the *Yoga Sutras, Thread of Yoga*, a work attributed to an ancient saint whose name, Patanjali (from *pata*, "falling," plus *anjali*, "the joined hands"), is explained by a legend of his having dropped from heaven in the shape of a small snake into the hands of the grammarian Panini, just as the latter was bringing his palms together in prayer.[5] Its date is under debate, some assigning it to the second century B.C., others to the fifth century A.D. or later;[6] all, however, recognizing that the ideas and disciplines represented are certainly older than this writing, some perhaps dating back even to the Indus civilization, ca. 2500-1500 B.C. For the earliest known evidences of yoga appear on a half-dozen or so of the Indus Valley seals, an example of which appears here. Two attendant serpents Fig. 250

250. Deity with Worshipers and Serpents. ca. 2000 B.C. Indus Valley

elevate their giant forms behind a pair of worshipers kneeling at either hand of an enthroned figure seated in what appears to be a posture of yoga. And the fact that the elevation of the so-called Serpent Power is one of the leading motifs of yogic symbolism suggests that we may have here an explicit pictorial reference not only to the legend of some prehistoric yogi, but also to the concept of the unfoldment through yoga of this subtle spiritual force.

If so, the question arises whether some sort of yoga may not have been practiced outside India at that time as well. For a number of the symbols that are interpreted in psychological terms in yogic lore appear also in the monuments of other ancient cultures—where, however, no explanatory texts such as those that can be studied from the Hindu-Buddhist sphere are known.

251. *Libation Cup of King Gudea of Lagash. ca. 2000 B.C. Sumer*

Here, for example, is an ornamented Sumerian ritual cup of the same period as Figs. 251, 252 the Indus Valley seal. Two composite beasts of a type called "lion-birds" draw back the portals of a sanctuary, where an apparition appears of the great Mesopotamian serpent-god Ningishzida, under the aspect of a pair of copulating vipers. The two are entwined about an axial rod in such a way as to suggest both the caduceus of cf. Figs. 218, 220, 226, 306 classical Hermes, guide of souls to rebirth in eternal life, and the Indian diagram of seven spinal centers touched and wakened to consciousness in Kundalini yoga by the rising Serpent Power.

252. *Extended Drawing of Figure 251*

Two "lion-birds" draw back the portals of a shrine to reveal the serpent-god Ningish-zida in his dual aspect, as a pair of copulating vipers.

Fig. 253

cf. Fig. 175

Figs. 255-258
Fig. 254

The Sumerian seal below shows a god enthroned before a caduceus, offering his worshiper (the owner of the seal) the cup of an immortal drink, held directly beneath the celestial vessel of the moon. The worshiper is being presented by his patron deity, while behind him stands the porter of the palace gate, wearing a sort of serpent cap and bearing in hand one of those ambrosia pails that we have already found associated with guardians of the tree of life. Opposite are more such portal guardians from the palace of an Assyrian king of the ninth century B.C.; and below, at the entrance to a Buddhist temple, is a typical Indian serpent king in the same

253. *God of the Caduceus.* 2350-2150 B.C.

Before the god is a fire-altar, behind him the sign of his nature and power in the form of the later caduceus. A devotee is led before him by a second god, as Hunefer before Osiris. The figure to the right, with a serpent dangling from his head, is the porter at the god's gate, who, admitting and excluding

aspirants, is a reduced or preliminary manifestation of the power of the god himself. Hence the contents of his pail must be a reduced or preliminary potion of the ambrosial drink given by the god. Compare him in this role to Anubis, Thoth, and Horus in the Egyptian judgment scene, or to Hermes in the Greek mysteries.

254. *Serpent King.* A.D. *12th century.*
Ceylon

255, 256, 257. *Assyrian Winged Genii.* 885-860 B.C.

The winged lion-bull with human head combines in one body those four signs of the zodiac that in the earliest period of Meso-potamian astronomy marked the solstices and equinoxes: the Bull (spring equinox and eastern quarter), Lion (summer solstice and southern quarter), Eagle (later Scorpio: autumn equinox and western quarter), and Water Carrier (winter solstice and northern quarter). These are the four "living crea-tures" of Ezekiel's vision and of the Apoca-lypse.

The conelike fruits held by the winged genii may represent either a bunch of dates from the tree of life or a staminate blossom of the date palm brought to fertilize the pistillate flower. The little pails or baskets are containers, accordingly, of either fruit or pollen symbolic of the life elixir. Compare the wine and milk pails of Figures 186 and 187; also, in the Olmec tablet of Figure 102, the copal pouch in the hand of the masked figure enthroned on the coils of the feathered serpent.

ig. 164

ig. 175

258. *Assyrian Winged Genie*

threshold-guarding role, bearing in his right hand a burgeoning stalk of the tree of life and in his left a jar of the liquor of immortality (Sanskrit *amrita*, Greek *ambrosia*), these being the very gifts that the serpent of Eden had in store for our first parents as the treasure of his second tree. For as the reader must by now have realized, the usual mythological association of the serpent is not, as in the Bible, with corruption, but with physical and spiritual health, as in the Greek caduceus.

259. *Votive Tablet from the Asklepieion.*
  4th century B.C. *Athens*

260. *Asklepios.* A.D. *2nd century. Roman copy*

Below are the snake and staff of the god of healing. Above, his right hand is administering medicine to a patient.

261. *The Serpent-god Amphiaraos.*
4th century B.C. *Attica*

Writing of the cures at the classical sanctuaries of healing, C. Kerényi remarks that "the patient himself was offered an opportunity to bring about the cure whose elements he bore within himself. To this end an environment was created which, as in modern spas and health resorts, was as far as possible removed from the disturbing and unhealthful elements of the outside world. The religious atmosphere also helped man's innermost depths to accomplish their curative potentialities. In principle the physician was excluded from the individual mystery of recovery."[8]

In this remarkable scene, representing the dream-cure of the temple sleep (*incubatio*), the deity is not Asklepios but a god of oracles acting his part. In the background is the invalid, dreaming, and at the right his own vision of himself standing, as though having just emerged in spirit from his ailing body. At the left this figure has advanced to be cured by the god, who is touching his ailing shoulder, while on the couch, simultaneously, the same shoulder is being licked by a snake, which (if I read the picture correctly) has emerged from the dreamer himself.

262. *Hygieia.* A.D. *late 4th century. Rome*

Here, as Dr. Kerényi points out, the snake emerging from the tripod is Apollonian, as at Delphi. Above are ritual utensils suggesting the symbolism of the mystery cults: to the right a wine pitcher with an emerging snake, to the left a basket (*cista mystica*) containing along with a second snake a divine child. Below, near the goddess, stands another appearance of the child. Asklepios appeared to his worshipers as either a child, a youth, or an elder.[9]

Fig. 253

cf. Fig. 102

cf. Figs. 91, 92

Fig. 263

Thus the porter and god of the old Sumerian seal represent two degrees of manifestation of the one principle of immortal life; and between that seal and the later image of the serpent guardian of the world-tree of the Buddha there extends a rainbow span of four thousand years. Yet the symbols have all remained the same, both in meaning and in form. And it was about midway of that four-millennium span that the serpent-sage Patanjali was supposed to have dropped from his threshold-guarding post above, to reveal on earth the secrets of the yogic way to those prepared to hear.

Still further: in America too, as already shown, a serpent god, the Feathered Serpent, was recognized as symbolic of the power that casts off death to be resurrected: and this from as early, apparently, as the Olmec site of La Venta, ca. 1200-800 B.C. Below, from an Aztec codex fully two millennia later, a worshiper offers gifts and incense to a serpent deity in the form of a slightly modified caduceus; and in an

263. Altar of the Caduceus. Aztec. Pre-Columbian

It is worth remarking in connection with this picture that an old Navaho medicine man, Jeff King (who died in 1964 at about the age of 110), declared to us in 1942 that the pollen paintings of the war ceremonial then used by him to bless young men of the reservation being drafted into the U. S. Army were derived "from a cave on the east slope of a certain mountain." He declared that he had visited the cave in his boyhood and could visit it again when he wished to refresh his memory of the paintings. "Outside the cave," he said, "was a stone carving of two snakes intertwined, the heads facing east and west." Since his last visit, however, the serpent-monument had been undermined by water and had collapsed, so that it now was no more.[10]

elegant work of Classic Mayan art, below, we see the Feathered Serpent rising from a vessel to receive the offerings of a priest.

264. *Kukulcan, The Feathered Serpent, Receives an Offering.* A.D. *3rd century. Mexico*

Fig. 265

Fig. 272

cf. Fig. 130

An extraordinarily interesting design from a still later American period appears on this stone disk from Moundville, Alabama. Interpreted in Oriental terms, its central sign would be said to represent the "fear-banishing gesture" (*abhaya-mudra*) of a Bodhisattva hand showing on its palm the compassionate Eye of Mercy, pierced by the sight of the sorrows of this world. The framing pair of rattlesnakes, like those of the Aztec Calendar Stone, would then symbolize the maya power binding us to this vortex of rebirths, and the opposed knots would stand for the two doors, east and west, of the ascent and descent, appearances and disappearances, of all things in the endless round. Furthermore, the fact that the eye is at the center of the composition would suggest, according to this reading, that compassion (the quality of the Bodhisattva) is the ultimate sustaining and moving power of the universe, transcending and overcoming its pain. And finally, the fact that the hand is represented as though viewed simultaneously from back and front would say that this Bodhisattva power unites opposites. For this manner of representation is deliberate here—a frequently repeated motif in the monuments of this particular American tradition.

265. Engraved Stone Disk. A.D. *1200-1600. Moundville, Alabama*

266, 267, 268, 269, 270. *Designs Engraved on Shells. Mississippi Culture. ca.* A.D. 1200-1600

In these renderings from another province of the same culminating period, the
so-called "Mississippi Culture Complex," A.D. ca. 1200-1600, the world-supporting and
-moving center is symbolized by an encircled cross (top left)—which in Mexico was
the symbol of Quetzalcoatl. The whirling carousel of winged rattlesnakes brings to
this serpent-symphony a certain humorous, joyous note, while the counterclockwise
lion-bird parade (top center) suggests comparison with the portal guardians of King
Gudea's cup. Next (top right) is a design that in India would be read (like the
caduceus of Gudea's cup) as symbolic of the opposed side nerves and central serpent
channel of the Kundalini.* The hand bearing an encircled cross (lower left) bal-
ances the symbol of death in the other bend of the serpent, and a pair of ornamented
serpent dancers bursting from a rattlesnake skin (lower right) reiterate the universal serpent-theme of renewal of life through the sloughing of death. And finally

Figs. 266-270

cf. Fig. 251

Fig. 306

* See below, pp. 331ff.

271. Mayan Maize God. A.D. *7th-8th century*   *272. The White Tara.* A.D. *19th century. Tibet*

Fig. 273   (opposite), is the unmistakable saint, savior, god, or bodhisattva of this heritage,
sitting cross-legged as he teaches, leaning slightly forward, with his right hand held
Fig. 102   in the "boon-bestowing" posture. Compare the left hand of the Olmec jaguar-man
(Figure 102); also, the whole symbolic presence of the Mayan maize god (upper
Fig. 271   left): the mask of death on his breast, and his two hands held in absolutely classic
Hindu-Buddhist style, with the left in the "fear-dispelling" and the right in the "boon-
bestowing" sign.

But are we justified in proposing such broad cross-cultural references? Or let us
put the case the other way: Is it reasonable to maintain, in cases where identical
motifs appear in identically structured compositions—with, in many instances,
analogous myths and legends to support them—that the informing ideas must not
be assumed to have been pretty much the same as well?

What, however, about that serpent of Eden, who was not worshiped as the lord
of life, but humbled, cursed, and rejected?

What is different about that fellow is simply that his role has been taken from him
and given to another, a late arrival in his garden, who was now to be revered in
his stead as "the Lord that kills and brings to life" (I Samuel 2:6, Hannah's song).

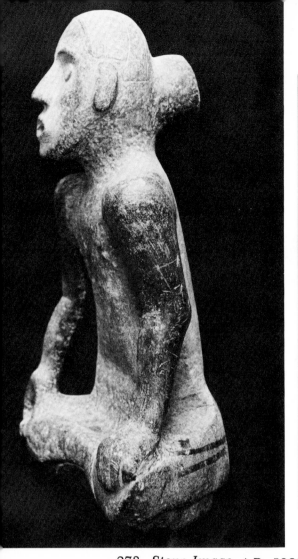

273. *Stone Image.* A.D. 1200-1600. *Raccoon Creek, Georgia*

Serpent gods, however, do not die, and history records that the subtle old master of the garden, recovering, took upon the newcomer an amusing and ironical revenge. For as we are told in II Kings 18: there was a brazen serpent worshiped in the very temple of Jerusalem along with an image of his spouse, the mighty goddess, who was known there as the Asherah. And the brazen serpent's name was Nehushtan. King Hezekiah (719-691 B.C.) had them both broken up and burned, but even that was not the end; for by the period of the Maccabees (second century B.C.) the serpent Fig. 274 had become attached to the image of Yahweh himself, and with that embarrassing development the question naturally arose as to who, after all, was Satan and who, or what, was God. Compare Titian's image of the serpent, and Blake's rendering of cf. Figs. 6, 180 Job's vision of his god.

274. "The Anguipede," Snake-footed Forms of Yahweh. 2nd-1st century B.C.

The Jewish Anguipede is represented normally as a war god, bearing on his right arm a shield and in his left hand the whip of Helios. On his head in one case we see the figure of Ares, Greek god of war. Another example shows him as Helios, standing on a lion which in turn is trampling a crocodile. The second, smaller human figure in this case is Horus the Child (Harpocrates), with his left hand to his mouth and a cornucopia on his right arm. (Compare the elements of this composition with those of Figure 10: the crocodile, the lion-legged throne supporting Min of the Uplifted arm, and before Min,

Horus the Child.) It is interesting to remark the varying combinations of bird and serpent themes: eagle and serpent, rooster and serpent. Both birds are solar symbols; hence the lion's head (also a solar symbol), which in one case replaces the cock. We note also the Anguipede in the sun chariot, between the moon and morning star, above an inscription reading (in Greek letters) Sabaō[th]. Professor Goodenough interprets the little animal-headed figure with the eagle as the Egyptian god Anubis bearing a sistrum in his left hand and "a peculiar pronged instrument in his right."[11]

Now according to Second Kings, the idol that Hezekiah destroyed was "the bronze serpent that Moses had made" on that curious occasion described in Numbers 21, when the people, hungry in the wilderness, having complained against both Moses and his god, "Yahweh sent fiery serpents among them and they bit the people, so that many people of Israel died. And the people came to Moses, and said, 'We have sinned, for we have spoken against Yahweh and against you; pray to Yahweh, that he take away the serpents from us.' So Moses prayed for the people. And Yahweh said to Moses, 'Make a fiery serpent and set it on a pole; and every one who is bitten, when he sees it, shall live.' " Fig. 278

275. *Goddess of the Tree of Life. ca.* 2500 B.C.

The female figure at the left, before the serpent, is almost certainly the goddess Gula-Bau of Figure 74-75, while the male on the right, who is a god, as we know from his horned lunar crown, is no less surely her son-husband Dumuzi, "Son of the Abyss," the ever-dying, ever-reviving Sumerian prototype of the resurrected savior.

276. *Demeter and Plutus. 5th century* B.C.

The goddess of the Eleusinian mysteries here is seen with her divine child Ploutos, or Plutus (not the same as Plouton or Pluto, god of the Netherworld, though frequently identified with him by assimilation of the names), of whom the poet Hesiod wrote:

> *Happy, happy is the mortal who*
> *doth meet him as he goes,*
> *For his hands are full of blessings*
> *and his treasure overflows.*
> (*Theogony* 973-974)[12]

277. *Zeus Meilichios. 4th century* B.C.

Here, as Jane Harrison has pointed out, "Zeus, father of gods and men, is figured by his worshipers as a snake. . . . The colossal size of the beast as it towers above its human adorers is the *Magnificat* of the artist echoed by the worshipers."[13]

278. *The Serpent Lifted Up.* A.D. *16th century. Germany*

"And as Moses lifted up the serpent in the wilderness, so must the Son of Man be lifted up . . ." (John 3:14). According to the Christian view, both Moses' lifting up of the healing serpent (Numbers 21:5-9) and Christ's Crucifixion were historical events, with the earlier to be read as a prefiguration of the latter. However, in Gnostic thought the two could be and were regarded as alternative manifestations of the same transcendant power, and since the thaler illustrated here dates from a period when Gnostic and Neoplatonic thought were fashionable in Europe, it is entirely possible that Hieronymus, the artist-craftsman who fashioned this Renaissance coin, may have intended to suggest behind its orthodox appearance a covert reference (for the learned) to the ageless theme of the saving wisdom of the serpent power.

It is not easy to reconcile this command with that of Exodus 20:4, to make no graven image. However, it accords well with the legend of Moses' rod, which he was taught to change into a snake to frighten Pharaoh (Exodus 4:1-5), and with which, some seasons later, he struck a rock in the desert to bring forth the life-restoring serpent element, water (Numbers 20:7-11).

Nor were these the only and last victories of the subtle serpent of Eden against the god who had taken away his garden with its tree. In the earliest Christian centuries there were actually Ophitic Christian sects (Greek ὄφις, "serpent") honoring the serpent of the garden as a first appearance of the Savior. For as in his second appearance, as Jesus, he had overthrown the Old Testament law (Romans 10:4), so in his first, as the serpent, he had urged on mankind disobedience of that newcomer to the garden who was now thinking to hoard for himself the fruit of the tree of eternal life. The fourth-century saint Epiphanius has given the following description of the manner of worship of one of these unorthodox Christian companies:

> They have a snake, which they keep in a certain chest—the *cista mystica*—and which at the hour of their mysteries they bring forth from its cave. They heap loaves upon the table and summon the serpent. Since the cave is open it comes out. It is a cunning beast and, knowing their foolish ways, it crawls up on the table and rolls in the loaves; this they say is the perfect sacrifice. Wherefore, as I have been told, they not only break the bread in which the snake has rolled and administer it to those present, but each one kisses the snake on the mouth, for the snake has been tamed by a spell, or has been made gentle for their fraud by some other diabolical method. And they fall down before it and call this the Eucharist, consummated by the beast rolling in the loaves. And through it, as they say, they send forth a hymn to the Father on high, thus concluding their mysteries."[14]

279. St. John the Evangelist

Like the *kantharos* of the Dionysian cult, the chalice of the Catholic Mass is an inexhaustible vessel, whence the blood of redemption pours without cease. And therein the wine of this earth, transubstantiated, becomes itself that saving blood. "No one has ascended into heaven," said Jesus to Nicodemus the Pharisee, "but he who descended from heaven, the Son of man. And as Moses lifted up the serpent in the wilderness, so must the Son of man be lifted up; that whoever believes in him may have eternal life" (John 3:13-15).

About a century earlier another scandalized saint, Hippolytus (who lived until ca. 230), had reported on a serpent sect of his own time known as Perates—from the Greek πέρᾶτος, "on the opposite side," which is a word exactly corresponding in sense to the Sanskrit *paramita*, "yonder shore," in the phrase *prajna-paramita*, "the Wisdom of the Yonder Shore."*

> Their cosmos consists of Father, Son, and Matter, each of which three principles contains many forces. Midway between the Father and Matter, the Son, the Logos, has his place, the Serpent that moves eternally toward the unmoved Father and moved Matter; now it turns to the Father and gathers up forces in its countenance; and now, after receiving the forces, it turns toward Matter, and upon Matter, which is without attribute and form, the Son imprints the ideas that had previously been imprinted upon the Son by the Father. Moreover, no one can be saved and rise up again without the Son, who is the serpent. For it is he who brought the paternal models down from aloft, and it is he who carries back up again those who have been awakened from sleep and have resumed the features of the Father.[15]

Figs. 280, 281 Here are the inside and the outside of an Ophitic communion bowl of Hippolytus' time. In the center, the forward part of a winged serpent (left wing lost) coils around a hemisphere, from the base of which there radiate spikes of flame. Sixteen naked figures, nine female, seven male, all regarding the winged serpent, stand in attitudes cf. Figs. 245-248 of worship, with five of the women in the Medici Venus pose.

Apparently we are viewing here the interior of a cult sanctuary symbolic of the highest heaven, where the cycling serpent, having ascended from the lower plane of time through the golden sun-door to eternity, is now beheld in the likeness, not of a lunar, but of a winged solar serpent, radiant with its own light. The mound or hemisphere in the center, about which it has wrapped itself, is the summit of the cosmic egg, inside of which all mortals dwell. The mystic company, that is to say, is here *above* the egg. They have ascended (spiritually) through the sun-door, which opens at the instant of noon at the summit of the sky. Its active panels, which at noon separate, have here closed again beneath, and the company is now (in knowledge) in eternity, beyond all pairs of opposites: death and birth, good and evil, light and dark. The normal limitations of human thought and sense, the clothing of the mind, have been destroyed in the fiery passage, the purging flames of which are now blazing at their feet; and the serpent wrapped around the mound, at which they gaze in silent rapture, combines the forms that would have been seen below as opposites: the serpent, earthbound, and the bird of air, in winged flight.

On the outside of the bowl is a view of the heavenly vault from below, with its circles of cycling spheres. Four cherubs blowing conch shells and trumpets are stationed at the quarters, symbolizing the four winds of the round of space and the four seasons of the round of time. Twenty-four columns support this structure, as hours the day. And finally, around the base there is an inscription in slightly incorrect Greek of four quotations from separate Orphic hymns:

---

* See pp. 215ff.

280-281. *Alabaster "Serpent Bowl."* A.D. *2nd or 3rd century.*
Probably Orphic. Provenance unknown. Above, interior; below, exteri

Hear, Thou who turnest forever the
  radiant sphere of distant motion. . . .

Originally Heaven and Earth were a
  single form—the Cosmic Egg. . . .

First, light—Phanes—appeared: named
  also Dionysus, because it moves in a
  circle round the infinitely lofty Mount
  Olympus. . . .

He is glittering Zeus, Father of All the World.[16]

Compare the two serpent kings with the figures at the foot of the Djed-pillar in Figure 17, the solar disk in that composition corresponding to the Buddha figure in this. Compare also Figures 283 and 284, the former from the "active imagination" of a patient of C. G. Jung, who states of it:

"This picture was made by a middle-aged woman who, without being neurotic, was struggling for spiritual development and used for this purpose the method of active imagination. These efforts induced her to make a drawing of the birth of a new insight or conscious awareness (eye) from the depths of the unconscious (sea). Here the eye signifies the self."[17]

283 (lower left). *Painting by a Patient of C. G. Jung*

284 (lower right). *Motif from a Roman Mosaic Floor. Tunis*

282. *Two Serpent Kings Supporting the Lotus of the Preaching Buddha.* A.D. *2nd century. India*

Now as the idea of transcending death can be interpreted in two ways, so too the image of the serpent. The first, more popular way is of reincarnation, eternal return, death, but then rebirth, as in the waning and waxing moon, or the serpent's sloughing its skin. However, one can also think of an ultimate transcendence of this everlasting round through an attainment of unfailing light, like that of the sun; and this is the aim of yoga. The waxing moon, night by night, approaches the fullness of the solar sphere, to which it attains the fifteenth night; after which, night by night, it again falls back into darkness. According to the mystical way of the Wisdom of the Yonder Shore, however, the ultimate aim of a life is to have one's light remain at the full—once having attained through many lifetimes to that apogee, to leap from Moon to Sun in consciousness and let the body go its way, like a waning moon: and
Fig. 282   it was just such a victory that the Buddha achieved in his final birth. Enthroned on
cf. Fig. 10 a lotus pedestal, he is shown here being borne up from the watery abyss by a pair of serpent kings. So may we too be raised by virtue of the serpent power to the status of a Buddha, a sun god, on a lotus throne of undiminishing light.

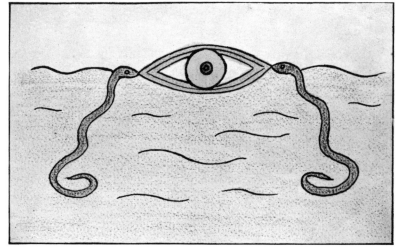

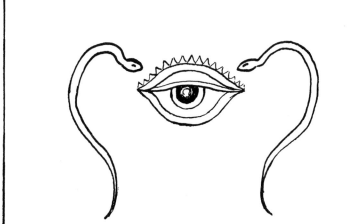

285. *Buddha in the Earth-Touching Posture.* A.D. *9th or 10th century. India*

The moment in the Buddha-life represented in this image immediately follows that of Figure 181. The two temptations represented there having failed, the god who rules all life and whose name is "Desire and Death" transformed himself into the god of "Duty," Dharma, and in that capacity challenged the right of the Blessed One to be sitting on the immovable spot beneath the axial tree, indifferent to the duties of his social role. To which the Blessed One replied by simply moving his right hand to his knee and letting the fingertips touch the earth, to summon the mother-goddess Earth herself to bear witness to his right to be there. And the goddess thundered with a hundred, a thousand, a hundred thousand roars: "I bear you witness." Whereupon the elephant on which the god Dharma sat bent its knees in worship. The army and three daughters of Mara dispersed. And that night the Blessed One acquired in the first watch the knowledge of previous existences; in the middle watch, the divine eye; in the last, knowledge of the Twelve Knots of Dependent Origination;[18] and at sunrise, omniscience.

286. Shakyamuni. A.D. *early 6th century. Hopei, China*

The hands, "fear-dispelling" (*abhaya*) and "boon-bestowing" (*varada*). Pedestal, above an inverted lotus.

3. The One Thus Come

THE word "yoga" is from the Sanskrit verbal root *yuj*, meaning "to yoke, to join," to yoke one thing to another. What is to be joined through yoga is consciousness to its source, so that one lives in the knowledge of identity with that source and not merely with the limited ego of the daylight personality. Or to recast the idea in terms of lunar and solar light: what is to be joined is the reflected light of a sublunar, temporal consciousness to the timeless solar source of all light and all consciousness whatsoever. Such an aim would seem to be essentially that expressed in the words of Saint Paul: "it is no longer I who live, but Christ who lives in me" (Galatians 2:20)—except that in the usual Christian view, no one is to believe that he is in any sense *identical* with Christ.

For here, as in all three of the great Levantine faiths sharing the Biblical concept of divinity (Judaism, Christianity, and Islam), where the godhead is regarded as a transcendental personality outside of and ontologically distinct from his creatures, a logic of duality is maintained, and the religious aim is not to achieve an experience of *identity* with godhood but to establish and maintain a *relationship* of some kind by virtue of membership in a social group believed to be supernaturally endowed: the Jewish race, the Christian church, or the Mohammedan *Sunna*.

287. *Shivaite Mendicant with a Trident*

Shivo-'ham, "I am Shiva." "I am neither male, female nor sexless, but Shiva, the Peaceful One, whose form is self-effulgent; whose form is powerful radiance. Neither a child, a youth, nor an ancient, I am of no age, but Shiva, the Blessed-Peaceful One, who is the only Cause of the Origin and Dissolution of the world."[19]

"The trident," states Heinrich Zimmer, "is one of the symbolic implements of the pil-grim-mendicants of the Shivaite creed. These Hindu monks in their apparel imitate their deity in his manifestation as the homeless wandering ascetic. To the simpler devotee of the god (in fear of their power and of their wrath, which is easily roused) such holy men are personifications of the god himself, who takes delight in assuming human form and thus approaching men to test their devotion and to confer on them his initiations."[20]

Fig. 287

The aim of Indian yoga, on the other hand, is a realization of identity, and the key phrase, the guiding thought to this experience is that announced in the *Chhandogya Upanishad*, as taught by the sage Aruni to his son: *tat tvam asi*, "thou art That"—you, my son, are already yourself that light of consciousness, that ground of being, that bliss in truth, which you wish to know.

Expressed in algebraic terms, if we let x stand for that mystery of being beyond categories which is to be known, and a for "you," Aruni's son (i.e., oneself), then the message of Aruni's teaching might at first seem to be $a = x$. However, on second thought, since it is obvious that the "you" intended cannot possibly be the temporal, named, ephemeral appearance with which, in one's daily consciousness, one identifies oneself, the meditation appropriate to the contemplation of that mere effect of maya would be, rather, *neti, neti*, "not this, not this"; for which thought the appropriate algebraic formula would have to be, $a \neq x$, "thou art *not* That." And so we arrive in effect at the apparently absurd formulation $a \neq = x$ (a does not, in its temporal aspect, yet does, in its immortal, equal x), as the clue to the mystical secret.

Moreover, this thought is to be applied not only to oneself, but to everything whether on earth, in heaven, or in hell. The yogi is to penetrate and cast aside (as the serpent sloughs its skin) the whole spectacle of phenomenality—forms, names, and relationships—letting only that which shines through all as undifferentiated consciousness remain to his contemplation.

Pick up, for example, any object at all. Draw mentally a ring around it, setting it off from the world. Forgetting its use, forgetting its name, not remembering that it was made, or how, or that names are given to its parts; not knowing *what* it is, but only *that* it is, simply regard it; and so then: What *is* it?

Anything at all, any stick, stone, cat, or bird, dissociated from every concept this way, will be seen as a wonder without "meaning," a beginning and end in itself—like the universe, "thus come" (*tathagata*). The Buddha is called the "One Thus Come," Tathagata, and "all things are Buddha-things." Or as James Joyce states in *Ulysses*: "Any object, intensely regarded, may be a gate of access to the incorruptible eon of the gods."[21] For contemplating it thus we are thrown back upon our own pure state, as subject to an object, each then the aspect of a mystery "thus come":

> *You light the fire;*
> *I'll show you something nice,—*
> *A great ball of snow!*[22]

288. *Shrike on a Dead Branch. Miyamoto Musashi*

289. *Wagtail on a Withered Lotus Leaf. Mu-ch'i*

290. *Heron. Tan-an Chiden*

291. *Tea Bowl and Whisk*

292. *Sunflowers. Vincent van Gogh*

293. *Old Shoes. Vincent van Gogh*

294. *Black Sun. Isamu Noguchi*

295. *Solitary Angler. Ma Yüan*

4. The Wisdom of the Yonder Shore

THE first aphorism of Patanjali's classic handbook of yoga supplies the key to the entire work:

> *Yoga consists in the intentional stopping*
> *of the spontaneous activity of the mind-stuff.*[23]

The idea is that within the gross gray matter of the brain there is an active "subtle substance" (*sukshma*) that is continually changing form. Responsive to sound, touch, sight, taste, and smell, this fluent inmost substance of the nerves takes on the shapes of all their sense impressions—which, indeed, is how and why we experience them. Moving the eyes quickly, one can observe the speed with which this sensitive matter assumes forms and dismisses them. There is a difficulty, however, in that its movement never ceases. Any person unused to meditation, desiring to fix in his mind a single image or thought, will find within seconds that he is already entertaining associated thoughts. The untrained mind will not stand still, and yoga is the intentional stopping of its movement.

It may be asked, why should anyone wish to bring about such a state?

The mind is likened, in reply, to the surface of a pond rippled by a wind. At the opening of the Book of Genesis we read that "the Wind of God moved upon the face of the waters." The wind (*spiritus, pneuma, ruach*) ruffled the waters, and that was the first act of creation. Only then did God say, "Let there be light." And there was light fluctuating on the waters.

The idea of yoga is to cause that wind to subside and let the waters return to rest. For when a wind blows and waters stir, the waves break and distort both the light and its reflections, so that all that can be seen are colliding broken forms. Not until the waters will have been stilled, cleansed of stirred-up sediment and made mirror-bright, will the one reflected image appear that on the rippling waves had been broken: that of the clouds and pure sky above, the trees along the shore, and down deep in the still, pure water itself, the sandy bottom and the fish. Then alone will that single image be known of which the wave-borne reflections are but fragments and distortions. And this single image can be likened to that of the Self realized in yoga. It is the Ultimate—the Form of forms—of which the phenomena of this world are but imperfectly seen, ephemeral distortions: the God-form, the Buddha-form, which is truly our own Knowledge-form, and with which it is the goal of yoga to unite us.

Fig. 296

And there are those who, once united, become so established in this knowledge of identity that the rippling field of secondary forms falls away. The body, as they say, "drops off"; or as others might say, those yogis die. But on the other hand, it is possible, also, to return to this world of continually breaking forms, open the eyes,

296. *Mount Fuji at Dawn Reflected in Lake Yamanaka*

let the winds again blow, and enjoy the kaleidoscopic changes in the knowledge that all these dancing figures are revelations of that one Form of forms of which each of us, in his own way, is an incarnation.

The method of stilling the wind, therefore, is the first problem of yoga. And it is a problem that is strictly psychological: mainly a matter of shifting the mind's concern from surfaces to inwardness. Whereupon a second problem arising will be, to bring the mind back again to the surface of things at play on the waters of life, blown about by the winds of the mind. A third and culminating task will then be that of holding both to the enjoyment of these changing things and to one's fixed centering within, recognizing in what was formerly experienced as *two* fields but one—which is the beginning and end of the ultimate, nondual "Wisdom (prajna) of the Yonder Shore (paramita)." As formulated in a Chinese guide to yoga, *The Book of the Secret of the Golden Flower*:

> Emptiness comes as the first of the three contemplations. All things are looked upon as empty. Then follows delusion. Although it is known that they are empty, things are not destroyed, but a man attends to his affairs in the midst of emptiness. Yet though one does not destroy things, neither does one pay attention to them: this is contemplation of the center.[24]

The term "emptiness" in a text of this kind is to be read as pointing beyond its usual meaning, "emptiness" as the opposite of "fullness." It is intended, in fact, to point beyond all categories altogether—including even the category "beyond." As D. T. Suzuki has written of this term:

> Emptiness (*shunyata*) does not mean "relativity," or "phenomenality," or "nothingness," but rather means the Absolute, or something of transcendental nature, although this rendering is also misleading. . . . When Buddhists declare all things to be empty, they are not advocating a nihilistic view; on the contrary an ultimate reality is hinted at, which cannot be subsumed under the categories of logic. With them, to proclaim the conditionality of things is to point to the existence of something altogether unconditioned and transcendent of all determination. Shunyata may thus often be most appropriately rendered by the Absolute.[25]

The classic Mahayana Buddhist document on this point is the *Prajnaparamita Hridaya Sutra, Guiding Thread to the Heart of the Wisdom of the Yonder Shore*, which is redacted in two versions, a longer and a shorter, of which the latter runs as follows:[26]

ADORATION TO THE ALL-KNOWING

When the venerable Bodhisattva Avalokiteshvara was engaged in the study of the profound Wisdom of the Yonder Shore, he thought thus: "There are five constituents of mundane consciousness: form, perception, thought, feeling, understanding." And he recognized that all were by nature empty.

Fig. 301

"O Shariputra," said he, "form here is emptiness, emptiness is form: emptiness is not different from form, form not different from emptiness. What is form is emptiness: what is emptiness is form. And the same applies to perception, thought, feeling and understanding.

"O Shariputra, all things here have the character of emptiness: no beginning, no end: they are faultless and not faultless: they do not increase, they do not diminish. Therefore, O Shariputra, there is in this emptiness no form—no perception—no thought—no disposition—no consciousness: no eye, ear, nose, tongue, body, mind, form, sound, color, touch, or objects; there is nothing for the eye, nothing for the ear, nothing for the nose, nothing for the tongue, nothing for the body, nothing for the mind:

> there is no knowledge, no ignorance;
> no extinction of knowledge, no extinction of ignorance;
> no action, no extinction of action;
> no consciousness, no extinction of consciousness;
> no name-and-form, no extinction of name-and-form;
> no six senses, no extinction of six senses;
> no contact, no extinction of contact;
> there is no perception, no extinction of perception;
> no desire, no extinction of desire;
> no attachment, no extinction of attachment;
> no being, no extinction of being;
> no birth, no extinction of birth;
> no suffering, no extinction of suffering;
> no path, no knowledge, no attainment.

"There are in the mind of the Bodhisattva dwelling in the Wisdom of the Yonder Shore no obstacles whatsoever. Going beyond the envelopment of consciousness, free of fear, beyond the course of change, he enjoys primal and final Nirvana. All the Buddhas of the past, of the present, and of the future, dwelling in the Wisdom of the Yonder Shore, awaken to this highest perfect knowledge.

"Therefore, one must know that the Wisdom of the Yonder Shore is the great 'magic formula' [*mantra*], the magic formula of the Great Wisdom, the most excellent magic formula, the peerless magic formula, capable of allaying all pain. It is truth, because it is not falsehood: a magic formula proclaimed in the Wisdom of the Yonder Shore. And it goes like this: '*Gaté gaté paragaté parasamgaté, bodhi svaha!* O Thou who art gone, gone, gone to the Yonder Shore, disembarked on the Yonder Shore, O Awakening! Hail!' "[27]

To appreciate the ultimate ranges of reference of the symbolism of great myths—whether of the Orient or of the Occident—we must now try to arrive at some sort of understanding of what this magic formula might mean.

297. The White Tara, with Eye in Palm. A.D. *19th century. Tibet*

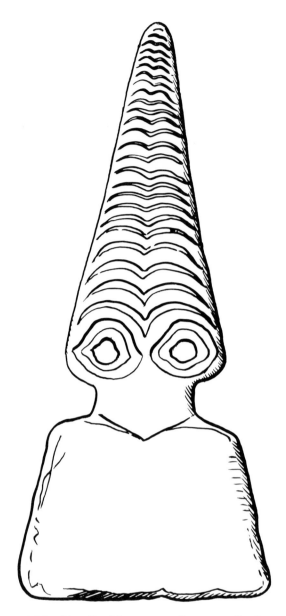

298. Eye Goddess. ca. 2800 B.C. Syria

299 (opposite). Bodhisattva Ushnishasitatapatra, "White Umbrella Diadem." A.D. *19th century. Tibet*

Surrounded by Buddhas and Bodhisattvas, and having one hundred and seventeen heads symbolizing her influence in all spheres of being, this augmented form of the White Tara holds in her left hand the world umbrella (*axis mundi*) and in her right the Wheel of the Law. Eyes of mercy innumerable bespangle the flaming trifold aureole and whole body of this infinitely compassionate divinity. Beneath her numerous feet stand those who have turned to her for enlightenment, while beneath the feet of the three "furious" powers at the bottom of the picture lie those still tortured by lust, resentment, and delusion. To the left and right of these are the two Taras, the white (in normal form) and the green, each with an eye in the palm of her boon-bestowing right hand and holding in her left the lotus-symbol of her grace. The sun and moon in the upper corners symbolize the unity in Buddha-consciousness of the virtues of eternity and time, nirvana and the world, while the lamas at the top center represent the orthodox line of Tibetan teachers of the doctrine.

300. Thousand-armed, Eleven-headed Avalokitesh–
vara, with an Eye in the Palm of each Hand.
A.D. *19th century. China*

The *Tsao Hsiang Liang-tu Ching*, a Chinese Lamaist text printed in 1748 and quoted, in part, in the script of this icon, declares that the innermost circle of eight arms belongs to the "Absolute," or "Truth Body" (*Dharmakaya*) of the Buddha; the next circle, of forty arms bearing tokens of power, to the "Meditation," or "Bliss Body" (*Sambhogakaya*); and the remaining five circles of nine hundred and fifty-two arms with open hands to the "Manifest," "Measured Out," "Temporal," or "Personalized Body" (*Nirmanakaya*) of the Buddha. This "Three Body" (*Trikaya*) doctrine is a fundamental Mahayana tenet, matching, essentially, those three planes or orders of Buddha consciousness that are represented respectively in the Chikhai, the Chönyid, and the Sidpa Bardo of the Tibetan *Book of the Dead*. As stated in the Chinese inscription, all three bodies have here become manifest in the one form of this Bodhisattva of inexhaustible compassion.

According to legend, when Avalokiteshvara looked down upon this suffering world he was filled with such compassion that his head burst into innumerable heads (iconographically represented as eleven), while from his body sprang a thousand helping arms and hands, like an aura of dazzling rays, and in the palm of each hand there appeared an eye of unimpeded vision. At the top of this picture he is seen among the gods in the "earth-touching" posture of mercy. To his left and right, below, are sun and moon. The topmost head of the pyramid is red and is the Buddha Amitabha's, of whose quality of compassion Avalokiteshvara is the chief ambassador in this world. The second head is indigo, and is that of Yama, the Lord of Death, whose judgments are transcended by the mercy of the all-regarding Bodhisattva. And finally, the nine remaining heads radiate through all three worlds the realization of the immanence through all change of nirvanic peace.

301. Avalokiteshvara-Padamapani. A.D. 600-642. *India*

The meaning of the title Padmapani is "Lotus in Hand." That of Avalokiteshvara is more obscure, and a number of suggestions have been made. The element *ava-* means "down"; *lok* means "to look at, to view, to contemplate," *lokita*, "looking" but also "looked at, seen, beheld," and *loka*, "the world," "space," or any "region of the universe"; *ishvara*, finally, means "lord." Hence, such readings have been given as: "Lord of What We See," i.e., of the present world; but also, "the Lord Whom We See, the Lord Revealed, the Lord Who Is Or Was Seen." Tibetans read: "the Lord Who Looks." ("He is so called," states a relevant text, "because he regards with compassion beings suffering from the evils of existence.")[29] Still another reading of the Sanskrit term is, "the Lord Who Looks Down From On High."

"The great Mahayana Bodhisattva Avalokiteshvara," states Heinrich Zimmer of this enormously popular and best-beloved Bodhisattva, "is a personification of the highest ideal of the Mahayana Buddhist career. His legend recounts that when, following a series of eminently virtuous incarnations, he was about to enter into the surcease of nirvana, an uproar, like the sound of a general thunder, rose in all the worlds. The great being knew that this was a wail of lament uttered by all created things—the rocks and stones as well as the trees, insects, gods, animals, demons, and human beings of all the spheres of the universe—at the prospect of his imminent departure from the realms of birth. And so, in his compassion, he renounced for himself the boon of nirvana until all beings without exception should be prepared to enter in before him—like the good shepherd who permits his flock to pass first through the gate and then goes through himself, closing it behind him."[30]

Every pore of the body of Avalokiteshvara contains and pours forth thousands of Buddhas, saints of all kinds, entire worlds. From his fingers flow rivers of ambrosia that cool the hells and feed the hungry ghosts. The Taras* are the tears of his eyes; and he is the giver, also, of the great formula of the Wisdom of the Yonder Shore,** as well as that of the prayer wheels of Tibet: OM MANI PADME HUM.*** The Dalai Lama is regarded as an incarnation of his presence; but he is present also in the intercourse of all beings insofar as they serve to illuminate each other. He appears to brahmans as a brahman, to merchants as a merchant, to insects as an insect, to each in the aspect of its kind; and he may have two arms, four, six, eight, or innumerable—with an eye in the palm of each hand, pierced as it were by the spectacle of the world's sorrow and compassionately sending forth Taras, i.e., saving tears.[31]

* See above, p. 52.
** See above, p. 316.
*** See above, p. 254.

302. *The "Warka Head." 4th millennium* B.C.
    Sumer

Originally the eyes and eyebrows of this
lovely head were inlaid with lapis lazuli and
shell, and the hair was no doubt brightly
tinted. The unique, sensitive rendering of
the cheeks, mouth, and chin announces—
like the brilliant opening statement of a great
symphony—the new spiritual role of the female power and the new spiritual aim of
humanity that were formulated for all future
time in the culture of that mysterious Sumerian race to which our whole world owes
all its basic arts of literate civilized life. No
longer a goddess merely of instinctual physical fecundity, the woman of this visage is a
divinity of spiritual light, as revealed through
that human organ of light, the eyes. The
primitive claims of biological and social ne-
cessities have been decisively surpassed in
the maturation of the ideal of a developed,
properly human character, endowed with the
qualities of a personal spiritual life. It would
be a mistake to classify such a divinity as a
"fertility goddess," unless by "fertility" something much more than the mere production
of crops and of herds and children is meant.
This might well be the portrait of a goddess-
priestess such as is depicted in the top range
of the contemporary Warka Vase (Figs. 70-
72), receiving offerings at the summit of the
cosmic mountain.

303. *Kwannon.* A.D. *early 8th century. Japan*

In China and Japan the feminine aspect of the Bodhisattva Avalokiteshvara is emphasized in the character of Kuan-yin (Japanese, Kwannon), of whose universal compassion the following legend is told.

THE LEGEND OF THE BRIDE OF MERO

In a certain rural, western province of old China, there was a time when the Buddha, his Law, and his Order were disdained, and men devoted themselves rather to riding swift horses and to archery. But the merciful Bodhisattva showered her compassionate benevolence upon them and led them in the following way to the Dharma.

In one of the villages of that province, situated on the banks of a remote upper reach of the Yellow River, there appeared early one summer day a strange young woman of the greatest beauty and most noble grace. Her almond eyes, jet black, flashed from beneath slender brows that were like little bows, and the lovely oval of her placid face was framed by soft waves of blackest hair. She carried a basket in her hands, woven of bamboo, lined with green leaves of the willow and filled with fresh golden-scaled fish of the river. Moreover, as she called her wares her voice suggested the play of a breeze among jade beads. The villagers stared and questioned each other, but none could say whence she had come or who she might be.

She appeared this way every morning, and as soon as her basket was emptied would disappear so quickly that the people sometimes doubted she had been among them at all. The young men, of course, having taken notice, daily watched for her appearances, and then, one morning, would not let her pass. They began begging her to marry them, but she answered, "O honorable young gentlemen, I do certainly wish to marry; but I cannot marry you all. If there were one among

you, however, who could recite by heart the entire Sutra of the Compassionate Kuan-yin, he would be the one I would wed."

So deep was the darkness of the minds of those young men that they had never even heard of that sutra. Nevertheless, when evening came they met and vied with each other, and when dawn broke there were thirty who had learned the text by heart. The young woman said, when these then accosted her, "But, O honorable young gentlemen, I am only one woman; I cannot marry thirty young men. However, if any one among you can explain the meaning of the sutra, he is the one I shall wed."

The following dawn found ten youths waiting to claim the young woman's hand; for ten now understood. But she replied, "O young sirs, I am but one woman; I cannot marry ten husbands. However, if any one of you will in three days have *experienced* the meaning of the Sutra of the Compassionate Kuan-yin, him surely shall I marry gladly."

And on the morning of that third day there was waiting for her just one, the young Mero. And when she saw him there, she smiled.

"O Son of the House of Me," she said, for she could recognize his bearing, "I perceive that you have indeed realized the meaning of the blessed Sutra of the Compassionate Kuan-yin and do gladly accept you as my husband. My house you will find this evening at the river bend, and my parents there to receive you."

And so, when evening fell, Mero, alone at

the bend of the shore, searched out and discovered her little house among the reeds and rocks. At its gate there were standing an old man and woman, beckoning. He approached and said to them, "I am the son of the House of Me, and have come to claim your daughter as my bride"; to which the old man responded, "We have been waiting for you a long time." And the old woman, leading the way, opened the door to her daughter's room and Mero went in.

But the room was empty. From the open window he saw a stretch of sand as far as to the river, and in the sand the prints of a woman's feet, which he followed, to find at the water's edge two golden sandals. He looked about in the increasing twilight, and saw no house now among the rocks. There was only a cluster of dry bamboo by the river softly rustling in an evening breeze. And then suddenly he knew: the fisher-maid had been none other than the Bodhisattva herself, and he comprehended fully how great is the merciful benevolence of the infinitely compassionate Kuan-yin.

> *She made a bridge of love, that he*
> *might cross to the shore of Bodhi.*
> *O Compassionate Avalokiteshvara,*
> *most benevolent!*

And ever since that time, in that rural western province, many have known and revered the Dharma of the Buddha.[32]

304. Flagstones. Katsura Palace Grounds. Kyoto, Japan

5. The Lotus Ladder

IT was during the centuries of the burgeoning of the various pagan, Jewish, and Christian Gnostic sects of Rome's Near Eastern provinces (the first four centuries of the Christian Era) that in Hindu and Buddhist India the first signs of what is known as Tantric practice appeared. The backgrounds of both movements, the Gnostic and the Tantric, are obscure, as are their connections with each other. Rome at the time was in direct commerce with India. Buddhist monks were teaching in Alexandria, Christian missionaries in Kerala. The halo (a Persian, Zoroastrian motif) had appeared abruptly in the Christian art of the time as well as in the Buddhist art of India and China; and in contemporary writings evidences abound of what must have been a very lively two-way traffic.

The elder Pliny (A.D. 23-79) wrote, for example:

> In no year does India drain us of less than 550,000,000 sesterces, giving back her own wares, which are sold among us at fully 100 times their first cost. . . . Our ladies glory in having pearls suspended from their fingers, or two or three of them dangling from their ears, delighted even with the rattling of the pearls as they knock against each other; and now, at the present day, even the poorer classes are affecting them, since people are in the habit of saying that "a pearl worn by a woman in public is as good as a lictor walking before her." Nay, even more than this, they put them on their feet, and that not only on the laces of their sandals but all over the shoes; it is not enough to wear pearls, but they must tread upon them, and walk with them under foot as well."[33]

Mircea Eliade, in his masterful *Yoga: Immortality and Freedom*, has suggested something of the obscurity and complexity of the problem of the origins and development of Tantric thought:

> It is not easy to define tantrism. Among the many meanings of the word *tantra* (root *tan*, "extend," "continue," "multiply"), one concerns us particularly—that of "succession," "unfolding," "continuous process." *Tantra* would be "what extends knowledge" (*tanyate, vistāryate, jñānam anena iti tantram*). In this acceptation, the term was already applied to certain philosophical systems (*Nyāya-tantreṣu*, etc.). We do not know why and under what circumstances it came to designate a great philosophical and religious movement, which, appearing as early as the fourth century of our era, assumed the form of a pan-Indian vogue from the sixth century onward. For it was really a vogue; quite suddenly, tantrism becomes immensely popular, not only among the active practitioners of the religious life (ascetics, yogins, etc.), and its prestige also reaches the "popular" strata. In a comparatively short time, Indian philosophy, mysticism, ritual, ethics, iconography, and even literature are influenced by tantrism. It is a pan-Indian movement, for it is assimilated by all the great Indian religions and by all the "sectarian" schools. There is a Buddhist tantrism and a Hindu tantrism, both of considerable proportions. But Jainism too

accepts certain tantric methods (never those of the "left hand"), and strong tantric influences can be seen in Kashmirian Shivaism, in the great Pāñcarātra movement (c. 550), in the *Bhāgavata Purāna* (c. 600), and in other Vishnuist devotional trends.[34]

It would be ridiculous to pretend that in a few pages, or even a considerable tome, anything more than a suggestion of the jewel tree—or rather, jewel jungle—of this truly astounding body of psychologized physiological and mythological lore might be offered. Even a glimpse will suffice to make the point, however, that there is evidence in this body of material of a highly developed *psychological* science: one, moreover, that has shaped and informed every significant development of Oriental doctrine—whether in India, Tibet, China, Korea, Japan, or Southeast Asia—from the first centuries of the Christian Era. And since there is evidence, furthermore, already in the earliest Upanishads—the *Brihadaranyaka* and *Chhandogya*—that something like an elementary foreview of the Tantric movement had been known to India long before the general vogue, we shall have to take into account the possibility that its sudden popularity, to which Professor Eliade alludes, represents not so much a novelty as a resurgence in freshly stated terms of principles long familiar to the pre-Aryan—or even, possibly, pre-Dravidian—populations of the timeless East.[35]

The essential alphabet of all Tantric lore is to be learned from the doctrine of the seven "circles" (*chakras*) or "lotuses" (*padmas*) of the *kundalinī* system of yoga. Fig. 306 The long terminal *ī* added to the Sanskrit adjective *kundalin*, meaning "circular, spiral, coiling, winding," makes a feminine noun signifying "snake," the reference in the present context being to the figure of a coiled female serpent—a serpent goddess not of "gross" but of "subtle" substance—which is to be thought of as residing in a torpid, slumbering state in a subtle center, the first of the seven, near the base of the spine: the aim of the yoga then being to rouse this serpent, lift her head, and bring her up a subtle nerve or channel of the spine to the so-called "thousand-petalled lotus" (*sahasrara*) at the crown of the head. This axial stem or channel, which is named *sushumna* ("rich in happiness, highly blessed"), is flanked and crossed by two others: a white, known as *ida* (meaning "refreshment, libation; stream or flow of praise and worship"), winding upward from the left testicle to right nostril and associated with the cool, ambrosial, "lunar" energies of the psyche; and a red, called *pingala* ("of a sunlike, tawny hue"), extending from the right testicle to left nostril, whose energy is "solar, fiery," and, like the solar heat of the tropics, desiccating and destructive.[36] The first task of the yogi is to bring the energies of these contrary powers together at the base of his sushumna and then to carry them up the central stem, along with the uncoiling serpent queen. She, rising from the lowest to the highest lotus center, will pass through and wake the five between, and with each waking the psychology and personality of the practitioner will be altogether and fundamentally transformed.

Fig. 306 Now there was in the last century a great Indian saint, Ramakrishna (1836-1886), who in the practices of this yoga was a veritable virtuoso. "There are," he once told his devotees, "five kinds of samadhi"; five kinds, that is to say, of spiritual rapture.

> In these samadhis one feels the sensation of the Spiritual Current to be like the movement of an ant, a fish, a monkey, a bird, or a serpent.
>
> Sometimes the Spiritual Current rises through the spine, crawling like an ant. Sometimes, in samadhi, the soul swims joyfully in the ocean of divine ecstasy, like a fish. Sometimes, when I lie down on my side, I feel the Spiritual Current pushing me like a monkey and playing with me joyfully. I remain still. That Current, like a monkey, suddenly with one jump reaches the Sahasrara. That is why you see me jump up with a start. Sometimes, again, the Spiritual Current rises like a bird hopping from one branch to another. The place where it rests feels like fire. . . . Sometimes the Spiritual Current moves up like a snake. Going in a zigzag way, at last it reaches the head and I go into samadhi. A man's spiritual consciousness is not awakened unless his Kundalini is aroused.

He goes on to describe a certain experience:

> Just before my attaining this state of mind, it had been revealed to me how the Kundalini is aroused, how the lotuses of the different centers blossom forth, and how all this culminates in samadhi. This is a very secret experience. I saw a boy twenty-two or twenty-three years old, exactly resembling me, enter the Sushumna nerve and commune with the lotuses, touching them with his tongue. He began with the first center at the anus, and passed through the centers at the sexual organ, navel, and so on. The different lotuses of those centers—four-petalled, six-petalled, ten-petalled, and so forth—had been drooping. At his touch they stood erect.
>
> When he reached the heart—I distinctly remember it—and communed with the lotus there, touching it with his tongue, the twelve-petalled lotus, which was hanging head down, stood erect and opened its petals. Then he came to the sixteen-petalled lotus in the throat and the two-petalled lotus in the forehead. And last of all, the thousand-petalled lotus in the head blossomed. Since then I have been in this state.[37]

The earliest serious studies in English of the principles of Tantra appeared during the first quarter of this century in the publications of Sir John Woodroffe (1865-1936), Supreme Court Judge at Calcutta, three of whose imposing volumes are indispensable to any Western reader seeking more than a passing knowledge of this learning: *Principles of Tantra* (Madras, 1914), *Shakti and Shākta* (Madras, 1928), and *The Serpent Power* (Madras, 3rd rev. edn. 1931). Add to these the more recent work by Dr. Shashibhusan Dasgupta, *Obscure Religious Cults as Background of Bengali Literature* (Calcutta, 1946), and the compendious handbook of Professor Eliade, already mentioned, and the patient student will be enabled to open to himself many hidden approaches to the interpretation of symbols and their relevance to his own interior life.

At the outset, however, two warnings are generally given: first, not to attempt to engage alone in the indicated exercises, since they activate unconscious centers, and improperly undertaken may lead to a psychosis; and second, not to overinterpret whatever signs of early success one may enjoy in the course of practice. Sir John Woodroffe explains:

> There is one simple test whether the Shakti is actually aroused. When she is aroused intense heat is felt at that spot, but when she leaves a particular center the part so left becomes as cold and apparently lifeless as a corpse. The progress upwards may thus be externally verified by others. When the Shakti (Power) has reached the upper brain (Sahasrara) the whole body is cold and corpse-like; except the top of the skull, where some warmth is felt, this being the place where the static and kinetic aspects of Consciousness unite.[38]

And so, to begin, then, at the beginning:

One is to sit in a posture of perfectly balanced repose, and in this so-called "lotus posture" to begin regulating the breath. The psychological theory underlying this primary exercise is that the mind or "mind power" (*manas*) and breathing or "breath power" (*prana*) interlock and are in fact the same. When one becomes angry, the breathing changes; also, when one is moved with erotic desire. In repose, it steadies down. Accordingly, control of the breath controls feeling and emotion, and can be made to serve as a mind-regulating factor. That is why in all serious Oriental mind-transforming enterprises the fundamental discipline is *pranayama*, "control of the breath." Steadying the breath one correspondingly steadies the mind, and the resultant aeration of the blood, furthermore, sets going in the body certain chemical processes that produce predictable effects.

Now this breathing will seem a little strange. One is to inhale through the right nostril, imagining the air as pouring down the white or "lunar" spinal course, ida, cleaning it out, as it were. One is to hold the breath a certain number of counts and to breathe out, then, with the air coming up through pingala, the tawny "solar" nerve. Next: in through the left, and after a hold, out through the right; and so on, strictly according to counts, the mind in this way being steadied down, the whole nervous system clarified; until presently, one fine day, the serpent goddess will be felt to stir.

I have been told that certain yogis, on becoming aware of this movement, press their hands to the ground and, elevating themselves a little from their lotus seats, bang down, to give the coiled-up one a physical jolt to rouse her. The waking and elevation are described in the texts in terms altogether physical. The references are to that "subtle" physical matter already mentioned, however, not the gross matter to which the observations of our scientists are directed. As Alain Danielou has remarked in his compact little volume, *Yoga: The Method of Reintegration*: "The Hindu will therefore speak indifferently of men or of subtle beings, he intermingles the geography of celestial worlds with that of terrestrial continents, and in this he sees no discontinuity but, on the contrary, a perfect coherence; for, to him, these worlds meet at many common points, and the passage from one to the other is easy for those who have the key."[39] Much the same could be said of almost any of the mythologically structured, protoscientific traditions of the ancient past.

So now we have got the serpent started: let us follow her up the spinal staff, which in this yoga is regarded as the microcosmic counterpart of the macrocosmic universal axis, its lotus stages being thus equivalent to the platforms of the many-storied ziggurats, and its summit to the lofty marriage chamber of the lunar and solar lights.

305. Ramakrishna. A.D. *1836-1886*

306. *Seven Lotus Centers of the Kundalini*

307. *Figure from Oseberg Bucket. Before* A.D. *800. Norway*

308 *(opposite). Dextra Dei (The Right Hand of God). Design on Stone Cross.* A.D. *10th century. Ireland*

309. *Mandala Paintings by Patients of C. G. Jung*

"This mandala," states Jung, "was made by a woman patient in her middle years, who first saw it in a dream. . . . The spiral is painted in the typical colors, red, green, yellow, and blue. According to the patient, the square in the center represents a *stone*, its four facets showing the four basic colors. The inner spiral represents the snake that, like Kundalini, winds three and a half times round the center.

"The dreamer herself had no notion what was going on in her, namely the beginning of a new orientation, nor would she have understood it consciously. Also, the parallels from Eastern symbolism were completely unknown to her, so that any influence is out of the question. The symbolic picture came to her spontaneously, when she had reached a certain point in her development."[40]

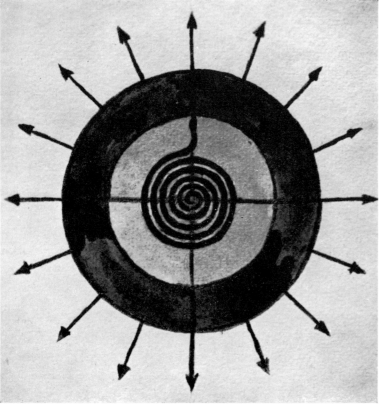

"The picture was made by a young woman. . . . The snake is coiled round the four-rayed middle point. It is trying to get out: it is the awakening of Kundalini, meaning that the patient's chthonic nature is becoming active. This is indicated by the arrows pointing outward."[41]

310. *Serpent Stone.* A.D. *1787. In the park, Weimar, Germany*

311. *The Basket of Isis. From Caligula's Temple to Isis.* A.D. *1st century. Rome*

The lotus at the base of the sushumna, called the "Root Support" (Muladhara), is Fig. 312 described as crimson in hue and having four petals, on each of which a Sanskrit syllable is inscribed (reading clockwise, from the upper right: *vam, śam, sham,* and *sam*). These are to be understood as sound-counterparts of the aspects of spiritual energy operative on this plane. In the white center is a yellow square symbolic of the element earth, wherein a white elephant stands waving seven trunks. This animal is Airavata, the mythic vehicle of Indra, the Vedic king of the gods, here supporting on its back the sign of the syllable *lam*, "which," Woodroffe writes, "is said to be the expression in gross sound of the subtle sound made by the vibration of forces of this center."[42] The elephant, he continues, is symbolic of the strength, firmness, and solidity of earth; but it is also* a cloud condemned to walk upon the earth, so that if it could be released from this condition it would rise. The supervising deity made visible in this lowest center is the world-creator Brahma, whose shakti, the goddess Savitri, is a personification of solar light. On the elephant's back is a downward-pointing triangle symbolic of the womb (*yoni*) of the goddess-mother of the universe, and within this "city of three sides," this "figure of desire," is seen the first or basal divine phallus (*lingam*) of the universal masculine principle, Shiva. The white serpent-goddess Kundalini, "fine as the fiber of a lotus-stalk," is coiled three and a half times around this lingam, asleep, and covering with her head its Brahma-door.[43]

Now to be exact, the precise locus of this center at the base of the human body is midway between the anus and the genitals, and the character of the spiritual energy at that point is of the lowest intensity. The world view is of uninspired materialism, governed by "hard facts"; the art, sentimental naturalism; and the psychology, adequately described in behavioristic terms, is reactive, not active. There is on this plane no zeal for life, no explicit impulse to expand. There is simply a lethargic avidity in hanging on to existence; and it is this grim grip that must finally be broken, so that the spirit may be quit of its dull zeal simply to be.

One may think of the Kundalini on this level as comparable to a dragon; for dragons, we are told by those who know, have a propensity to hoard and guard things; and their favorite things to hoard and guard are jewels and beautiful young girls. They are unable to make use of either, but just hang on, and so the values in their treasury are unrealized, lost to themselves and to the world. On this level, the serpent-queen Kundalini is held captive by her own dragon-lethargy. She neither knows nor can communicate to the life that she controls any joy; yet will not relax her hold and let go. Her key motto is a stubborn "Here I am, and here I stay."

The first task of the yogi, then, must be to break at this level the cold dragon grip cf. Figs. 315ff. of his own spiritual lethargy and release the jewel-maid, his own shakti, for ascent to those higher spheres where she will become his spiritual teacher and guide to the bliss of an immortal life beyond sleep.

* See above, p. 244.

312-314 (opposite). *Chakra 1: Muladhara (bottom); Chakra 2: Svadisthana
(center); Chakra 3: Manipura (top)*

315. *Cadmus Fighting the Dragon. Laconian Cup*

316. *St. George and the Dragon. Raphael*

317. *"Scroll of the Nine Dragons"* (detail). A.D. 12th century. China

318. *Sigurd and Fafnir.* A.D. 10th century. Rock Engraving. Sweden

On the right Sigurd drives his sword through the monster Fafnir, who is represented by a long serpentine band with a runic inscription. In the center a tree can be distinguished, to which Sigurd's steed Grani has been tied. In it are perched the two birds that have come to warn Sigurd against the knavish designs of Regin (Wagner's dwarf Mimir). The personage to the left of the horse is again Sigurd. He is here roasting Fafnir's heart over a fire, and raises to his mouth a finger that he has burned by touching the heart to see if it is ready. Thus he has unintentionally tasted the monster's blood and will henceforth understand the language of the birds: the language of nature. The final scene, on the left, represents Regin's forge. We see the tongs, anvil, bellows, the hammer, and the body of Regin himself, whose head Sigurd has cut off.[44]

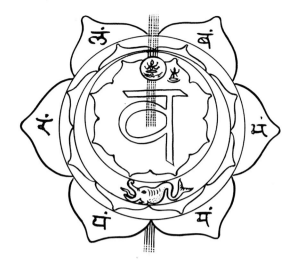

Chakra 2: Svadishthana

The second lotus of the series, called Svadhisthana, "Her Special Abode," is at the level of the genitals. It is a vermilion lotus of six petals, bearing the syllables *bam, bham, mam, yam, ram,* and *lam*. Water being the element of this center, its inner field is the shape of a crescent moon, within which a mythological water monster known as a *makara* is to be seen, supporting the sign of the water syllable *vam*. This is the seed sound of the Vedic god Varuna, lord of the rhythmic order of the universe. The presiding Hindu (as distinct from early Vedic) deity here is Vishnu in the pride of early youth, clothed in yellow and holding a noose in his hand. Beside him sits a wrathful form of his shakti, Rakini by name, of the color of a blue lotus, bearing in her four hands a lotus, a drum, a sharp battle-ax, and a spear, her teeth showing fiercely, her three eyes blazing red, and her mind exalted from the drinking of ambrosia.[45]

When the Kundalini is active at this level, the whole aim of life is in sex. Not only is every thought and act sexually motivated, either as a means toward sexual ends or as a compensating sublimation of frustrated sexual zeal, but everything seen and heard is interpreted compulsively, both consciously and unconsciously, as symbolic of sexual themes. Psychic energy, that is to say, has the character here of the Freudian libido. Myths, deities, and religious rites are understood and experienced in sexual terms.

Now of course there are in fact a great many myths and rites directly addressed to the concerns of this important center of life—fertility rites, marriage rites, orgiastic festivals, and so on—and a Freudian approach to the reading and explanation of these may not be altogether inappropriate. However, according to Tantric learning, even though the obsession of the life-energies functioning from this psychological center is sexual, sexuality is not the primal ground, end, or even sole motivation of life. Any fixation at this level is consequently pathological. Everything then reminds the blocked and tortured victim of sex. But if it also reminds his doctor of sex, what is the likelihood of a cure? The method of the Kundalini is rather to recognize affirmatively the force and importance of this center and let the energies pass on *through* it, to become naturally transformed to other aims at the higher centers of the "rich in happiness" sushumna.

319. *Head of the Young Dionysos. Late Hellenistic Carving.*
Found near Rome

320. *Eros and Psyche. Antique Sculpture. Rome*

321. *Venus, Cupid, and the Passions of Love. Bronzino*

322. *Danaë and the Shower of Gold. Titian*

Chakra 3: Manipura

Fig. 314 Chakra three, at the level of the navel, is called Manipura, "City of the Shining Jewel," for its fiery heat and light. Here the energy turns to violence and its aim is to consume, to master, to turn the world into oneself and one's own. The appropriate Occidental psychology would be the Adlerian of the "will to power"; for now even sex becomes an occasion, not of erotic experience, but of achievement, conquest, self-reassurance, and frequently, also, revenge. The lotus has ten petals, dark as thunderheads heavy laden, bearing the seed syllables *ḍam, ḍham, ṇam, tam, tham, dam, dham, nam, pam,* and *pham.* Its central triangle, in a white field, is the sign of the element fire, shining like the rising sun, with swastika marks on its sides. The ram, its symbolic animal, is the vehicle of Agni, Vedic god of the sacrificial fire, bearing on its back the syllable *ram,* which is the seed syllable or sound form of this god and his fiery element. The presiding Hindu (as distinct from Vedic) deity is Shiva in his terrible guise as an ascetic smeared with the ashes of funeral pyres, seated on his white bull Nandi. And at his side is his goddess shakti, enthroned on a ruby lotus in her hideous character of Lakini. Lakini is blue, with three faces, three eyes to each; fierce of aspect, with protruding teeth. She is fond of meat: her breast is smeared with grease and blood that have dripped from her ravenous jaws; yet she is radiant, elegant with ornaments, and exalted from the drinking of ambrosia. She is the goddess who presides over all rites of human sacrifice and over the battlefields of mankind, terrible as death to behold, though to her devotees gracious, beautiful, and sweet as life.

323. The Devouring Kali. A.D. *18th-19th century. Nepal*

324 (above). *The Great Hunt of King Ashurbanipal (detail). 7th century* B.C

325 (below). Foot Race of Athenian Youths. 6th century B.C.

326 (opposite). St. Dominic Burning Books. A.D. 15th century

327. *The Battle of Anghiari. Copy by Rubens of the lost painting by Leonardo da Vinci*

328. *Saturn. Francisco de Goya*

Now all three of these lower chakras are of the modes of man's living in the world in his naïve state, outward turned: the modes of the lovers, the fighters, the builders, the accomplishers. Joys and sorrows on these levels are functions of achievements in the world "out there": what people think of one, what has been gained, what lost. And throughout the history of our species, people functioning only on these levels (who, of course, have been in the majority) have had to be tamed and brought to heel through the inculcation of a controlling sense of social duty and shared social values, enforced not only by secular authority but also by all those grandiose myths of an unchallengeable divine authority to which every social order—each in its own way—has had to lay claim. Wherever motivations of these kinds are not checked effectively, men, as the old texts say, "become wolves unto men."

However, it is obvious that a religion operating only on these levels, having little or nothing to do with the fostering of inward, mystical realizations, would hardly merit the name of religion at all. It would be little more than an adjunct to police authority, offering in addition to ethical rules and advice intangible consolations for life's losses and a promise of future rewards for social duties fulfilled. Hence, to interpret the imagery, powers, and values of the higher chakras in terms of the values of these lower systems is to mistranslate them miserably, and to lose contact in oneself, thereby, with the whole history and heritage of mankind's life in the spirit.

Fig. 332 And so we ascend to chakra four, at the level of the heart, where what Dante called *La Vita Nuova,* "The New Life," begins. And the name of this center is Anahata, "Not Struck"; for it is the place where the sound is heard "that is not made by any two things striking together."

Every sound normally heard is of two things striking together; that of the voice, for example, being the sound of the breath striking our vocal cords. The only sound *not* so made is that of the creative energy of the universe, the hum, so to speak, of the void, which is antecedent to things, and of which things are precipitations. This, they say, is heard as from within, within oneself and simultaneously within space. It is the sound beyond silence, heard as OM (very deeply intoned, I am told, somewhere about C below low C). "The word OM," said Ramakrishna to his friends, "is Brahman. Following the trail of OM, one attains to Brahman."[46]

cf. Fig. 331 In the Sanskrit Devanagari script OM is written either as ॐ or as आঁ , and in the posture of the dancing Shiva image the pose of the head, hands, and lifted foot suggests the outline of this sign—which makes the point that in the appearance of this god the sound resounds of the wonder of existence. OM is interpreted as the seed sound, the energy sound, the shakti, of all being, and in that sense analyzed in the following way by the seers and teachers of the Upanishads.

Firstly, since the vowel o in Sanskrit is regarded as a fusion of A and U, the syllable OM can be written also as AUM— अाঁ —and in that augmented form is called the syllable of *four* elements; namely, A, U, M, and the SILENCE that is before, after,

329. *The Last Judgment. Michelangelo*

The upper right hand of the dancing god holds a little drum shaped like an hourglass, the rhythm of which is the world-creating beat of time, which draws a veil across the face of eternity, projecting temporality and thereby the temporal world. The extended left hand holds the flame of spiritual light that burns the veil away, thus annihilating the world and revealing the void of eternity. The second right hand is in the "fear-dispelling" posture, and the second left, lifted across the chest, pointing to the raised left foot, is in a position known as "elephant hand," signifying "teaching"; for where an elephant has gone through jungles all animals can follow, and where a teacher leads the way disciples follow. The left foot, to which the "teaching hand" points, is lifted to symbolize "release," while the right stamping on the back of a dwarf named "Forgetfulness" drives souls into the vortex of rebirth. The dwarf is gazing in fascination at the poisonous world-serpent, representing thus man's psychological attraction to the realm

f. Fig. 127

of his bondage in unending birth, suffering, and death. (Cf. dwarf, fig. 127.)

The god's head, meanwhile, is poised, serene and still, in the midst of all the movement of creation and destruction represented in the rhythm of the rocking arms and slowly stamping right heel. His right earring is a man's, his left a woman's; for he includes and transcends opposites. His streaming hair is that of a yogi, flying now however in a dance of life. Among its strands is tucked a skull, but also a crescent moon; a datura flower, from the plant of which an intoxicant is distilled; and finally, a tiny image of the goddess Ganges—for it is Shiva, we are told, who receives on his head the first impact of that heavenly stream as it falls to earth from on high.

From the mouths of a double-headed mythological water monster called a makara the flaming aureole issues by which the dancer is enclosed; and the posture of his head, arms, and lifted leg within this frame suggests the sign of the syllable OM:

331. The Syllable OM.

and around it, out of which it rises and back into which it falls—as the universe, out of and back into the void.

The A is announced with open throat; the U carries the sound-mass forward; and the M, then, somewhat nasalized, brings all to a close at the lips. So pronounced, the utterance will have filled the whole mouth with sound and so have contained (as they say) all the vowels. Moreover, since consonants are regarded in this thinking as interruptions of vowel sounds, the seeds of all words will have been contained in this enunciation of AUM, and in these, the seed sounds of all things. Thus words, they say, are but fragments or particles of AUM, as all forms are particles of that one Form of forms that is beheld when the rippling surface of the mind is stilled in yoga.* And accordingly, AUM is the one sound spelled in all possible inflections on the petals of the Kundalini series.

Allegorically, the initial A of AUM is said to represent the field and state of Waking Consciousness, where objects are of "gross matter" (*sthula*) and are separate both from each other and from the consciousness beholding them. On this plane of experience, I am not you, nor is this that; A is not *not-A*; cause and effect, God and his world, are not the same, and all mystical statements are absurd. Moreover, the gross objects of this daylight sphere, to be seen, must be illuminated from without. They are not self-luminous, except, of course, in the instances of fire, lightning, stars, and the sun, which suggest gates to another order of existence. Anything perceived by the waking senses, furthermore, must already have come into being, and so is already a thing of the past. Science, the wisdom of the mind awake, and of "hard facts," can consequently be a knowledge only of what has already become, or of what in the future is to repeat and continue the past. The unpredictably creative, immediate present is inaccessible to its light.

And so we come to the letter U, which is said to represent the field and state of Dream Consciousness, where, although subject and object may *appear* to be different and separate from each other, they are actually one and the same. A dreamer is surprised, even threatened, by his dream, not knowing what it means; yet even while dreaming he is himself inventing it; so that two aspects of the one subject are here playing hide-and-seek: one in creative action, the other in half-ignorance. And the objects of this world of dream, furthermore, being of "subtle matter" (*sukshma*), shine of themselves, rapidly changing shape, and therefore are of the order of fire and the radiant nature of gods. In fact, the Indo-European verbal root *div*, from which the Latin *dīvus* and *deus*, Greek Ζεύς, and Old Irish *dīa* as well as Sanskrit *deva* (all meaning "deity") derive, signifies "to shine"; for the gods, like the figures of dream, shine of themselves. They are the macrocosmic counterparts of the images of dream, personifications of the same powers of nature that are manifest in dreams; so that on this plane the two worlds of the microcosm and

* See above, p. 313.

332-334 (opposite). Chakra 4: Anahata (bottom); Chakra 5: Vishuddha
    (center); Chakra 6: Ajna (top)

Cf. Figs. 203, 337, 338

macrocosm, interior and exterior, individual and collective, particular and general, are one. The individual dream opens to the universal myth, and gods in vision descend to the dreamer as returning aspects of himself.

Mythologies are in fact the public dreams that move and shape societies; and conversely, one's own dreams are the little myths of the private gods, antigods, and guardian powers that are moving and shaping oneself: revelations of the actual fears, desires, aims, and values by which one's life is subliminally ordered. On the level, therefore, of Dream Consciousness one is at the quick, the immediate initiating creative *now*, of one's life, experiencing those activating forces that in due time will bring to pass unpredicted events on the plane of Waking Consciousness and be there observed and experienced as "facts."

So then, if A is of Waking Consciousness, gross objects, and what has become (the past), and U of Dream Consciousness, subtle objects, and what is becoming (the present), M is of Deep Dreamless Sleep, where (as we say) we have "lost" consciousness, and the mind (as described in the Indian texts) is "an undifferentiated mass or continuum of consciousness unqualified," lost in darkness. That which when awake is conscious only of what has become and in dream of what is becoming, is in Deep Dreamless Sleep dissociated from all commitments whatsoever, and so is returned to that primal, undifferentiated, and unspecified state of latency, chaos, or potentiality from which all that will ever be must in time arise. But alas! The mind that there contains all is lost in sleep. As the *Chhandogya Upanishad* describes it: "Just as those who do not know the spot might pass over a hidden treasure of gold again and again but not find it, even so do all creatures here go to that Brahma-world, day after day, in deep sleep, and not find it."[47]

So also in C. G. Jung's account: "The deeper 'layers' of the psyche lose their in-dividual uniqueness as they retreat farther and farther into darkness. 'Lower down,' that is to say as they approach the autonomous functional systems, they become increasingly collective until they are universalized and extinguished in the body's materiality, i.e., in chemical substances. The body's carbon is simply carbon. Hence, 'at bottom' the psyche is simply 'world.' "[48]

Briefly stated, then: the goal of every yoga is to go into that zone awake; to sink to where there is no longer any resting on this object or on that, whether of the waking world or of dream, but there is met the innate light that is called, in Buddhist lore, the Mother Light. And this then, this inconceivable sphere of undifferentiated consciousness, experienced not as extinction but as light unmitigated, is the refer-ence of the fourth element of AUM: the Silence that is before, after, within, and around the sounding syllable. It is silent because words, which do not reach it, refer only to the names, forms, and relationships of objects either of the daylight world or of dream.

The sound AUM, then, "not made by any two things striking together," and float-

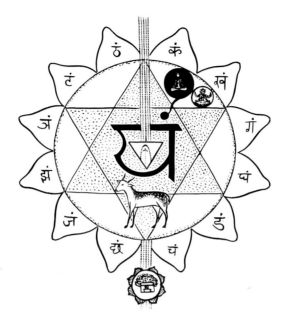

Chakra 4: Anahata

Fig. 332

ing as it were in a setting of silence, is the seed sound of creation, heard when the rising Kundalini reaches the level of the heart. For there, as they say, the Great Self abides and portals open to the void. The lotus of twelve red petals, marked with the syllables *kam, kham, gam, gham, ngam, cham, chham, jam, jham, nyam, tam,* and *tham,* is of the element air. In its bright red center is an interlocking double triangle, the color of smoke, signifying "juncture" and containing its seed syllable *yam* displayed above an antelope, which is the beast, swift as wind, of the Vedic wind-god Vayu. The female triangle within this letter holds a lingam like shining gold, and the patron Hindu deity is Shiva in a gentle, boon-bestowing aspect. His shakti, known here as Kakini, lifts a noose and a skull in two hands, while exhibiting with her other two the "boon-bestowing" and "fear-dispelling" gestures.

Just below this lotus of the heart there is pictured a lesser, uninscribed lotus, at about the level of the solar plexus, supporting on a jeweled altar an image of the Wish-Fulfilling Tree. For it is here that the first intimations are heard of the sound OM in the Silence, and that sound itself is the Wish-Fulfilling Tree. Once heard, it can be rediscovered everywhere and no longer do we have to *seek* our good. It is here—within—and through all things, all space. We can now give up our struggle for achievement, for love and power and the good, and may rest in peace.

Or so, at first, it will seem.

However, there is a new zeal, a new frenzy, now stirring in the blood. For, as Dante states at the opening of *La Vita Nuova,* describing the moment when he first beheld Beatrice:

> At that moment, I say truly, the spirit of life, which dwells in the most secret chamber of the heart, began to tremble with such violence that it appeared fear-

fully in the least pulses, and, trembling, said these words: "Behold a god stronger than I, who coming shall rule over me."

At that instant the spirit of the soul, which dwells in the high chamber to which all the spirits of the senses carry their perceptions, began to marvel greatly, and, speaking especially to the spirit of the sight, said these words: "Now has appeared your bliss."

At that instant the natural spirit, which dwells in that part where our nourishment is supplied, began to weep, and, weeping, said these words: "Woe is me, wretched! because often from this time forth shall I be hindered."[49]

335. *The Sacred Heart of Jesus. St. Marguerite Marie.* A.D. *1685.*
Preserved in the Monastery of the Visitatio, Turin, Italy

336. *Mandala Painting by a Patient of C. G. Jung*

"This picture was made by a young woman patient with a schizoid disposition. The pathological element is revealed in the 'breaking lines' that split up the center. The sharp, pointed forms of these breaking lines indicate evil, hurtful, and destructive impulses which might hinder the desired synthesis of the personality. But it seems as if the regular structure of the surrounding mandala might be able to restrain the dangerous tendencies to dissociation. And this proved to be the case in the further course of the treatment and subsequent development of the patient."[50]

338. St. John the Evangelist on Patmos. Titian

337 (opposite). Dr. Faustus in his Study. Rembrandt

Chakra 5: Vishuddha

Once the great mystery-sound has been heard, the whole desire of the heart will be to learn to know it more fully, to hear it, not through things and within during certain fortunate moments only, but immediately and forever. And the attainment of this end will be the project of the next chakra, the fifth, which is at the level of the larynx and is called Vishuddha, "Purified." "When the Kundalini reaches this plane," said Ramakrishna, "the devotee longs to talk and to hear only of God."[51]

Fig. 333

The lotus has sixteen petals of a smoky purple hue, on each of which is engraved one of the sixteen Sanskrit vowels, namely, *am, ām, im, īm, um, ūm, rm, r̄m, lrm, lr̄m, em, aim, om, aum, am,* and *ah.* In the middle of its pure white central triangle is a white disk, the full moon, wherein the syllable *ham,* of the element space or ether, rests on the back of a pure white elephant. The patron of this center is Shiva in his hermaphroditic form known as Ardhanareshvara, "Half-Woman Lord," five-faced, clothed in a tiger's skin, and with ten radiant arms. One hand makes a "fear-dispelling" gesture and the rest are exhibiting his trident, battle-ax, sword, and thunderbolt, a fire, a snake-ring, a bell, a goad, and a noose, while beside him his goddess, here called Sakini, holds in her own four hands a bow, an arrow, a noose, and a goad. "This region," we are told in a Tantric text, "is the gateway of the Great Liberation."[52] It is the place variously represented in the myths and legends of the world as a threshold where the frightening Gate Guardians stand, the Sirens sing, the Clashing Rocks come together, and a ferry sets forth to the Land of No Return, the Land Below Waves, the Land of Eternal Youth. However, as told in the *Katha Upanishad*: "It is the sharpened edge of a razor, hard to traverse."[53]

Fig. 339

Figs. 340-345

339. *Shiva Ardhanari, "Half-woman Lord."* A.D. *8th century. India*

340. Kongorikishi. A.D. *12th century. Japan*

In the Buddhism of the Far East the typical temple guardians are the paired warrior sentries known in Japan as Kongo-rikishi (Sanskrit, Vajrapani), "Thunderbolt Carriers," of whom the most famous examples

are undoubtedly the two prodigious fellows at the Great South Gate of the Todaiji Temple at Nara. They are counterparts of the cherubim and flaming sword that Yahweh placed "at the east of the garden of Eden . . . to guard the way to the tree of life" (Genesis 3:24). In Buddhist thought, however, we are not to be intimidated, but to pass between.

341. Odysseus and the Sirens. 5th century B.C. *Greece*

"Meanwhile our good ship quickly came to the island of the Sirens twain, for a gentle breeze sped her on her way. Then straightway the wind ceased, and lo, there was a windless calm, and some god lulled the waves. Then my company rose up and drew in the ship's sails, and stowed them in the hold of the ship, while they sat at the oars and whitened the water with their polished pine blades. But I with my sharp sword cleft in pieces a great circle of wax, and with my strong hands kneaded it. And soon the wax grew warm, for that my great might constrained it and the beam of the lord Helios, son of Hyperion. And I anointed therewith the ears of all my men in their order [that they might not hear the Sirens' song], and in the ship they bound me hand and foot [as I had instructed them] upright in the maststead, and from the mast they fastened rope-ends and themselves sat down and smote the grey water with their oars. But when the ship was within the sound of a man's shout from the land, we fleeing swiftly on our way, the Sirens espied the swift ship speeding toward them, and they raised their clear-toned song:

"'Hither, come hither, renowned Odysseus, great glory of the Achaeans, here stay thy barque, that thou mayest listen to the voice of us twain. For none hath ever driven by this way in his black ship, till he hath heard from our lips the voice sweet as the honeycomb, and hath had joy thereof and gone on his way the wiser. For lo, we know all things, all the travail that in wide Troy-land the Argives and Trojans bare by the gods' designs, yea, and we know all that shall hereafter be upon the fruitful earth.'

"So spake they uttering a sweet voice, and my heart was fain to listen, and I bade my company unbind me, nodding at them with a frown, but they bent to their oars and rowed on."[54]

342. *The Temptation of St. Anthony. Martin Schongauer.* A.D. *15th century. Germany*

343. *The Annihilation of Self-hood. William Blake*

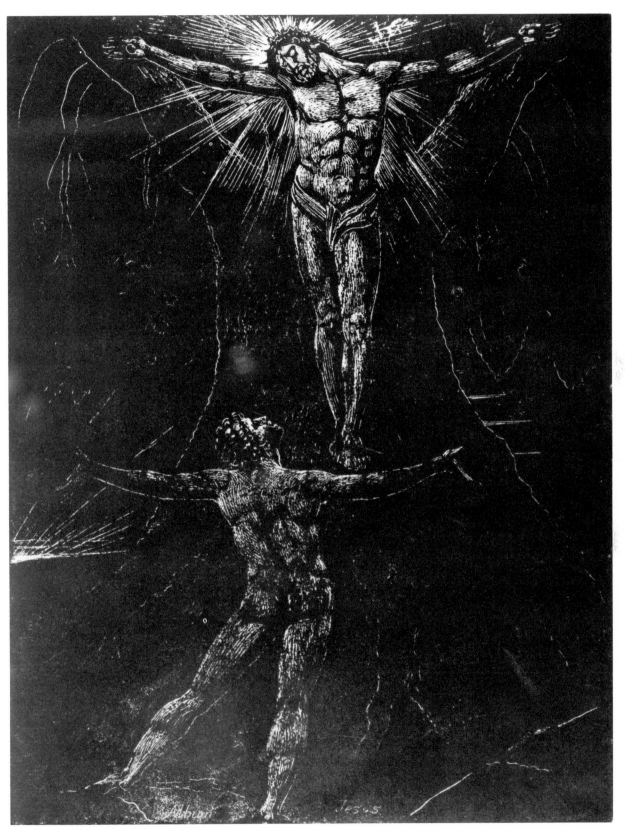

344. *Albion Contemplating Jesus Crucified. William Blake*

345. The River Styx. Joachim Patinir

346. *St. Anthony the Abbot and St. Paul the Hermit. Diego Velásquez*

Fig. 333 The yogi at the purgatorial fifth chakra, striving to clear his consciousness of the turbulence of secondary things and to experience unveiled the voice and light of the Lord that is the Being and Becoming of the universe, has at his command a number of means by which to achieve this aim. There is a discipline for instance, known as the yoga of heat or fire, formerly practiced in Tibet and known there as *Dumo (gTum-Mo)*, which is a term denoting "a fierce woman who can destroy all desires and passions"[55]—and I wonder whether the classical legend of the Maenads beheading Orpheus, who had been brooding on his lost Euridice, may not have been a covert reference to some esoteric mystery of this kind. What this yoga first requires is the activation of the energy at the navel chakra, Manipura (chakra three), through a special type of breath control and the visualization of an increasing fire at the intersection (just below the navel) of all three spiritual channels:

> At the start the blazing tongue of Dumo should not be visualized as more than the height of a finger's breadth; then gradually it increases in height to two, three, and four fingers' breadth. The blazing tongue of Dumo is thin and long, shaped like a twisted needle or the long hair of a hog; it also possesses all four characteristics of the Four Elements—the firmness of the earth, the wetness of water, the warmth of fire, and the mobility of air; but its outstanding quality still lies in its great heat—which can evaporate the life breaths (*pranas*) and produce the bliss.[56]

What is happening here is that the powers of the lower chakras are being activated and intensified, to force them to open and to release the energies they enclose; for these are the energies that in the higher chakras are to lead to sheerly spiritual fulfillments. In this introverted exercise, the aggressive fires of chakra three are being turned inward, against enemies that are not outside but within: to burn away obstructions to the Mother Light that are lodged within oneself. Thin as a needle, the Dumo fire is to be lengthened upward from the navel chakra to the higher centers of the head, to release from these an ambrosial seminal dew (as it is called), which is to be pictured as dripping, white, into the red Dumo fire. The white nerve ida is of this seminal dew, and the red, pingala, of the Dumo fire. The imagery is obviously sexual: the fire is female and the dew that it receives and consumes is male. Moreover, as the Tantric texts advise: "If these measures still fail to produce a Great Bliss, one may apply the *Wisdom-Mother-Mudra* by visualizing the sexual act with a Dakini, while using the breathing to incite the Dumo heat."[57] Thus in this yoga cf. Figs. 358-360 the energies either of the sex instinct or of the will to power may be employed to assist in shattering and surpassing the limits of the lower instinct system itself.

A second type of exercise in this Tibetan series is known as "Illusory Body Yoga," the aim of which is to realize in experience—not simply to be told to believe—that all appearances are void. One is to regard the reflection of one's own body in a mirror and to consider (as the texts advise), "how this image is produced by a combination of various factors—the mirror, the body, light, space, etc.,—under certain conditions. It is an object of 'dependent-arising' (*pratitya-samutpada*) without any self-substance—appearing, yet void. . . ." One is then to consider how one's own self, as one knows it, is equally an appearance.

Or one may practice in the same way a meditation on echoes. Go to some place where echoes abound. "Then shout loudly many pleasing and displeasing words to praise or malign yourself, and observe the reactions of pleasure and displeasure. Practicing thus, you will soon realize that all words, pleasant or unpleasant, are as illusory as the echoes themselves."[58]

In a third yoga, known as the "Dream Yoga," we immediately recognize a resemblance to certain modern psychotherapeutic techniques; for the yogi here is to cultivate and pay close attention to his dreams, analyzing them in relation to his feelings, thoughts, and other reactions. "When the yogi has a frightening dream, he should guard against unwarranted fear by saying, 'This is a dream. How can fire burn me or water drown me in a dream? How can this animal or devil, etc., harm me?' Keeping this awareness, he should trample on the fire, walk through the water, or transform himself into a great fireball and fly into the heart of the threatening devil or beast and burn it up. . . ."

Next:

The yogi who can recognize dreams fairly well and steadily should proceed to practice the *Transformation of Dreams*. This is to say that in the Dream state, he should try to transform his body into a bird, a tiger, a lion, a Brahman, a king, a house, a rock, a forest. . . . or anything he likes. When this practice is stabilized, he should then transform himself into his Patron Buddha Body in various forms, sitting or standing, large or small, and so forth. Also, he should transform the things that he sees in dreams into different objects—for instance, an animal into a man, water into fire, earth into space, one into many, or many into one. . . . After this the yogi should practice the Journey to Buddha's Lands. . . .

Finally—and here the sense of it all becomes clear:

The Dream Yoga should be regarded as supplementary to the Illusory Body Yoga. . . . for in this way, the clinging-to-time manifested in the dichotomy of Dream and Waking states can eventually be conquered.[59]

Still another yoga of this series, going past the illusory forms of both waking and dream, is the "Light Yoga," where one is to visualize one's entire body as dissolving into the syllable of the heart center (in Tibet this syllable is HUM) and this syllable itself, then, as dissolving into light. And there are four degrees of this light: (1) the Light of Revelation, (2) the Light of Augmentation, (3) the Light of Attainment, and (4) the Light of the Innate. Moreover, anyone able to do so should concentrate, just before going to sleep, on the fourth of these, the Innate Light, and holding to it even on passing into sleep, dissolve both dreams and darkness in that light.[60]

And with that, indeed, one will have passed into the state of Deep Dreamless Sleep awake.*

* See above, p. 362.

When the tasks of the fifth chakra have been accomplished, two degrees of illumination become available to the perfected saint, that at the sixth, known as *savikalpa samadhi*, "conditioned rapture," and finally, supremely, at the seventh chakra, *nirvikalpa samadhi*, "unconditioned rapture." Ramakrishna used to ask those approaching him for instruction: "Do you like to speak of God with form or without?"[61] And we have the words of the great *doctor ecstaticus* Meister Eckhart, referring to the passage from six to seven: "Man's last and highest leave-taking is the leaving of God for God."[62]

Chakra 6: Ajna

Fig. 334   The center of the first of these two ecstasies, known as the lotus of "Command,"
cf. Fig. 347   Ajna, is above and between the brows. The uraeus serpent in Egyptian portraits of the pharaohs appears exactly as though from this point of the forehead. The center is described as a lotus of two pure white petals, bearing the syllables *ham* and *ksham*. Seated on a white lotus near its heart is the radiant six-headed goddess Hakini, holding in four of her six hands a book, a drum, a rosary, and a skull, while the remaining two make the "fear-dispelling" and "boon-bestowing" signs. Within the yoni-triangle is a Shiva lingam, shining "like a chain of lightning flashes,"[63] supporting the sign of the syllable OM, of which the sound is here fully heard. And here, too,
Fig. 348   the form is seen of one's ultimate vision of God, which is called in Sanskrit *Saguna Brahman*, "the Qualified Absolute." As expounded by Ramakrishna:

> When the mind reaches this plane, one witnesses divine revelations day and night. Yet even then there remains a slight consciousness of "I." Having seen the unique manifestation man becomes mad with joy as it were and wishes to be one with the all-pervading Divine, but cannot do so. It is like the light of a lamp inside a glass case. One feels as if one could touch the light, but the glass intervenes and prevents it.[64]

347. Portrait of Pharaoh Sesostris III. 19th century B.C. *Egypt*

For where there is a "Thou" there is an "I," whereas the ultimate aim of the mystic, as Eckhart has declared, is identity: "God is love, and he who is in love is in God and God in him."[65]

If we remove that glasslike barrier of which Ramakrishna spoke, both our God Fig. 349 and ourselves will explode then into light, sheer light, one light, beyond names and forms, beyond thought and experience, beyond even the concepts "being" and "non-being." "The soul in God," Eckhart has said, "has naught in common with naught and is naught to aught."[66] And again: "There is something in the soul so nearly kin to God that it is one and not united."[67]

The Sanskrit term *Nirguna Brahman*, "the Unqualified Absolute," refers to the realization of this chakra. Its lotus, Sahasrara, "Thousand Petalled," hangs head downward, shedding nectarous rays more lustrous than the moon; while at its center, brilliant as a lightning flash, is the ultimate yoni-triangle, within which, well concealed and very difficult to approach, is the great shining void in secret served by all gods.[68] "Any flea as it is in God," declared Eckhart, "is nobler than the highest of the angels in himself."[69]

One single moment only is for me greater oblivion
    Than five and twenty centuries to the emprise
    That made Neptune wonder at the shadow of Argo.
Thus my mind, wholly rapt,
    Was gazing fixed, motionless and intent
    And ever with gazing grew enkindled.
In that Light one becomes such
    That it is impossible he should ever
    Consent to turn himself from it for other sight;
Because the Good which is the object of the will
    Is all collected in it, and outside of it
    That is defective which is perfect there.
Now will my speech fall more short,
    Even in respect to that which I remember, than that of an infant
    Who still bathes his tongue at the breast.
Not because more than one simple semblance
    Was in the Living Light wherein I was gazing,
    Which is always such as it was before;
But through my sight, which was growing strong
    In me as I looked, one sole appearance,
    As I myself changed, was altering itself to me.
Within the profound and clear substance
    Of the lofty Light appeared to me three circles
    Of three colors and one dimension;
And one seemed reflected in the other,
    As Iris by Iris, and the third seemed fire
    Which from the one as from the other is equally breathed forth.
O how inadequate is speech, and how feeble
    Toward my conception! and this toward what I saw
    Is such that it suffices not to call it little.
O Light Eternal, that sole abidest in Thyself,
    Sole understandest Thyself, and, by Thyself understood
    And understanding, lovest and smilest on Thyself!
That circle which appeared in Thee
    Generated as a reflected light,
    Being awhile surveyed by my eyes,
Seemed to me depicted with our effigy
    Within itself, of its own very color;
    Wherefore my sight was wholly set upon it.
As is the geometer who wholly applies himself
    To measure the circle, and finds not
    By thinking that principle of which he is in need,
Such was I at that new sight:
    I wished to see how the image was conformed.
    To the circle, and how it has its place therein.
                    (*Paradiso XXXIII, 94-138.*)

348. Dante Introduced by Beatrice to the Beatific Vision of God. A.D. *14th century. Italy*

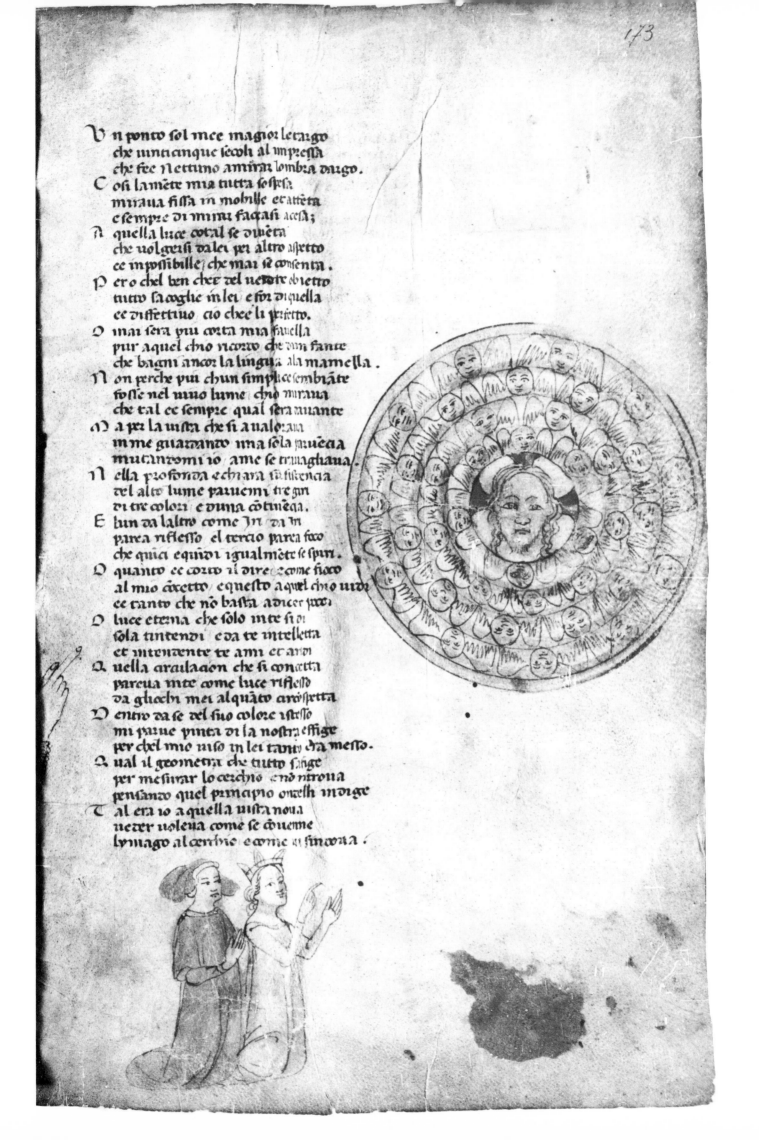

Vn ponto sol mee magior letargo
che uintianque secoli al impresa
che fee Nettuno amirar lombra daugo.

Cosi lamete mia tutta sospesa
miraua fissa in mobille et atteta
e sempre di mirar facasi acesa;

A quella luce cotal se diueta
che uolgersi dalei per altro aspetto
ee impssibille che mai se consenta.

Pero chel ben chee del uolire obietto
tutto sacoglie in lei e for diquella
ee diffettiuo cio chee li perfetto.

O mai sera piu corta mia fauella
pur aquel chio ricorto che dun fante
che bagni ancor la lingua ala mamella.

Non perche piu chun simplice sembiante
fosse nel uiuo lume chio miraua
che tal ee sempre qual sera muante.

Ma per la uista che si aualoraua
in me guardando una sola parueaa
mutanromi io ame se trauaghaua.

Nella profonda echiara sussistencia
del alto lume paruemi tre giri
di tre colori e duna cotinnega.

E lun da laltro come Iri da iri
parea riflesso el tercio parea foco
che quici equindi igualmete se spiri.

O quanto ee corto il dire ecome fioco
al mio coretto e questo aquel chio uidi
ee tanto che no basta adicer poci.

O luce eterna che solo inte sidi
sola tintendi e da te intelletta
et intendente te ami et ardi.

Quella auuluccion che si concetta
pareua inte come luce riflesso
da ghueohi mei alquato acirspetta.

Dentro da se del suo colore istesso
mi parue pinta di la nostra effige
per chel mio uiso in lei tanto ora messo.

Qual il geometra che tutto safige
per mesurar lo cerchio end ntroua
pensando quel principio ondelli indige.

Tal era io aquella uista noua
ueder uoleua come se coueme
lymago al cerchio e come ui sincoua.

349. *Mandala of the Admantine Bolt.*

"The mandala shown here," notes C. G. Jung, "depicts the state of one who has emerged from contemplation into the absolute state. That is why representation of hell and the horrors of the burial ground are missing. The diamond thunderbolt, the *dorje* [Sanskrit *vajra*], in the center symbolizes the perfect state where masculine and feminine are united. The world of illusions has finally vanished. All energy has gathered together in the initial state.

"The four *dorjes* in the gates of the inner courtyard are meant to indicate that life's energy is streaming inwards; it has detached itself from objects and now returns to the center. When the perfect union of all energies in the four aspects of wholeness is attained, there arises a static state called the 'Diamond Body,' corresponding to the *corpus incorruptibile* of medieval alchemy, which is identical with the *corpus glorificationis* of Christian tradition. This mandala shows, then, the union of all opposites, and is embedded between *yang* and *yin*, heaven and earth; the state of everlasting balance and immutable duration.

"For our more modest psychological purposes we must abandon the colorful metaphysical language of the East. What yoga aims at in this exercise is undoubtedly a psychic change in the adept. The ego is the expression of individual existence. The yogin exchanges his ego for Shiva or the Buddha; in this way he induces a shifting of the psychological center of personality from the personal ego to the impersonal non-ego, which is now experienced as the real 'Ground' of the personality."[70]

Compare the words of Paul: "it is no longer I who live, but Christ who lives in me" (Galatians 2:20).

350 (*opposite, upper*). *The Living Light and the Angelic Choirs.* A.D. *9th century. Breviary of St. Hildegarde*

351 (*opposite, lower*). *Shri Yantra. Tantric Mandala. India*

352. *The Ladder of Judgement. John of Climax.* A.D. *7th century*

Unearthed in the year 1837 near the town of Pietroasa, in the area of Buzau, Rumania, this Orphic bowl had been buried with twenty-one other precious pieces, possibly at the time of the Huns. Taken to Moscow during the First World War for protection from the Germans, the whole collection was melted down for its gold by the Communists. Fortunately, however, during the winter of 1867-1868 it had been on loan for six months in England, where it had been photographed and galvanoplastically reproduced. The forms are crude according to classical standards, and may represent the work of a provincial craftsman.

The figures of the outer circle may be interpreted as follows:

1. *Orpheus the Fisherman*, with his fishing pole, line wound around it, a mesh bag in his elevated hand, and a fish lying at his feet. (One thinks of Christ's words to his fisherman apostles, "I shall make you fishers of men.") Orpheus in this role is the announcer, guide, and guardian of the mysteries.

2. *A naked figure in attendance at the entrance*, bearing on his head the sacred chest (*cista mystica*), and with an ear of grain in hand. (In classical reliefs such figures, bearing sacred chests, are frequently smaller than those around them: this attendant is not to be interpreted as a child.) The contents of the chest are offered to:

3. *A kilted male, the neophyte.* He holds in his left hand a torch, symbol of the goddess Persephone of the Netherworld, to whose mystery (the truth about death) he is about to be introduced. Yet his eyes still hold to those of his mystagogue, the Fisherman. The raven of death perches on his shoulder, while with his right hand he lifts from the mystic chest an immense pinecone symbolic of the life-renewing principle of the seed, which the death and decay of its vehicle, the cone, are to set free. Compare the words of Paul: "What you sow does not come to life unless it dies. . . . What is sown is perishable, what is raised is imperishable" (I Corinthians 15:36, 42).

4. *A draped female figure, porteress of the*

sanctuary, bearing in her left hand a bowl and in her right a pail (compare Figures 161, 173, and 174; also 244 and 245). She conducts the neophyte within, to the sanctuary of the two goddesses:

5. *Demeter enthroned*, holding in her right hand the flowering scepter of terrestrial life and in her left the open shears by which life's thread is cut; and

6. *Her daughter, Persephone*, as mistress of the Netherworld, enthroned beyond the reign of Demeter's scepter and shears. The torch, her emblem, is symbolic of the light of the Netherworld, a regenerative spiritual fire. As the female power resident in the earth releases the seed life from the cone, so the knowledge of the two goddesses releases the mind of the neophyte from its commitment to what Paul (using the language of the mysteries) termed "this body of death" (Romans 7:24).

The neophyte has now learned the meaning of the raven that perched on his shoulder when he entered the mystic way; also the meanings of the torch and cone that were placed in his hands. We see him next, therefore, as:

7. *The initiated mystes*, standing with his left hand reverently to his breast, holding a chaplet in his right.

8. *Tyche, the goddess of fortune*, touches the initiate with a wand that elevates his spirit above mortality, holding on her left arm a cornucopia symbolic of the abundance she bestows. We are now halfway around the circle, at the point, as it were, of midnight, where:

9. *Agathodaemon, the god of good fortune*, holding in his right hand the poppy stalk of the sleep of death, turned downward, and in his left, pointing upward, a large ear of the grain of life, is to introduce the initiate to:

10. *The Lord of the Abyss.* With his hammer in his right hand and on his left arm a cornucopia, this dark and terrible god is enthroned upon a scaly sea-beast, a sort of modified crocodile. His hammer is the instrument of Plato's divine artificer, by whom the temporal world is fashioned on the model of

cf. Fig. 1(

353. *The Pietroasa Bowl (drawn without the center figure)*

eternal forms; but the same hammer is symbolic, also, of the lightning bolt of illumination (Sanskrit, *vajra*), by which ignorance concerning this same temporal world is destroyed. (Compare the central symbol of Figure 349.) What the mystes has learned at this station of the way is that the god of the creative abyss, whether known as Hades or as Poseidon (Pluto or Neptune), is an aspect of himself, to be experienced within as well as without. And so we move to the next station, that of:

11. *The mystes, fully initiate.* He bears a bowl, as though endowed with a new capacity. His hair is long, and his right hand, on his belly, suggests a woman who has conceived. Yet the chest is clearly male. Thus an androgyne theme is suggested, symbolic of a spiritual experience uniting the opposed ways of knowledge of the male and female; and fused with this idea is that of a new life conceived within. Above the crown of the head, symbolic center of realization, are spiritual wings.

The initiate is now fit to return to the world of daylight. There follow:

12. and 13. *Two young men regarding each other, the classical twin horsemen,* the immortal Pollux and the mortal Castor, respectively. For the mystes, departing from the sanctuary of his experience of androgyny (beyond the opposites not only of femininity and masculinity but also of life and death, time and eternity), must resume his place in the daylight world without forfeiting the wisdom gained; and exactly proper to the sense of such a passage is the dual symbol of the twins, immortal and mortal. Both were horsemen; hence the whips. On the shoulder of Castor, the mortal twin, perches the raven that has not been seen since the neophyte crossed the threshold of the two goddesses, opposite, where the passage was *into* the realm of knowledge beyond death, from which we are now emerging. The raven on Castor's right shoulder and the torch in his left hand correspond to the raven and torch of station 3, and the whip in his right hand adds a token of the initiate's acquired knowledge of his immortal part as a member of the symbolic twin-horsemen syzygy. The whip can be read as the urging instrument of consciousness, driving man's animal nature to its goal.

The last three figures of the series return us to the daylight world:

14. *The returning mystes,* clothed exactly as at station 3, now bears in his left hand a basket of abundance and in his right a sage's staff. He is conducted by:

353a. Center of the Pietroasa Bowl (detail)

15. *A draped female figure with pail and bowl,* counterpart of the figure at station 4. Vines and fruit are to her right and left: fulfillment has been attained. She leads the initiate toward the god to whose vision he has at last arrived and on whom his eyes are fixed:

16. *Hyperborean Apollo,* the mythopoetic personification of the *transcendent* aspect of the Being of beings, as the Lord of the Abyss at station 10 represented the *immanent* aspect of the same. He sits gracefully with lyre in hand and a griffin reposing at his feet— the very god addressed in Orphic hymns as the Lord of both Day and Night:

> *For thou surveyest this boundless ether all,*
> *And every part of this terrestrial ball*
> *Abundant, blessed; and thy piercing sight*
> *Extends beneath the gloomy, silent night;*
> *The world's wide bounds, all-flourishing, are thine,*
> *Thyself of all the source and end divine.*[71]

Having circled the full round, the mystes now is in possession of the knowledge of that mover beyond the motions of the universe, from whose substance the sun derives its light and the dark its light of another kind. The lyre suggests the Pythagorean "harmony of the spheres," and the griffin at the god's feet, combining the forms of the solar bird and solar beast, eagle and lion, is the counterpart of the symbolic animal-fish, the crocodile of night of station 10.

In the inner circle of the mystic bowl, sur-   Fig. 353 rounding the pivotal deity, there is a reclining human being, apparently a shepherd, by whose legs there lies (or runs?) a dog. In front of the dog's nose is a recumbent (or fleeing?) donkey colt. The reclining figure, in contrast to the upright figures of the outer series, suggests sleep ("There is a dream,   cf. Fig. dreaming us"!), the spiritual state of the un-initiated natural man, who sees without understanding; whereas the knowledge gained by the mystes in the outer circle is of those eternal forms, or Platonic ideas, that are the structuring principles of all things, inherent in all, and to be recognized by the wakened mind.

In this inner circle, furthermore, at the point opposite the dreamer, two asses—recumbent and standing—browsing on a plant, are themselves about to be consumed by a leopard and a lion. The one ever-dying, ever-reviving life which is the reality of all beings our mortal eyes see only as the consumer and the consumed. However, the initiate who has penetrated the veil of nature knows that the one life immortal lives in all, which is namely the very god whose symbol is the vine, here proceeding from the feet of the world goddess and encircling the entire composition. "I am the vine, you are the branches" (John 15:5).[72]

In the center of the sacramental bowl, as the pivotal form around which all revolves, sits the Great Goddess, by whatever name, within whose universal womb both night and day (the two knowledges of stations 10 and 16) are enclosed. She is the one mother, both of life, as symbolized by Demeter (5), and of death, life's daughter, Persephone (6). The grapevine entwining her throne matches that of the outer margin of the bowl, and she holds with both hands a large chalice of the ambrosia of this vine of the universe: the blood of her ever-reviving, every-dying, slain and resurrected son, Dionysus-Bacchus-Zagreus (or in the older, Sumero-Babylonian myths, Dumuzi-absu, Tammuz), the "child of the abyss." His blood thus offered, is the pagan prototype of the wine of the Christian sacrifice of the Mass, which has been transubstantiated by the words of consecration into the blood of the Son of the Virgin. For it is only through her that the god-substance pours into this field of space and time in its continuous act of world-creative self-giving* and through her, in return—her guidance and her teaching—that these many who are here her children are led back, beyond her reign, to the light beyond dark from which we all proceed.

cf. Fig. 223

* Compare the Indian "Hymn to the Mother of the World," above, p. 8.

354. Center Figure from the Pietroasa Bowl

6. The Return to Earth

In the now ravished land of high Tibet there were maintained, up to the time of the Chinese Communist entry and desecration of the lamaseries,[73] a number of Tantric Buddhist practices of the greatest psychological interest. The curious *Tibetan Book of the Dead, Bardo Thödol*—"Book of Liberation through Hearing (*thödol*) on the After-Death Plane (*bardo*)"[74]—is perhaps the most important single document to have been brought to us from that last surviving sanctuary and treasury of the mystic lore of antiquity. It is an account, in detail, of the ordeals to be experienced by a reincarnating soul during the seven weeks, or forty-nine days, between death and reentry into life. In the opinion of Jung, the book "belongs to that class of writings which not only are of interest to specialists in Mahayana Buddhism, but also, because of their deep humanity and still deeper insight into the secrets of the human psyche, make an especial appeal to the layman seeking to broaden his knowledge of life." "For years," he adds, "ever since it was first published, the *Bardo Thödol* has been my constant companion, and to it I owe not only many stimulating ideas and discoveries, but also many fundamental insights."[75]

The Lama Anagarika Govinda in a foreword states that though presented and actually used as a guide for the dying and the dead, the *Bardo Thödol* was originally intended to serve as a guide also for the living, "for initiates, and for those who are seeking the spiritual path of liberation." For, as he reminds us: "It is one of the oldest and most universal practices for the initiate to go through the experience of death before he can be spiritually reborn."[76]

What we are to recognize in this work, therefore, is a reflex, from the last surviving outpost of antiquity, of hidden rites of revelation that for centuries flourished throughout the ancient world, such as even Socrates celebrates in the *Phaedo*, where he speaks of "practicing death" and of the value of religious initiations.

"Of course you know," said Socrates to his two friends Simmias and Cebes,

> "that when a person dies, although it is natural for the visible and the physical part of him, which lies here in the visible world and which we call his corpse, to decay and fall to pieces and be dissipated, none of this happens to it immediately. It remains as it is for quite a long time, even if death takes place when the body is well nourished and in the warm season. Indeed, when the body is dried and embalmed, as in Egypt, it remains almost intact for an incredible time, and even if the rest of the body decays, some parts of it—the bones and sinews and anything else like them—are practically everlasting. . . . But the soul, the invisible part, which goes away to a place that is, like itself, glorious, pure, and invisible—the true Hades or unseen world—into the presence of the good and wise God, where, if God so wills, my soul must shortly go: will it, if its very nature is such as I have described, be dispersed and destroyed at the moment of its release from the body, as is the popular

view? Far from it, my dear Simmias and Cebes. The truth is much more like this:

"If at its release the soul is pure and carries with it no contamination of the body, because it has never willingly associated with it in life, but has shunned it and kept itself separate as its regular practice—in other words, if it has pursued philosophy in the right way and really practiced how to face death easily—this is what 'practicing death' means. Isn't it?"

"Most decidedly."

"Very well, if this is its condition, then it departs to that place which is, like itself, invisible, divine, immortal, and wise, where, on its arrival, happiness awaits it, and release from uncertainty and folly, from fears and uncontrolled desires, and all other human evils, and where, as they say of the initiates in the Mysteries, it really spends the rest of time with God. Shall we adopt this view, Cebes, or some other?"

"This one by all means," said Cebes.

"But, I suppose, if at the time of its release the soul is tainted and impure, because it has always associated with the body and cared for it and loved it, and has been so beguiled by the body and its passions and pleasures that nothing seems real to it but those physical things which can be touched and seen and eaten and drunk and used for sexual enjoyment, and if it is accustomed to hate and fear and avoid what is invisible and hidden from our eyes, but intelligible and comprehensible by philosophy—if the soul is in this state, do you think that it will escape independent and uncontaminated?"

"On the contrary, it will, I imagine, be permeated by the corporeal, which fellowship and intercourse with the body will have ingrained in its very nature through constant association and long practice."

"Certainly."

"And we must suppose, my dear fellow, that the corporeal is heavy, oppressive, earthly, and visible. So the soul which is tainted by its presence is weighed down and dragged back into the visible world, through fear, as they say, of Hades or the invisible, and hovers about tombs and graveyards. The shadowy apparitions which have actually been seen there are the ghosts of those souls which have not got clear away, but still retain some portion of the visible, which is why they can be seen."

"That seems likely enough, Socrates."

"Yes, it does, Cebes. Of course these are not the souls of the good, but of the wicked, and they are compelled to wander about these places as a punishment for their bad conduct in the past. They continue wandering until at last through craving for the corporeal, which unceasingly pursues them, they are imprisoned once more in a body. As you might expect, they are attached to the same sort of character or nature which they have developed during life."

"What sort do you mean, Socrates?"

"Well, those who have cultivated gluttony or selfishness or drunkenness, instead of taking pains to avoid them, are likely to assume the form of donkeys and other perverse animals. Don't you think so?"

"Yes, that is very likely."

"And those who have deliberately preferred a life of irresponsible lawlessness and violence become wolves and hawks and kites, unless we can suggest any other more likely animals."

"No, the ones which you mention are exactly right."

"So it is easy to imagine into what sort of animals all the other kinds of soul will go, in accordance with their conduct during life."

"Yes, certainly."

"I suppose that the happiest people, and those who reach the best destination, are the ones who have cultivated the goodness of an ordinary citizen—what is called self-control and integrity—which is acquired by habit and practice, without the help of philosophy and reason."

"How are these the happiest?"

"Because they will probably pass into some other kind of social and disciplined creature like bees, wasps, and ants, or even back into the human race again, becoming decent citizens."

"Very likely."

"But no soul which has not practiced philosophy, and is not absolutely pure when it leaves the body, may attain to the divine nature; that is only for the lover of wisdom. This is the reason, my dear Simmias and Cebes, why true philosophers abstain from all bodily desires and withstand them and do not yield to them. It is not because they are afraid of financial loss or poverty, like the average man who thinks of money first, nor because they shrink from dishonor and a bad reputation, like those who are ambitious for distinction and authority."

"No, those would be unworthy motives, Socrates," said Cebes.

"They would indeed," he agreed. "And so, Cebes, those who care about their souls and do not subordinate them to the body dissociate themselves firmly from these others and refuse to accompany them on their haphazard journey, and, believing that it is wrong to oppose philosophy with her offer of liberation and purification, they turn and follow her wherever she leads. . . ."[77]

"Perhaps," said Socrates at the start of this dialogue, "these people who direct the religious initiations are not so far from the mark; and all the time there has been an allegorical meaning beneath their doctrine that he who enters the next world uninitiated and unenlightened shall lie in the mire, but he who arrives there purified and enlightened shall dwell among the gods."[78]

The leading idea of the *Bardo Thödol* is that the Innate Clear Light is beheld immediately at the moment of death, so that the end experience of yoga is to be at that moment attained by each. However, those still clinging to ego find the blaze of that light unendurable, and for them a graded descent then begins through planes of increasing opacity, until, at the end of forty-nine days, unless arrested on the way, they will have been carried back to life in the womb of another birth.

Three distinct stages mark the course of this way of return:

I. The *Chikhai Bardo*: "Intermediate State of the Moment of Death," corresponding in its two sub-stages to the states of the Kundalini chakras seven and six.

II. The *Chönyid Bardo*: "Intermediate State of Glimpsing Reality," corresponding in its two sub-stages to the trials of chakra five.

III. The *Sidpa Bardo*: "Intermediate State of Seeking Rebirth," corresponding in its two sub-stages to the states of chakra four and of chakras three, two, and one.

I. CHIKHAI BARDO: THE MOMENT OF DEATH

Stage 1: Of the Primary Clear Light

The person dying having been turned on his right side by the attendant lama at his bedside, with his limbs arranged in the so-called "lion-posture" assumed by the Buddha when he was about to pass from the world of rebirths, he is reminded by the lama's voice of the teachings that have prepared him for this critical moment, which if lost will not soon return; and the minute his breathing stops: "O nobly born (so and so by name)," says the lama, "you are now experiencing the Primary Clear Light in its Reality in the Bardo state, where all is like the void of a cloudless sky. Try to abide in that state. Your own clear intellect, now voidness unobstructed—shining, thrilling and blissful—is now the very consciousness of the All-good Buddha, himself. This and that are indistinguishable; and their union is the Dharma-kaya, Body of Truth."[79]

Fig. 355

355. *Parinirvana of the Buddha.* A.D. *12th century. Ceylon*

Stage 2: Appearance of the Apparitional Form
of the Secondary Clear Light

Should there be reason to fear, however, that the Primary Clear Light has not been recognized and accepted, "then," the text advises, "it can certainly be assumed that there is dawning upon the deceased the manifestation called the Secondary Clear Light, which dawns in somewhat more than a mealtime period after breathing has ceased"; and the lama now is to urge his charge to meditate on his chosen deity: the particular Buddha on whose name and form he had meditated throughout life. "Meditate," he is told, "on your tutelary deity as though his image were the reflection of the moon in water—apparent, yet in itself inexistent."[80]

Fig. 209   The form beheld may be, for example, that of the "Great Sun Buddha," Mahavairo-
Fig. 356   chana; or of the Buddha and his shakti in union. The mystery of the Chikhai
Fig. 348   Bardo is thus exactly that of Dante's vision of God at once as light and in human form. And the duration of such a vision at the Moment of Death will vary, it is said, according to the subject's readiness to endure it: "In those who have had even a little practical experience of the firm, tranquil state of meditation, and in those who have sound nerves, the confrontation of the Primary Clear Light endures only so long as it would take to snap a finger."[81] And further: "If the first stage of the *Bardo* has been taken by the forelock, that is best. But even where the Primary Clear Light has not been recognized, if the Clear Light of the second stage is recognized, Liberation will be attained. If not liberated even by that, then the *Chönyid Bardo* dawns, where the karmic illusions of the worlds of action come to shine."[82]

356. The Adi Buddha and His Shakti (detail). A.D. *18th century. Tibet*

II. CHÖNYID BARDO: THE GLIMPSING
OF REALITY

The very name Chönyid Bardo, "The Intermediate State (*bar-do*) of the Glimpsing of Reality (*chö-nyid*)," announces the nature of the problem now to be confronted. It is to distinguish between the temporal and eternal aspects of phenomenality; for in terms of the Kundalini system: having dropped from the seventh to the sixth lotus stage and having lost our place even there, we are now to experience a series of trials in the purgatorial center, the fifth stage. This is *Vishuddha*, where for a season of some fourteen days two series of seven visions each will be endured: the first seven of the Peaceful and the second of the Wrathful Deities, the first seven of inflections of the *voidness* of the Body of Truth and the second of its *radiance*. In effect, we are following in reverse Dante's course through purgatory, with the bed-side lama in the role of Virgil. At this juncture he will be saying:

> "O nobly born, whatever fears and terrors may come to you, bear the meaning of this prayer in your heart; for in it lies the vital secret of recognition:
> "*May I recognize whatever visions appear, as the reflections of my own consciousness.*
> "*May I know them to be of the nature of apparitions in the Intermediate State.*
> "*May I not fear the troops of my own thought forms, the Peaceful Deities and the Wrathful.*"[83]

The figures about to appear will be transformations of the five Meditation Buddhas that are represented as five jewels in the crown of the Buddha of Clear Light, and they will appear, first, in their peaceful, beneficent forms, to draw the ready spirit to release through the radiance of their respective modes of nirvanic rapture; but failing in that, they will next put on dynamic, nightmarish forms, to shatter with frightening awe the binding, self-protective hindrances of a tenacious ego-consciousness. So then:

Stage 1: Apparitions of the Peaceful Deities

As the apparitional form of the Great Sun Buddha, Mahavairochana, fades, there will be seen appearing from a central point called the "Spreading Forth of the Seeds

357 (*opposite*). *The Five Dhyani Buddhas.*
A.D. *19th century. Tibet*

Center: Vairochana, the Sun Buddha, white (or blue), on a lion throne, holding the Wheel of Truth.

Lower left (East): Vajrasattva, "Whose Being is the Adamantine Bolt," blue (or white), on an elephant throne, holding a vajra.

Upper left (South): Ratnasambhava,

"Jewel Born," yellow, on a horse throne, holding a jewel.

Upper right (West): Amitabha, "Unmeasured Radiance," red, on a lotus throne (with water birds), holding a lotus.

Lower right (North): Amoghasiddhi, "Unerring Victory in Achievement," green, on a harpy throne, holding a thunderbolt (usually double and crossed ✳).

of All Things" the Lesser Sun Buddha, Vairochana, embraced by his shakti, "the Mother of Space." White in color, he is seated on a lion throne, holding an eight-spoked Wheel of Truth and emitting such a dazzling azure Light of Truth that the unready consciousness, overwhelmed with fear, turns to a lesser, dull white light that will also have appeared and is not of Buddha-consciousness, but of the gods (devas). "Be not fond of the dull white light of the gods," the lama will be saying. "If attached to it, you will stray into the mansions of the gods and so be drawn to the round of six worlds."[84]

Fig. 358

The second day of this series of apparitions, if the first vision is allowed to fade, there will appear from the deep blue East the form of the Buddha known as "Un-shakable" (Akshobhya), "Whose Being is the Adamantine Bolt" (Vajrasattva). Bearing a five-pronged thunderbolt, he is seated on an elephant throne, embraced by his shakti Mamaki, whose name means "My and Mine," or "Greed"; for the same natural appetite that binds us to the goods of this world may become, when turned about to the aim of illumination, our very vehicle of release. So in Tantric thought and practice, that by which we fall is to be converted into that by which we rise again, and the "turning about," as it is called, "of our shakti in the deepest seat of consciousness" is treated and regarded as the first and ultimate necessary step of the religious life. In terms of the Kundalini system: the energy of chakra three is to be turned to the work of five; that of chakra two to the rapture of six; and the deep, dark sleep of chakra one to extinction in the light of the silent void.

Now from the father-mother vision of the Buddha "Whose Being is the Adaman-tine Bolt" embraced by his shakti "My and Mine" there comes pouring such a daz-zling beam of mirrored radiance that the mind unready for such glory may turn

358. *The Wheel of Becoming.* A.D. *19th century. Tibet*

In the center revolve the motivating "Three Poisons": ignorance (pig), desire (cock), hostility (serpent). Next circle: souls descending and ascending in round of rebirth. Next, the six realms of rebirth, a teaching Bodhisattva in each (from top, circling clockwise): realms of 1. gods, 2. titans, 3. hungry ghosts, 4. hell beings, 5. beasts, 6. mankind. In the rim, holding all enclosed, the "Twelve Interdependent Causes" (clockwise from lower left): 1. ignorance (blind woman being led), 2. karmic formations (potter), 3. consciousness (monkeys), 4. mind and body (man ferrying another), 5. senses (houses with windows), 6. contact (lovers), 7. sensation (man, eye pierced by arrow), 8. desire (man drinking), 9. attachment (men reaching hands across chasm), 10. existence (man by tree), 11. birth (woman giving birth), 12. old age and death (corpse carried to be eaten by jackals and vultures).

359. *Lion-headed Dakini.* A.D. *18th-19th century. Tibet*

360. *Sarva-Buddha Dakini.* A.D. *18th-19th century. Tibet*

away in terror to a dull smoke-colored light from hell that is also shining in this Buddha-field. "Those Buddha-rays that you see," the lama will be assuring the deceased, "are the hook of the rays of grace of the Lord Unshakable, come to save you from the terror of the Intermediate State. Do not turn to the dull, smoke-colored light from Hell."[85] But this opportunity too may fade, and the next apparition then arises.

The Lord Buddha "Jewel Born" (Ratnasambhava) will be seen appearing from the South: yellow in hue, bearing a jewel, seated on a horse throne, and embraced by his shakti "Buddha-Eyes." For the virtue of this Buddha-land is beauty, and its obscuring passion pride. There will be glowing a dull, bluish-yellow light rising from the world of human life, to which the mind may turn for relief from the dazzling yellow Wisdom-Light of Harmony of this father-mother Buddha pair. The shakti of one's own pride, that is to say, may not have turned about to regard the beauty, not of one's body and its temporal world, but of the Holder of the Jewel of Immortal Light; and again, the vision of this saving Buddha pair will fade and another be seen arising from the West.

The fourth Meditation Buddha is Amitabha, the great Lord of "Unmeasured Radiance," of the Western Paradise,* red in color, bearing a lotus, enthroned on a lotus and embraced by his shakti, known as "Woman in White." Their saving virtue is compassion, of which the obscuring passion, however, is attachment; and if one's gaze cannot endure the rainbow radiance of the light of this pair, there will be seen a dull red glow to which the mind may turn, arising from the world of the Hungry Ghosts—which is a miserable domain of inconsolable spirits, having large, insatiable stomachs and tiny, pinpoint mouths.

The fifth Buddha to appear will be of the North, Amoghasiddhi, the Lord of "Unerring Victory in Achievement." Of a dazzling green, glorious and terrifying, bearing a crossed thunderbolt and with radiant orbs surrounded by satellite orbs pouring from his Buddha-heart, he is seated on a flying harpy throne, embraced by his shakti, the glorious Green Tara, who is radiant with the light of her all-achieving wisdom. And from the world of the pugnacious Titans a dull green light will also be glowing here, of the sentiment of jealousy, which may attract the gaze and draw one into the brutal Titan-world of quarreling and war.

The sixth day, all five father-mother Buddha pairs appear together in a splendid multicolored mandala, each with a galaxy of attendants, and along with these the illusory lights of all six temporal worlds simultaneously: the dull white of the world of the gods, the smoke color of hell, the bluish-yellow of humanity, the dark red of the Hungry Ghosts, the green of the Titans, and along with all these, the murky blue of the beasts. "O nobly born," the lama will be saying, "these realms have not appeared from outside yourself. They are from within the directions of your heart. . . . They are the compassionate Radiances of Wisdom of the Five Orders of Those-Who-

---

* See above, pp. 221-232.

Have-Passed-into-Happiness, here come to draw you from the vortex. Do not be drawn instead to the impure lights of the worlds of this round of pain."[86]

Figs. 359, 360

On the seventh and final day of this peaceful stage of the Bardo, a new, inferior set of powers becomes visible in a great mandala of dancers, the Knowledge-Holding Deities, together with innumerable fairylike female figures known as Dakinis, which may appear in either alluring or frightening forms and are embodiments of the knowledge of unveiled reality. The pathway to the brute world, meanwhile, is marked by the dull blue light of the obscuring passion of stupidity, which is the danger inherent in this context. In the center of the brilliant dancing throng there appears the many-armed Lotus Lord of the Dance, haloed in a rainbow light and radiant with all five colors. He is flourishing in one raised hand a crescent knife, bears in another a skull full of blood, and, holding aloft a third in the posture of fascination,[*87] dances embraced by a Red Dakini. Simultaneously, from the East the Earth-Abiding Knowledge-Holder appears, white and with smiling countenance, embraced by the White Dakini; from the South, the Knowledge-Holder Having Power Over the Duration of Life, yellow, radiant, and smiling, dancing with the Yellow Dakini; from the West, the Knowledge-Holder of the Middle Path, red of hue, smiling, embraced by a Red Dakini; and from the North, the Knowledge-Holder Self-Evolved,

* Second finger touching thumb, third folded to the palm, index and little finger upright.

361. Chakra-Samvaraja and His Shakti, Vajra-Yogini

Discriminating Wisdom, which distinguishes between the ephemeral and essential aspects of experience, is the active, temporally operative energy (shakti) of the Perfection of Wisdom and is here personified as the radiant, fiery "Thunderbolt Mistress of Spiritual Union," Vajra-Yogini, in her zeal for the "Lord or King" (raja) of the "Comprehending and Enclosing" (samvara) "Wheel or Cycle" (chakra) of space-time. And he, the personification of Buddha-consciousness delighting in its own reflections mirrored in the cycles, responds to her zeal for his all-suffusing presence. There is a relevant meditation:

"Identifying yourself with Vajra-Yogini, visualize her [i.e., yourself infected with her zeal] as active in the purgatorial throat center [Chakra 5, above, pp. 368-379], red and vividly radiant as the cleansing fire of Divine Speech, and epitomized in the syllable AH. Concentrating mentally on this sound as that which is enduring, recognize all phenomenal things as forms reflected in a mirror, which,

though apparent, have no self-existence. So shall you understand the Great Dream."[89]

Above the symbolic couple is a representation of their transcendent peaceful dimension known as Sahaja-Samvara, "Naturally Co-existent Comprehension," flanked to their right (our left) by Hevajra, the "Joyous or Eternal Thunderbolt," and left (our right) by Kalachakra, the "Wheel of Time"; while directly beneath is the personification of their effect upon phenomenal forms as Bhairavavajra, the "Thunderbolt of Terror," known also as Yamantaka, "Slayer of the Lord Death," flanked to his right by Vajrapani, "Thunderbolt in Hand," and left by a magical Phurbu, or "Spirit Nail," with its guardian, for the nailing down (in meditation) of obstructing demons. Samvara is a Tantric, purely visionary deity: not a god in the sense of a supernatural "fact" of some kind, but the personification of a state of consciousness to be striven for, achieved, and retained.

who is green, half-angry, half-smiling, radiant of countenance and embraced by the Green Dakini. Dakinis also of many classes, pouring from many residences, come dancing from all sides, together with heroes, heroines, celestial warriors, and faith-protecting guardians, all bedecked with ornaments of bone, bearing drums and thigh-bone trumpets, skull timbrels, banners of gigantic human hides, human-hide canopies and banners, incense of human fat, and with a noise of many instruments, such as to make the whole world-system quake, vibrate, and tremble, and to dazzle a person's brain. Moreover, within that din there reverberates like a thousand thunders the natural sound of Truth, together with a repeated cry, "Slay! Slay!" while from the guiding lama at the bedside admonitions are coming now continually: "Fear not. Flee not. Be not terrified. Know these sounds to be of the intellectual faculties of your own inner light: know their wisdom to be your own. Be not drawn to the dull blue light of the brute world of stupidity, lest you be carried thither to miseries illimitable of slavery and stupor, from which release will not come soon."[88]

Stage 2: *Apparitions of the Wrathful Deities*

Multitudes, it is said, obtain release in one or another of the Buddha-realms of the Peaceful Deities. Those who do not, pass to the Wrathful; and the first of these greatly frightening forms to appear will be of Vairochana again, but in the aspect known as the Great and Glorious Buddha Heruka:

> . . . dark brown in color, with three heads, six hands and four feet firmly postured; the right face white, the left red, and the central, dark brown; the nine eyes widely opened in terrifying gaze, eyebrows quivering like lightning; the protruding teeth all glistening, set one over another: body emitting flames of radiance, throats giving vent to sonorous utterances of "a-la-la" and "ha-ha," and piercing whistling sounds: hair of a reddish yellow, standing on end, emitting a radiance; the heads adorned with dried human skulls and the symbols of sun and moon; black serpents and raw human heads forming a garland for the body, and the upper right hand holding a wheel, the middle a sword, the lower a battle-ax; the upper left, a bell, the middle, a skull-bowl, the last a ploughshare.
>
> Moreover his body is embraced by the Mighty Wrathful Buddha-Mother, right hand clinging to his neck, left holding a red shell of blood to his mouth, making with her own mouth a loud clacking clashing sound and a rumbling sound, as of thunder. Radiant flames of Wisdom blaze from every hair pore of these two, each blaze containing a flaming thunderbolt, and they stand, each with one leg bent, the other straight and tense, on a dais supported by horned eagles. . . .

"Be not afraid," says the guiding lama, "for this deity, come from your own mind, is in reality the blessed Father-Mother Vairochana."[90]

From East, South, West, and North, successively, then, the father-mother Buddha pairs of those quarters, likewise in horrendous aspects, day by day, will appear and, if unrecognized, fade away: the dark blue couple of the adamantine thunderbolt;

darkish yellow pair of the jewel; the reddish black, of the lotus; and dark green, of victorious action. Then, as before, all five will appear at once, but now surrounded by ghouls: eight wrathful Cemetery Goddesses from the eight points of the compass, one brandishing a human corpse, another chewing entrails, a third stirring with her thunderbolt the contents of a skull-bowl from which she drinks with majestic relish; still another tearing the head from a corpse and eating it like a fruit. Following which, from the same eight world-regions, animal-headed ghouls appear: lion-headed and tiger-headed, fox-, wolf-, vulture-, and owl-headed, crow- and cemetery-bird-headed; all together, horribly.

On the fourteenth day, the last of this purgatorial course, there appear from the quarters the four animal-headed fiends who watch the gates to the plane below: from the East, the white, tiger-headed, goad-holding goddess; from the South, the yellow, sow-headed, with a noose; from the West, the red, lion-headed; and from the North, the green, serpent-headed, with a chain. Thereafter, moreover, many more: yak-headed, leopard- and monkey-headed, snowbear-headed, and so on, flourishing clubs, thunderbolts, tridents, wheels, intestine-nooses, and what not, to the full number of twenty-eight. And in all of these, again, one is to recognize only emanations of the radiance of the Body of Truth; for indeed, these horrible killers and ghouls are but "glimpses of reality" seen from that archetypal plane of mythic truth that we enter in death and in dream.

III. SIDPA BARDO: THE SEEKING OF REBIRTH

As C. G. Jung has observed in his commentary, it is only in the Sidpa Bardo, these last and lowest stages of the Tibetan spiritual adventure, that the Oriental experience approaches (from the opposite direction, however) those ranges of psychological symbolism and stress that have been recognized, named, and studied in our modern psychoanalytic schools. And here again, as in each of the higher Bardos, the stages numbered are two.

Stage 1: Of the Judgment Scene

In terms of the Kundalini system, the lotus center of this critical conflict of eternal and temporal values is the fourth, Anahata, at the level of the heart, where on the ascending scale the sound was first heard that is *not* made by any two things striking together. For it was there that the great decision was made to follow the lure of that sound, to let go the clash of phenomena and press on into the mystery of one's own and the world's inward dimension; whereas now, coming down into that same center from above, the crisis will be faced with opposite results. We are now, that is to say, on the way to acquiring, not to abandoning, a body—although, as the lama at the bedside tells, even now, by an act of fearless, desireless, recognition of the voidness of the apparitions, release can still be gained.

"This moment," he gravely warns, "is one of supreme importance. Should you be distracted now, innumerable eons of time will be required for you to emerge from the Quagmire of Misery."[91]

"Up to the other day, you were unable to recognize the apparitional nature of the Chönyid Bardo and have had to wander down this far. Now, if you are to hold fast to the real Truth, *you must allow your mind to rest undistractedly in the nothing-to-do, nothing-to-hold condition of the unobscured, primordial, bright, void state of your intellect*"[92]—which, as Dr. Evans-Wentz points out, is exactly the unmodified, unmoving state of the mind-stuff defined in the first aphorism of the *Yoga Sutras* of Patanjali.*

The descending, returning consciousness may remain on this plane of proofs and tests for as long as thirty days or more, even up to the last few minutes before conception. It will, in fact, already have put on a body of its own—a Bardo body, as it is called, not of gross but of subtle matter—which will be able to see and to recognize earthly forms, to hear the sounds of this world, and to pass through walls, rock masses, hills, and mountains, traverse distances in a moment, and assume a variety of shapes. In short, the soul's condition here is that of those same unhappy graveyard ghosts remarked by Socrates. The ghost may see its former relatives weeping and realize, "I am dead! What shall I do?" If it is to return as a human being, the sights seen will be of the human sphere; if as a god or a titan, hell-being or brute beast, the sights will be of those. And there will begin to be felt fierce winds blowing, driving one ever downward, hard to resist; the eight fierce winds of earthly karma: of gain and loss, joy and sorrow, praise and blame, eulogy and defamation: winds rippling intelligence, breaking the repose of the nothing-to-do, nothing-to-hold state.

A thick, awesome darkness gathers. Cries of "Strike!" and "Slay!" are heard. Flesh-eating ghouls appear, and if the mind allows itself to be set moving by all or any of these, three massive walls will arise behind, to block retreat: the imprisoning walls of Stupidity, Lust, and Anger, which are the forces, namely, of the Kundalini centers one, two, and three, now gaining hold. They are represented in Figure 362, in the center of the mandala, as (1) a pig, signifying stupidity (2) a cock, signifying lust, and (3) a serpent, anger. And when these walls have arisen, behold! The Lord of Death himself appears for the judgment, gazing in his karmic mirror, where the victim's good and evil deeds are shown. He will summon his executioners, and these, as the lama warns his charge, "will place a rope around your neck, drag you about, cut off your head, dig out your heart, pull out your guts, drink your blood, lick up your brain, eat your flesh and gnaw your bones; but you will not be able to die."

"Be not terrified," he advises, however, "do not tremble, do not fear the Lord of Death. Your body is of the nature of voidness and this Lord of Judgment and his

Fig. 358

Fig. 362

* Above, p. 313.

362. *Yama and Yami, The Lord Death and His Shakti*

Furies too are void: they are your own hallucinations. What you are suffering is your own doing. Voidness cannot hurt voidness."[93]

So too will it be, we are given to know, during life on the gross earthly plane of this world, this world of earthly fact, whenever like terrors attack: as they attacked, indeed, in the present century, the Buddhist lamas of Tibet when the People's Army of China appeared to reproduce on their bodies of flesh all the atrocities of this mythic Bardo scene. If at such a time the monk—or anyone at all—should succeed in retaining the perfect Buddha-composure of this Buddhist "Great Symbol Practice" (the outer world recognized as an apparitional great mandala and one's own body therein as one's tutelary Buddha, like a moon reflected in water), Buddhahood would be immediately attained.

"O nobly born, be not distracted. Should you become distracted now, the chords of divine compassion will break and you will go into a place from which there is no immediate liberation."[94]

Stage 2: The Passage to Rebirth

For the plunge next is to be through the fields of the lower Kundalini chakras, the past life becoming less and less recollectable, the future beginning to materialize, and the lama at the bedside reduced to the final desperate pass of attempting, as the text declares, "to close the womb door" to his now rapidly descending charge.

At the first level of this plunge, corresponding the Kundalini chakra three, the deceased, moving now swiftly toward rebirth, is advised that when he sees before him visions of males and females in union, he must keep from going between them.[95] Failing this, he will be on his way to the lotus of desire, chakra two, and certain rebirth. If he is to be born as a male, attraction for the mother will be felt and of hatred for the father, but if female, the opposite. As Jung remarks, such references at this juncture have a distinctly Freudian ring, and, occurring here as they do, help to explain the inaccessibility of higher chakras to the probings of Freudian thought:

> Freudian psychoanalysis, in all essential aspects never went beyond the experiences of the *Sidpa Bardo*; that is, it was unable to extricate itself from sexual fantasies and similar "incompatible" tendencies which cause anxiety and other affective states. Nevertheless, Freud's theory is the first attempt made by the West to investigate, as if from below, from the animal sphere of instinct, the psychic territory that corresponds in Tantric Lamaism to the *Sidpa Bardo*. A very justifiable fear of metaphysics prevented Freud from penetrating into the sphere of the "occult." In addition to this, the *Sidpa* state, if we are to accept the psychology of the *Sidpa Bardo*, is characterized by the fierce wind of *karma*, which whirls the dead man along until he comes to the "womb-door." In other words, the *Sidpa* state permits of no going back, because it is sealed off against the *Chönyid* state by an intense striving downwards, towards the animal sphere of instinct and physical rebirth. That is to say, anyone who penetrates into the unconscious with purely biological assumptions will become stuck in the instinctual sphere and be unable to advance beyond it, for he will be pulled back again and again into physical existence. It is therefore not possible for Freudian theory to reach anything except an essentially negative valuation of the unconscious. It is a "nothing but."
>
> At the same time, it must be admitted that this view of the psyche is typically Western, only it is expressed more blatantly, more plainly, and more ruthlessly [by Freud] than others would have dared to express it. . . .
>
> I believe that we can state it as a fact that with the aid of psychoanalysis the rationalizing mind of the West has pushed forward into what one might call the neuroticism of the *Sidpa* state, and has there been brought to an inevitable standstill by the uncritical assumption that everything psychological is subjective and personal. Even so, this advance has been a great gain, inasmuch as it has enabled us to take one more step behind our conscious lives. This knowledge also gives us a hint of how we ought to read the *Bardo Thödol*—that is, backwards. If, with the help of our Western science, we have to some extent succeeded in understanding the psychological character of the *Sidpa Bardo*, our next task is to see if we can make anything of the preceding *Chönyid Bardo*.[96]

363. The Goddess Tlazolteotl Giving Birth to the Sun-god. Aztec. Mexico

The karmic wind, the irresistible downward draft, the last desperate effort to close the door of the womb at the level of chakra three, and then at the level of chakra two (the lotus land of Eros, youngest and oldest of the gods that rule the world), one begins to feel an attraction for the place from which one is to be born. . . . And the next thing the world knows is the growing in the body of its mother of a new creature, dark with the avidity of chakra one and lost in forgetfulness of all it has experienced: to be brought to light in due time in the field of Waking Consciousness, full of ignorance, sleep, bewilderment, terrors, and unconsidered urges, to prepare again, through another life, to make good the opportunities missed.

V. THE SACRIFICE

364. *Luther Preaching the Word. Lucas Cranach the Younger.* A.D. *16th century*

1. The Willing Victim

"CHRIST JESUS," wrote the apostle Paul to his congregation in Philippi, "though he was in the form of God, did not count equality with God a thing to be grasped, but emptied himself, taking the form of a servant, being born in the likeness of men. And being found in human form he humbled himself and became obedient unto death, even death on a cross" (2:6-8).

The apostle urged his flock therefore to be of the same mind as Christ. "Do nothing," he wrote, "from selfishness or conceit, but in humility count others better than yourselves. Let each of you look not only to his own interests, but also to the interests of others. Have this mind among yourselves, which you have in Christ Jesus . . ." (2:2-5).

This woodcut by Lucas Cranach gives a Reformational, Protestant turn to the sense of this teaching of Paul. Consigning the Roman Catholic clergy—monks, cardinals, popes, and all—to the flaming jaws of hell, the preaching Luther points away from those celibates, now torn from their sanctuaries of pomp and ease, to the lay community of men and women, humble in their engagement to life, as representing best in this troubled world the obedience of Christ to the Cross.

In contemporary German Catholic art, meanwhile, the Pauline theme of the willing victim was being rendered in those charming Rhineland "Annunciation" Fig. 218 scenes already noticed, where the infant Jesus, joyfully descending to his mother, is already bearing his Cross. In the Buddhist sphere a like idea is embodied in the figure of the Bodhisattva: that one "released while living," whose "essence" (*sattva*) is "enlightenment" (*bodhi*), and who yet refuses release from this world of sorrows for himself that he may remain to instruct, comfort, and release others—with the implication, paradoxically, that if they accept this ideal, they too will refuse release and remain through innumerable lifetimes, giving of themselves selflessly to all.

365. *The Way of the Bodhisattva: Almsgiving.* A.D. *8th-9th century. Borobudur, Java*

The Buddha is normally pictured as a monk; the Bodhisattva, on the contrary, in the garments of a secular role (above). Not resisting the karmic winds* but accepting and affirming them, not holding to the *voidness* of the Body of Truth but coming to birth as an incarnation of its *radiance*, this kind of Savior enters the world not as the teacher of a way out of it but as witness to a divine dimension within it, opening the way to Buddhahood through what in *The Lotus of the Good Law* is called "joyful acceptance."

* See above, p. 408.

366. *Standing Bodhisattva.* A.D. *2nd-3rd century. Gandhara, India*

In one of the small but profoundly impressive Buddhist cave temples of Aurangabad, there are two great standing Bodhisattvas, each holding a lotus stalk supporting on its corolla a meditating Buddha, and with a joyous young serpent prince at its root, urging the lotus upward. The first and most obvious lesson of these imposing presences is that the infinite compassion of the Bodhisattva is what sends forth Buddhas for the teaching of the world. The compassion of the Bodhisattva, not the absolute release of the Buddha from sorrow, is thus represented here as the higher principle. Further, since the Buddhist and Hindu divinities of this period—the eighth century A.D.—are to be understood in Tantric terms, as personifications of powers inward and essential to ourselves, not gods and powers simply "out there," the second wordless message of these images is an address of encouragement to that potential within ourselves which is their counterpart and which is matched in the life-zeal and irrepressible spontaneity of nature. In contrast to the Hindu vision of Vishnu as the world-dreamer, these Buddhist messengers are not asleep but awake; nor does the lotus spring from their body: it is consciously held in the hand and elevated, not just the blossom but the whole, in total affirmation of the whole length and range of the lotus stalk, the lotus-ladder of human experience, all the way from the deep dark center at "Root Support" to the summit light of nirvanic realization at the level of the lotus "Thousand Petalled," knowing and holding all in hand as one entity, one whole. And the little serpent prince at the root is now alert and awake, joyous, charming, and altogether aware of what he is doing.

Comparing this image with that of the Old Germanic world ash, Yggdrasil*— where the dragon Nithhogg gnaws at the root, the solar eagle perches on top, and the wonderful squirrel Ratatosk goes running up and down the trunk—we may presume to guess for what knowledge Othin hung on the "windy tree," a sacrifice (as the poet tells) to Othin, himself to himself. "Whoever seeks to gain his life will lose it," we read in the gospel according to Luke (17:33), "but whoever loses his life will preserve it." That is a message truly from the Yonder Shore, where the Wisdom-Self resides.

When the Bodhisattva teaches, we have been told, he assumes the outward forms of his auditors; but his message is addressed to the Wisdom-Self within each, to wake and call it to life. When shown with many arms, many hands, many heads, gazing and serving in all directions, this awakener is an image of that consciousness within all which through pain, sorrow, and suffering yet affirms the phenomenal world—and affirms it not as some might think it "ought" to be, but as it is. He is known, accordingly, as the "god of the present," and his character, free of passion, is benevolence without intention. Known also as "He Who Bears the World," he absorbs in his infinite person the sorrows and pains of the world, transforming all to that ambrosial knowledge on the plane of Buddha-consciousness which, pouring from his fingertips, going forth from every pore of his luminous being, yields comfort and sustaining bliss even to souls in the hells. And in doing this, he is not a

* See above, p. 192.

power "out there" in someone else, or in some god somewhere, but within each living thing, within ourselves, inward, essential, and to be found.

In the long view of history, this positive, life-supporting attitude of the willing victim, moving with full knowledge not away from but ever more generously into the vortex of this world of painful joy and joyful pain, is infinitely older, and at once more primitive and sophisticated, than its opposite of the hermit cell and the will either to a painless bliss in some paradise or to extinction. The young Mayan

Fig. 273 maize god holding his hands in the Asian Bodhisattva "fear-dispelling" and "boon-bestowing" postures bears on his chest the mask of death. One reference of this mask must be to the mythic theme—for which Frazer in *The Golden Bough* has cited no end of examples from all over the world—of the sacrificed divinity from the buried fragments of whose dismembered body the food plants sustaining human life arose: wheat and rice in the Old World; in the Americas maize and manioc; coconuts, taro, breadfruit, and yams in the Pacific. But in addition, throughout the Mayan-Toltec-Aztec sphere there was also the idea expressed in the myth, recounted above,* of the universe set in motion through the sacrifice of a god. And finally,

Figs. 368-370 as suggested in the Bodhisattva posture of the richly bejeweled priestly or godly personage of Figure 369, there is the possibility also of a direct trans-Pacific influence from the seafaring Buddhist civilizations of East and Southeast Asia and Oceania, which would have added to the vegetal and cosmogonic references of the mythological sacrifice an emphatically inward, psychological order of meaning.

In the year 1524 a delegation of Aztec nobles defended their religious heritage before a council of twelve Spanish friars, and in the recorded account of their profession of faith the theme of sacrifice dominates:

"You have said," they are reported to have argued,

> that we do not know the Lord of the Close Vicinity, to whom the heavens and earth belong. You have said that our gods are not true gods. These words you speak are new to us. Because of them we are disturbed, because of them we are troubled. For our ancestors before us, who lived upon this earth, were not accustomed to speak that way. From them we have inherited our pattern of life, which they held in truth and in reverence. They honored our gods. Therefore we prostrate ourselves before them; bleed ourselves in their names, keep our oaths, burn incense, and offer sacrifices. It was the doctrine of the elders that there is life because of the gods: with their sacrifice, they gave us life. In what manner? When?—When there still was darkness.[1]

* See above, p. 158.

The Bodhisattva Samantabhadra. A.D. 8th-9th century.
Borobudur, Java

369. Mayan Figure, Lotus in Hand ("The Madrid Stele").
A.D. 7th-8th century

370 (opposite). Marine Scene.
A.D. 8th-9th century. Borobudur, Java

Note the outrigger and compare with those of Figure 385.

V · 421

Fig. 375
cf. Fig. 273
Fig. 376 Opposite, a sculptured stone lintel of approximately the same period as the image of the maize god shows a Mayan priest in the penitential act of drawing blood from his tongue, and next a divinity (unidentified) is depicted pouring down his boons. Note, in this last, the right hand in the bestowing posture, the left holding a vessel of some kind, and, strapped to the back, a severed head.

"They make sacrifices of their own blood," wrote the Bishop Diego de Landa in his *Relación de las cosas de Yucatán,*

> sometimes cutting the edges of their ears to shreds and thus leaving them as a sign of their devotion. At other times they pierced their cheeks, other times the lower lips; again they scarify parts of the body; or again they perforate their tongues in a slanting direction from side to side, passing pieces of straw through the holes with horrible suffering; and yet again they slit the foreskin of the virile member, leaving it like their ears, which deceived the general historian of the Indies [Gonzalo Fernández de Oviedo y Valdes, 1478-1559] into saying that they practiced circumcision. . . . Furthermore, with the blood of all things that they possess, whether birds of the sky, beasts of the earth, or fish of the sea, they were always anointing the face of the demon [i.e. of the images of their gods].[2]

Human sacrifices also were offered up—copiously by the Aztecs, abundantly enough by the Mayas and the rest—to keep the sun in motion and to increase the Figs. 371, 372 bounty of nature. Two sketches below, from the temple ruins at Chichén Itzá (Yucatan), show the method of the rite by which the heart was torn from the victim and Figs. 373, 374
cf. Fig. 239 flung, beating still, at the image of the god; while those opposite illustrate the mythic sense of the sacrifice: the tree of life itself arising from the open body of the victim.

371, 372, 373, 374. Mayan Scenes of Human Sacrifice. Above, Chichen Itza, Yucatan. Opposite, upper, Piedras Negras; lower, Dresden Codex

375. *Mayan Penance: Priest Drawing Blood from His Tongue.* A.D. *7th-8th century. Mexico*

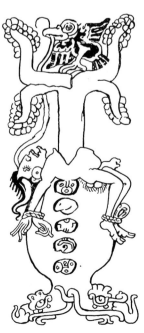

376. *Mayan God Bestowing Boons.* A.D. *8th century. Piedras Negras, Guatemala*

Figs. 377, 378   Two analogous scenes from South Africa appear in the rock paintings below. In the first, from the Rusapi District of South Rhodesia, a female body lies beneath a tree and a man stands by with uplifted hands, either praying or conjuring heaven, while above, a second, larger female form, also with uplifted hands, bends forward over a slanting field of nine parallel lines, beneath which rain descends to refresh and fertilize the earth. The second, also of South Rhodesia, from the Marandelles District, shows again a reclining human form, and rising from it some sort of stretching tree or heaven-ladder which at the top turns into a serpent, both the tree and the snake showing lightning spikes; while above, there is again a female form leaning forward in response.

378. Rain Sacrifice. Rock Painting. Mirandelles District, Rhodesia

377. Rain Sacrifice. Rock Painting. Rusapi District, Rhodesia

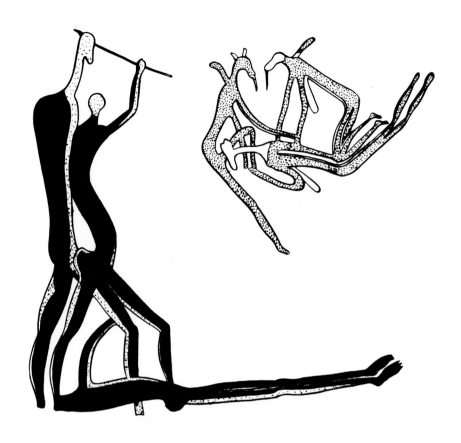

379. *Ritual Murder Scenes. Rock Paintings. Basutoland, South Africa*

Two more South African rock paintings are of special interest in this context. Fig. 379
They are from the Drakensberg Mountains, south of the Transvaal. In that at the
right, from Advance Point (Teyateyaneng, Basutoland), all the characters are
masked, the victim as well as his slayers, and from the mouths of the latter blood is
dripping. In the painting at the left (as Professor James Walton, to whom we owe
these "medicine murder" scenes, observes) the head of the victim is blotted out by
a mass of color and cannot be seen, only one of the officiants is masked, and the
other is flourishing a weapon. "Both these scenes," states Professor Walton, "represent a medicine man with the murderer, preparing to remove or removing blood, and
probably flesh, from the victim. The scene is so similar to that of the present day
liretlo murders," he continues, "that it seems safe to conclude that such murders
are what are here actually depicted."[3]

The estimated date for these last two rock paintings of ritual murder is A.D. 1700-
1750, and yet, for all the years between, they suggest remarkably both the forms of
the main actors and the mythological meaning of the ancient Egyptian scenes of
the embalming of the slain god-king Osiris. In Figure 22 (p. 27) an Egyptian priest, Fig. 22
assuming the mask of the jackal-god Anubis preparing the body of Osiris for rebirth,

Fig. 380

Fig. 381

cf. Figs. 371-374,
377, 378
is shown preparing the mummy of one deceased for a like rebirth. Below is a profile view of the earliest animal form of the slayer of Osiris.* And a bas-relief from Philae shows the sacrificed Osiris with wheat growing from his body—in essentially the same mythic role as the sacrificed South Rhodesian maidens and the Mayan victims. From another South Rhodesian rock wall** comes a great reclining personage, beneath whose stylized masked form a lively multitude of village folk are engaged in a celebration that Leo Frobenius, whose 1928 Basutoland expedition brought knowledge of this monument to us, interprets as a late, East African counterpart of the Early Bronze Age ritual regicide studied by Frazer in *The Golden Bough*:

Fig. 3
> Here lies the king in the typical posture of the dead in the rock-painted "Pietàs" of this region. The ornamental waist-band is typical; likewise, the body wrapped in tight bands. Over the face there is a horned mask. The upper hand clutches an unidentified object. On his lifted knee is a little bird. There are a number of striding or soaring human figures round about, and to the right, beneath him, lies a larger figure among what appear to be rocks. Meanwhile, beneath and set apart from this whole group by a number of wavy parallel lines, is a confused multitude of folk amid gift-offerings. Such wavy parallel lines, as may be judged from other examples in this region, are meant to represent the shoreline of the mythical other-world sea: the Dsivoa.[4]

* See above, pp. 21-29.
** See Figure 3, p. 5.

380. Animal Form of Seth, Slayer of Osiris

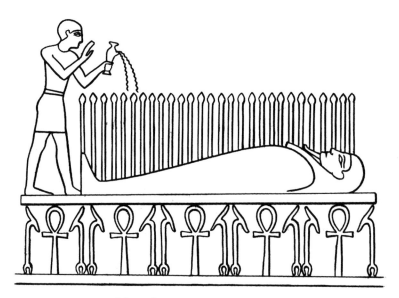

381. Osiris-mummy with Growing Grain

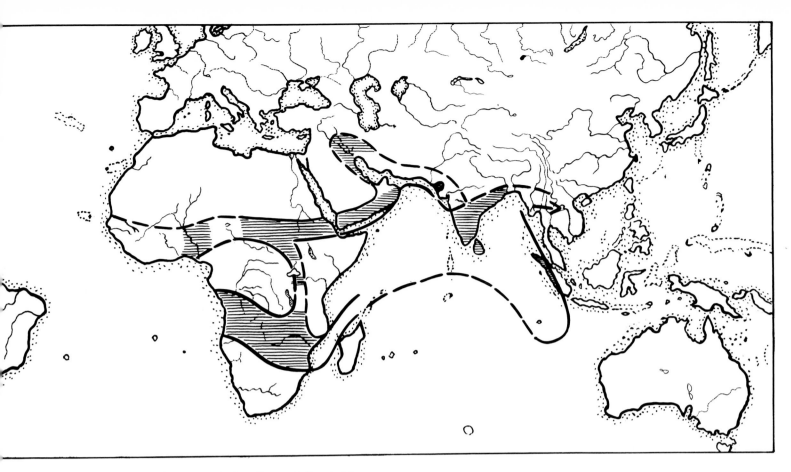

Map 5. *Distribution of the Sacred Regicide.*

382. *Palace Company Assembled for Burial Alive, at Tomb of Sacrificed Lady and Lord.*
     Royal Tomb, Ur. Reconstruction Drawing

On November 28, 1928 Leo Frobenius recorded the following legend from the lips of
a wandering native peddler of rings in South
Rhodesia:

THE LEGEND OF THE SACRIFICE
OF THE MAIDEN

"Once upon a time, very long ago, there
fell no rain for an entire year. The chief
priest declared that a sacrifice had to be offered. The priests said: 'It must be a nubile
princess who has not yet slept with a man.
The sacrifice must be immaculate.' So the
king, the mambo, summoned his chief wife
and said to her: 'Search out among my
daughters one who is nubile and untouched,
to be offered up as a sacrifice.' And the chief
wife left the king's presence.

"The king's chief wife caused all the
princesses to be brought together, and she
asked: 'Which of you has not yet had to do
with a man?' The king's daughters laughed
and answered: 'Is it expected that princesses
should behave like other maids?' The king's
chief wife commanded: 'Lie down, all of you,
on a mat.' The king's daughters laughed and
lay down on a mat. The king's chief wife
found not a single princess among the king's
nubile daughters who had had nothing to do
with a man.

"The king's chief wife went to the mambo.
'Mambo!' she said. 'Among your nubile
daughters there is not one who has not yet
had to do with a man.' The mambo summoned the priests and said to them: 'There
is not one among the nubile princesses who
has not already had something to do with a
man. Tell me what now is to be done.' And
the priests replied: 'Mambo, the sacrifice
must be offered. If no untouched nubile

princess can be found, then the eldest of your
not yet nubile daughters has to be found. She
must be kept in the offering place and held
there until she is ready. She will then be fit
to be the sacrifice.' The king summoned his
chief wife and said to her: 'Search out among
my not yet nubile daughters the eldest who
has not yet had to do with a man.' And the
king's chief wife called together all the little
girls of the royal compound. She discovered
among them a child who had as yet had nothing to do with a man. The maiden had as yet
no breasts.

"The little girl was taken to the offering
place [a place enclosed, the storyteller explained, by a circular high wall like that of
a hut and with an entrance, but of stone, not
wood or clay: his reference apparently being
to something like the ruined "Acropolis" of
the great Rhodesian monument site of Zim-
babwe]. In the middle there was a high termite hill, and on the termite hill stood a big
tree. The maiden was taken to that offering
place and its entrance was closed with
stones. Every day the older princesses
brought to the little sacrifice food and water,
which they reached over the wall. And the
priests saw to it that no man ever approached
that sanctuary.

"The maiden matured there. It was two
years before she developed and had breasts.
In the course of those two years there fell no
rain. All the cattle died. Many people died as

well. The streams dried up. The crops languished. One day the maiden became nubile and the priests proceeded to the king. The priests said: 'The sacrifice is nubile. The ritual can commence.' The king called together all the people. These gathered about the offering place. The priests removed the stones from the entrance. The priests dug a pit into the termite hill among the roots of the big tree. The priests were chanting. They strangled the sacrifice. The people danced about the offering place. The priests buried the maiden in the termite hill among the roots of the big tree. They shouted out the ritual chant and the people danced about the offering scene.

"As the sacrifice was being buried among its roots, the tree began to grow. It grew and grew. The tree grew that whole night long. And the people danced the whole night long. For three whole days the tree was growing, and for three whole days the people danced. Just as the fourth day was about to dawn the crown of the tree touched the sky. In the sky the Morning Star appeared. The treetop spread across the sky and one could no longer see the stars or the moon. A mighty wind arose. The leaves of the tree turned into clouds. It began to rain. It rained for thirty days.

"And ever since that time," the storyteller added, "when there is lack of rain for too long a time, the Wazeguro people sacrifice a maiden."

Leo Frobenius comments:

"In spite of every effort, I was able to discover only one more bit of information touching such a legend—recounted by a man from the place known as Umbowe, near Sinoya. He, too, knew of a legend of a maiden sacrificed for rain, and again in a termite hill within a stone-wall enclosure. In this case, the maiden was buried alive. On the termite hill there stood a tree that began to grow when the sacrifice was placed among its roots. And the novelty in this version was, that, as the top of the tree approached the sky it turned into a snake, or perhaps the snake rose out of the crown of the tree and from the sky then sent down the rain. The account, unfortunately, was so unclear that I had all I could do to catch the main idea, without being able to learn more about the matter of the snake."[5]

Rain sacrifices, Frobenius learned, were still being offered in 1928 by a number of peoples of Mozambique and Rhodesia. They were celebrated in circular sanctuaries; and besides rites in times of drought, there were others, scheduled every two years, "when the planet Venus disappeared as Evening Star and reappeared as the Morning Star.[6]*

* Cf. the whole Feathered Serpent complex of the Mayan-Aztec Lord of the Morning and Evening Star (above, pp. 150 and 176ff).

2. The Magical, Moral, and Mystical Orders of Sacrifice

IT IS APPALLING what a systematic wallowing in human—not to mention animal—blood has marked the history of religions in every quarter of the globe, in high as well as low culture contexts, and with very little difference, furthermore, between the aims, the methods, and even the offered rationalizations—high and low—of the contingent practices. The grim Tahitian scene following, therefore, will be an appropriate introduction to the whole range of this negative side of our subject: the dark and really horrible *exoteric*, magico-religious side of it, in contrast to the inward, *esoteric*, mystical and psychological.

Fig. 383

Engraved in the year 1777 by the artist John Webber, a member of Captain Cook's third expedition to the Pacific, this scene, taken together with Captain Cook's detailed account of the associated ceremonial, well deserves our notice as the earliest scientifically recorded anthropological documentation of a human sacrifice. And I believe this evidence is worth reviewing in full, not only for the memorable account it renders of the event but also for the conversations between Cook and the two Tahitian chieftains for whom the ceremony was performed. It was a rite supposed to bring to their support the *Eatooa* (local deity) of a certain sanctuary or *morai* for an attack that they were proposing to launch against the neighboring island of Moorea. The sacrifice, along with their subsequent explanations and indignant reactions to criticism, illustrates both the typical motifs of a magico-religious liturgy and the underlying presumption that constitutes its supporting superstition.

In *The Golden Bough* Frazer defines religion in the following terms:

> By religion, I understand *a propitiation or conciliation of powers superior to man, which are believed to direct and control the course of nature and of human life.* Thus defined, religion consists of two elements, a theoretical and a practical, namely, *a belief in powers higher than man and an attempt to propitiate and please them.* Of the two, belief clearly comes first, since we must believe in the existence of a divine being before we can attempt to please him. But unless the belief leads to a corresponding practice, it is not a religion but merely a theology; in the language of St. James, "faith, if it hath not works, is dead, being alone." In other words, no man is religious who does not govern his conduct in some measure by the fear of God. On the other hand, mere practice, divested of all religious belief is also not religious. Two men may behave in exactly the same way, and yet one of them may be religious and the other not. If one acts from the love or fear of God, he is religious; if the other acts from the love or fear of man, he is moral or immoral according as his behaviour comports or conflicts with the general good.[7]

To which dichotomy a third class must be added, however, if the point of view that has been represented in earlier pages of this volume is to be taken into account:

namely, that of the mystic or the poet, thinking neither of God nor of man as an ultimate term but simply in awe of the marvel of being and absorbed in the difficult task of self-transformation, striving to extend the range of his own realization of the Body of Truth.

I would say that in the last of these three orders of thought there is something of religion and something of morality as well; for insofar as the mystery of one's identity with the All in all will have been realized, one will have achieved in experience, and not merely in belief, a sense of participation in the consubstantiality of all beings, which is finally the ultimate ground and inspiration of all self-subordination—whether to a principle higher than phenomenal man or in the willing sacrifice of oneself for the good of another human being. If we set aside what Frazer has termed the *moral* order of judgment, as representing a rational manner of thought, requiring no mysterious mythological, metaphysical, or transcendental symbolization—in fact, embarrassed and disordered by such thinking; and if we gather under one rubric the *religious* (in Frazer's definition) and the *mystical* (in mine), it will then appear, I believe, that these last two have shared through all time a common set of symbols. These symbols are read, however, in two distinctly different ways: by the religious man as relevant to substantial gods or entities "out there" who are to be (as Frazer states) conciliated or propitiated; but by the mystic, on the other hand, as challenges and guiding signs to an inward transformation ultimately justified as rendering its willing victim (in the words and sense of Paul) "obedient unto death. . . . Look[ing] not only to his own interests, but also to the interest of others." Such can hardly be called the end of prayers, incense, or the odor of the burnt flesh of some creature *other* than oneself, sent up for the purpose of insuring one's own health and wealth, long life and fruitfulness, or victory in war.

383 (overleaf). A Human Sacrifice, in a Morai. Otaheite (Tahiti). September 1, 1777

384. *Omai. Sir Joshua Reynolds. Painted about* A.D. *1776*

3. The Altar of Blood

THE great mariner and scientist James Cook (1728-1779) had already visited Tahiti in the course of both his first Pacific voyage, 1769 to 1771, and his second, 1771 to 1775, so that he was already on familiar terms with the native king, Otoo, in whose interest the rite that he was about to observe was to be enacted. He had aboard his craft as interpreter, furthermore, an altogether charming young Polynesian, Omai, from the island of Raiatea, who in 1774 had joined his second expedition and sailed with him to England. There he had seemed to all to represent so perfectly Jean Jacques Rousseau's romantic notion of the Noble Savage that he had become, as soon as he stepped ashore, absolutely the rage. "Amazing Omai," he was called by the London press, and the "Lyon of Lyons." "Omai seems to shame education," Fanny Burney wrote enthusiastically in her journal, after witnessing at the home of Sir Joseph Banks the youth's execution of a stunning bow when introduced to the Duchess of Gloucester. "He is so polite, attentive, and easy that you would have thought he came from some foreign court."[8] He became a favorite of Mrs. Thrale, and handled himself so well at her receptions that even Samuel Johnson—no lover of "savages"—had to give him ungrudging praise. King George himself endowed him with a sword, which he received in both hands with perfect grace. Sir Joshua Reynolds painted one or more portraits, and Sir Nathaniel Dance another. By the time he set foot on ship again, popular gossip was reckoning every lady of fashion of that London season to his credit. And yet he was glad to set sail for his islands and island friends, after an absence of three incredible years.

It was just as the sun was setting, on Saturday, August 23, 1777, that the hand-some British square-rigger *Resolution*, bearing the fabulous Omai homeward and Captain Cook on his last great voyage, rounded Matavai Point, Tahiti, and came to anchor in the bay. Next morning Cook's second ship, *Discovery*, with Captains Clerke and Gore aboard, likewise came around the point, hove to, and cast anchor. "About nine o'clock in the morning," states Cook's account of the events of that day,

> Otoo, the King of the whole island, attended by a great number of canoes full of people, came from Oparre, his place of residence, and having landed on Matavai Point, sent a message on board expressing his desire to see me there. Accordingly, I landed accompanied by Omai and some of the officers. We found a prodigious number of people assembled on this occasion, and in the midst of them was the king, attended by his father, his two brothers, and three sisters.
>
> I went up first and saluted him, being followed by Omai, who kneeled and embraced his legs. He had prepared himself for this ceremony, by dressing himself in his very best suit of clothes, and behaved with a great deal of respect and modesty. Nevertheless, very little notice was taken of him. Perhaps envy had some share in producing this cold reception. He made the Chief a present of a large piece of red

feathers, and about two or three yards of gold cloth; and I gave him a suit of fine linen, a gold-laced hat, some tools, and what was of more value than all other articles, a quantity of red feathers, and one of the bonnets in use at the Friendly Islands.[9]

For about a week the mutual giving of presents and exchange of visits continued, until on Sunday, August 30, messengers abruptly arrived with the news that the people of a neighboring island, Moorea (at that time called Eimeo), were preparing for war. Next day a second message arrived, from a subordinate chief, Towha by name, to say that he had just had a man killed to be offered at the morai at Atta-hooroo, in the hope of gaining that divinity's aid in the coming interisland conflict. Captain Cook too was asked to give aid. But as he reports at length in his journal, he contrived to refuse without alienating his host and depriving himself thus of the opportunity to observe the coming sacrificial rite.

"Omai was sent for to be my interpreter," he records of the occasion, "but, as he could not be found, I was obliged to speak for myself, and told them, as well as I could, that as I was not thoroughly acquainted with the dispute, and as the people of Eimeo had never offended me, I could not think myself at liberty to engage in hostilities against them."

There had long been rumors of human sacrifices on those islands, yet no one had ever had ocular confirmation. Cook therefore strongly desired to observe and record the occasion, and on proposing his attendance to King Otoo was readily accepted as a guest. Immediately, as he tells, things then got started.

"We set out in my boat, with my old friend Potatou, Mr. Anderson [the First Officer], and Mr. Webber [the artist]; Omai following in a canoe." On the way, the party stopped briefly to visit the donor of the sacrifice, who, in contrast to King Otoo, seemed angry when the British captain refused to assist their cause. This Chief Towha gave to the king two or three red feathers for the ceremony and a lean half-starved dog; a priest to preside then stepped into the boat and they sailed, leaving Towha behind—at which point in the Captain's journal, his eyewitness account of the sacrifice begins.

385. Captain Cook's Two Ships in Kealakekua Bay, Hawaii. A.D. *1779*

386. *Great Morai. Pappara, Otaheite (Tahiti).* A.D. *late 18th century. Engraving*

A PARTICULAR RELATION
OF THE
CEREMONIES OF THE GREAT MORAI
WHERE THE SACRIFICE
WAS OFFERED

An Account, also of other
Barbarous Customs of this People

AS soon as we landed at Attahooroo, which was about two o'clock in the afternoon, Otoo expressed his desire that the seamen might be ordered to remain in the boat; and that Mr. Anderson, Mr. Webber, and myself might take off our hats as soon as we should come to the *morai*, to which we immediately proceeded, attended by a great many men, and some boys; but not one woman. We found four priests, and their attendants, or assistants, waiting for us. The dead body, or sacrifice, was in a small canoe that lay on the beach, and partly in the wash of the sea, fronting the *morai*. Two of the priests, with some of their attendants, were sitting by the canoe; the others at the *morai*. Our company stopped about twenty or thirty paces from the priests. Here Otoo placed himself; we, and a few others standing by him; while the bulk of the people remained at a greater distance.

The ceremonies now began. One of the priest's attendants brought a young plantain-tree, and laid it down before Otoo. Another approached with a small tuft of red feathers, twisted on some fibres of the cocoa-nut husk, with which he touched one of the king's feet, and then retired with it to his companions. One of the priests, seated at the *morai*, facing those who were upon the beach, now began a long prayer; and, at certain times, sent down young plantain trees, which were laid upon the sacrifice. During this prayer, a man, who stood by the officiating priest, held in his hands two bundles, seemingly of cloth. In one of them, as we afterward found, was the royal *maro* [loin-cloth]; and the other, if I may be allowed the expression, was the ark of the *Eatooa* [the deity of this morai]. As soon as the prayer was ended, the priests at the *morai*, with their attendants, went and sat down by those upon the beach, carrying with them the two bundles. Here they renewed their prayers; during which the plantain trees were taken, one by one, at different times, from off the sacrifice; which was partly wrapped up in cocoa leaves and small branches. It was now taken out of the canoe, and laid upon the beach, with the feet to the sea. The priests placed themselves around it, some sitting and others standing; and one, or more of them, repeated sentences for about ten minutes. The dead body was now uncovered, by removing the leaves and branches, and laid in a parallel direction with the sea-shore. One of the priests then, standing at the feet of it, pronounced a long prayer, in which he was, at times, joined by the others; each holding in his hand a tuft of red feathers. In the course of this prayer, some hair was pulled off the head of the sacrifice, and the left eye taken out; both of which were presented to Otoo, wrapped up in a green leaf. He did not, however touch it; but gave, to the man who presented it, the tuft of feathers, which he had received from Towha. This, with the hair and eye, was carried back to the priests. Soon after, Otoo sent to them another piece of feathers, which he had given me in the morning to keep in my pocket. During some part of this last ceremony, a kingfisher making a noise in the trees, Otoo turned to me, saying, That is the Eatooa; and seemed to look upon it to be a good omen.

The body was then carried a little way, with its head toward the *morai*, and laid under a tree; near which were fixed three broad thin pieces of wood, differently, but rudely, carved. The bundles of cloth were laid on a part of the *morai*; and the tufts of red feathers were placed at the feet of the sacrifice; round which the priests took their stations; and we were now allowed to go as near as we pleased. He who seemed to be the chief priest sat at a small distance, and spoke for a quarter of an hour, but with different tones and gestures; so that he seemed often to expostulate with the dead person, to whom he constantly addressed himself, and, sometimes, asked several questions, seemingly with respect to the propriety of his having been killed. At other times, he made several demands, as if the deceased either now had power himself, or interest with the Divinity, to engage him to comply with such requests. Amongst which, we understood, he asked him to deliver Eimeo, Maheine its chief, the hogs, women, and other things of the island, into their hands; which was, indeed, the express intention of the sacrifice. He then chanted a prayer, which lasted near half an hour, in a whining, melancholy tone, accompanied by two other priests; and in which Potatou, and some others, joined. In the course of this prayer, some more hair was plucked by a priest from the head of the corpse, and put upon one of the bundles. After this, the chief priest prayed alone, holding in his hand the feathers which came from Towha. When he had finished, he gave them to another, who prayed in like manner. Then all the tufts of feathers were laid upon the bundles of cloth; which closed the ceremony at this place.

The corpse was then carried up to the most conspicuous part of the *morai*, with the feathers, the two bundles of cloth, and the drums; the last of which beat slowly. The feathers and bundles were laid against the pile of stones and the corpse at the foot of them. The priests having again seated themselves round it, renewed their prayers; while some of their attendants dug a hole about two feet deep, into which they threw the unhappy victim, and covered it over with earth and stones. While they were putting him into the grave, a boy squeaked aloud, and Omai said to me that it was the *Eatooa*. During this time, a fire having been made, the dog, before mentioned, was produced, and killed, by twisting his neck, and suffocating him. The hair was singed off, and the entrails taken out, and thrown into the fire, where they were left to consume. But the heart, liver, and kidneys were only roasted, by being laid on hot stones for a few minutes; and the body of the dog, after being besmeared with the blood, which had been collected into a cocoa-nut shell, and dried over the fire, was, with the liver, etc. carried and laid down before the priests, who sat praying, round the grave. They continued their ejaculations over the dog, for some time, while two men, at intervals, beat on two drums very loud; and a boy screamed, as before, in a loud, shrill voice, three different times. This, as we were told, was to invite the *Eatooa* to feast on the banquet that they had prepared for him. As soon as the priests had ended their prayers, the carcase of the dog, with what belonged to it, were laid on a *whatta*, or scaffold, about six feet high, that stood close by, on which lay the remains of two other dogs, and of two pigs, which had lately been sacrificed, and, at this time, emitted an intolerable stench. This kept us at a greater distance, than would, otherwise, have been required of us. For, after the victim was removed from the sea-side toward the *morai*, we were allowed to approach as near as we pleased. Indeed, after that, neither seriousness nor attention were much observed by the spectators. When the dog was put upon the *whatta*, the priests and attendants gave a kind of shout, which closed the ceremonies for the present. The day being now also closed, we were conducted to a house belonging to Potatou, where we were entertained, and lodged for the night. We had been told, that the religious rites were to be renewed in the morning; and I would not leave the place, while any thing remained to be seen.

TUESDAY, SEPTEMBER 2.

BEING unwilling to lose any part of the solemnity, some of us repaired to the scene of action pretty early, but found nothing going forward. However, soon after, a pig was sacrificed, and laid upon the same *whatta* with the others. About eight o'clock, Otoo took us again to the *morai*, where the priests, and a great number of men, were, by this time, assembled. The two bundles occupied the place in which we had seen them deposited the preceding evening; the two drums stood in the front of the *morai*, but somewhat nearer it than before; and the priests were beyond them. Otoo placed himself between the two drums, and desired me to stand by him.

The ceremony began, as usual, with bringing a young plantain-tree, and laying it down at the king's feet. After this a prayer was repeated by the priests, who held in their hands several tufts of red feathers, and also a plume of ostrich feathers, which I had given to Otoo on my first arrival, and had been consecrated to this use. When the priests had made an end of the prayer, they changed their station, placing themselves between us and the *morai*; and one of them, the same person who had acted the principal part the day before, began another prayer, which lasted about half an hour. During the continuance of this, the tufts of feathers were, one by one, carried and laid upon the ark of the *Eatooa*.

Some little time after, four pigs were produced; one of which was immediately killed; and the others were taken to a sty, hard by, probably reserved for some future occasion of sacrifice. One of the bundles was now untied; and it was found, as I have before observed, to contain the *maro*, with which these people invest their kings; and which seems to answer, in some degree, to the European ensigns of royalty. It was carefully taken out of

Fig. 381

387. *Royal Malo. Ceremonial Belt of Feathers and Shells.* A.D. *19th century. Hawaii*

the cloth, in which it had been wrapped up, and spread, at full length, upon the ground before the priests. It is a girdle, about five yards long, and fifteen inches broad; and, from its name, seems to be put on in the same manner as is the common *maro*, or piece of cloth, used, by these people, to wrap round the waist. It was ornamented with red and yellow feathers; but mostly with the latter, taken from a dove found upon the island. The one end was bordered with eight pieces, each about the size and shape of a horse-shoe, having their edges fringed with black feathers. The other end was forked, and the points were of different lengths. The feathers were in square compartments, ranged in two rows, and, otherwise, so disposed as to produce a pleasing effect. They had been first pasted and fixed upon some of their own country cloth; and then sewed to the upper end of the pendant which Captain Wallis had displayed, and left flying ashore, the first time that he landed at Matavai. This was what they told us; and we had no reason to doubt it, as we could easily trace the remains of an English pendant. About six or eight inches square of the *maro* was unornamented; there being no feathers upon that space, except a few that had been sent by Waheadooa, as already mentioned. The priests made a long prayer, relative to this part of the ceremony; and, if I mistook not, they called it the prayer of the *maro*. When it was finished, the badge of royalty was carefully folded up, put into the cloth, and deposited again upon the *morai*.

The other bundle, which I have distinguished by the name of the ark, was next opened, at one end. But we were not allowed to go near enough to examine its mysterious contents. The information we received was, that the *Eatooa*, to whom they had been sacrificing, and whose name is *Ooro*, was concealed in it; or rather, what is supposed to represent him. This sacred repository is made of the twisted fibres of the husk of the cocoa-nut, shaped somewhat like a large fid or sugar loaf; that is, roundish, with one end much thicker than the other. We had, very often, got small ones from different people, but never knew their use before.

By this time, the pig, that had been killed, was cleaned, and the entrails taken out. These happened to have a considerable share of those convulsive motions, which often appear, in different parts, after an animal is killed; and this was considered by the spectators as a very favorable omen to the expedition, on account of which the sacrifices had been offered. After being exposed for some time, that those who chose, might examine their appearances, the entrails were carried to the priests, and laid down before them. While one of their number prayed, another inspected the entrails more narrowly, and kept turning them gently with a stick. When they had been sufficiently examined, they were thrown into the fire, and left to consume. The sacrificed pig, and its liver, etc. were now put upon the *whatta*, where the dog had been deposited the day before; and then all the feathers, except the ostrich plume, were inclosed with the *Eatooa*, in the ark; and the solemnity finally closed.

Four double canoes lay upon the beach, before the place of sacrifice, all the morning. On the fore-part of each of these, was fixed a small platform, covered with palm-leaves, tied in mysterious knots; and this also is called a *morai*. Some cocoa-nuts, plaintains, pieces of bread-fruit, fish, and other things, lay upon each of these naval *morais*. We were told, that they belonged to the *Eatooa*; and that they were to attend the fleet designed to go against Eimeo.

388. *Polynesian Execution Scene. ca.* A.D. *1818. Hawaii*

The unhappy victim, offered to the object of their worship upon this occasion, seemed to be a middle-aged man; and, as we were told, was a *towtow*; that is, one of the lowest class of the people. But, after all my inquiries, I could not learn, that he had been pitched upon, on account of any particular crime, committed by him, meriting death. It is certain, however, that they generally make choice of such guilty persons for their sacrifices; or else of common, low, fellows, who stroll about, from place to place, and from island to island, without having any fixed abode, or any visible way of getting an honest livelihood; of which description of men, enough are to be met with at these islands. Having had an opportunity of examining the appearance of the body of the poor sufferer, now offered up, I could observe, that it was bloody about the head and face, and a good deal bruised upon the right temple; which marked the manner of his being killed. And we were told, that he had been privately knocked on the head with a stone.

Those who are devoted to suffer, in order to perform this bloody act of worship, are never apprised of their fate, till the blow is given that puts an end to their existence. Whenever any one of the great Chiefs thinks a human sacrifice necessary, on any particular emergency, he pitches upon the victim. Some of his trusty servants are then sent, who fall upon him suddenly, and put him to death with a club, or by stoning him. The king is next acquainted with it, whose presence, at the solemn rites that follow, is, as I was told, absolutely necessary; and, indeed, on the present occasion, we could observe that Otoo bore a principal part. The solemnity itself is called *Poore Eree*, or Chief's Prayer; and the victim who is offered up, *Taata-taboo*, or consecrated man. This is the only instance where we have heard the word *taboo* used at this island, where it seems to have the same mysterious signification as at Tonga; though it is there applied to all cases where things are not to be touched. But at Otaheite [Tahiti], the word *raa* serves the same purpose, and is full as extensive in its meaning.

The *morai* (which, undoubtedly, is a place of worship, sacrifice, and burial, at the same time), where the sacrifice was now offered, is that where the supreme Chief of the whole island, is always buried, and is appropriated to his family, and some of the principal people. It differs little from the common ones, except in extent. Its principal part, is a large, oblong pile of stones, lying loosely upon each other, about twelve or fourteen feet high, contracted towards the top, with a square area, on each side, loosely paved with pebble stones, under which the bones of the Chiefs are buried. At a little distance from the end nearest the sea, is the place where the sacrifices are offered; which, for a considerable extent, is also loosely paved. There is here a very large scaffold, or *whatta*, on which the offerings of fruits, and other vegetables, are laid. But the animals are deposited on a smaller one, already mentioned, and the human sacrifices are buried under different parts of the pavement. There are several other reliques which ignorant superstition had scattered about this place; such as small stones, raised in different parts of the pavement; some with bits of cloth tied round them; others covered with it; and upon the side of the large pile, which fronts the area, are placed a great many pieces of carved wood, which are supposed to be sometimes the residence of their divinities, and, consequently, held sacred. But one place, more particular than the rest, is a heap of stones, at one end of the large *whatta*, before which the sacrifice was offered, with a kind of platform at one side. On this are laid the skulls of all the human sacrifices, which are taken up after they have been several months under ground. Just above them, are placed a great number of the pieces of wood; and it was also here, where the *maro*, and the other bundle, supposed to contain the god *Ooro* (which I call the ark), were laid, during the ceremony; a circumstance which denotes its agreement with the altar of other nations.

It is much to be regretted, that a practice so horrid in its own nature, and so destructive of that inviolable right of self-preservation, which every one is born with, should be found still existing; and (such is the power of superstition to counteract the first principles of humanity!) existing amongst a people, in many other respects, emerged from the brutal manners of savage life. What is still worse, it is probable, that these bloody rites of worship are prevalent throughout all the wide extended islands of the Pacific Ocean. The similarity of customs and language, which our last voyages have enabled us to trace, between the most distant of these islands, makes it not unlikely, that some of the more important articles of their religious institutions should agree. And, indeed, we had the most authentic information, that human sacrifices continue to be offered at the Friendly Islands. When I described the *Natche* at *Tonga-taboo*, I mentioned that, on the approaching sequel of that festival, we had been told, that ten men were to be sacrificed. This may give us an idea of the extent of this religious massacre, in that island. And though we should suppose, that never more than one person is sacrificed, on any single occasion, at Otaheite, it is more than probable, that these occasions happen so frequently, as to make a shocking waste of the human race; for I counted no less than forty-nine skulls, of former victims, lying before the *morai*, where we saw one more added to the number. And as none of those skulls had, as yet, suffered any considerable change from the weather, it may hence be inferred, that no great length of time had elapsed, since, at least, this considerable number of uphappy wretches had been offered upon this altar of blood.

The custom, though no consideration can make it cease to be abominable, might be thought less detrimental, in some respects, if it served to impress any awe for the divinity, or reverence for religion, upon the minds of the multitude. But this is so far from being the case, that though a great number of people had assembled at the *morai*, on this occasion, they did not seem to shew any proper reverence for what was doing, or saying, during the celebration of the rites. And Omai happening to arrive, after they had begun, many of the spectators flocked round him, and were engaged, the remainder of the time, in making him relate some of his adventures, which they listened to with great attention, regardless of the solemn offices performed by their priests. Indeed, the priests themselves, except the one who chiefly repeated the prayers, either from their being familiarized to such objects, or from want of confidence in the efficacy of their institutions, observed very little of that solemnity, which is necessary to give to religious performances their due weight. Their dress was only an ordinary one; they conversed together, without scruple; and the only attempt made by them to preserve any appearance of decency, was by exerting their authority, to prevent the people from coming upon the very spot where the ceremonies were performed; and to suffer us, as strangers, to advance a little forward. They were, however, very candid in their answers to any questions that were put to them, concerning the institution. And, particularly, on being asked, what the intention of it was? They said, that it was an old custom, and was agreeable to their god, who delighted in, or, in other words, came and fed upon the sacrifices; in consequence of which, he complied with their petitions. Upon its being objected, that he could not feed on these, as he was neither seen to do it, nor were the bodies of the animals quickly consumed, and that as to the human victim, they prevented his feeding on him, by burying him. But to all this they answered, that he came in the night, but invisibly; and fed only on the soul, or immaterial part, which, according to their doctrine, remains about the place of sacrifice, until the body of the victim be entirely wasted by putrefaction.

It were much to be wished, that this deluded people may learn to entertain the same horror of murdering their fellow-creatures, in order to furnish such an invisible banquet to their god, as they now have of feeding, corporeally, on human flesh themselves. And, yet, we have reason to believe, that there was a time when they were cannibals. We were told (and indeed partly saw it), that it is a necessary ceremony, when a poor wretch is sacrificed, for the priest to take out the left eye. This he presents to the king, holding it to his mouth, which he desires him to open; but, instead of putting it in, immediately withdraws it. This they call "eating the man," or "food for the Chief"; and, perhaps, we may observe here some traces of former times, when the dead body was really feasted upon.

But not to insist upon this; it is certain, that human sacrifices are not the only barbarous custom we find still prevailing amongst this benevolent, humane people. For, besides cutting out the jaw-bones of their enemies slain in battle, which they carry about as trophies, they, in some measure, offer their bodies as a sacrifice to the *Eatooa*. Soon after a battle, in which they have been victors, they collect all the dead that have fallen into their hands, and bring them to the *morai*, where, with a great deal of ceremony, they dig a hole, and bury them all in it, as so many offerings to the gods; but their skulls are never after taken up.

Their own great Chiefs, that fall in battle, are treated in a different manner. We were informed, that their late king Tootaha, Tubourai-tamaide, and another Chief, who fell with them in the battle, fought with those of Tiaraboo, and were brought to this *morai*, at Attahooroo. There their bowels were cut out by the priests, before the great altar; and the bodies afterward buried in three different places, which were pointed out to us, in the great pile of stones, that compose the most conspicuous part of the *morai*. And their common men, who also fell in this battle, were all buried in one hole at the foot of the pile. This, Omai, who was present, told me, was done the day after the battle, with much pomp and ceremony, and in the midst of a great concourse of people, as a thanksgiving offering to *Eatooa*, for the victory they had obtained; while the vanquished had taken refuge in the mountains. There they remained a week, or ten days, till the fury of the victors was over, and a treaty set on foot, by which it was agreed, that Otoo should be declared king of the whole island; and the solemnity of investing him with the *maro*, was performed at the same *morai*, with great pomp, in the presence of all the principal men of the country.

The close of the very singular scene, exhibited at the *morai*, leaving us no other business in Attahooroo, we embarked about noon, in order to return to Matavai; and, in our way, visited Towha, who had remained on the little island, where we met him the day before.

Some conversation passed between Otoo and him, on the present posture of public affairs; and then the latter solicited me, once more, to join them in their war against Eimeo. By my positive refusal I entirely lost the good graces of this Chief.

Before we parted, he asked us, if the solemnity, at which we had been present, answered our expectations; what opinion we had of its efficacy; and whether we performed such acts of worship in our own country? During the celebration of the horrid ceremony, we had preserved a profound silence; but as soon as it was closed, had made no scruple in expressing our sentiments very freely about it, to Otoo, and those who attended him; of course, therefore, I did not conceal my detestation of it, in this conversation with Towha. Besides the cruelty of the bloody custom, I strongly urged the unreasonableness of it; telling the Chief, that such a sacrifice, far from making the *Eatooa* propitious to their nation, as they ignorantly believed, would be the means of drawing down his vengeance; and that, from this very circumstance, I took upon me to judge, that their intended expedition against Maheine would be unsuccessful. This was venturing pretty far upon conjecture; but still, I thought, that there was little danger of being mistaken. For I found, that there were three parties in the island, with regard to this war; one extremely violent for it; another perfectly indifferent about the matter; and the third openly declaring themselves friends to Maheine, and his cause. Under these circumstances, of disunion distracting their councils, it was not likely that such a plan of military operations would be settled, as could insure even a probability of success. In conveying our sentiments to Towha, on the subject of the late sacrifice, Omai was made use of as our interpreter; and he entered into our arguments with so much spirit, that the Chief seemed to be in great wrath; especially when he was told, that if he had put a man to death in England, as he had done here, his rank would not have protected him from being hanged for it. Upon this, he exclaimed, *maeno! maeno!* [vile! vile!] and would not hear another word. During this debate, many of the natives were present, chiefly the attendants and servants of Towha himself; and when Omai began to explain the punishment that would be inflicted in England, upon the greatest man, if he killed the meanest servant, they seemed to listen with great attention; and were, probably, of a different opinion from that of their master, on this subject.

389. *The Body of Tee, a Chief, Prepared after Death. Otaheite (Tahiti).* A.D. 1777

4. The Myth

*Take to thyself the Eye of Horus, he brings it to thee; put it in thy mouth.
Behold, we bring thee the great left eye as healer.
I have brought thee the Eye of Horus, that thou mayest equip with it thy face,
that it may purify thee, that its odor may come to thee. . . . It defends thee against
the violence of the arm of Seth.*[10]

390. *The Eye of Horus*

Can there possibly be a relationship between these ancient Egyptian funerary charms from the earliest body of religious writings known to us—the Pyramid Texts of the Fifth and Sixth Dynasties, ca. 2350-2175 B.C.—and that grisly act observed by Captain Cook, of a Tahitian priest presenting to the lips of his king the left eye of a human victim?

The pyramid charms were addressed to the well-being of the dead kings on whose tomb walls they were inscribed, the pharaohs to be resurrected in the likeness of
Fig. 390 Osiris; and their reference was to the eye that Horus, the son of Osiris, had lost in his avenging battle with Seth, the slayer of his father. As we have seen,* it was only by virtue of this sacrificed eye, presented to the dead Osiris as an offering, that his mummy was given eternal life; and by analogy, the offerings presented to the embalmed pharaohs for their resurrection in the Netherworld were identified with that "great left eye." Hence we read, for example, in these texts:

*Take to thyself the Eye of Horus, which thou tastest. One loaf.
Take to thyself the Eye of Horus, which thou shalt embrace. One joint of meat.
Take to thyself the Eye of Horus, which is free from Seth, and which thou shalt
   take to thy mouth, and with which thou shalt open thy mouth. Wine; one
   white stone jar.*[11]

* Above, p. 29.

In a passage of *The Book of the Dead* (the chief Egyptian funerary text of ca. 1500 B.C. and thereafter) it is related that Seth, in the course of his battle with Horus, transformed himself in a whirlwind of fire into a black pig, which when Horus looked upon it burned out his left eye. And Re then said to all the gods: "The pig is an abominable thing unto Horus." To which the followers of Horus answered: "Let sacrifices be made to the gods, of his bulls, and of his goats, and of his pigs."[12]

We think of all those sacrificed pigs in the Polynesian morai. Nor were those and the ritual of the eye the only features of that gruesome ceremony reminiscent of antiquity. The form of the morai itself recalls an ancient temple compound. The inspection of entrails for auspices suggests Etruria and Babylon. The special burial of chiefs, furthermore, with the removal of their entrails before embalmment, again calls to mind Egypt. And finally, a point of special interest was the lack of signs of reverence or even serious attention—not to mention religious awe—that Captain Cook observed among those present at the ceremony. The prayers, offerings, and other elements of the liturgy seem to have been expected, if accurately rendered, to work automatically, of themselves, moving the power believed to reside in the sacred bundle called by Cook "the ark"—which suggests a familiar routine handed down over long years rather than any immediate sense of an actual spiritual presence.

Fig. 386

cf. Fig. 389

391. Seth Represented as a Pig in Osiris' Judgment Scene

The ritual lore and mythology of the pig hold a place of the greatest importance throughout Oceania, not only in Polynesia but also in Melanesia, both the rites and the animal itself having been carried to the Pacific isles by successive waves of immigrants in catamarans from Indonesia and Southeast Asia. There is in Hawaii the popular legendary cycle of a shape-shifter known as "Hog-child," Kamapua'a, who was the lover and for a time the spouse, of the great underworld fire-goddess Pele of the volcanic crater Kilauea;[13] and in the temples, known there as *heiau*, pigs and human victims were the principal sacrifices to the inhabiting spirits or gods. We know also that throughout Melanesia the tusked boar is the principal sacrifice in rites of the men's secret societies, and that associated with these is a lore of the mysteries of the afterworld, to which the deceased gains entrance only by virtue of his spiritual identification with a ritually bred tusked boar—his "death pig"—which is sacrificed instead of himself to the guardian goddess of the fiery gate.[14]

Fig. 394

392-1. Hawaiian Figure.
Before A.D. *1819.*
Function unknown

392-2 (left). *Figure Ornamenting Top of a Wooden Staff. Before* A.D. *1819. Maui, Hawaii*

392-3 (right). *Hawaiian Temple Image of Kauila Wood. ca.* A.D. *1800*

393. *Reconstructions of an* A.D. *18th century Heiau. "The City of Refuge," Hawaii*

394. *Tusked Jaw of a Sacrificial Boar.* A.D. *19th century. New Hebrides*

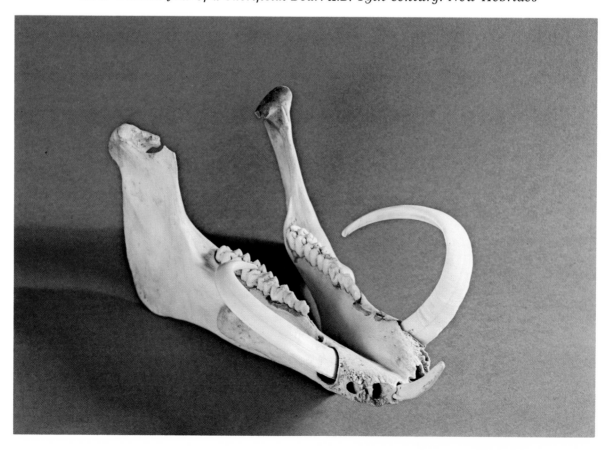

395. *Temple Guardian Figure.*
Before A.D. *1819. Hawaii*

396. *The War God, Ku Ka'ili Moku. Feather Image.*
Before A.D. *1819. Hawaii*

As John Layard has demonstrated in his richly documented *Stone Men of Male-*
Fig. 397 *kula*, megalithic altars and monoliths suggesting the dolmens and menhirs of Bronze-
Age Europe are associated with such rites; as are also certain labyrinth designs
supposed to represent the way of access to the land of the immortal dead. In the
Fig. 398 culminating festivals of a great fifteen-year-long ceremonial known in Malekula
as the Maki, the chief tuskers are sacrificed on the megalithic altars, two hundred
or more being offered on a single day, and, as Layard comments:

> The efficacy of this sacrifice results from the fact that the sacrificial animals have
> themselves previously been consecrated through sacrifice of yet other boars, and
> have by this means become identified with the Guardian Ghost, and in the highest
> grades have been invested with a title similar to its own. At the moment of sacrifice
> the ghost of the boar passes into the sacrificer, who by this means himself becomes
> identified with this Being, and in this way builds up a power within him that he
> hopes will ensure him from being devoured when he dies.[15]

Through years of increasingly costly sacrifices offered to the animal each male
Malekulan's death pig becomes identified in its owner's mind with the consuming
power of the Guardian Ghost that eats souls on their way to the afterworld; and
with the sacrifice then of the death pig itself, that consuming power passes to the
owner, who is thereby advanced to the spiritual status of one who is no longer a
potential victim but a master of the power of death, and can now say in truth, "It
is no longer I who live, but my sacrifice that lives in me."

397. Stone Monuments and Upright Slit Gongs for Malekulan Megalithic Rite. A.D. *20th century.*
New Hebrides

Original stone-platform on which canni-
bal feasts were held. The roots of the
banyan tree surrounding it are hollowed
out to form a cave, in which the victim
was cooked and eaten.

Stone-platform

Old Dolmen

Old Monoliths

Existing Orchestra of Upright slit Gongs
(note the native, giving the scale)

Old gongs

Rack displaying tusked jaws
of sacrificed boars

398. *Racks Displaying the Tusked Jaws of Boars Sacrificed during a Single Ceremony.*
New Hebrides

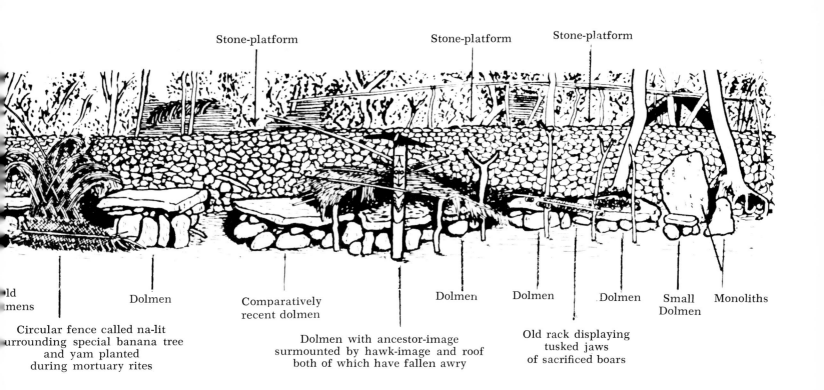

Stone-platform   Stone-platform   Stone-platform

ld
tmens   Dolmen   Comparatively   Dolmen   Dolmen   Dolmen   Small   Monoliths
                            recent dolmen   Dolmen

Circular fence called na-lit
urrounding special banana tree   Dolmen with ancestor-image   Old rack displaying
    and yam planted   surmounted by hawk-image and roof   tusked jaws
during mortuary rites   both of which have fallen awry   of sacrificed boars

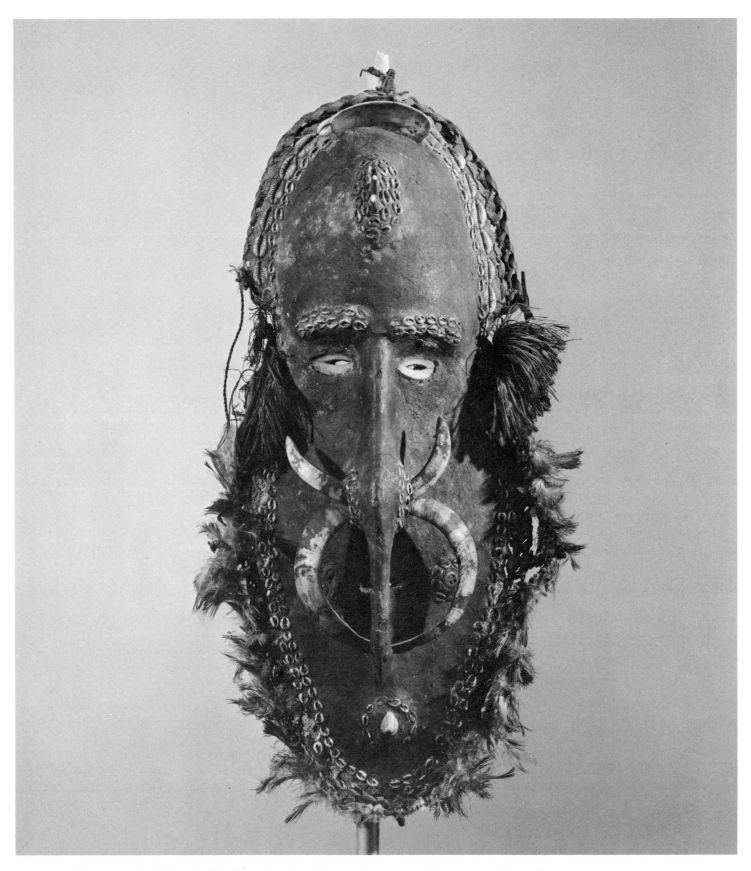

399. *Mask of Wood, Shell, and other Materials.* A.D. *20th century. New Guinea*

As observed and interpreted by Layard, the Malekulan boy's first ritual act, undertaken at the age of about five or six under the guidance of his father, is the sacrifice of a pet boar, at which time he gives up eating with his mother and joins the older boys in a special house for bachelors, where he is given more boars to rear and sacrifice. The effect of such repeated rites at this early stage of life is a conquest in the developing male child of his infantile dependency on the mother: the mother as a protecting, but also as a retaining, "devouring" mother, and himself as a mother-devouring child. The youngster's feelings of dependency and affection are transferred from the mother to the boars, which are male and yet also food, like the mother, as well as eaters of food, like the boy himself. And when the cherished pig is then sacrificed, the system of dependency that it stands for and supports is overcome and transcended, the "ghost" or "spirit" of the boar going into the sacrificer and he incorporating in himself the support formerly sought from without.

The boars bred and sacrificed by the older men have had their upper canines knocked out, so that the tusks, having nothing to bite against, and following their natural curve, curl backward, then downward and around, piercing the cheek and then the jaw. And at various stages of this cycling growth ceremonials of sacrifice are undertaken, during which the owner offers hecatombs of pigs of his own breeding, the powers of which are assimilated by both his chief porker and himself. Nor does a completion of one cycle terminate the adventure; for as Layard notes:

> The jaw is no obstacle, for, growing now forwards again through the bone, the tusks finally emerge once more, each having completed a whole circle, with the tip of the tusk just inside the spot at which it first appeared. When the tusk has pushed its way up for the second time so that the tip is visible outside the animal's lip, it is considered perfect from a ritual point of view. This is, however, by no means the highest possible stage of growth. Tusks so treated can, with luck and good management, be induced to describe two complete circles, and there are cases in which they have been known to describe three.[18]

The motive behind the tremendous labor and endless care lavished on these pigs is that the boar with the brilliantly curving tusks should become (in Layard's words) "the sacrificial animal, through the slaying of which, with due ritual, a man attains life after death."[19] The shining tusks themselves represent, according to Layard, the waxing and waning moon, and the black body of the boar between corresponds to the "new" or "black" invisible moon at the time of her apparent death. "Consequently," as Layard observes, "it is not surprising to find the tusked boar throughout all Malekula to be not only the food of the ancestral ghosts, but also intimately associated with the Devouring Mother in all her aspects."[20]

In the mask opposite, cowrie shells, which are female symbols, frame the ominous black face, whereas the tusks surrounding the cavernous mouth are phallic; and so the boar is both male and female, continuing thus for the adult Malekulan the "conquest of the mother" motif first announced in the sacrifices performed by the growing

Fig. 400

Fig. 401

boy. Only now the Devouring Mother to be overcome is not the beloved, protecting, holding mother of childhood, but the ultimate, cosmic Mother Night of death, which must be incorporated and transcended. Also, the sentiments invested in the pigs of these later years are not so much those of tenderness, love, and affection as of manly enterprise and pride, the chief symbolic carriers of all this spiritual weight being the great two- and three-circle tuskers, the death pigs loaded with both mythic and economic worth. The growth of every inch of tusk will have been celebrated, through the years, with increasingly elaborate ceremonials of lavish sacrifice, in former times even human offerings being required for the highest masonic degrees.[21]

And so highly charged can a great three-circle porker become as a consequence of such operations conducted in the service of its waxing lunar tusks, that if its owner, equivalently charged, should die before sacrificing it there would be left no one of rank high enough to dare to take the owner's place, and the priceless beast would be left to die a natural death, all the years of its expensive rearing wasted and its power-laden soul passing on without conferring its exalted rank upon anyone at all. For as Layard states: "If a man were to sacrifice a boar advanced to a grade too far beyond his own in the Maki hierarchy, the passage of the boar's soul into his own would overwhelm him, and disaster would be sure to follow."[23] Whereas, on the other hand, the sacrifice of such a pig by a master eligible to assimilate its spiritual charge confers a degree of authority beyond the touch of any threat whatsoever, either of life or of death. He becomes one who has incorporated in his person not only the powers of all pairs of opposites—male and female, life and death, being and nonbeing, and the rest—but also whatever powers beyond such polarizations a man who had become verily a superman might be imagined to subsume.

400. Moon Design. A.D. *20th century. Malekula*

cf. Fig. 399

"The design inside each crescent," states Bernard Deacon, to whom this drawing is credited, "is said to represent a face; while the two sides of the figure are supposed to be either the waxing and waning moon, or, according to some men, the light and dark halves of the moon."[22]

401. *Ancestral Figure.* A.D. *20th century. New Ireland*

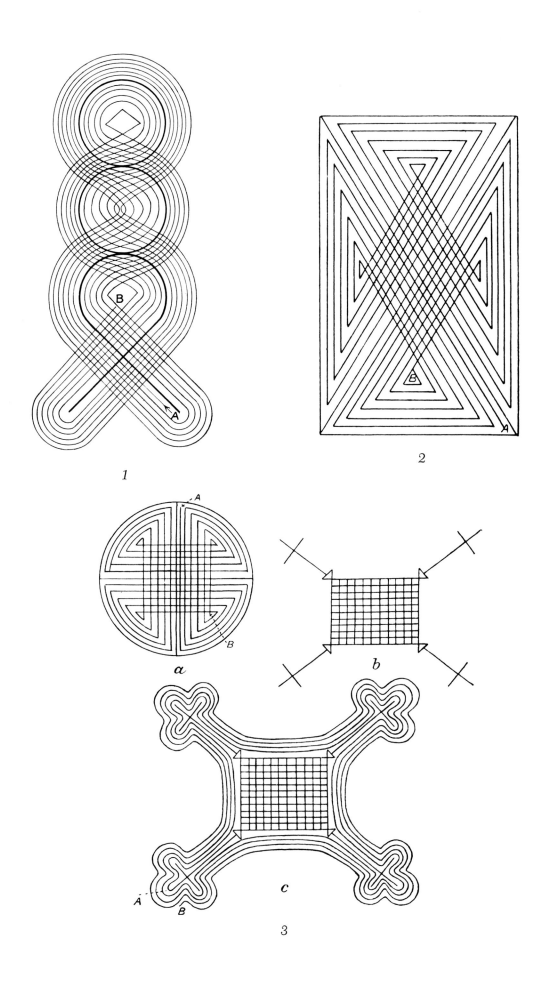

1. Linear framework denoted by thick line. Continuous line starts externally at *A* and ends internally at *B*.

2. The framework is a rectangle, with diagonals joining the corners. The continuous line starts on the periphery at *A* and ends internally at *B*.

3. The first part of the design to be drawn is *a*, of which the framework consists of a circle intersected by two lines at right angles to each other. Here the continuous line begins at *A* and ends at *B*. Next, the outer contours are rubbed out and four crosses drawn at the corners, as shown in *b*. A continuous line is now begun at the tip of one cross and traced all around the figure four times from *A* to *B*, as shown in *c*.[16]

"This drawing," states Dr. Layard of labyrinth 3, "is strikingly reminiscent of the church labyrinths of Europe, although there is no question here of European influence. In the Middle Ages such labyrinths were used for penance; the penitent had to make his way through them until he finally found Jerusalem, heaven, or a saint in the center. In his work on the labyrinth, Hermann Güntert [*Labyrinth; eine sprachwissentschaftliche Untersuchung*, Heidelberg, 1932] demonstrates the close relationship between the structure of such labyrinths, together with the purpose for which they were constructed, and that of the megalithic tombs of the pre-Indo-Germanic peoples of the Mediterranean region.

"What is the real meaning of these labyrinths? The best starting point for such an inquiry is provided by the important discovery of C. N. Deedes ["The Labyrinth," in S. H. Hooke, *The Labyrinth*, London and New York, 1935], who, on the basis of detailed studies of Egyptian and Mesopotamian seals, found that the labyrinths, from which the later mazes were derived, originally served to safeguard the kings' tombs against intrusion by uninitiates. The author traces the architectural development of the tomb from simple to complex form with labyrinthine passages.

"With the removal of the mortuary temple to outside the tomb proper, the labyrinth came in time to be transferred from tomb to temple, where 'the funerary rites of the dead king-god were performed. Here was his portrait statue and here he was daily fed.' Summing up a considerable body of evidence, the author [C. N. Deedes] declares:

" 'The labyrinth was the center of activities concerned with those greatest of mysteries, Life and Death. There men tried by every means known to them to overcome death and to renew life. . . . There the living king-god went to renew and strengthen his own vitality by association with the immortal lives of his dead ancestors. . . . The break-up of the archaic civilizations, together with the diffusion and democratization of the ancient pattern of religious belief and ritual, resulted in degradation of ritual, confusion of beliefs, and loss of technical knowledge and ability to reproduce the old forms. . . . Labyrinth forms . . . were preserved as art-motives in decoration.'

"The same observations apply also," Layard resumes, "to Malekula. Here, too, the motivation for the Journey of the Dead is to be sought not in the fact of death itself, but in the desire for the renewal of life through contact with the dead ancestors who are already leading a life beyond the grave. The juxtaposition of tomb, labyrinth, and portrait statue of the dead, which we find in Egyptian funerary monuments, can accordingly be brought into a direct parallel with that Malekulan variant of the Journey of the Dead in which the female figure of the Devouring Ghost sits beside a stone with which she is identified; she sits outside the Cave, which represents the tomb, having before her a labyrinthine design, whose mazes the dead man, who is said to have lost his way, must understand if he is to pass through."[17]

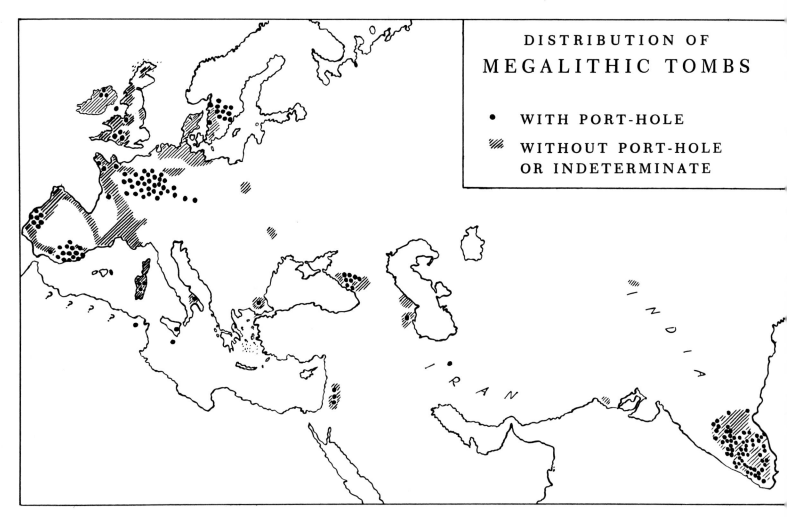

Map 6. *Distribution of Megalithic Monuments in Europe and Asia.*

Dating: European series, ca. 2500-1500 B.C.; South Indian, ca. 250 B.C.-A.D. 50.

" 'Megalithic' tombs and related monuments constructed usually of large slabs or blocks of stone, either in their natural form or roughly quarried and trimmed, are more abundant in the Deccan and South India than any other category of ancient structures. . . . Many of them show a similarity, seemingly amounting to kinship, with megaliths in other parts of the world—in the lands bordering upon the Mediterranean and the Atlantic, in the Caucasus, in Iran. . . . Some have portals, and not only so, but portals carved in a single stone slab in the form called a port-hole stone in western and northern Europe. . . . [which] seems to me a highly specialized trait suitable for defining a generalized 'megalithic' culture if any such exist. . . . It would seem likely that the complex originated around the eastern Mediterranean, presuming it had a single origin at all."[24]

Now since there were in Oceania no wild pigs when the first seafarers arrived in their sailing catamarans from Asia, the mythic theme of the wild boar hunt, which plays such a prominent role in the legends of antiquity, is lacking in the islands. The association of the pig with ideas of survival in the afterworld has been retained, however; also, the notion of the labyrinth as a guide to the afterworld, along Fig. 402 with the idea of a body of esoteric knowledge to be gained through participation in graded rites insuring the initiate against disaster in his journey through the afterworld-maze to a seat of immortal life.

This map shows the distribution of megalithic tombs throughout both Europe Map #6 and South India—with little or no evidence of such structures between: the European date roughly from ca. 2500 to 1500 B.C., in association with the Bronze Age civilizations of Egypt, Crete, and Southwest Asia; the Indian, on the other hand, are of a much later period, ca. 250 B.C.-A.D. 50 or so, and associated with a relatively primitive iron-using complex that had arrived apparently from the southeast. Dr. Layard has described the role of megalithic elements in the Malekulan sacrificial rites, and we have reports also of megalithic rituals among a number of the so-called Hill Tribes of India: the Maria Gonds of Bastar, Bondos and Gadabas of Orissa, Oraons and Mundas of Chola Nagpur, Nagas and Khasis of Assam.[25] As Professor V. Gordon Childe has remarked of these phenomena: "The significance of this apparent interrelationship over many thousands of miles of the earth's surface cannot yet be appraised."[62] It is still largely an unsolved problem, which will perhaps one day be explained. However, in the meantime, whether an explanation is forthcoming or not, it is at any rate fortunate for all students of mythology that such absolutely undeniable evidences of cultural continuity across enormous distances and through incredible reaches of time do in fact exist and can be seen, touched, photographed, and pondered; for otherwise, any such recognition of a common intangible heritage as must be taken for granted when describing and discussing the mythologies of this single great continuum would be difficult to argue and confirm.

Who would have expected, for example, that an explanation of the image given in *The Book of the Dead*, of Seth as a black pig that burned out the left eye (the lunar eye) of Horus, would be found in the New Hebrides—in the identification of the black body between the waxing and waning crescent tusks of a boar with the "new" or "black" invisible moon at the time of its apparent death? The flesh of swine is, of course, tabu in Malekula: not eaten under any circumstances by women, and by men only as communion food in connection with the sacrifice, when only male pigs are consumed. The whole art of herding swine, therefore, is holy, having nothing to do with secular, materialistic economics.[27] And as the distinguished Egyptologist Adolf Erman has pointed out in his comment on the passage of *The Book of the Dead* which explains why the pig is "an abominable thing to Horus," the eating of pork was avoided in ancient Egypt too, because of this identification of the black pig with Seth, who not only put out the lunar eye of Horus but also brought about the disappearance of Osiris.[28]

Frazer in *The Golden Bough* has discussed further implications of this avoidance:

> The Egyptians are generally said by Greek writers, to have abhorred the pig as a foul and loathsome animal. If a man so much as touched a pig in passing, he stepped into the river with all his clothes on, to wash off the taint. To drink pig's milk was believed to cause leprosy to the drinker. Swineherds, though natives of Egypt, were forbidden to enter any temple, and they were the only men who were thus excluded. No one would give his daughter in marriage to a swineherd, or marry a swineherd's daughter; the swineherds married among themselves. Yet *once a year the Egyptians sacrificed pigs to the moon and to Osiris*, and not only sacrificed them, but ate their flesh, though on any other day of the year they would neither sacrifice them nor taste of their flesh. Those who were too poor to offer a pig on this day baked cakes of dough, and offered them instead. This can hardly be explained except by the supposition that the pig was a sacred animal which was eaten sacramentally by his worshippers once a year.[29]

Concerning the Jewish avoidance of the flesh of the pig, Frazer remarks that there too the attitude is ambiguous:

> The Greeks could not decide whether the Jews worshipped swine or abominated them. On the one hand they might not eat swine; but on the other hand they might not kill them. And if the former rule speaks for the uncleanness, the latter speaks still more strongly for the sanctity of the animal. For whereas both rules may, and one rule must, be explained on the supposition that the pig was sacred; neither rule must, and one rule cannot, be explained on the supposition that the pig was unclean. If, therefore, we prefer the former supposition, we must conclude that, originally at least, the pig was revered rather than abhorred by the Israelites. We are confirmed in this opinion by observing that down to the time of Isaiah some of the Jews used to meet secretly in gardens to eat the flesh of swine and mice as a religious rite. Doubtless this was a very ancient ceremony, dating from a time when both the pig and the mouse were venerated as divine, and when their flesh was partaken of sacramentally on rare and solemn occasions as the body and blood of gods. And in general it may perhaps be said that all so-called unclean animals were originally sacred; the reason for not eating them was that they were divine.[32]

But the Greeks themselves, meanwhile, made a great deal of the pig as well. Odysseus, it may be recalled, was introduced to the mysteries of the underworld by Circe of the Braided Locks, who turned men into swine; and when she turned them back again, they were younger and more handsome than before. Moreover, when Odysseus returned to his own shore from his twenty-year adventure, it was in his own swineherd's shelter that he was reunited with his son. Frazer has pointed out that since the pig was such an essential feature of the rites of Demeter and Persephone, those two goddesses of the mysteries must themselves have originally been pigs:

Fig. 403

> The pig was sacred to Demeter; in art she was portrayed carrying or accompanied

by a pig; and the pig was regularly sacrificed in her mysteries, the reason assigned being that the pig injures the corn and is therefore an enemy of the goddess. But after an animal has been conceived as a god, or a god as an animal, it sometimes happens that the god sloughs off his animal form and becomes purely anthropomorphic; and that then the animal, which at first had been slain in the character of the god, comes to be viewed as a victim offered to the god on the ground of its hostility to the deity; in short, the god is sacrificed to himself on the ground that he is his own enemy. This happened to Dionysus, and it may have happened to Demeter also. And in fact the rites of one of her festivals, the Thesmophoria, bear out the view that originally the pig was an embodiment of the corn-goddess herself, either Demeter or her daughter and double Persephone. The Attic Thesmophoria was an autumn festival, celebrated by women alone in October, and appears to have represented with mourning rites the descent of Persephone (or Demeter) into the lower world, and with joy her return from the dead. Hence the name Descent or Ascent variously applied to the first, and the name *Kalligeneia* (fair-born) applied to the third day of the festival. Now it was customary at the Thesmophoria to throw pigs, cakes of dough, and branches of pine-trees [cf. p. 439, plantain boughs at Attahooroo] into "the chasms of Demeter and Persephone," which appear to have been sacred caverns or vaults. In these caverns or vaults there were said to be serpents, which guarded the caverns and consumed most of the flesh of the pigs and dough-cakes which were thrown in. Afterwards—apparently at the next annual festival—the decayed remains of the pigs, the cakes, and the pine branches were

Fig. 404

Fig. 405

403. *Odysseus Forces Circe to Restore His Men to Human Form. 4th century* B.C.

404. *Pig Sacrifice. Date unknown. Greece*

"Art," states Jane Harrison, "has left us no certain representation of the Thesmophoria; but in the charming little vase-painting from a lekythos in the National Museum at Athens, a woman is represented sacrificing a pig. He is obviously held over a trench and the three planted torches indicate an underworld service. In her left hand the woman holds a basket, no doubt containing *sacra*. There seems to be a reminiscence of the rites of the Thesmophoria, though we cannot say that they are actually represented.

"It is practically certain that the ceremonies of the burying and resurrection of the pigs took place on the first day of the Thesmophoria called variously the *Kathodos* and the *Anodos*. It is further probable from the name *Kalligeneia*, Fairborn, that on the third day took place the strewing of the rotten flesh on the fields. The second, intervening day, also called μέση, middle day, was a solemn fast, *Nesteia*; probably on this day the magical *sacra* lay upon the altars where the women placed them."[30]

cf. Fig. 383

fetched by women called "drawers," who, after observing rules of ceremonial purity for three days, descended into the caverns, and, frightening away the serpents by clapping their hands, brought up the remains and placed them on the altar. [Compare the exhumed skulls on the *morai*.] Whoever got a piece of the decayed flesh and cakes, and sowed it with the seed-corn in his field, was believed to be sure of a good crop.

To explain the rude and ancient ritual of the Thesmophoria the following legend was told. At the moment when Pluto carried off Persephone, a swineherd called Eubuleus chanced to be herding his swine on the spot, and his herd was engulfed in the chasm down which Pluto vanished with Persephone. Accordingly at the Thesmophoria pigs were annually thrown into caverns to commemorate the disap-

405. *Return of the Maiden. Date and origin unknown. Greece*

406. *The Purification of Orestes.*
    5th century B.C. *Greece*

A sacrifice of a pig is here being performed to turn away the wrath of the Furies, the Erinyes, who have arrived to avenge Orestes' murder of his mother Clytemnestra. As described by Jane Harrison: "Orestes, sword in hand, is seated close to the Omphalos. Above his head Apollo holds the pig of purification, in his left hand the laurel; to the right is Artemis as huntress with spears; to the left are two sleeping wingless Erinyes; the ghost of Clytaemnestra beckons them to wake. From the ground rises another Erinyes, a veritable earth demon. The euphemism of the vase-painter makes the Erinyes not only wingless but beautiful, as fair to see as Clytaemnestra."[31]

407 (opposite). Venus and Adonis. Titian. After A.D. 1560

Venus to Adonis, in Shakespeare's version of their parting:

O! be advis'd thou know'st not what it is
With javelin's point a churlish swine to
*   gore,*
*   Whose tushes never sheath'd he*
*   whetteth still,*
*   Like to a mortal butcher, bent to kill.*

On his bow-back he hath a battle set
Of bristly pikes, that ever threat his
*   foes;*
His eyes like glow-worms shine when he
*   doth fret;*
His snout dig sepulchres where'er he
*   goes;*
*   Being mov'd, he strikes whate'er is in*
*   his way,*
*   And whom he strikes his crooked*
*   tushes slay.*

His brawny sides, with hairy bristles
*   arm'd,*
Are better proof than thy spear's point
*   can enter;*

His short thick neck cannot be easily
*   harm'd;*
Being ireful, on the lion he will venture:
*   The thorny brambles and embracing*
*   bushes,*
*   As fearful of him part, through whom*
*   he rushes.*

Alas! he nought esteems that face of
*   thine,*
To which Love's eyes pay tributary
*   gazes;*
Nor thy soft hands, sweet lips and
*   crystal eyne,*
Whose full perfection all the world
*   amazes;*
*   But having thee at vantage, wondrous*
*   dread!*
*   Would root these beauties as he roots*
*   the mead.*

O! let him keep his loathsome cabin
*   still;*
Beauty hath nought to do with such
*   of foul fiends.*[38]

---

pearance of the swine of Eubuleus. It follows from this that the casting of the pigs into the vaults at the Thesmophoria formed part of the dramatic representation of Persephone's descent into the lower world; and as no image of Persephone appears to have been thrown in, we may infer that the descent of the pigs was not so much an accompaniment of her descent as the descent itself, in short, that the pigs were Persephone. Afterwards when Persephone or Demeter (for the two are equivalent) took on human form, a reason had to be found for the custom of throwing pigs into caverns at her festival; and this was done by saying that when Pluto carried off Persephone there happened to be some swine browsing near, which were swallowed up along with her.[33]

It is worth remarking in this connection that the name Eubuleus, "Giver of Good Counsel," was equally an appellation of the abductor, Hades-Pluto himself; further, that according to a Welsh version of the Tristan legend the lover and abductor of King Mark's queen once disguised himself as the king's swineherd and, taking charge then of the pigs, sent the real swineherd with a message to Isolt.[34] Like Odysseus, Tristan bore on his thigh a scar from the tusk of a boar, and in Gottfried

of Strassburg's version of the legend Tristan's shield is described as inlaid with the image of a boar, "as sable-black as coal,"[35] while he himself is compared in a memorable image to a charging boar, crashing into Mark's bedchamber and ravaging the king's bed.[36] Magical swine play prominent roles, in fact, throughout the myths and fairy lore of the Celtic world, and the tales in which they occur share many motifs with those of classical antiquity. There is an Irish fairytale—told to this day, for example, in Connaught—of the daughter of the king of the Land of Youth. She appeared to Oisin, son of Finn McCool, wearing a pig's head (Circe! Persephone!), which he had the wit, however, to kiss away. And when he had done so he found himself with a supernatural bride, and she the queen of the timeless Land of Youth below Waves.[37] And there is the famous legend, also, of Diarmuid, the young lover and abductor of Grianne, the promised bride of Finn McCool, who was killed and gored by a magical boar that he simultaneously slew—as was in classical legend Adonis, the young lover of the greatest goddess of antiquity, when, against her passionate pleading, he had torn himself from her arms.

Among the Irish folk the megalithic dolmens about the country are called "Diarmuid and Grianne's bed," while the upright menhirs are "Finn's Thumb." For the pursuit by Finn was close and threatening and the flight of the lovers extensive in its course, until Finn let up and the couple was left in peace—but only for a time.

For there was a geis on Diarmuid (a special type of tabu) never to hear the baying of hunting hounds without following the sound; and Finn, his uncle, knew this. Consequently, when he one fateful day spied the whittlings of a stick coming down the waters of a brook, each speel of them curled nine times in a way that no knife in Ireland other than Diarmuid's could have contrived, he knew that his enemy was nigh, and that night released his hounds for the hunting of a monstrous boar that had for some time been ranging thereabouts. Diarmuid heard the voice of one of Finn's hounds and started out of his sleep. Grianne caught him, threw her two arms about him, and asked what he had seen.

"It is the voice of a hound I have heard," he said, "and I marvel to hear it at night."

"It is the fairy people that are doing this to you," she answered, and lulled him back to their bed. Twice more he heard and started out of sleep; and the last time, at dawn, went forth with his favorite hound.

Now it was in Sligo that the terrible adventure occurred, on the summit of the flat-topped Mount Ben Bulben, up the face of which came the wild boar at him with all the troop of Finn's warriors after. Diarmuid's hound tucked tail and took flight, and himself, hurling his javelin, struck the oncoming tusker in the middle of its face, with no effect. His sword, which he brought down upon its back without injuring a bristle, broke in two, leaving only the hilt in his hand. And when the animal wheeled, tripping him, he tumbled astride its back, facing backward, to be carried thus down the hill and up again, at the summit of which he was tossed, and the boar ripped him open with a tusk. However, he had just flung at the beast with a prodigious blow the hilt of his sword, which dashed the animal's brains out, and it fell beside him, dead. Whereupon Finn arrived to survey with satisfaction the scene of the dual sacrifice, like some deity appearing to accept with relish an offering: the great boar destroyed, and Diarmuid dying, with his entrails out upon the ground.

"Well it pleases me to see you in this plight," said Finn, "and it grieves me only that all of the women of Erin are not now gazing upon you; for your extraordinary beauty is now ugliness, and your choice form a deformity."

"You might nevertheless heal me, O Finn, if you had a mind to it," Diarmuid said.

"And in what way," asked Finn, "could that be done?"

"When as a lad you received the gift of knowledge from the salmon in the pool beneath the Tree of Knowledge," Diarmuid answered, "you received with it the gift that anyone to whom you would give a drink from the palms of your hands would be young and well again from any sickness."

"I know of no well on this hill," said Finn.

"That," Diarmuid answered, "is not true. For not nine footsteps away from you is the well of the best fresh water in the world."

408. *Sacred Boar. Probably 1st century* B.C. *Hounslow, England.
Shown actual size*

409. *Bronze Boar. Late Gallic period, ca. 100* B.C. *Dept. Loiret, France.
H: 2′ 2¾″; L: 4′ 1½″; W: 1′ 1″*

Finn went to the well. He took up the full of his two hands of water, and during the nine steps back let it trickle away through his fingers. Again he went, and again let it go. And so again; at the end of which third venture, Diarmuid was dead.[40]

Fig. 410

Opposite is an image from Druidic Gaul of the century of Vercingetorix (died ca. 50 B.C.), executed in a style continuing the old menhir-statue tradition of the megalithic Bronze Age; and what is most remarkable is the fact that this god has engraved along his sides in place of arms two huge eyes, exactly as long as the boar and disposed on the same vertical axis. The fact that they are exactly the same length as the boar cannot be accidental; nor can the interesting, bodhisattva-like tilt of the head. The mythology and name of the god are unknown, but he wears an Irish torque of gold and is certainly a deity of the ancient Celtic Druidic faith, out of which the legends of Diarmuid and Finn McCool derived their mythological matter and themes. The great eyes along his sides suggest an influence, dating from the megalithic

cf. Figs. 298, 302, 411

age, of the old Sumerian eye goddess whose cult (we know)[41] was transported westward along early Bronze Age sea routes. And they suggest, too, in relation to the

Map #7

fairy themes of later Celtic legend, the great gift of omniscience that Finn was supposed to have acquired when as a boy he ate the salmon drawn from the pool beneath the Tree of Knowledge, where it had been feeding its life long on the hazelnuts of wisdom continually dropping from the broadly spreading branches. Finn had received at that time, also, the ability to heal and restore life and youth by giving

cf. Fig. 413

water from the palms of his hands, like ambrosia from the palms of the Bodhisattva. However, in the Finn of this episode at least, there is no sign of a Bodhisattva's boundless compassion for the abductor of his bride. His attitude is rather that of Shiva in the legend of the "Face of Glory,"* where the god let fly at one who had come to abduct his goddess a lightning flash of wrath from his middle eye of transcendental vision. In the vocabulary of the lama of the Tibetan *Book of the Dead*, Finn here would have to be termed a manifestation of the *wrathful* aspect of the Body of Truth, while the god of the Gallo-Roman image would represent the *peaceful* aspect—the force and character of all such mythical apparitions being but reflexes determined by the qualities of ego-will in the persons to whom they appear. And such a compulsive passion as that of Diarmuid for Finn's bride would certainly have merited—from the point of view, at least, of the Body of Truth—a good thunderbolt or two, or perhaps three.

In the Adonis legend, as Frazer has shown, the boar is an aspect of the deity himself: "the god," in Frazer's words, "is sacrificed to himself." In our legend, Diarmuid is sacrificed to Finn; the boar is the animal agent or vehicle of Finn's wrath, but an aspect equally of Diarmuid. In the ancient legend of the slain and resurrected

Fig. 39

Phrygian divinity, Attis, beloved of the great mother and earth-goddess Cybele, the young god, according to one version of his death, was gored and slain by a boar, but according to another, died from loss of blood when he unmanned himself beneath

* See above, p. 118.

410a. Detail of Figure 410

410. *Gaulish God with Boar.*
   ca. 1st century B.C. *France*

"Although this is probably only of the Gallo-Roman period, it has been dated earlier, and is a continuation of the menhir-statue tradition by virtue of its stone-bound lines. But at the same time the work is reminiscent of wood-carving and in overall composition and in detail is purely 'Celtic': mixture of the human form with animal figures, incorporated in the god. Stylized face still recognizable despite mutilation; shape of eyes, height of ears, massive neck, hair-style (so far as this is preserved), necklace or *torques*. Alongside the limbless trunk, instead of arms, huge eyes, exactly as long as the boar and disposed on the same axis as the latter."[39]

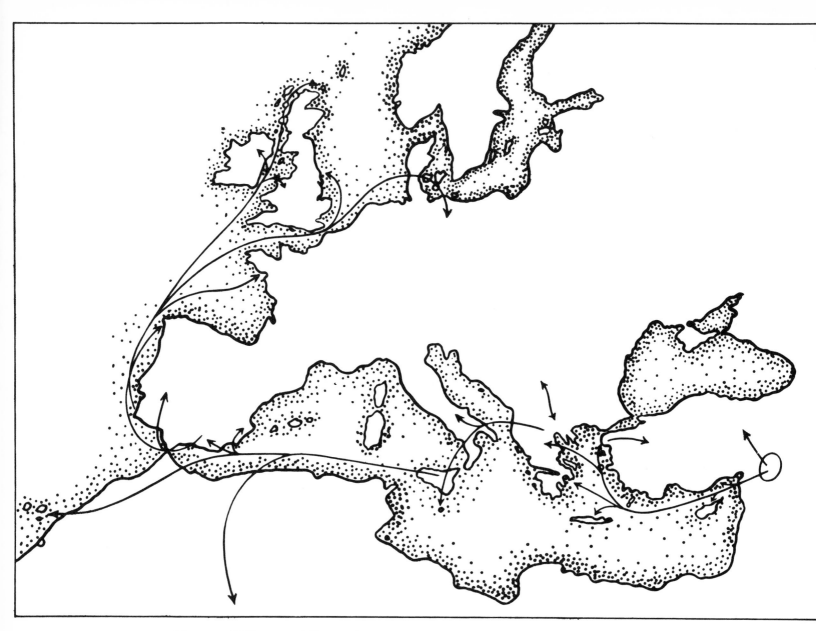

Map 7. *Diffusion of Eye-goddess Monuments and Tradition from S.W. Asian Matrix via sea routes to N.W. African and W. European zones.*

411. Early Sumerian Eye Goddess Figurines.
3500-3000 B.C. Northwest Syria

Votive figurines of black or white alabaster, from strata deep beneath a temple floor of ca. 2800 B.C. See also Fig. 298.

412. Spearing the Boar. ca. 2000 B.C. *Sumer*

"The meaning of the scene is obscure," states Stephen Langdon in discussing this mythic episode; "and the figure of the person lancing a spear from the top of a palm tree may not be a divinity." On the other hand, of course, he may; and Professor Langdon's guess is that the scene refers to an episode in the mythology of the god Ninurta, who was regent of the month Tammuz (Tammuz, like Adonis and others, was slain by a boar), and whose title was Ninkilim, "Lord of Swine." We note the tree, the crescent moon, and remarkably, the two tails of the beast. "It is certain," declares Langdon, "that the pig was sacred to Ninurta, and possible that he was known both in Babylonia and throughout the West as 'Lord of Swine.' In any case as War-god, he was associated with the western War-god, who is there always the Sky- and Thunder-god Adad, Ishar, Yāw.

This probably explains why the pig, at least among the worshippers of Yāw, i.e., the Hebrews, was tabu and its flesh forbidden to be eaten. This animal was well known in Sumer and Babylonia, but, in the innumerable records of offerings and economic transactions, it practically never occurs as a food, and a temple calendar forbids it to be eaten on the thirtieth of the fifth month. A fable in Assyrian states that the pig is unclean and an abomination to the gods. It is difficult to understand why the Sumerians, Babylonians, and Canaanites kept pigs at all; for it seems clear that none of these people used them much for food."

"This seal from Kish," Langdon concludes, "where Ninurta's principal cult under the name Zamama as War-god existed from prehistoric times, may possibly be connected with a legend of the killing of Nikilim by a wild boar."[42]

a pine tree—which, in the light of Frazer's demonstration, would amount to the same thing. In either case, furthermore, such a mythological death is but the foreground view of a resurrection; the symbolism of the image being susceptible to interpretation not only in the popular sense of a restoration to life following a physical death, but also, more properly, in the mystical, of an awakening to immortality through an act of psychological self-divestiture: and this second is the understanding sym-

Fig. 390 bolized in the eye, the EYE OF HORUS, by which the one thought to be dead is disclosed to himself and to all to be in fact alive eternally, both in himself and in the person of his son. And it was Seth, furthermore, the black boar—who was finally metaphysically consubstantial and so at one with both Horus and Osiris—who had provided the occasion for the lesson.

For what is in the mystical dimension one, is in the temporal-spatial two—and many—the very form of our "knowledge" (in mystical terms, our "ignorance") being multiplicity. Here in this field of Waking Consciousness we are separate from each other, *A* is not *not-A*, and so long as we hold to this ego-consciousness, that will continue to be the way things are. However, as Dr. Ananda K. Coomaraswamy once

413. Divinity with Overflowing Vase. ca. 2100 B.C. Sumer

formulated the mystery: "for this *ignorantia divisiva* an expiation is provided in the Sacrifice, where by the sacrificer's surrender of himself and the building up again of the dismembered deity, whole and complete, the multiple selves are reduced to their single principle."[43] As symbolized in the imagery of myth, it is at the summit of the mountain (Mount Ben Bulben, for example), where the opposite sides come together (and where there is "the best fresh water in the world"), that the mystery of this coming together of *all* opposites is realized, recognized, and solemnized in the symbolic adventure of the sacrifice or its equivalent, a sacred marriage: for there the eye of knowledge opens to behold—as in the symbol at the summit of the pyramid in the Great Seal of the United States, which we carry in our pockets on every dollar bill—the *coincidentia oppositorum*. It's as easy as that! In the mythological mystery play, as Coomaraswamy describes it, "Slayer and Dragon, sacrificer and victim are of one mind behind the scenes, where there is no polarity of contraries; but mortal enemies on the stage, where the everlasting war of the Gods and the Titans is displayed."[44]

Hence, wherever a knowledge of this unity in duality informs and inspires the arts and artists of a culture—as it did supremely in the creative Tantric periods of India—even the simplest folklore theme becomes enlarged, illuminated, and marvelously transformed; as, for example, in the legend illustrated in the powerful image of the mighty Indian world-dreamer Vishnu seen as a great wild boar rescuing the goddess Earth from the ocean of a universal flood. The theme there represented is known to folklorists as the earth diver motif, and in the authoritative *Motif-Index of Folk-Literature* it is concisely described as follows: "From a raft in the primeval sea, the creator sends down animals to try to bring up the earth. After a number of animals have failed, one (often a muskrat) succeeds. The earth is made from the bit brought up."[45] Numerous North American Indian and Siberian examples are recorded, many humorous, all charming, none, however, equalling either the beauty or the wonder of this classic Hindu example, where the diver is the cosmic sleeper himself, whose recurrent dream—fading and reappearing before his inward vision—is the entire universe. So that the situation here is comparable to that earlier case, where the same god, soaring on his golden-plumaged sun bird, entered into the plot and context of his dream to rescue an imperiled elephant—except that whereas there the rescue had been of a single dream character, here it is of the whole dream, as though a sleeper, feeling that a night's vision for which he greatly cared was about to fade, should suddenly see himself in some phantasmagoric dream-disguise plunging into the night to find and bring it back to view.

The adventure, as recorded in a number of puranas (the basic mythic texts of popular Hinduism, dating largely from the first millennium A.D.), is supposed to have occurred at the dawn of the present world-eon, when Brahma the Creator, seated on the lotus of Vishnu's world-dream,* awoke from his long night of sleep

Fig. 414

cf. Fig. 5

* Cf. above, p. 142.

and, looking about, saw nothing but a void, in the midst of which he, on his lotus, was hovering alone. Concluding that within the waters of that void there must lie the earth submerged, Brahma was moved by a desire to have it brought to light. The rhythm of his breathing altered and there issued from his nostril the tiny figure of a boar the size of a thumb, which immediately increased, swelling mightily, to prodigious size, until—as described in the *Vayu* and *Matsya Puranas*:

> the boar was some fifty miles broad, five thousand high, and of the color of a dark cloud. His roar was like thunder; his bulk, vast as a mountain. His tusks were white, sharp, and fearful; fire flashed from his eyes; and he was radiant as the sun. His shoulders were plump, rounded, huge; he strode like a powerful lion; his haunches also were plump; his loins, however, slender; his smooth body, beautiful.[46]

And immediately on achieving this stature that immense boar plunged into the cosmic sea. Whereupon the goddess Earth, beholding him thus descending through the night-sea to her rescue, bowed in adoration and glorified her god:

> "Hail to thee, who art all creatures! Elevate me now from this place, as already many times before, in the ever-recurring cycles of time, thou hast upraised me. From thee, O Lord, have I proceeded. Of thee do I consist, as do the skies and all existing things. No one knows thy true nature. Even the gods adore thee only in the forms it has pleased thee to assume. Whatever may be apprehended by the mind, perceived by the senses, discovered by the intellect, is all but a name and a form of thee. Of thee am I, upheld by thee: my creator, thou! to thee do I fly for refuge. Hence, in this world I am known as 'Vishnu's Bride.' Triumph to thee, the essence of all wisdom, unchangeable, imperishable! Triumph to Eternity, the undefined essence of all definable things! Triumph to him who is both cause and effect, the universe, the sacrifice, the mystic syllable OM, the sacrificial fires, the scriptures and their sciences! Hail to the sun, the stars, the planets and whole world: all that is formless, all that has form, whether visible or invisible: all that I have said or left unsaid, all this art thou, Supreme Being of beings! Hail to thee, again, again, and again! All hail! All hail!"
>
> And he, approaching, luminous, through the waters of the cosmic night, auspicious supporter of the universe, thus welcomed by the goddess Earth, emitted a low murmuring sound, like a chanting of the Veda. He came plunging, a mighty boar whose eyes were like luminous lotuses and whose body, great as the Cosmic Mountain, was dark, of the color of lotus leaves. With his radiant white tusks he arrived and with those ample tusks elevated the goddess of his dream from those darkest regions.

In the powerful relief we see the moment of the rescue. The great serpent king and queen of the cosmic sea—of whom those of the elephant relief (Figure 5) are but minor, local representatives—coil back in awe and reverence as the precious goddess Earth is by the invincible saving power of Vishnu liberated from their toils.* And along the back wall of the sanctuary gods and sages can be seen watching amazed as the mighty form comes surging upward through the waters.

* Cf. the serpents of the classical Thesmophoria (above, p. 468).

414. *Vishnu, as the Cosmic Boar, Rescues the Goddess Earth.* ca. A.D. *6th century. Badami, India*

As he reared his head the waters shed and splashing from his brow purified the great sages residing in the heavens of the saints. Through the prints of his hoofs the waters with thundering sound rushed pouring to the netherworlds. The pious denizens of that heaven where the radiant sons of Brahma dwell were scattered before his breath, like leaves before a great wind. And the immortal sages clung for safety to the bristles of his body, trembling as he uprose bearing on his tusk the fair goddess Earth, shedding in all directions the rich brine of the cosmic sea. . . .[47]

VI. THE WAKING

THERE is a tradition which attributes the Buddha's death to a meal of boar's flesh eaten at the invitation of a disciple, Chunda by name, who was a master blacksmith. It has baffled many interpreters. However, in the light of what we now know of the world history of the archetype of the dying god through whose death the dominion of the Lord Death is transcended, the role of the boar as slayer here can be recognized as normal.

So too is the role of the blacksmith, in whose fiery forge the ore is "sacrificed" to extract its enduring essence, the precious metal. Professor Mircea Eliade, in a richly documented study, *Forgerons et alchimistes*, has brought together a multitude of examples to support the argument for a mystical mythology of metallurgy that originated ca. 1200-1000 B.C. in Armenia and was then diffused, east and west, with the spread of the arts of the metalworker's forge. "From the earliest stages of culture, fire," as Eliade points out, "has been employed as the agent of 'transmutation': the immunity of shamans to fire, for example, demonstrates that they have transcended the human state and participate in that of 'spirits' (whence the ritual enactment of fire tricks, which confirm and validate periodically the prestigious powers of the shamans). As an agent of transmutation fire is evident equally in certain rites of initiation of which traces remain even in the myths and legends of the Greeks. Who knows, furthermore, but that the rite of cremation itself may not have originated as an expression of the hope of a transmutation by fire?"[1]

The legend of the last meal of the Buddha has been handed down in the early Pali scripture known as the "Great Snuffing-Out Text" (*Mahaparinibbana-sutta*), which dates from approximately 80 B.C.; and there is about the legend as it appears there a distinct suggestion—though with totally different accent—of a common tradition somehow shared with the Gospel account of the Last Supper: Chunda in the role of Judas; Ananda as Peter; and the Buddha, of course, the willing victim.

415. *The Parinirvana of the Buddha.* A.D. 1086. Japan

Now The Blessed One having remained at Bhogagama as long as he desired, addressed the venerable Ananda: "Come, Ananda," he said, "let us proceed to Pava." To which the venerable Ananda replied, in assent to The Blessed One, "Even so, my Lord!" And with a great company of the brethren The Blessed One proceeded to Pava. And there at Pava The Blessed One stayed at the Mango Grove of Chunda, who was by family a smith.

Chunda, the worker in metals, heard that The Blessed One had come to Pava and that he was staying there in his Mango Grove. He went to the place where The Blessed One was staying and, saluting him, took his seat respectfully on one side. And when he was thus seated, The Blessed One instructed, aroused, incited, and gladdened him with religious discourse.

Then Chunda, the worker in metals, instructed, aroused, incited, and gladdened by the religious discourse of The Blessed One, addressed The Blessed One, and said: "May The Blessed One do me the honor of taking his meal, together with the brethren, tomorrow, at my home?" And The Blessed One, by silence, signified his consent.

Then seeing that The Blessed One had consented, Chunda, the worker in metals, rose from his seat and bowed down before The Blessed One, and keeping him on his right side as he passed him, departed thence. And by the end of that night, Chunda, the worker in metals, had made ready in his dwelling sweet rice and cakes and a quantity of succulent boar's meat; and he announced the hour to The Blessed One, saying, "The hour, Lord, has come, and the meal is ready."

And The Blessed One robed himself early in the morning and, taking his bowl, went with the brethren to the dwelling-place of Chunda, the worker in metals. When he had come thither he seated himself on the seat prepared for him. And when he was seated he addressed Chunda, the worker in metals, and said: "As to the succulent boar's flesh that you have made ready, serve me with it, Chunda; and as to the other food, the sweet rice and cakes, serve the brethren with it."

"Very well, my Lord!" said the worker in metals, Chunda, in assent to The Blessed One, and he served to The Blessed One the succulent boar's flesh that he had made ready, while to the members of the order he served the other food, the sweet rice and cakes.

And now The Blessed One addressed Chunda, the worker in metals, saying: "Whatever succulent boar's flesh is left over to thee, Chunda, bury it in a hole. I see no one on earth, Chunda, nor in Mara's heaven nor in Brahma's heaven, no one among monks and brahmans, among gods and men, no one by whom that food, when eaten, could be assimilated save the Tathagata."*

"Very well, my Lord!" said Chunda, the worker in metals, in assent to The Blessed One, and whatever succulent boar's flesh remained over he buried in a hole. Then he went to the place where The Blessed One sat; and when he had come there he took his seat respectfully on one side. And when he was seated, The Blessed One instructed and aroused and incited and gladdened Chunda, the worker in metals, with religious discourse. And The Blessed One then arose from his seat and departed thence.

But now, after The Blessed One had eaten the food prepared by Chunda, the worker in metal, there fell upon him a dire sickness, the sickness of dysentery, and

* See above, pp. 456-460.

416. *The Last Supper. Albrecht Dürer. Germany*

a sharp pain befell him, even unto death. But The Blessed One, mindful and self-possessed, bore it without complaint, and he addressed the venerable Ananda. "Come, Ananda," he said, "let us proceed to Kusinara." To which the venerable Ananda, in assent to The Blessed One, answered, "Even so, my Lord!"

And as we read somewhat further on:

> The Blessed One addressed again the venerable Ananda. "Now Ananda, it may happen," he said, "that some one should stir remorse in Chunda the smith by saying: 'It is unfortunate and a loss to thee, Chunda, in that when the Tathagata had eaten his last meal from thy provision, he died.' Any such remorse, Ananda, in Chunda the smith should be checked by saying: 'Chunda, it is fortunate and a gain for thee, in that when the Tathagata had eaten his last meal from thy provision, he died. From the very mouth of The Blessed One I have heard this, Chunda, from his own mouth I have received this teaching: "These two offerings of food," I have heard, "are of equal profit, and of much greater fruit and much greater profit than any other: and which are the two? The offering of food after which, when a Tathagata has eaten, he attains to supreme and perfect insight; and the offering of food after which, when a Tathagata has eaten, he passes away by that utter passing away in which nothing whatever remains behind: these two offerings of food are of equal fruit and of equal profit, and of much greater fruit and much greater profit than any others. There has been laid up by Chunda the smith a karma redounding to length of life, redounding to good birth, redounding to good fortune, redounding to good fame, redounding to the inheritance of heaven, and of sovereign power." ' In this way, Ananda, any remorse should be checked in Chunda the smith."[2]

cf. Fig. 1

Our birth, wrote the poet Wordsworth, *is but a sleep and a forgetting.*[3]

In a symbolic painting of the Parinirvana, "The Ultimate Snuffing Out" of the Buddha Shakyamuni, opposite, the resemblance of the posture to that of Vishnu

cf. Fig. 4

the world-dreamer is eloquent of the message. As we have heard, the very title "Buddha" means "The One Who Has Waked," the one who has passed from dream, neither into the state of Deep Dreamless Sleep nor back to this other state of dream that we know as Waking Consciousness, but to that state which is no state, beyond names and forms, beyond namelessness and formlessness, beyond the concept "beyond," which is connoted in the Zen directive attributed to the Patriarch Hui-neng: "Show me the face you had before you were born." Reclining in the so-called "lion-posture," head pillowed on his right hand, left leg directly upon right, and left arm flat along his side, with his cousin, loyal Ananda, standing by in sorrow, he who at the age of thirty-five had absolutely quenched in his heart desire, loathing, and delusion, now, at the age of eighty—having for forty-five years taught compassionately of suffering, its origin, its passing away and the way that leads to its passing away—like a fading coal, went out. "As a flame blown about by the wind goes out and no one knows where," we read in an early Buddhist text, "so the saint released from name and body vanishes, no one knows where. . . . For him who has disappeared there is no form: that by which he might be said to be, no longer exists: when all things have been cut off, all disputes [concerning being or nonbeing] also are cut off."[4]

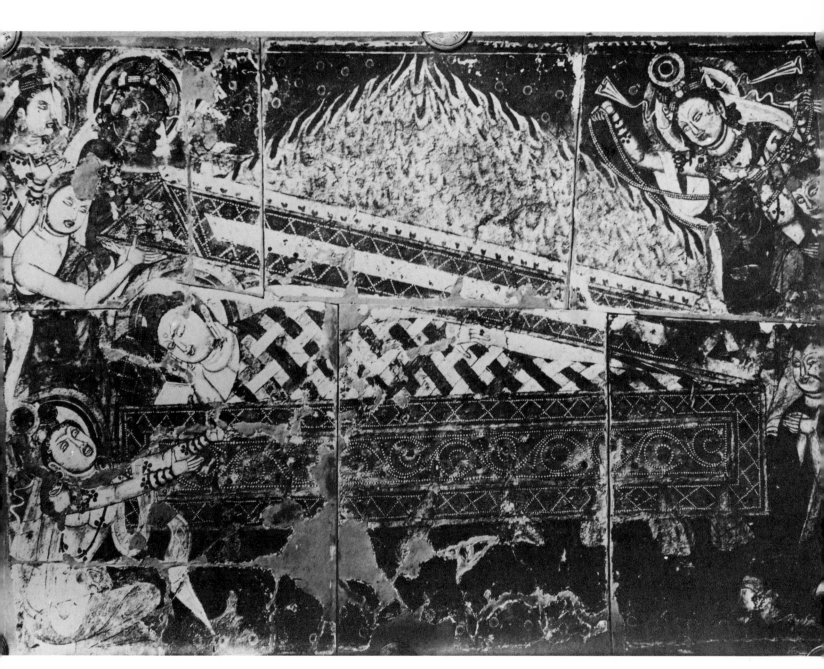

417. *Cremation of the Buddha.* A.D. *6th century. Central Asia*

Schopenhauer in his poetically speculative essay *On an Apparent Intention in the Fate of the Individual* proposes an image of this whole vast universe, this marvelous "multiplicity of phenomena conditioned by time and space," as "a vast dream, dreamed by a single being, in such a way that all the dream characters dream too; so that everything interlocks and harmonizes with everything else."[5]

James Joyce puts forth the same idea in his own way when he writes of the contending powers—male and female, active and contemplative, light and dark—as "equals of opposites, evolved by a onesame power of nature or of spirit as the sole condition and means of its himundher manifestation and polarised for reunion by the symphysis of their antipathies."[6]

Figs. 312, 313, 314

Figs. 331, 332, 333

Figs. 315, 316, 318

On the plane of understanding of the dream itself conflict is experienced as between the wills of contending characters, and in this limited context the desired end is normally a victory of the hero, of the higher, saving and releasing power over the lower, binding and limiting. Such is the mode of understanding associated with the first three lotus stages of the ladder of the uncoiling Kundalini.* But on the other hand, when the aim is to dissolve and surpass the limitations even of the highest names, forms, and modes of understanding of the dream-bound will, the desired end becomes the opposite, namely the sacrifice of the hero-form itself, as itself limiting and binding, this being the mode and aspiration of the higher chakras. The aim is then not the conquest of the dragon by the hero but the reverse, an immolation of the hero by the dragon; that is to say, self-divestiture through interiorization of the sacrifice.

In the language of the Buddha:

Fig. 417

All things, O monks, are on fire. And what, O monks, are all these things that are on fire? The eye is on fire; forms are on fire; impressions received by the eye are on fire; and whatever sensation, pleasant, unpleasant, or indifferent, originates in dependence on impressions received by the eye, that also is on fire. And with what are these on fire? With the fire of passion, say I; with the fire of hatred, with the fire of infatuation; with birth, old age, death, sorrow, lamentation, misery, grief and despair, they are on fire.

The ear is on fire: sounds are on fire. The nose is on fire: odors are on fire. The tongue is on fire: tastes are on fire. The body is on fire: things tangible are on fire. The mind is on fire: ideas are on fire. Mind-consciousness is on fire: impressions received by the mind are on fire; and whatever sensation, pleasant, unpleasant or indifferent, originates in dependence on impressions received by the mind, that also is on fire. And with what are these on fire? With the fire of passion, say I; with the fire of hatred, with the fire of infatuation: with birth, old age, death, sorrow, lamentation, misery, grief, and despair they are on fire.

Perceiving this, O monks, the learned and noble disciple conceives an aversion for the eye, conceives an aversion for forms, conceives an aversion for eye-consciousness, conceives an aversion for the impressions received by the eye; and whatever

* See above, p. 340.

418. *Pentecost. El Greco*

419. *End of a Monster. Pablo Picasso*

sensation, pleasant, unpleasant, or indifferent, originates in dependence on impressions received by the eye, for that also he conceives an aversion. He conceives an aversion for the ear, conceives an aversion for sounds; conceives an aversion for the nose, conceives an aversion for odors; conceives an aversion for the tongue, conceives an aversion for tastes; conceives an aversion for the body, conceives an aversion for things tangible; conceives an aversion for the mind, conceives an aversion for ideas; conceives an aversion for mind-consciousness, conceives an aversion for the impressions received by the mind; and whatever sensation, pleasant, unpleasant, or indifferent, originates in dependence on impressions received by the mind, for this also he conceives an aversion.

And in conceiving this aversion, he becomes divested of passion, and by the absence of passion he becomes free, and when he is free he becomes aware that he is free; and he knows that rebirth is exhausted, that he has lived the holy life, that he has done what it behooved him to do, and that he is no more for this world.[7]

Thus in emptiness the wisdom of the Buddha was fulfilled. But we have also heard those words delivered from the Yonder Shore of the *Prajnaparamita Sutra*: "Form is emptiness; emptiness, form. What is form, that is emptiness; what is emptiness, that is form. Thus perception, thought, feeling, and understanding also are emptiness."[8]

For when the bounding categories of this sphere of our life-dream are transcended, when all things are cut off and all disputes also, there remains no ground for dispute or for Hamlet's question, "To be or not to be." At the center of the wheel of the standard Tibetan-Buddhist representation of the vortex of existence there is the figure of a pig or boar signifying "ignorance": i.e., that condition of restricted consciousness from which it was the aim of the Buddha to release us; this dream-bounded fascination with forms out of which arise the delusory fears, desires, and quarrels that in general determine human life. It was the recognition of the nature of that boar—symbolically, the assimilation of the flesh of that boar to the flesh of his own body—that completely released the Blessed One from the general identification of consciousness with the limitations put upon it by our bodies of boar's flesh, fleshly senses and concerns. In the posture of the Great Sleeper, with the blaze of full consciousness burning his fleshly form to extinction (the same blaze by which, in reduced fervor, the fervent forms of this world are inflamed) he is that one who is no longer anyone at all; nor, indeed, had he ever been anyone at all, since, as taught in his illumination: "All things are without a self."

Fig 362

Stars, darkness, a lamp, a phantom, dew, a bubble;
A dream, a flash of lightning, and a cloud:
Thus should we look upon the world.[9]

420. *Autumn Rhythm. Jackson Pollack* (*detail*).

421. Beheld by the heavenly gods and sages, Vishnu, as the Cosmic Boar, rescues the Lotus-goddess Earth from the Waters of the Cosmic Serpent-king. ca. A.D. 400. Udayagiri (Bhopal), India

In the puranic figure of Vishnu as the cosmic boar, on the other hand, a willing affirmation is symbolized of those same limitations of consciousness upon which the wonder of this round of illusory existence depends for its motivation. Whereas the very title Buddha means "Awakened," the root syllable *vish* of the name Vishnu means, "to penetrate, to pervade, to invest, to spread through, to embrace, to go to (or against), to accomplish, to obtain, to convey."[10] Like the willing victim, who, "though he was in the form of God . . . humbled himself and became obedient unto death, even death on a cross" (Philippians 2:6-8), so in his incarnation as the cosmic boar the dreamer of this universal dream entered, in full knowledge, into the action of his theater piece, in a spirit of playful participation. Simultaneously engaged as actor and disengaged as knower, the god participates in the world-illusion; and by analogy: any and each of us might live thus disengaged, as witness, even while, as actor, being fully engaged on one side or the other of the ineluctable combats and disputes of the world play. These pairs of opposites are the Clashing Rocks at the bounds of all space-time existence, between which the illumined mind, even while struggling here, may pass to the Wisdom of the Yonder Shore.

For all action in this visionary theater of space-time is limited, directed, and implies not only an end to be gained, but also resistance, difficulty, and something to be conquered. Hence, in the legend of the rescue by the boar there is not only a goddess to be saved, but also a serpent king, the ocean king, to be overcome; and all of these are aspects of the one great dream and dreamer. That is to say, not only is the mighty Savior one with the cosmic dreamer of the dream into which he has entered as an incarnation, but *all* beings, all *things*, are also of the substance of that dream, at one with it in essential peace. That is the realization expressed in the prayer of the goddess Earth addressed to the boar descending to her rescue. And so also, in the words of another Indian sacred text, the *Shatapatha Brahmana*: "He is one as He is there, but many as He is in his children here."[11]

We opened this work with a motto from the lips of a Kalahari bushman: *There is a dream dreaming us*; and we are closing under the spell of a suggestion from the pen of Schopenhauer, of this whole universe of milky ways and ourselves within it as *a vast dream, dreamed by a single being, in such a way that all the dream characters dream too.* Obviously, there is here a certain accord of inspiration; but obviously also, there are differences. And we have neither cast a glance into the world of the Kalahari huntsman, nor asked ourselves what really remains to us—and remained to Schopenhauer—of myth. What is the dream we dream and that is dreaming us, today? Of what kind was the waking of the Renaissance that inspired Titian's brush and the fluent pen of Shakespeare; brought forth a Galileo, a Newton, and our flights of astronauts to the moon?

cf. Fig. 414

Cf. Figs. 150-152

Cf. Figs. 151, 218

What are you doing, Earth, in
   Heaven?
Tell me, what are you doing, Silent
   Earth?[12]

Notes

ABBREVIATIONS

CWJ *The Collected Works of C. G. Jung*, translated by R.F.C. Hull. Princeton: Princeton University Press (Bollingen Series XX). London: Routledge and Kegan Paul, Ltd.

PEY *Papers from the Eranos Yearbooks*, edited by Joseph Campbell. Princeton: Princeton University Press (Bollingen Series XXX). London: Routledge and Kegan Paul, Ltd.

KJV *King James Version*. Unless otherwise indicated Biblical quotations are from RSV, the Revised Standard Version (New York: Thomas Nelson and Sons, 1953), occasionally modified.

Translations, unless otherwise indicated, are by the author.

Transliterations of Oriental terms are styled throughout to omit diacritics.

CHAPTER I

[1] C. G. Jung, "The Meaning of Psychology for Modern Man," *Civilization in Transition, CWJ*, X, par. 304-305.

[2] Robinson Jeffers, "Roan Stallion," *Roan Stallion, Tamar, and Other Poems* (New York: Horace Liveright, 1925), p. 24.

[3] "Jagadambika" ("Hymn to the Mother of the World"), *Devibhagavata Purana* 29.5. Translation by Arthur and Ellen Avalon, *Hymns to the Goddess* (London: Luzac and Co., 1913), p. 147, modified.

[4] Blake's rendition of Job 7:14.

[5] Jung, "Basic Postulates of Analytical Psychology," *The Structure and Dynamics of the Psyche, CWJ*, VIII, par. 673.

[6] *The Book of the Dead*, Chapter LXIV, Papyrus of Nebseni (British Museum, No. 9,900, Sheets 23-24), translation by E.A.W. Budge, *The Chapters of the Coming Forth by Day* (London: Kegan Paul, Trench, Trübner and Co., 1898), pp. 112-113.

[7] *Mythological Papyri*, trans. Alexandre Piankoff, ed. N. Rambova, Bollingen Series XL.3 (New York: Pantheon Books, 1957), I, 100-101.

[8] E. A. Wallis Budge, *Osiris and the Egyptian Resurrection* (New York: G. P. Putnam's Sons, 1911), I, 303.

[9] *Mythological Papyri*, trans. Piankoff, I, 149. Papyrus No. 17.

[10] *Ibid.*, I, 114.

[11] Budge, *Osiris*, II, Frontispiece.

[12] *Panarion* 51.22.8ff.; II. 285ff.; as cited, translated, and interpreted by Hans Leisegang, "The Mystery of the Serpent," in Joseph Campbell (ed.), *The Mysteries*, Papers from the Eranos Yearbooks, Vol. 2. Bollingen Series XXX.2 (New York: Pantheon Books, 1955), pp. 238-239.

[13] Hieronymus, *Epistulae ad Paulinum* 58, 3.5, as cited and interpreted by William Bousset, *Kyrios Christos: Geschichte des Christus glaubens von den Anfangen des Christentums bis Irenaeus* (Goettingen: Vandergoeck and Ruprecht, 1926), p. 275.

[14] As quoted by Huntington Cairns and John Walker, *A Pageant of Painting from the National Gallery of Art* (Washington, D.C.: National Gallery of Art, 1966), I, 6.

[15] André Michel, *Histoire de l'art, depuis les premiers temps chrétiens jusqu'à nos jours* (Paris: A. Colin, 1905-1929), Vol. I, Part 1, p. 34, text to Figure 21.

[16] André Grabar, *Christian Iconography: A Study of Its Origins*, Bollingen Series XXXV.10 (Princeton: Princeton University Press, 1968), p. 36.

[17] *Ibid.*, p. 36.

[18] James Mellaart, *Çatal Hüyük: A Neolithic Town in Anatolia* (New York: McGraw-Hill Book Co., 1967), text to Plate 83, facing p. 149.

[19] *Ibid.*, text to Plate 67.

[20] Otto Rank, *Der Mythus von der Geburt des Helden* (Leipzig and Vienna: Franz Deuticke, 1922).

[21] Sigmund Freud, *Moses and Monotheism* (New York: Alfred A. Knopf, 1939).

[22] Hesiod, *Theogony* 459-491.

[23] Strabo, *Geography* 10.486ff.

[24] *Vishnu Purana* 5.1-4 (translation by H. H. Wilson, *The Vishnu Purana* [London: Oriental Translation Fund, 1840], pp. 491-505, abridged and modified), supplemented by additions from the *Bhagavata Purana* 10.1-4.

[25] Monier Monier-Williams, *A Sanskrit-English Dictionary* (Oxford: The Clarendon Press, 1888), pp. 370, 383, 1143-1144.

[26] Louis de la Vallée-Poussin, *Le Bouddhisme* (Paris: G. Beauchesne and Cie, 1909), p. 140.

[27] *Katha Upanishad* 3.12.

[28] *Vakyashudha* 13.

[29] *The Poetical Works of William Wordsworth*, ed. Thomas Hutchinson (London: Oxford University Press, 1910), p. 207.

[30] *Chhandogya Upanishad* 7.25.1-2, abridged.

[31] Kuo Hsi, *Lin Ch'üan Kao Chih* (eleventh century), cited by Cairns and Walker, *Pageant*, II, 352.

[31a] Translation supplied by Cleveland Museum.

[32] Translation from the *Manual of Prayers* enjoined by the Third Plenary Council of Baltimore (New York: P. J. Kennedy and Sons, 1930), pp. 676-677.

[33] *Ibid.*, pp. 71-72.

[34] Coptic text established and translated by A. Guillaumont, H.-Ch. Puech, G. Quispel, W. Till, and Yassah 'Abd Al-Masīḥ (New York: Harper and Brothers; Leiden: E. J. Brill, 1959), pp. 3, 55, 29, 43, 57.

[35] *Meister Eckhart*, ed. Franz Pfeiffer, trans. C. de B. Evans (London: John M. Watkins, 1924-1931), No. LXXXVIII ("The Virgin Birth"), I, 221-222.

[36] Angelus Silesius, *Cherubinischer Wandersmann* (1657):

> *Was hilft mich's, Gabriel, dass du Mariam grüsst,*
> *Wenn du nicht auch bei mir derselbe Bote bist!* (2.102)

[37] *Meister Eckhart*, trans. Evans, No. LXXXVII ("The Poor in Spirit"), I, 220.

[38] Silesius, *Cherubinischer Wandersmann* 3.148:

> *Gott ist mein Mittelpunkt, wenn ich ihn in mich schliess:*
> *Mein Umkreis dann, wenn ich aus Lieb in ihn zerfliesse.*

[39] Thomas Mann, *Joseph und seine Brüder* (Berlin: S. Fischer Verlag, 1933-1943), I, 79.

[40] Emile Mâle, *L'art religieux du XIIᵉ siècle en France* (Paris: Librairie Armand Colin, 1953), pp. 373-374.

[41] Erich Neumann, *The Great Mother: An Analysis of the Archetype*, trans. Ralph Manheim, Bollingen Series XLVII (New York: Pantheon Books, 1963), pp. 145-146, to Plate 62.

CHAPTER II

[1] Sir James G. Frazer, *The Golden Bough*, 1 vol. edn. (New York: Macmillan Co., 1922), p. 386.

[2] *Grimnismol* 23.

[3] Berossos' lost *History of Babylonia* is known only through fragmentary references and quotations from Polyhistor and Apollodorus, preserved by Eusebius and George the Syncellus. A reconstruction of his system was achieved by Alfred von Gutschmid, "Zu den Fragmenten des Berosos und Ktesias," *Rheinisches Museum* VIII (1853): 256. For a comparison of Berossos' figures with those of the recently discovered and deciphered Sumerian mythological tablets, much earlier in date, see Thorkild Jacobsen, *The Sumerian King Lists* (Chicago: Chicago University Press, 1939).

[4] André Parrot, *Sumer, the Dawn of Art*, trans. Stuart Gilbert and James Emmons (New York: Golden Press, 1961), p. 305.

[5] Henri de Genouillac, *Textes religieux sumériens du Louvre*, Vols. I-II (Paris: Musée du Louvre, Département des antiquités orientales, 1930), 10. 36-37; cited and translated by Samuel N. Kramer, *Sumerian Mythology* (Philadelphia: The American Philosophical Society, 1944), p. 39.

[6] André Parrot, *Ziggurats et Tour de Babel* (Paris: Editions Albin Michel, 1949), pp. 37-38.

[7] Translation by Kramer, *Sumerian Mythology*, p. 40, from Tablet 13877 in the Nippur collection of the University Museum, Philadelphia, lines 2-5.

[8] *Theogony* 176-182. Translation by Richmond Lattimore, *Hesiod* (Ann Arbor: University of Michigan Press, 1959), pp. 133-134.

[9] Antony Alpers, *Maori Myths and Tribal Legends* (Boston: Houghton Mifflin Co., 1966), pp. 16-18.

[10] Apollo delivered oracles at Patara during the six winter months, and at Delos during the six summer months.

[11] Herodotus, *The Persian Wars* 1.181-183. Translation by George Rawlinson, in *The Greek Historians*, ed. Francis B. Godolphin (New York: Random House, 1942), I, 77-78.

[12] Parrot, *Sumer*, pp. 70-72.

[13] Alfred Jeremias, *Die Weltanschauung der Sumerer* (Leipzig: J. C. Hinrichs'sche Buchhandlung, 1929), pp. 9-11.

[14] For these identifications, see William J. Hinke, *A New Boundary Stone of Nebuchadnezzar I from Nippur*, The Babylonian Expedition, Series D, Vol. IV (Philadelphia: University of Pennsylvania, 1907); and William Hayes Ward, *The Seal Cylinders of Western Asia* (Washington, D.C.: The Carnegie Institute of Washington, 1910), pp. 394-407.

[15] Heinrich Zimmer, *Philosophies of India*, ed. Joseph Campbell, Bollingen Series XXVI (New York: Pantheon Books, 1951), pp. 327-328.

[16] Sylvanus G. Morley, *The Ancient Maya*, 2nd edn. (Stanford, Cal.: Stanford University Press, 1947), p. 216.

[17] *Ibid.*, p. 221.

[18] Philip Drucker, Robert F. Heizer, and Robert J. Squier, *Excavations at La Venta, Tabasco,*

1955, Smithsonian Institution, Bureau of American Ethnology, Bulletin 170 (Washington, D.C.: Government Printing Office, 1959). See also Michael D. Coe, "Archaeological Synthesis of Southern Veracruz and Tabasco," in *Handbook of Middle American Indians*, ed. Robert Wauchope, 8 vols. (Austin, Tex.: University of Texas Press, 1964-1969), III, 686-693.

[19] Robert F. Heizer, "New Observations on La Venta," in *Dumbarton Oaks Conference on the Olmec: October 28th and 29th, 1967*, ed. Elizabeth P. Benson (Washington, D.C.: Dumbarton Oaks Research Library and Collection, 1968), pp. 9-36.

[20] Drucker, Heizer, and Squier, *Excavations at La Venta*; and Heizer, "New Observations on La Venta," *passim*. See also Coe, "Archaeological Synthesis of Southern Veracruz and Tabasco."

[21] Heizer, "New Observations on La Venta," p. 19.

[22] Matthew W. Stirling, "Monumental Sculpture of Southern Veracruz and Tabasco," in *Handbook*, ed. Wauchope, III, 733-735.

[23] See Drucker, Heizer, and Squier, *Excavations at La Venta*, pp. 267-271; also *Dumbarton Oaks Conference on the Olmec*, ed. Benson, pp. 65 and 72.

[24] Drucker, Heizer, and Squier, *Excavations at La Venta*, pp. 280-283.

[25] *Ibid.*, pp. 152-156, abridged.

[26] Peter T. Furst, "The Olmec Were-Jaguar Motif," in *Dumbarton Oaks Conference on the Olmec*, ed. Benson, p. 148.

[27] *Ibid.*, p. 170.

[28] Hermann Baumann, *Das doppelte Geschlecht* (Berlin: Dietrich Reimer, 1955), pp. 24-25.

[29] Matthew W. Stirling, "Stone monuments of the Río Chiquito, Veracruz, Mexico," in *Anthropological Papers*, Nos. 43-48, Smithsonian Institution, Bureau of American Ethnology, Bulletin 157 (Washington, D.C.: Government Printing Office, 1955), pp. 8 and 19-20; Plates 2 and 25, 26.

[30] See Drucker, Heizer, and Squier, *Excavations at La Venta*, p. 199.

[31] *Skanda Purana* II (Vishnukanda, Karttikamasa Mahatmya). 17. *Rupam*, No. 1 (Calcutta; Jan. 1920): pp. 11-19.

[32] Heinrich Zimmer, *Myths and Symbols in Indian Art and Civilization*, Bollingen Series VI (New York: Pantheon Books, 1946), pp. 182-184.

[33] Footnote to Zimmer, *Myths and Symbols*, p. 175.

[34] G.H.S. Bushnell, *Peru*, rev. edn. (New York: Praeger Paperbacks, 1963), p. 51.

[35] Robert Heine-Geldern, "The Problem of Transpacific Influences in Mesoamerica," in *Handbook*, ed. Wauchope, IV, 277-295, where an ample bibliography on the subject will be found.

[36] William Willetts, *Foundations of Chinese Art: From Neolithic Pottery to Modern Architecture* (New York, Toronto, London: McGraw-Hill Book Co., 1965), p. 97.

[37] See Robert Heine-Geldern, "The Problem of Transpacific Influences in Mesoamerica"; also Miguel Covarrubias, *The Eagle, The Jaguar, and The Serpent* (New York: Alfred A. Knopf, 1954), pp. 29-72.

[38] Philip Phillips, "The Role of Transpacific Contacts in the Development of New World Pre-Columbian Civilizations," in *Handbook*, ed. Wauchope, IV, 296-315; also Gordon R. Willey, *An Introduction to American Archaeology* (Englewood Cliffs, N.J.: Prentice-Hall, 1966), I, 21-24.

[39] A. L. Kroeber, *Anthropology* (New York: Harcourt, Brace and Co., 1923), p. 216.

[40] Mss *Cantares Mexicanos*, fol. 62, r, as quoted by Miguel Léon-Portilla, *Aztec Thought and Culture*, trans. Jack Emory Davis (Norman, Okla.: University of Oklahoma Press, 1963), p. 124, slightly modified.

[41] *Taittiriya Upanishad* 3.10.5-6. Translation by Robert Ernest Hume, *The Thirteen Principal Upanishads* (London: Oxford University Press, 1921), p. 293.

[42] Betty J. Meggers, Clifford Evans, and Emilio Estrada, *Early Formative Period of Coastal Ecuador: The Valdivia and Machililla Phases* (Washington, D.C.: Smithsonian Institution Press, 1965).

[43] James A. Ford, *A Comparison of Formative Cultures in the Americas* (Washington, D.C.: Smithsonian Institution Press, 1969), pp. 183-185.

[44] *Ibid.*, pp. 187-188.

[45] *Ibid.*, p. 189.

[46] *Ibid.*, p. 188.

[47] *Ibid.*, p. 190.

[48] Robert Heine-Geldern, "Chinese Influences in Mexico and Central America: The Tajín style of Mexico and the Marble Vases from Honduras," *Actas del 33 Congreso Internacional de Americanistas, Costa Rica* (San José, 1958), pp. 195-206, and "Representation of the Asiatic Tiger in the Art of the Chavin culture: A Proof of Early Contacts between China and Peru," *ibid.*, pp. 321-326.

[49] Ford, *A Comparison of Formative Cultures*, p. 188.

[50] *Ibid.*, p. 183.

[51] *Ibid.*, p. 187.

[52] *Ibid.*

[53] *Ibid.*, p. 189. James cites J. Edward Kidder, Jr., *The Jomon Pottery of Japan*, Artibus Asiae, Supplementum 17 (New York: Institute of Fine Arts, 1957), pp. 123, 149, and Figure 26.

[54] Ford, *A Comparison of Formative Cultures*, p. 188.

[55] *Ibid.*, pp. 189-190.

[56] Robert Heine-Geldern, "The Origin of Ancient Civilizations and Toynbee's Theories," *Diogenes*, No. 13 (Spring 1956): 92-99; here, p. 93.

[57] *Ibid.*, p. 93.

[58] *Ibid.*, pp. 93-94.

[59] *Ibid.*, p. 94.

[60] See Cyrus H. Gordon, *Before Columbus: Links between the Old World and Ancient America* (New York: Crown Publishers, 1971). In connection with the Roman head he cites Robert Heine-Geldern, "Ein römischer Fund aus dem vorkolumbischen Mexica," *Anzeiger der Oesterreichischen Akademie der Wissenschaften, Philosophische-historische Klasse* 98 (1961): 117-119.

[61] For full discussion, see Meggers, Evans, and Estrada, *Early Formative Period of Coastal Ecuador*, pp. 147-169.

[62] Pilot Chart number 1401 (November 1960), Hydrographic Office, Navy Dept., Washington, D.C., as interpreted by Meggers, Evans, and Estrada, Figure 103.

[63] Ford, *A Comparison of Formative Cultures*, pp. 41-47.

[64] *Ibid.*, Chart 2, and pp. 41-47.

[65] *Ibid.*, Chart 10 and pp. 78-82.

[66] Kenneth H. Cooper, M.D., *Aerobics* (New York: Bantam Books, 1968), p. 101: "A conditioned man, who exercises regularly, will have a resting heart rate of about 60 beats per minute or less. . . . Sixty per minute, times 60 minutes, equals 3600 beats per hour. Times 24 **hours**, equals 86,400 beats per day."

[67] This dream was interpreted by the prophet Daniel as referring to historical kingdoms. "You, O king, the king of kings," he announced, "to whom the God of heaven has given the kingdom, the power, and the might, and the glory, and into whose hand he has given, wherever they dwell, the sons of men, the beasts of the field, and the birds of the air, making you rule over them all—you are the head of gold. After you shall arise another kingdom inferior to you, and yet a third kingdom of bronze, which shall rule over the earth. And there shall be a fourth kingdom, strong as iron, because iron breaks to pieces and shatters all things; and like iron which crushes, it shall break and crush all these. And as you saw the feet and toes partly of potter's clay and partly of iron, it shall be a divided kingdom; but some of the firmness of iron shall be in it, just as you saw iron mixed with the miry clay. And as the toes of the feet were partly iron and partly clay, so the kingdom shall be partly strong and partly brittle. As you saw the iron mixed with miry clay, so they will mix with one another in marriage, but they will not hold together, just as iron does not mix with clay" (Daniel 2:37-44).

[68] Zimmer, *Myths and Symbols*, pp. 36-37, citing *Matsya Purana* 167.13-25.

[69] Sylvanus G. Morley, *An Introduction to the Study of Maya Hieroglyphics*, Smithsonian Institution, Bureau of American Ethnology, Bulletin 57 (Washington, D.C.: Government Printing Office, 1915), p. 32.

[70] Morley, *The Ancient Maya*, pp. 295-296.

[71] C. E. Guthe, "A Possible Solution of the Number Series on Pages 51 to 58 of the Dresden Codex," *Papers, Peabody Museum, Harvard University*, 6, No. 2 (1921).

[72] Nathan Sivin, *Cosmos and Computation in Early Chinese Mathematical Astronomy* (Leiden: E. J. Brill, 1969), pp. 5-7.

[73] *Ibid.*, pp. 13, 26-64.

[74] The Mayan cycle is discussed by Linton Satterthwaite, "Calendrics of the Maya Lowlands," in *Handbook*, ed. Wauchope, III, 622-623.

[75] Sivin, *Cosmos and Computation*, p. 43.

[76] Joseph Needham and Wang Ling, *Science and Civilisation in China* (Cambridge, Eng.: Cambridge University Press, 1954-19—), III, 459.

[77] Alfonso Caso, "Zapotec Writing and Calendar," in *Handbook*, ed. Wauchope, III, 932.

[78] Heine-Geldern, "The Problem of Transpacific Influences in Mesoamerica," pp. 280ff.

[79] Morley, *The Ancient Maya*, pp. 284-285.

[80] Hermann Jacobi, "Indian Ages of the World," in *Encyclopaedia of Religion and Ethics*, ed. James Hastings (New York: Charles Scribner's Sons, 1928), I, 201.

[81] Seneca, *Fragmenti, historia, Graeciae* 2.50; as quoted by Alfred Jeremias, "Ages of the World (Babylonian)," *ibid.*, I, 183.

[82] *Ibid.*, I, 184.

[83] Eduard Seler, *Gesammelte Abhandlungen zur amerikanischen Sprach- und Altertumskunde*, 5 vols. (Berlin: Ascher & Co. and Behrend & Co., 1902-1923), IV, 38-39.

[84] León-Portilla, *Aztec Thought and Culture*, p. 80, quoting *Colección de Cantares Mexicanos*, ed. Antonio Peñafiel (National Library of Mexico), fol. 62r.

[85] *Ibid.*, p. 35.

[86] Justino Fernández, *Coatlicue, estética del arte indigena antiguo*, 2nd edn. (Mexico City:

Centro de Estudios Filosóficos, 1959), p. 215; as quoted by León-Portilla, *Aztec Thought and Culture*, pp. 52-53.

[87] Mss *Cantares Mexicanos*, fol. 21v. Translation by León-Portilla, *Aztec Thought and Culture*, pp. 81-85.

[88] Eduard Seler, *Codex Vaticanus No. 3773: An Old Mexican Pictorial Manuscript in the Vatican Library* (Berlin and London: privately printed for the Duke of Loubat, 1902-1903), pp. 160-165.

[89] Mss *Cantares Mexicanos*, fol. 13r, 62r, 5v. Translation by León-Portilla, *Aztec Thought and Culture*, pp. 74-75 and 77.

[90] Schuyler Cammann, "The TLV Pattern on the Cosmic Mirrors of the Han Dynasty," *Journal of the American Oriental Society* 68 (1948): 159ff.

[91] Needham and Ling, *Science and Civilisation in China*, II, 255.

[92] *Ibid.*, II, 238.

[93] Fragment 26. Translation by John Burnet, *Early Greek Philosophy* (New York: Meridian Books, 1957), p. 210.

[94] Fragment 80. Translation by F. M. Cornford, *Greek Religious Thought* (London: J. M. Dent and Sons, 1923), p. 84.

[95] Fragment 30. *Ibid.*, p. 80.

[96] León-Portilla, *Aztec Thought and Culture*, p. 30.

[97] Heinrich Zimmer, *The Art of Indian Asia*, ed. Joseph Campbell, Bollingen Series XXXIX, 2nd edn. (Princeton: Princeton University Press, 1960), I, 339-340, quoting *Sutta Nipata* 5.7.8.

[98] In this abstract of the legend I have largely followed Daniel H. Brinton, *American Hero Myths* (Philadelphia: H. C. Watts and Co., 1882), pp. 90-136; with material, also, from Bernadino de Sahagún, *Historia general de las cosas de Nueva España* (Mexico, 1829), Bk. III, Chaps. xii-xiv.

[99] This interpretation closely follows Eduard Seler, *Codex Borgia: Eine altmexikanische Bilderschrift der Bibliothek der Congregatio de Propaganda Fide* (Berlin: privately printed for the Duke of Loubat, 1904-1906), II, 2-6 and Plate 30.

[100] John of Salisbury, *Policraticus* 1.6, as quoted by Otto von Simson, *The Gothic Cathedral*, Bollingen Series XLVII, 2nd edn. (New York: Pantheon Books, 1962), p. 191.

[101] *Ibid.*, p. 231.

[102] Translations by Samuel A. B. Mercer, *The Pyramid Texts in Translation and Commentary*, 4 vols. (New York, London, Toronto: Longmans, Green and Co., 1952), I, 92, 176, 169, 174 (slightly modified).

[103] T.G.H. Strehlow, *Aranda Traditions* (Melbourne: Melbourne University Press, 1947), pp. 7-9 and Figure 4.

[104] *Ibid.*

[105] C. G. Jung, *Analytical Psychology: Its Theory and Practice* (New York: Pantheon Books, 1968), p. 46.

[106] *Black Elk Speaks: Being the Life Story of a Holy Man of the Oglala Sioux, as Told to John G. Neihardt* (New York: William Morrow and Co., 1932), picture facing p. 40; p. 43 and note. (A paperback edition is also available: University of Nebraska Press, 1961.)

[107] *Ibid.*, p. 38.

[108] *Beautyway: A Navajo Ceremonial*, Bollingen Series LIII (New York: Pantheon Books, 1957), pp. 17-18. See also Jeff King, Maud Oakes, and Joseph Campbell, *Where the Two Came to Their Father*, Bollingen Series I, 2nd edn. (Princeton: Princeton University Press, 1970).

[109] *Hovamol* 139. Translation by Henry Adams Bellows, *The Poetic Edda* (New York: The American-Scandinavian Foundation, 1923), p. 60.

[110] *Grimnismol* 32-33. *Ibid.*, pp. 97-98.

[111] *Katha Upanishad* 6.1. The Sanskrit word for "fig tree," *aśvattha*, comes from the word *aśva*, meaning "horse." Compare Yggdrasil, "Othin's Steed."

[112] John of Ruysbroeck, *The Adornment of the Spiritual Marriage*. Translation by Dom C. A. Wynschek (London: J. M. Dent and Sons, 1916), p. 47.

[113] *Zohar, Beha Alothekha* (Num.), 148b (ET, V, 203), as quoted by Erwin R. Goodenough, *Jewish Symbols in the Greco-Roman Period*, Bollingen Series XXXVII, 13 vols. (New York: Pantheon Books and Princeton: Princeton University Press, 1953-1965), IV, 92-93.

[114] *Purgatorio* 22. 131-135. Translation by Charles Eliot Norton, *The Divine Comedy of Dante Alighieri* (Boston and New York: Houghton Mifflin Co., 1902), II, 173.

[115] *Purgatorio* 32. 37-42. *Ibid.*, II, 245.

[116] *Dhammapada* 16.6.

[117] Jane Harrison, *Prolegomena to a Study of Greek Religion*, 3rd edn. (Cambridge, Eng.: Cambridge University Press, 1922), pp. 406-407.

[118] *Paradiso* 33. 1-2. *The Divine Comedy*, trans. Norton, III, 252.

[119] Harrison, *Prolegomena*, pp. 448-449.

[120] *Corpus Hermeticum* 4.4. Translation by G.R.S. Mead, *Thrice-Greatest Hermes: Studies in Hellenistic Theosophy and Gnosis* (London and Benares: The Theosophical Publishing Society, 1906), II, 86-87.

[121] Goodenough, *Jewish Symbols*, I, 241-253.

[122] *Ibid.*, I, 250.

[123] *Corpus Hermeticum* 12.23. Mead, *Thrice-Greatest Hermes*, II, 212.

[124] Goodenough, *Jewish Symbols*, I, 253.

[125] *Ibid.*, I, 253.

[126] *Ibid.*, I, 252.

[127] Bernard Goldman, *The Sacred Portal: A Primary Symbol in Ancient Judaic Art* (Detroit, Mich.: Wayne State University Press, 1966), p. 56.

[128] *Ibid.*, pp. 57-58.

[129] Goodenough, *Jewish Symbols*, I, 247.

CHAPTER III

[1] Trans. Norton, *The Divine Comedy*, III, 238.

[2] *Ibid.*, III, 255-257.

[3] Emile Mâle, *L'Art religieux du XIIIe siècle en France* (Paris: Librairie Armand Colin, 1923), pp. 236-237.

[4] Ananda K. Coomaraswamy and Duggirāla Gopālakrishnāyya, *The Mirror of Gesture* (New York: E. Weyhe, 1936), pp. 50 and 60, Plates XIV B and XVI A.

[5] Zimmer, *The Art of Indian Asia*, I, 141-144.

[6] James Joyce, *Finnegans Wake* (New York: The Viking Press, 1939), p. 29.

[7] *Poetry and Prose of William Blake*, ed. Geoffrey Keynes (New York: Random House, Inc., 1932), p. 107.

[8] Rokusōdankyō, as quoted by R. H. Blyth, *Zen in English Literature and Oriental Classics* (Tokyo: Hokuseido Press, 1948), p. 120.

[9] From Hakuin's "Song of Meditation," as translated by D. T. Suzuki, *Manual of Zen Buddhism* (London: Rider and Co., 1950), p 152.

[10] *The Gospel According to Thomas* 99:16-18, trans. Guillaumont et al., p. 57.

[11] James Joyce, *Ulysses* (New York: Random House, Inc., 1934), p. 584.

[12] E. Dale Saunders, *Mudrā: A Study of Symbolic Gestures in Japanese Buddhist Sculpture*, Bollingen Series LVIII (New York: Pantheon Books, 1960), pp. 102-107, 235-237.

[13] From Hui-neng's *Tan-ching*, as quoted by Suzuki, *Manual of Zen Buddhism*, p. 88.

[14] Sherman E. Lee, *A History of Far Eastern Art* (New York: Prentice-Hall, Inc. and Harry N. Abrams, Inc., n.d.), pp. 299-300.

[15] The *Larger Sukhavati Vyuha* 3-11, summarized; from *The Sacred Books of the East*, ed. F. Max Müller, 50 vols. (Oxford: The Clarendon Press, 1879-1910), XLIX, 7-28.

[16] Ovid, *Metamorphoses* 15.165-168. Translated by Frank Justus Miller, Loeb Classical Library edn. (Cambridge, Mass.: Harvard University Press, 1916), II, 377.

[17] *Amitayur Dhyana Sutra* 9-30, summarized; from *The Sacred Books of the East*, XLIX, 169-199.

[18] Lee, *A History of Far Eastern Art*, p. 159.

[19] *Maitri Upanishad* 6.1-2 (abridged). Translation largely follows Hume, *The Thirteen Principal Upanishads*, pp. 424-425.

[20] Jeffers, *Roan Stallion*, p. 24.

[21] *Paradiso* 33.115-145. *The Divine Comedy*, trans. Norton, III, 256-257.

[22] Henry Adams, *Mont-Saint-Michel and Chartres* (Boston and New York: Houghton Mifflin Co., 1904), p. 195.

[23] *Ibid.*, pp. 185-186.

[24] Zimmer, *The Art of Indian Asia*, I, 165.

[25] Matangalila I; as related by Zimmer, *Myths and Symbols*, p. 106.

[26] Alleluia of the Mass, March 25, in honor of the Annunciation and of Mary as Θεοτόκος, "Mother of God." *Daily Missal*, ed. Dom Gaspar Lefebvre (Saint Paul, Minn.: E. M. Lohmann, Co., 1934), p. 1311.

[27] IHS, representing the Greek IHΣ, is a contraction of IH(ΣOY)Σ, Jesus: often read, however, as an abbreviation of the Latin *Jesus Hominum Salvator*, "Jesus Savior of Men," as well as of *In Hoc Signo* (*vinces*), "In this Sign (thou shalt conquer)," words supposedly seen written in the sky beneath an apparition of the Cross by Constantine and his army on the eve of his victory over Maxentius on October 28, 312, at Saxa Rubra—which, in the long view of history, is now taken to mark the moment of decision when Christian prevailed over Pagan Rome.

[28] Mâle, *L'art religieux du XIIIe siècle en France*, pp. 166-167.

[29] *Shvetashvatara Upanishad* 5.9-10.

[30] *Katha Upanishad* 3.12.

[31] For an elucidation of the symbolism of Figure 226, see Joseph Campbell, *The Masks of God: Creative Mythology* (New York: The Viking Press, 1968), pp. 278ff.

[32] Jung, "The Psychology of the Transference," *The Practice of Psychotherapy*, CWJ, XVI, par. 454 and Figure 4.

[33] *Ibid.*

[34] *Jataka* 1.52-53. Adapted from Henry Clarke Warren, *Buddhism in Translations* (Cambridge, Mass.: Harvard University Press, 1896), pp. 45-47.

[35] *Mohenjo-Daro and the Indus Civilization*, ed. Sir John Marshall (London: Arthur Probesthain, 1931), I, 52.

[36] Campbell, *The Masks of God: Primitive Mythology* (New York: The Viking Press, 1959), pp. 165-225.

[37] Ernest Mackay, *The Indus Civilization*

(London: Lovat Dickson and Thompson, 1935), p. 73.

[38] Zimmer, *The Art of Indian Asia*, I, 206-207.

[39] *Ibid.*, I, 155-156.

[40] Kenneth Clark, *The Nude: A Study in Ideal Form*, Bollingen Series XXXV.2 (New York: Pantheon Books, 1956), pp. 84-87.

CHAPTER IV

[1] C. G. Jung, Foreword to Daisetz Teitaro Suzuki, *An Introduction to Zen Buddhism* (New York: The Philosophical Library, 1949), p. 26.

[2] *Brihadaranyaka Upanishad* 1.4.6-10, abridged.

[3] Translation by Guillaumont et al., pp. 43, 55.

[4] *Katha Upanishad* 3.12.

[5] Monier-Williams, *A Sanskrit-English Dictionary*, p. 528.

[6] For a summary of the argument and a bibliography on this subject see Mircea Eliade, *Yoga: Immortality and Freedom*, Bollingen Series LVI, 2nd edn. (Princeton: Princeton University Press, 1969), pp. 370-372 ("Patañjali and the Texts of Classic Yoga").

[7] *Bhagavad Gita* 2.22.

[8] C. Kerényi, *Asklepios: Archetypal Image of the Physician's Existence*, trans. Ralph Manheim, Bollingen Series LXV.3 (New York: Pantheon Books, 1959), p. 50.

[9] *Ibid.*, p. 57.

[10] King, Oakes, and Campbell, *Where the Two Came to Their Father*, p. 8.

[11] Goodenough, *Jewish Symbols*, II, 248.

[12] Translation, Jane Ellen Harrison, *Prolegomena to the Study of Greek Religion* (Cambridge University Press, 3rd ed., 1922), p. 565.

[13] Harrison, *Prolegomena*, pp. 18, 19.

[14] Epiphanius, *Panarion* 1.37.5 (272Aff), as quoted by Hans Leisegang, "The Mystery of the Serpent," in *PEY*, II, 231.

[15] Hippolytus, *Elenchos* 5.17.1-2 and 8, as quoted *ibid.*, II, 230.

[16] *Ibid.*, II, 194-260.

[17] Jung, "Concerning Mandala Symbolism," *The Archetypes and the Collective Unconscious*, *CWJ*, IX.1, par. 698.

[18] These Twelve Knots or Binding Links (*nidanas*) of the wheel of causation are named as follows: (1) Ignorance (2) Misperceptions (3) Cognitions (4) Names and Forms (5) Sense Experiences (6) Contact (7) Emotion (8) Craving (9) Attachment (10) Becoming (11) Birth (12) Sorrow, Sickness, Old Age, and Death (*Digha-nikaya* 14, 15; *Majjhima-nikaya* 1.140). Compare Fig. 358.

[19] Shankaracharya, *Nirvanamanjari*, as quoted by Zimmer, *Philosophies of India*, p. 463.

[20] Zimmer, *The Art of Indian Asia*, I, 27.

[21] James Joyce, *Ulysses*, p. 409.

[22] Haiku by Basho. Translation by R. H. Blyth, as quoted by Alan Watts, *The Way of Zen* (New York: Pantheon Books, 1957), p. 184.

[23] Patanjali, *Yoga Sutras* 1.2 Cf. Zimmer, *Philosophies of India*, p. 284.

[24] *The Secret of the Golden Flower*, trans. Richard Wilhelm, with a commentary by C. G. Jung (New York: Harcourt, Brace and Co., 1938), p. 66.

[25] Suzuki, *Manual of Zen Buddhism*, p. 29.

[26] Commonly, but inexactly, translated, "Heart of the Perfection of Wisdom."

[27] Translation mine. Others can be found in *The Sacred Books of the East*, ed. Müller, Vol. XLIX, Part II, pp. 153-154; Suzuki, *Manual of Zen Buddhism*, pp. 26-27; and Edward Conze, *Buddhist Texts Through the Ages* (New York: Philosophical Library, 1954), pp. 152-153.

[28] "Deep down in the artificial platform which supported the Brak Eye Temple there was a series of four older buildings. . . . Unique amongst the many thousands of objects discovered in these lower levels are the 'eye-idols' in black and white alabaster of which there are thousands of examples. They consist normally of a thin biscuit-like body surmounted by a pair of eyes in human form once tinted with malachite paint. Most probably they represent dedications by every member of the populace to an all-seeing god who watched over the fortunes of the city. There were moreover many different varieties of the idol, including figures with three eyes, pairs with four eyes, and pairs with engravings of smaller idols on the front of the body which were possibly family dedications." M.E.L. Mallowan, *Early Mesopotamia and Iran* (New York: McGraw-Hill Book Company, 1965), p. 48. See also Figure 411.

[29] Louis de la Vallée Poussin in his article "Avalokitesvara," *Encyclopaedia of Religion and Ethics*, ed. Hastings, I, 256-257, citing the versified *Karanda*.

[30] Zimmer, *Philosophies of India*, p. 534.

[31] De la Vallée Poussin, "Avalokitesvara," pp. 258-261.

[32] Adapted from *Cat's Yawn* (New York: First Zen Institute of America, 1947), p. 11.

[33] Pliny, *Natural History* 6.26.101, 9.57.114, as quoted by Wilfred H. Schoff, *The Periplus of the Erythraean Sea: Travel and Trade in the Indian Ocean by a Merchant of the First Century* (New York: David McKay Co., 1916), pp. 219, 240.

34 Eliade, *Yoga*, pp. 200-201.

35 I have discussed this matter at some length in *The Masks of God: Oriental Mythology* (New York: The Viking Press, 1962), pp. 197-206. The critical texts are *Brihadaranyaka Upanishad* 2.1; *Chhandogya Upanishad* 5.3-10, 5.11-24, 7.1-25; and *Kena Upanishad* 3.1-4.2.

36 Arthur Avalon (Sir John Woodroffe), *The Serpent Power*, 3rd rev. edn. (Madras: Ganesh and Co., 1931), p. 111, note 2.

37 *The Gospel of Sri Ramakrishna*, trans. Swami Nikhilananda (New York: Ramakrishna-Vivekananda Center, 1942), pp. 829-830.

38 Avalon, *The Serpent Power*, pp. 21-22.

39 Alain Danielou, *Yoga: The Method of Re-integration* (New York: University Books, 1955), p. 11.

40 Jung, "Concerning Mandala Symbolism," *The Archetypes and the Collective Unconscious*, *CWJ*, IX.1, par. 647-649.

41 *Ibid.*, IX.1, par. 667.

42 Avalon, *The Serpent Power*, p. 117.

43 *Ibid.*, pp. 115-118, 330-354, and Plate 2.

44 *Larousse Encyclopedia of Mythology* (New York: Prometheus Press, 1959), p. 261.

45 Avalon, *The Serpent Power*, pp. 118-119, 355-363, and Plate 3.

46 *The Gospel of Sri Ramakrishna*, trans. Nikhilananda, p. 404.

47 *Chhandogya Upanishad* 8.3.2.

48 Jung, "The Psychology of the Child Archetype," *The Archetypes and the Collective Unconscious*, *CWJ*, IX.1, par. 291.

49 Dante, *La Vita Nuova*, II. Translation by Charles Eliot Norton, *The New Life of Dante Alighieri* (Boston and New York: Houghton Mifflin Co., 1867), p. 2.

50 Jung, "Concerning Mandala Symbolism," *The Archetypes and the Collective Unconscious*, IX.1, par. 696.

51 *The Gospel of Sri Ramakrishna*, trans. Nikhilananda, p. 499.

52 *Shatchakra Nirupana* 30. Avalon, *The Serpent Power*, p. 386.

53 *Katha Upanishad* 3.14.

54 *Odyssey* 12.166-194. Translation by S. H. Butcher and Andrew Lang, *The Odyssey of Homer* (London and New York: The Macmillan Co., 1879), pp. 197-198.

55 Garma C. C. Chang, *Teachings of Tibetan Yoga* (New Hyde Park, N.Y.: University Books, 1963), p. 73.

56 "The Epitome of an Introduction to the Profound Path of the Six Yogas of Naropa," translated by Chang, *ibid.*, pp. 63-64.

57 *Ibid.*, p. 68.

58 *Ibid.*, pp. 82-83.

59 *Ibid.*, pp. 92-94.

60 *Ibid.*, pp. 96-101.

61 *The Gospel of Sri Ramakrishna*, trans. Nikhilananda, pp. 80, 148, 180, 191, 217, 370, 802, 858.

62 *Meister Eckhart*, trans. Evans, No. XCVI ("Riddance"), I, 239.

63 *Shatchakra Nirupana* 33. Avalon, *The Serpent Power*, p. 395.

64 Swami Yatiswarananda, "A Glimpse into Hindu Religious Symbology," in Sri Ramakrishna Centenary Committee (ed.), *Cultural Heritage of India*, 3 vols. (Calcutta: Belur Math, 1937), Vol. II, p. 15.

65 "The Soul Is One with God," *Meister Eckhart*, trans. Evans, II, 89.

66 "Riddance," *ibid.*, I, 239.

67 "The Soul Is One with God," *ibid.*, II, 89.

68 *Shatchakra Nirupana* 40-41. Avalon, *The Serpent Power*, pp. 417-428.

69 "The Soul Is One with God," *Meister Eckhart*, trans. Evans, II, 89.

70 Jung, "Concerning Mandala Symbolism," *The Archetypes and the Collective Unconscious*, *CWJ*, IX.1, par. 636-638.

71 Orphic Hymn XXXIV. Translation by Thomas Taylor, *The Mystical Hymns of Orpheus* (Chiswick: O. Whittingham, 1824), pp. 77-79.

72 For a justification and development of this interpretation of the symbolism of the Pietroasa Bowl, see Campbell, *The Masks of God: Creative Mythology*, pp. 9-27, of which the above is largely an abridgment. See also my chief source, Hans Leisegang's "The Mystery of the Serpent," in *PEY*, II, 194-260.

73 For testimony and eyewitness accounts, see *The Masks of God: Oriental Mythology*, pp. 505-516, citing "A Report to the International Jurists by Its Legal Inquiry Committee on Tibet," *Tibet and the Chinese People's Republic* (Geneva: International Commission of Jurists, 1960).

74 *The Tibetan Book of the Dead, or The After-Death Experiences on the Bardo Plane, According to Lama Kazi Dawa-Samdup's English Rendering*, ed. W. Y. Evans-Wentz, with a Commentary by C. G. Jung and Forewords by the Lama Anagirika Govinda and Sir John Woodroffe (New York: Oxford University Press, 1960).

75 Jung, "Psychological Commentary," *ibid.*, p. xxxvi.

76 Lama Anagarika Govinda, "Introductory Foreword," *ibid.*, p. lix.

77 *Phaedo* 80c-82d. Translation by Hugh Tredennick, in *The Collected Dialogues of Plato*, ed. Edith Hamilton and Huntington Cairns, Bol-

lingen Series LXXI (New York: Pantheon Books, 1961), pp. 63-65.

[78] *Phaedo* 69c. *Ibid.*, p. 52.

[79] *The Tibetan Book of the Dead*, pp. 95-96, abridged and slightly modified.

[80] *Ibid.*, pp. 97-99.

[81] *Ibid.*, pp. 92-93.

[82] *Ibid.*, pp. 100-101, abridged.

[83] *Ibid.*, p. 103.

[84] *Ibid.*, p. 107.

[85] *Ibid.*, p. 109.

[86] *Ibid.*, pp. 121, 125.

[87] *Ibid.*, p. 127.

[88] *Ibid.*, pp. 126-130.

[89] *Epitome of the Six Doctrines*: III. "Doctrine of the Dream State," published in translation by W. Y. Evans-Wentz, *Tibetan Yoga and Secret Doctrine* (London: Humphrey Milford, 1935), pp. 171-252. My passage, III. 9-10, appears p. 217.

[90] Evans-Wentz, *The Tibetan Book of the Dead*, p. 137.

[91] *Ibid.*, p. 168.

[92] *Ibid.*, p. 157 and note 3 (italics mine).

[93] *Ibid.*, pp. 165-168.

[94] *Ibid.*, p. 168.

[95] *Ibid.*, pp. 177-178.

[96] Jung, "Psychological Commentary," *ibid.*, pp. xlii-xliii.

CHAPTER V

[1] Walter Lehmann, *Sterbende Götter und Christliche Heilsbotschaft, Wechselreden Indianischer Vornehmer und Spanischer Glaubenapostel in Mexiko, 1524* (Stuttgart, 1949), as quoted by Léon-Portilla, *Aztec Thought and Culture*, p. 64.

[2] Diego de Landa, *Relación de las cosas de Yucatán* (Mórida, 1938), as quoted by Morley, *The Ancient Maya*, p. 218.

[3] James Walton, "The Rock Paintings of Basutoland," in *Third Pan-African Congress on Prehistory, Livingstone, 1955*, ed. J. Desmond Clark (London: Chatto and Windus, 1957), pp. 277-281.

[4] Leo Frobenius, *Erythräa: Länder und Zeiten des heiligen Königsmordes* (Berlin and Zurich: Atlantis-Verlag, 1931), p. 309, text to Plates 34-35.

[5] *Ibid.*, pp. 204-206.

[6] *Ibid.*, pp. 201-202.

[7] Frazer, *The Golden Bough*, p. 50 (italics mine).

[8] As quoted by Thomas Blake Clark, *Omai, First Polynesian Ambassador to England* (San Francisco: The Colt Press, 1940), p. 47. My whole knowledge of Omai comes from this attractive little volume.

[9] *A Voyage to the Pacific Ocean, Undertaken by the Command of His Majesty, for Making Discoveries in the Northern Hemisphere, To Determine The Position and Extent of the West Side of North America; its Distance from Asia; and the Practicability of a Northern Passage to Europe. Performed under the Direction of Captains Cook, Clerke, and Gore, In his Majesty's Ships the Resolution and Discovery. In the Years 1776, 1777, 1778, 1779, and 1780*. In Three Volumes. Vol. I and II written by Captain James Cook F.R.S. Vol. III by Captain James King LL.D. and F.R.S. Published by Order of the Lords Commissioners of the Admiralty London: 1784. Quotes here and below are from Vol. II, pp. 27-48.

[10] Pyramid Text Utterances, 39, 301:451a, and 29. Translation by Mercer, *The Pyramid Texts*, I, 27, 100, 24-25, slightly abridged.

[11] Utterances 51, 53, and 47. *Ibid.*, I, 28, 29.

[12] *The Book of the Dead*, Chapter CXII, Papyrus of Nu (British Museum, No. 10,477, Sheet 18), translation by E.A.W. Budge, *The Chapters of the Coming Forth by Day* (London: Kegan Paul, Trench, Trübner and Co., 1898), p. 177.

[13] See W. D. Westervelt, *Hawaiian Legends of Volcanoes* (Boston: Ellis Press, 1916), pp. 45-54, and Martha Beckwith, *Hawaiian Mythology* (New Haven: Yale University Press, 1940), pp. 201-213.

[14] John Layard, *Stone Men of Malekula* (London: Chatto and Windus, 1942), pp. 255ff. and *passim*.

[15] *Ibid.*, p. 14.

[16] John Layard, "The Malekulan Journey of the Dead," in *PEY*, IV, 139-141, Figures 2, 3a, and 4.

[17] *Ibid.*, IV, 141-143.

[18] Layard, *Stone Men of Malekula*, pp. 240-241.

[19] *Ibid.*

[20] John Layard, "The Making of Man in Malekula," *Eranos-Jahrbuch 1948* (Zurich: Rhein-Verlag, 1949), p. 235.

[21] John Layard, "Identification with the Sacrificial Animal," *Eranos-Jahrbuch 1955* (Zurich: Rhein-Verlag, 1956), pp. 373-389.

[22] Layard, "The Making of Man in Malekula," p. 234, citing Bernard Deacon, "Geometrical Drawings from Malekula and other islands of the New Hebrides, *Journal of the Royal Anthropological Institute*, LXIV, Jan.-June, 1934, Figure 39.

[23] Layard, *Stone Men of Malekula*, pp. 261-262.

[24] V. Gordon Childe, "Megaliths," *Ancient India*, No. 4 (July 1947-Jan. 1948): 5-12.

[25] V. D. Krishnaswami, "Megalithic Types of South India," *Ancient India*, No. 5 (Jan. 1949): 41.

[26] Childe, "Megaliths," p. 5.

[27] Layard, *Stone Men of Malekula*, p. 242.

[28] Adolf Erman, *Die Ägyptische Religion* (Berlin: Georg Riemer Verlag, 1905), p. 181.

[29] Frazer, *The Golden Bough*, pp. 472-473 (italics mine).

[30] Harrison, *Prolegomena*, p. 126.

[31] *Ibid.*, p. 229, text to Figure 48.

[32] Frazer, *The Golden Bough*, p. 472.

[33] *Ibid.*, pp. 469-470.

[34] Gertrude Schoepperle, *Tristan and Isolt* (London: David Nutt, 1913), p. 227.

[35] Gottfried von Strassburg, *Tristan und Isold*, ed. Friedrich Ranke (Berlin: Weidmannsche Verlagsbuchhandlung, 1959), ll. 6611-6616, p. 83.

[36] *Ibid.*, ll. 13513-13536, pp. 169-170.

[37] Jeremiah Curtin, *Myths and Folklore of Ireland* (Boston: Little, Brown and Co., 1890), pp. 327-332.

[38] *Venus and Adonis*, ll. 615-638, *The Complete Works of Shakespeare*, ed. W. J. Craig (Oxford University Press, 1925), p. 1251.

[39] Marcel Pobé and Jean Roubier, *The Art of Roman Gaul* (Toronto: University of Toronto Press, 1961), p. 51, text to Plate 6.

[40] Adapted from *The Pursuit after Diarmuid O'Duibhne, and Grianne, the Daughter of Cormac MacAirt, King of Ireland in the Third Century*, Transactions of the Ossianic Society for the year 1855, ed. Standish Hayes O'Grady (Dublin: John O'Daly, 1857), III, pp. 173-193, greatly abridged.

[41] O.G.S. Crawford, *The Eye Goddess* (New York: The Macmillan Co., n.d.).

[42] Stephen Herbert Langdon, *Semitic Mythology*, pp. 132-133. *Semitic Mythology* is Volume V of *The Mythology of All Races*, ed. John Arnott MacCulloch, 13 vols. (Boston: Marshall Jones Co., 1916-1932), pp. 133 and 132.

[43] Ananda K. Coomaraswamy, *Hinduism and Buddhism* (New York: Philosophical Library, n.d.), p. 9.

[44] *Ibid.*, p. 7.

[45] Stith Thompson, *Motif-Index of Folk-Literature* (Bloomington, Ind.: Indiana University, 1932-1936), Item A 812.

[46] Passage from *Vayu Purana* as quoted by Wilson, *The Vishnu Purana*, p. 30, note 6.

[47] *Vishnu Purana* 1.4; translation from Wilson, *op.cit.*, pp. 29-31, adapted and abridged.

CHAPTER VI

[1] Mircea Eliade, *Forgerons et alchimistes* (Paris: Flammarion, 1956), pp. 176-177.

[2] *Mahaparinibbana Sutta* 4.13-22 and 57. Translation from the Pali by T. W. Rhys David, *The Sacred Books of the East*, ed. Müller, XI, 70-73 and 83-84, slightly modified. I follow J. F. Fleet (*Journal of the Royal Asiatic Society* [1906]: 658, 881f.) in rendering the words *sūkara maddava* as "succulent boar's flesh" rather than "dried boar's flesh," as in Rhys David's translation.

[3] "Ode: Intimations of Immortality," l. 58, *Poetical Works*, ed. Hutchinson, p. 588.

[4] *Sutta Nipata* 1073, 1075.

[5] Arthur Schopenhauer, *Transcendente Spekulation über die anscheinende Absichtlichkeit im Schicksale des einzelnen*, in *Sämtliche Werke* (Stuttgart: Cotta'sche Bibliothek der Weltlitteratur, n.d.), VIII, 220-225.

[6] James Joyce, *Finnegans Wake*, p. 92.

[7] *Maha Vagga* ("The Fire-Sermon") 1.21.1-4. Translation by Warren, *Buddhism in Translations*, pp. 350-351, slightly modified.

[8] *Prajnaparamita Hridaya Sutra*. See above, pp. 315-316.

[9] *Vajracchedika* 32. *The Sacred Books of the East*, ed. Müller, Vol. XLIX, Part II, p. 144.

[10] Monier-Williams, *A Sanskrit-English Dictionary*, pp. 946 and 949.

[11] *Shatapatha Brahmana* 10.5.2.16. Coomaraswamy, *Hinduism and Buddhism*, p. 7.

[12] Giuseppe Ungaretti, poem to the earth as seen from the moon. Published in *Epoca* XX.983 (July 27, 1969).

List of Illustrations

Notes to the Sources

Unless otherwise indicated, photographs have been obtained from the institution of repository.

Abbreviations are listed on page 538.

AUTHOR'S NOTE: To reflect the whole range and continuity of Bollingen Series publications, special note is here given to refer the reader to those Bollingen Series volumes from which pictorial material was selected.*

*EDITOR'S NOTE: Those Bollingen Series volumes are listed in brackets [ ] preceding the original source in instances when the reproduction for this volume was made from photographs loaned from the files of the Bollingen Series, through the courtesy of Princeton University Press, publishers of the Bollingen Series since 1967; when photographs were obtained from other sources, the appropriate Bollingen Series volume number is listed in parentheses ( ) following the source for the photograph given with the listing; in cases where no photograph was available, the name of the volume from which the illustration here was actually reproduced is given in the listing. For full details, see the Abbreviations.

530

MAPS

UNNUMBERED ILLUSTRATIONS INTRODUCING CHAPTERS

Alinari-Art
    Reference Bureau
See Art Reference Bureau.

Anderson-Art
    Reference Bureau
See Art Reference Bureau.

Avalon
Arthur Avalon (Sir John Woodroffe), *The Serpent Power*, 3rd rev. edn. (Madras [India]: Ganesh and Co., 1931).

Art Reference
    Bureau
Permissions granted by Art Reference Bureau, Ancram, New York, agents in the U.S.A. for archives of Alinari, Anderson, Bruckmann, Mas, Wurzburg.

Beautyway: A
    Navaho Ceremonial
See Bollingen Series LIII.

BOLLINGEN SERIES

BS VI
Heinrich Zimmer, *Myths and Symbols in Indian Art and Civilization* (1946).

BS XIV
Corpus of Ancient Near Eastern Seals in North American Collections, catalogued and edited by Edith Porada and Briggs Buchanan, vol. I (1948), The Collection of the Pierpont Morgan Library.

BS XVII
Joseph Campbell, *The Hero with a Thousand Faces* (1949; 2nd edn., 1968).

BS XX.5
C. G. Jung, *Symbols of Transformation* (Collected Works, 1956; 2nd edn., 1967).

BS XX.9.i
C. G. Jung, *The Archetypes and the Collective Unconscious* (Collected Works, 1959; 2nd edn., 1969).

BS XX.12
C. G. Jung, *Psychology and Alchemy* (Collected Works, 1953; 2nd edn., 1968).

BS XX.16
C. G. Jung, *The Practice of Psychotherapy* (Collected Works, 1954; 2nd edn., 1966).

The Collected Works of C. G. Jung are translated by R.F.C. Hull.

BS XXVI
Heinrich Zimmer, *Philosophies of India* (1951).

BS XXX.2
The Mysteries (Papers from the Eranos Yearbooks, ed. by Joseph Campbell, translated by Ralph Manheim; 1955).

BS XXX.4
Spiritual Disciplines (Papers from the Eranos Yearbooks, ed. *ibid.*; 1960).

BS XXXV.2
Kenneth Clark, *The Nude: A Study in Ideal Form* (The A. W. Mellon Lectures in the Fine Arts, pub. 1956).

BS XXXV.7   Anthony Blunt, *Nicolas Poussin* (The A. W. Mellon Lectures in the Fine Arts, pub. 1967).

BS XXXV.10   André Grabar, *Christian Iconography: A Study of Its Origins* (The A. W. Mellon Lectures in the Fine Arts, pub. 1968).

BS XXXV.11   Kathleen Raine, *Blake and Tradition* (The A. W. Mellon Lectures in the Fine Arts, pub. 1968).

BS XXXV.15   David Cecil, *Visionary and Dreamer, Two Poetic Painters: Samuel Palmer and Edward Burne-Jones* (The A. W. Mellon Lectures in the Fine Arts, pub. 1969).

BS XXXV.16   Mario Praz, *Mnemosyne, The Parallel between Literature and the Visual Arts* (The A. W. Mellon Lectures in the Fine Arts, pub. 1970).

BS XXXVII   Erwin R. Goodenough, *Jewish Symbols in the Greco-Roman Period*, 13 vols. (1953-1968).

BS XXXIX   Heinrich Zimmer, *The Art of Indian Asia*, edited by Joseph Campbell (1955; 2nd edn., 1960).

BS XL.2   *The Shrines of Tut-Ankh-Amon* (Egyptian Religious Texts and Representations, translated, by Alexandre Piankoff; edited by N. Rambova; 1955).

BS XL.3   *Mythological Papyri* (Egyptian Religious Texts and Representations, translated by Alexandre Piankoff; edited by N. Rambova; 1957).

BS XLVII   Erich Neumann, *The Great Mother, An Analysis of the Archetype*, translated by Ralph Manheim (1955; 2nd edn., 1963).

BS LIII   *Beautyway: A Navaho Ceremonial*, texts recorded or translated by Father Berard Haile and Maud Oakes; edited by Leland C. Wyman (1957).

BS LXV.3   C. Kerényi, *Asklepios: Archetypal Image of the Physician's Existence* (Archetypal Images in Greek Religion, translated by Ralph Manheim, 1959).

BS LXXXI   Peter Brieger, Millard Meiss, and Charles S. Singleton, *Illuminated Manuscripts of the Divine Comedy*, 2 vols. (1969).

Budge   E. A. Wallis Budge, *Osiris and the Egyptian Resurrection* (London: Philip Lee Warner; New York: G. P. Putnam's Sons, 1911), 2 vols.

Campbell, *The Masks of God*   Joseph Campbell, *The Masks of God* (New York: The Viking Press): Vol. I, *Primitive Mythology* (1959); Vol. II, *Oriental Mythology* (1962); Vol. III, *Occidental Mythology* (1964); Vol. IV, *Creative Mythology* (1968).

Corpus of Ancient Near Eastern Seals   *See Bollingen Series XIV.*

Covarrubias	Miguel Covarrubias, *Indian Art of Mexico and Central America* (New York: Alfred A. Knopf, Inc., Borzoi Books, 1957).
Erman	Adolf Erman, *Die Aegyptische Religion* (Berlin: Georg Reimer, 1905).
Giraudon	Photographie Giraudon, Paris.
Goodenough, *Jewish Symbols*	*See Bollingen Series XXXVII.*
Harrison	Jane Ellen Harrison, *Themis*, 2nd edn. (Cambridge [England]: Cambridge University Press, 1927).
Isles of the Pacific	*Isles of the Pacific*: Book of Plates to *Cook's Third Voyage*, London, 1784; from a copy in the author's collection.
Jung, *The Archetypes and the Collective Unconscious*	*See Bollingen Series XX.9.i.*
Jung, *The Practice of Psychotherapy*	*See Bollingen Series XX.16.*
Jung, *Symbols of Transformation*	*See Bollingen Series XX.5.*
Lauros-Giraudon	*See Giraudon.*
Moor	Edward Moor, *The Hindu Pantheon* (London: J. Johnson, 1810).
Musées Nationaux	Service de Documentation Photographique de la Réunion des Musées Nationaux, Versailles, France.
Mythological Papyri	*See Bollingen Series XL.3.*
NYPL	New York Public Library, New York.
Papers from the Eranos Yearbooks, vol. II, "The Mysteries"	*See Bollingen Series XXX.2.*
Shrines of Tut-Ankh-Amon, The	*See Bollingen Series XL.2.*
Suzuki, *Zen and Japanese Culture*	*See Bollingen Series LXIV.*
Willetts	William Willetts, *Foundations of Chinese Art: From Neolithic Pottery to Modern Architecture* (London: Thames & Hudson; New York, McGraw-Hill Book Co., 1965).
Zimmer, *Myths & Symbols*	*See Bollingen Series VI.*
Zimmer, *The Art of Indian Asia*	*See Bollingen Series XXXIX.*

Index

Numbers printed in italic type in parentheses ( ) refer to illustration numbers of subject; the number preceding is the page number on which the illustration appears, *e.g.*, Pyramid, 124, 128, 142 (*117*).